NAPOLEON: PASSION, DEATH AND RESURRECTION, 1815–1840

Citizen Emperor: Napoleon in Power, 1799–1815
Napoleon: The Path to Power, 1769–1799
Talleyrand
Violence, Colonialism and Empire in the Modern World (co-editor)
War Stories: The War Memoir in History and Literature (editor)
Theatres of Violence: Massacre, Mass Killing and Atrocity throughout History (co-editor)
Napoleon and his Empire: Europe 1804–1814 (co-editor)
The French Revolution and Napoleon: A Sourcebook (co-editor)
Napoleon and Europe (editor)
Modern Prussian History, 1830–1947 (editor)
The Rise of Prussia, 1700–1830 (editor)

NAPOLEON

Passion, Death and Resurrection, 1815–1840

Philip Dwyer

BLOOMSBURY PUBLISHING
LONDON • OXFORD • NEW YORK • NEW DELHI • SYDNEY

BLOOMSBURY PUBLISHING
Bloomsbury Publishing Plc
50 Bedford Square, London, WC1B 3DP, UK

BLOOMSBURY, BLOOMSBURY PUBLISHING and the Diana logo are trademarks of
Bloomsbury Publishing Plc

First published in Great Britain 2018

Map by John Gilkes, based on a map in Gilbert Martineau,
La vie quotidienne à Sainte-Hélène au temps de Napoléon (Paris, 2005)

A catalogue record for this book is available from the British Library

ISBN: HB: 978-1-4088-9176-6; TPB: 978-1-4088-9175-9; eBook: 978-1-4088-9174-2

2 4 6 8 10 9 7 5 3 1

Typeset by Newgen KnowledgeWorks Pvt. Ltd., Chennai, India
Printed and bound in Great Britain by CPI Group (UK) Ltd, Croydon CR0 4YY

To find out more about our authors and books visit www.bloomsbury.com
and sign up for our newsletters

For Andrea

Contents

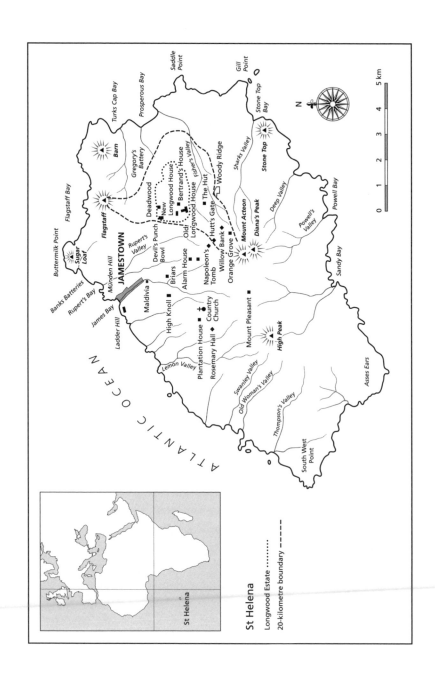

St Helena

Longwood Estate ·········
20-kilometre boundary – – – – –

Yes! where is he, the champion and the child
Of all that's great or little – wise or wild;
Whose game was Empire, and whose stakes were thrones;
Whose table Earth – whose dice were human bones?
Behold the grand result in yon lone Isle,
And, as thy nature urges – weep or smile.

Byron, The Age of Bronze (1823)

EXILE

1815

I

The Fallen Hero

In the evening of 23 July 1815, the *Bellerophon* or the 'Billy Ruffian' as it was known to those who manned it, came in sight of land off the English coast.[1] By morning, the seventy-four-gun warship had sailed into Torbay on the Devon coast, with Captain Frederick Maitland and a small group of French officers watching from the poop. Napoleon, in a flannel dressing gown over which he had thrown his greatcoat, exclaimed in French, 'What a beautiful country.' It was the closest Napoleon had ever come to English shores. In 1803, he had wanted to do so at the head of an army; now he had arrived as an English prisoner. The ship did not approach port, however, but was kept anchored about a mile out from the fishing village of Brixham on the southern side of the bay, 'quarantined' for political reasons.[2]

Maitland received instructions from Lord Keith, commander-in-chief of the Channel fleet, ordering him not to allow any contact whatsoever between the French on board and the English on land.[3] Keith, a big man over six feet tall with ruddy cheeks and a shock of thick white hair, disliked Napoleon and had referred to him in his correspondence as a 'reptile'.[4] It was, however, customary for ships that had just arrived from long stints at sea to be approached by shore boats trying to sell bread, tobacco, fruit and vegetables, and even women, but on this occasion they were warned off, and soon armed patrol boats were put out to keep them away. According to the most commonly accepted account, a local baker by the name of Michelmore approached the *Bellerophon* and saw a man signal to him through one of the portholes (they had all been closed for secrecy). Accompanying Michelmore was his apprentice and three boys who would normally have been at school, except that they had been given an extra week's summer vacation to celebrate the victory at Waterloo. Told to pull off, along with all the other provision boats that had come out, Michelmore circled the ship a few times, avoiding the patrol boat also circling the ship until someone on board supposedly threw a small 'foreign-looking' bottle into the sea. It contained a note simply saying, 'We have got Bonaparte on board.'[5]

Whether it was by this or other means that news of Napoleon's arrival reached the shore, it was impossible to keep his presence a secret for long. Officers of the *Bellerophon*, such as Midshipman George Home, had their part to play in this, letting it be known when they went ashore what was going on. Lieutenant Fletcher, who had been sent to London with dispatches, was indiscreetly telling people along the way what had happened. The word, in short, quickly spread so that, within hours, boats filled with locals and, within days, boats bringing the curious from as far afield as Torquay, Paignton and Dartmouth had surrounded the *Bellerophon*, everyone wanting to catch a glimpse of Napoleon. John Smart, one of the boys who had been in the boat with the baker Michelmore, recalled that Napoleon looked 'little' and 'rather fat'. 'He took off his hat which had a cockade on it and bowed to the people, who took off their hats and shouted "Hooray!" I recall a feeling of triumph mixed with a natural satisfaction at seeing a wonderful sight.'[6] Before long, people in London had heard of the attraction. 'The boats and yachts continued to arrive all day – and on that day all the country seemed to come in. Gentlemen and ladies on horseback and in carriages; other people in carts and wagons; and to judge by the number of people, all the world inland was flocking to see Bonaparte. The Brixham boatmen had a busy time of it and must have taken more money in two days than in an ordinary month.'[7]

The crowds were so thick that, on 26 July at three in the morning, less than two days after arriving in Torbay, Maitland received the order to move the ship to Plymouth Sound.[8] It was from that time on that Napoleon, or at least those in his entourage, began to complain about his treatment. The move coincides with a report by Napoleon's chief valet, Louis-Joseph-Narcisse Marchand, who claims that an

Irish Catholic soldier on sentry duty outside the dining room of the *Bellerophon* whispered to Marchand, 'No good for Emperor Saint Helena,' although he says he kept the news to himself.[9] It became obvious then that they were not going to be allowed to land (since he was being sent further away from London). If there was any doubt in the minds of some in Napoleon's entourage, they soon realised that they were prisoners when, on reaching Plymouth, two boats full of armed seamen were placed on watch around the *Bellerophon*.

Plymouth was likely to attract more people, but it was in more secure surrounds. By the time the *Bellerophon* reached Plymouth, coaches full of people from London and the surrounding areas were travelling down to get a glimpse of the man maligned by the English press for the last fifteen years. They lined the beaches, put out in whatever boats they could hire, and generally pressed as closely as possible to the *Bellerophon*. The day of 27 July was perfect for it; hot and sunny with a light breeze. By midday, the Sound was full of every imaginable craft from fishing boats and rowing boats to yachts. The crowds – between 8,000 and 10,000 people in as many as 1,000 boats[10] – were boisterous, singing, playing music, openly applauding Napoleon, with men removing their hats and cheering him 'apparently with the view of soothing his fallen fortunes and treating him with respect and consideration',[11] wearing red carnations in their buttonholes (these quickly became a Napoleonic symbol, possibly because the Legion of Honour was carnation red). Keith grew concerned that if Napoleon somehow managed to force his way on to a boat and set foot on shore, no power could then remove him. 'They [Napoleon and his entourage] are determined to make the attempt if at all possible, they are becoming most refractory and talk of resisting the Emperor's being taken out of the ship.'[12] 'I am miserable,' Keith wrote to his daughter, 'with all the idle people in England coming to see this man. Here is among others my niece Anne, with "dear friends" she never saw before, arrived from Exmouth! Sir J. Hippisley and Sir H. McLean and family – people all the way from Birmingham – not a bed in all the town.'[13] And again two days later, 'I am worried to death with idle folk coming, even from Glasgow, to see him; there is no nation as foolish as we are.'[14] The only day that the crowds did not turn out was on Saturday 29 July, when thick weather had set in. The waters around the *Bellerophon* were empty except for the guard boats.

The very next day, however, was a complete turnaround. It was still a rainy, cloudy afternoon but there were as many boats as on any previous day. 'I am certain that I speak within bounds,' Maitland wrote, 'when I state, that upward of a thousand were collected round the ship, in each of which, on an average, there were not fewer than eight people. The crush was so great as to render it quite impossible for the guard-boats to keep them off.'[15] Bands of musicians played French tunes in some of the boats in the hope of attracting Napoleon's attention. But that was not all. All around the Sound, on the breakwater and on the surrounding hills, people who could not afford boats gathered, where possible with telescope or glasses in hand, in the hope of viewing the most famous prisoner in the world. That day, Napoleon kept them waiting. He did not appear on deck until about five-thirty in the evening, but the acclamations became so loud that he became 'mortified and displeased and not a little agitated'.[16] He went back down below deck. He may have been dejected; it was the first time he had appeared before the English public unshaven.

Napoleon was *the* international celebrity of his age, and had been a constant presence in the English press ever since the coup of Brumaire in 1799.[17] Now, after his defeat, he was an object of both curiosity and pity, still possessed of an immense power of attraction because of his fall.[18] Many could not believe that he was 'actually in Plymouth Sound. How incredible all this is! How astonishing!' wrote one witness. 'I cannot think of it coolly, it bewilders me.'[19] Although Napoleon was generally lampooned in countless political cartoons, there were also those within English politics sympathetic to him and what they thought he represented, namely, liberty and the values of the French Revolution. For many of these people, whether they expected to see a man with 'horns or hoofs' or the greatest general of the age, it was a once-in-a-lifetime opportunity to lay their eyes on him.[20] And they were often people of means; they had to be able to afford to rent boats to take them out, and that cost anywhere between twenty and fifty guineas a day.[21] Boats were so full that some of the passengers were made to stand, so that they tottered with the waves. Many of these people were so taken with the idea of Napoleon as disconsolate hero that 'respectable' Britons among them considered it an honour 'to put on, for a moment, a shirt, a waistcoat, a neck-cloth' that had been worn by Napoleon (although where they may have got hold of articles of his clothing is another matter).[22] The few attempts made by the naval authorities to keep the boats at bay and to form a cordon of at least a hundred metres around the *Bellerophon* – firing warning shots, pushing back boats – seem not to have worked. This comic farce turned tragic when boats accidentally overturned and their occupants spilled into the sea, so that some were drowned.[23]

Napoleon quickly learnt to play to the crowds, appearing regularly on deck at around five or six o'clock every evening, acknowledging the people by raising his hat and bowing.[24] Sailors on the *Bellerophon* would hold up bulletins chalked on boards to keep the curious informed of his every movement – 'At breakfast', 'Resting', 'Going to Dinner', 'In the Cabin with Captain Maitland', and so on. When the board announced that Napoleon was 'Coming on Deck', the crowd's excitement would reach fever pitch. Harriet Haviland, the sister of the painter Benjamin Haydon, managed to see Napoleon from a boat near the *Bellerophon*. 'He seems a good figure and dignified,' she wrote to her brother, 'and to the disgrace of the Plymothians be it said, yesterday, as he withdrew, the people rose up in their boats and applauded him.'[25] Of course, there were not only Plymothians present, but English people from all quarters of life.

It was not just the gawking crowds that Napoleon played to; he was playing to the British on the national scene as well.

NAPOLEOMANIA

The British had been at war with France for over twenty years, and more than half that time with Napoleon. Their fascination for him, tinged with a degree of horror or fear, reached its paroxysm in that week in August 1815.

A number of exhibitions, as well as publications, paintings and prints depicting various aspects of the Napoleonic wars appeared in England and Europe after the fall of Napoleon in 1815, which greatly contributed to the development of both the black and the gilded legends. The battlefield of Waterloo almost immediately became a tourist attraction for Britons,[26] but for those unable to make the trip to the

Continent, there were alternatives in the form of plays, panoramas and virtual tours of the battlefield (and other Napoleonic sites) where for as little as a shilling the viewer could walk through canvas and wood reconstructions of the sites.[27] Napoleon and especially Waterloo were among the most popular subjects for British theatre-going audiences,[28] and as many as 200,000 people viewed the panorama of the Battle of Waterloo in Leicester Square in 1816. However, the biggest show in London centred on Napoleon's carriage and Arab stallion, Marengo, both captured at the battle.[29]

The Prussian officer Major von Keller, who had captured the carriage at Waterloo, gave it to Generalfeldmarschall Gebhard Leberecht von Blücher, in charge of the Prussian forces at the battle, who then gave it to the Prince Regent. The prince then sold it on to William Bullock for 2,500 guineas.[30] Bullock displayed it in his own private museum, in the Egyptian Hall, Piccadilly. The carriage, one of three made, served as campaign kitchen, dining room, study, bathroom and sleeper. Its bulletproof panels (a novelty for the period), silver-gilt furniture and the laurelled 'N' caused a sensation.[31] Around 800,000 people paid a shilling to see and touch the carriage. 'You cannot imagine the eagerness of the English to examine this carriage,' wrote one French tourist. 'It is an endless procession; men, women and children enter by one carriage door, pose for a moment on the back of the seat, and exit out the other carriage door, looking at each other with an air of satisfaction.'[32]

A booklet on sale at the exhibition forewarned the reader of what to expect: 'The diversity of thought that must arise, and the energy of those feelings that must be involved in regarding this object, surpass those which could be excited by almost any other upon earth.'[33] This was meant to be an experience, both physical and spiritual, as if by touching the object that was once Napoleon's some insight into the nature of the man could be gleaned. But it was also understood to be a war trophy, a material reminder that, had it not been for Great Britain, 'the civilised world would at this hour have continued under the dominion of usurped authority'.[34] This somewhat lofty description did not prevent the leading caricaturists of the day, Thomas Rowlandson and George Cruikshank, from making fun of the visiting crowds.

Alongside the carriage were items that had been captured with it – the four large brown horses that had drawn the carriage, personal

items of clothing belonging to Napoleon and, most curious of all,
Napoleon's Dutch coachman, Jean Hornn, who had lost his right arm
when the carriage was captured at Waterloo, and who later published
his recollections of the great man.[35] Hornn would drive the carriage
through the streets of the major cities the exhibition toured – Bristol,
Dublin and Edinburgh – no doubt drumming up business in the process, since his presence was supposed proof of the authenticity of the
carriage. It was eventually bought by Madame Tussaud's and displayed as part of her Napoleon Gallery in Baker Street, only to be
destroyed by fire there in 1925.[36]

THE BLACK LEGEND

The fascination for Napoleon in England is in stark contrast to a considerable body of critical works – what is referred to as the 'black legend' – that had begun to appear in France after his fall from power in
1814, often translated into English, German and Italian. An example is
the *Précis historique sur Napoléon Buonaparte* (An historical summary
of Napoleon Buonaparte), a work filled with anecdotes that illustrate
Napoleon's lack of humanity, his excessive ambition and his utter
impassivity before the carnage at Eylau.[37] Of a very different genre
are the *Histoire amoureuse de Napoléon Bonaparte* (The love story of
Napoleon Bonaparte), published in 1815, and the *Amours secrètes de
Napoléon Bonaparte* (The secret loves of Napoleon Bonaparte). Both
of these works reduced Napoleon's life to a crude sexual romp.[38] In
the *Amours secrètes*, the reader could find proof of Napoleon's per-
verse nature: he tried to 'abuse' a cousin at the impossibly young age of
nine; he seduced a young bourgeoise at Brienne; in Paris he frequented
brothels to the point where he soon had to be treated by a doctor. Once
cured, he rejoined his regiment, only to launch into a series of scandalous exploits, going from women of little repute to respectable daughters of good families, abducted by his men at arms. These activities, the
author went on, explain how he came to marry the mistress of Paul
Barras, Josephine, and was given as a wedding gift the Army of Italy.
Of course, his marriage could not calm his ardour, since he was taken
with Josephine's daughter, Hortense, whom he raped at Spa.[39] Once he
had tired of Hortense, he passed her to his brother Louis. In Egypt, he

had a harem of Georgian and Circassian women. During the Empire, he seduced one of Josephine's readers, Mlle George (which happened to be true, except that she was an actress). When Napoleon read a copy of the *Amours secrètes* on St Helena, he laughed 'very heartily' and observed that it was 'monstrous silly'.[40]

These sensationalist narratives, designed in part to legitimate the restoration of the Bourbon monarchy in 1814, flourished in the first years after their return.[41] Historians have suggested that they were the work of people in the pay of the Bourbon regime as much as an expression of a particular popular current.[42] Many of these biographies were political statements, designed to disparage the 'usurper' as well as throwing some light on the French character that had allowed these circumstances to pass.[43] The overriding theme in these works was, first, that Napoleon was not French, that is, he was a foreigner in habit, character and language, and second, that he was driven by an unbounded ambition.[44] He was variously portrayed as a Corsican brigand; as an exterminator of men; as Apollyon, the angel of the Apocalypse; as Nero, Attila, Genghis Khan, Tamerlane; as a cruel tyrant.[45] The Bonaparte family too came in for a drubbing and was portrayed in a state of frenetic libertinage:[46] gambling houses and brothels kept by the mother, Letizia, and her daughters; rape; incest between Lucien and Caroline, Pauline and Napoleon, and Pauline and Lucien; venereal disease and so on. In Italy, a comic opera called *La Snapoleonazione* ridiculed the whole family, and showed how the earth darkened at Napoleon's name.[47] The purpose of these 'histories' was to 'demythify' Napoleon's political and military genius, to set the reader on the right path by pointing to his true character – a man who was not only sexually depraved, but ungrateful, cowardly and an enemy of Christianity (an absence of religion was meant to demonstrate moral inferiority).[48] The author of the *Apothéose de Napoleone Bonaparte* calculated that the letters in his name added up to 666, the sign of the devil.

'A MOOD OF RECRIMINATION'

Napoleon's apparent popularity among the English, however, did not facilitate the task of the British government, which had to decide what to do with him, a debate documented in the English press.[49] Before boarding the *Bellerophon*, Napoleon wrote a letter to the Prince Regent, comparing himself to Themistocles, come 'to throw [himself] upon the hospitality of the British people'.[50] General Gaspard, Baron de Gourgaud, who as we shall see plays a considerable role in the years to come, was sent to England to deliver in person Napoleon's letter to the prince, accompanied by Captain Sartorious of the sloop *Slaney*. Gourgaud was also to deliver a request, namely, that Napoleon should be allowed to go to America, but, failing that, that he should live in England, preferably on an estate in the country. Napoleon no doubt had in mind his brother Lucien, who had lived as a prisoner in Shropshire from 1810 to 1814.[51]

The first rude awakening Napoleon got about his situation was the discovery that Gourgaud, who had arrived at Plymouth on 22 July, was refused permission to land. It is true that Captain Sartorious had taken a copy of Napoleon's letter to the Prince Regent, but no answer had been forthcoming.[52] The fate of the letter was of the utmost importance to Napoleon.[53] If the Prince Regent accepted it and entered into a correspondence with him, then the British government would have to deal directly with the former Emperor himself in any discussions about his future. If, however, the letter was not officially received, as was the case, then it meant that the government did not formally recognise Napoleon and could go about organising his fate without consulting him. In the end, the government never acknowledged receipt of the letter, despite the fact that it somehow found its way into the newspapers.

The lack of communication with the mainland increased the discomfort felt among Napoleon's party; it was completely at odds with the deference he had been shown on board the *Bellerophon*. The newspaper accounts were another rude awakening. Gourgaud, who came on board the *Bellerophon* on 24 July, brought with him a bunch of newspapers.[54] Although largely divided along party lines, they were almost uniformly hostile. The Tory press described Napoleon as 'the tyrant of the human race', as 'the ex-tyrant, the ex-rebel' and as 'that bloody miscreant who had so long tortured Europe'.[55] There was even a proposal by the English polemicist Lewis Goldsmith that Napoleon, as well as those who had betrayed the French king, Louis XVIII, should appear before a 'Grand European Tribunal', a sort of Nuremberg tribunal before its time, in order to answer for their war crimes. *The Times* in particular pursued this line, with other newspapers taking up the refrain.[56] Its editor, John Stoddart, deeply conservative and Francophobe to boot, railed against Napoleon, demanding he be treated like any other criminal and condemned to a dishonourable death by hanging.[57] Stoddart's vindictive editorials led to a riposte by the radical journalist William Hone, who published a pamphlet called *Buonaparte-phobia ou La malédiction rendue facile* (Buonaparte-phobia or the curse made easy), in which he accused Stoddart of being seduced by simple epithets and easy invectives.[58] The desire to see Napoleon executed was nevertheless common enough among British conservatives – there was a 'mood of recrimination' against him for having left the island to which he had been exiled in 1814, Elba, and causing another war[59] – but it is not something that was taken seriously by the allies. That is, there was no formal discussion about putting Napoleon on trial, even if at the meeting convened by the European powers at the Congress of Vienna in 1815 the allies declared Napoleon 'liable to public vengeance'.

The newspapers also speculated about what would become of Napoleon and where he might be sent – Gibraltar, Malta, Scotland. The Whig press was necessarily inclined to be more moderate, and was in favour of welcoming Napoleon as an exile. Once an enemy had surrendered his person, commented the *Courier*, 'you no longer had any right over his life'.[60] Other moderate papers considered the notion of exile and St Helena as distinct possibilities. The first time this was raised in the press, it was probably leaked by the government in an attempt to prepare public opinion.[61] *The Times* lamented the fact that the British were 'to impose upon ourselves the disgraceful trouble of conveying his body to a distant island, and there watching it',[62] while the *Independent Whig* protested that it was up to the law, and not ministers, to decide his fate.[63]

Reading these reports in the English newspapers would have increased the unease felt by Napoleon and his party. 'It would be difficult to describe our anxiety and our torment,' wrote Napoleon's chamberlain, Emmanuel de Las Cases, 'most of us seemed hardly to be living: the least circumstance that came from land, the most vulgar opinion of anyone on board, the least authentic newspaper article was the subject of the most serious arguments and the cause of constant swings between hope and fear.'[64] At first Napoleon appears to have remained unperturbed by these rumours and insisted that they could not let themselves be influenced by the 'rantings of journalists'.[65] He knew full well that newspaper accounts were not government policy and should therefore not be taken too seriously. There were other more encouraging signs that the English would receive them well, including the boatloads of sightseers that had ventured out to see him.

That was not to be. The British government had to decide what status to impose on Napoleon, that is, whether he was to be treated as a European sovereign, as a simple general or as an outlaw, and whether he was to be held prisoner in England, sent back to France or banished to another place of exile. The prime minister, Lord Liverpool, was at first more inclined to hand him over to Louis XVIII, who would 'hang or shoot Buonaparte, as the best termination of the business'.[66] Liverpool had been present during the storming of the Bastille in Paris as a young man in 1789 and associated all things revolutionary with the mob. As a result, he was not inclined to show Napoleon any leniency. The option was quickly rejected not because it would have led to Napoleon's death, but because it was feared it would have unforeseen repercussions on the stability of the newly reinstalled Bourbon monarchy. Besides, Louis XVIII did not insist on the English handing over Napoleon, so the cabinet decided the best thing was for them to take control of the situation.

The British foreign secretary, Robert Stewart, Viscount Castlereagh, who was in Vienna, later wrote that the allies saw no difficulty in 'leaving the unrestricted custody of Buonaparte's person to the British Government, under perhaps some engagement with the other Powers not to turn him loose without their consent'.[67] A formal convention was later drawn up in Paris, and signed on 2 August, that left Britain to assume responsibility for Napoleon, but the other allied powers were also insisting that commissioners be stationed at Napoleon's place of detention so that they could keep an eye on him. Castlereagh assured the allies that commissioners would be attached to any place of imprisonment.[68] The Duke of Wellington thought Napoleon ought to be imprisoned in Fort St George in Scotland.[69] Other places were discussed, including the Tower of London and Dumbarton Castle on the Clyde. The possibility that Napoleon should remain a prisoner on English soil, on the other hand, while offering some political advantages, was discarded as too complicated and too risky. The great-est fear of the British government was that, if Napoleon did remain in Britain, not only would he become 'an object of curiosity', but he would inevitably influence the course of domestic politics in France, and thereby destabilise the Bourbon monarchy.[70]

'THE PLACE IN THE WORLD BEST CALCULATED FOR CONFINEMENT'

The only sensible option other than sending Napoleon back to France or letting him remain in England was exile. The cabinet got parlia-ment to pass a law to that effect, and obtained the approval of the allies to carry it out. A few places were considered – Mauritius, for example – and abandoned finally in favour of St Helena in the South Atlantic. The ministers' goal was to remove him from the European scene, to get him away as far as they could, so that he would 'soon be forgotten'.[71] St Helena was, moreover, a possibility that had been raised on previous occasions, as early as 1800 when a few conspira-tors considered kidnapping the First Consul and transporting him to the island,[72] and more seriously in 1814 when the delegates at the Congress of Vienna envisaged transferring Napoleon from Elba to more secure surroundings.[73] Liverpool told Castlereagh as early as 15 July that the choice was between the Cape of Good Hope and St Helena.[74] By 21 July, the decision had been made. Discussions between Liverpool, the first lord of the Admiralty, Lord Melville, and John Barrow, a civil servant who was permanent secretary of the Board of Admiralty, had come to the conclusion that the 'place in the world the best calculated for the confinement of such a person' was St Helena.[75] Owned by the East India Company, about 3,500 kilo-metres from the Brazilian coast and 2,500 kilometres from Africa, it was the island furthest from any mainland anywhere in the world.

It would be some time yet before Napoleon was told of the deci-sion. The cabinet met on 24 July, the same day the *Bellerophon* sailed into Torbay. Their first task was to isolate Napoleon from all contact with anyone not on board the ship. There was no precedent for what to do in this situation; the British cabinet did not at all feel as though they were on solid legal grounds. When Napoleon had disembarked with 400 troops at Golfe Juan on 1 March 1815, it was to all intents and purposes a case of one monarch declaring war on another. If he were classified as a prisoner of war – debatable since he had freely given himself up, asking to benefit from English laws – then he would have to be released on the conclusion of peace. Moreover, the manner in which Napoleon had been greeted by Maitland off Rochefort, with a certain amount of deference but not full honours, complicated matters; Maitland had treated him as more than a simple general but somewhat less than a sovereign. In a letter to Keith dated 28 July, Melville informed him of the decision to 'restrain' General Bonaparte 'in his personal liberty' and to deny him the opportunity of ever again disturbing the peace of Europe.[76] The insistence on the part of the British government not to recognise Napoleon's imperial title appears mean-spirited in hindsight, an unnecessary belittling of a man who had fallen from grace. However, the cabinet took this decision, deliberately marking Napoleon out as a prisoner – indeed, he was referred to as the 'prisoner' in official dispatches – a distinction they wanted to press home so that there could be no repeat of Elba.[77] This was something Napoleon should have thought of before handing himself over to the British, since he had never been recognised as emperor or addressed as such by Britain the whole time he had been in power; and yet it does not seem to have occurred to him or to anyone in his entourage in their discussions about where best to seek refuge.

One of the apparent reasons for sending Napoleon to St Helena, apart from attempting to isolate him and to keep him so far from Europe that he and the memory of him would fall into oblivion, was the Duke of Wellington's impression of the island. He had stayed there for three weeks in June 1805 on his return voyage from India. He visited the interior of the island and described it as beautiful and the climate as the healthiest he had ever encountered.[78] He was not alone in his assessment. Melville also believed that the island possessed an excellent climate.[79]

The English were mistaken.[80] The main town, Jamestown, may have been considered healthy; other parts of the island were not. There was a considerable literature on St Helena available to contemporaries, in part because it represented such an important staging point on the Indian trading route. Much of it, however, was outdated and coloured by the fact that sailors had had a tendency to project on to it Edenesque qualities – normal for men seeing land after many months at sea – that it certainly no longer possessed by the beginning of the nineteenth century. In 1647, one voyager was able to write that St Helena was 'so fertile' that no other province in Europe was able to provide 'such plenty of excellent fruits' and 'so many creatures'.[81] The island maintained its paradisiacal reputation until the 1670s. Well after that, travelogues were reporting that the climate was 'peculiarly adapted to the constitution of Europeans'.[82] By the eighteenth century, however, the forests that had once covered St Helena were completely gone in a terrible example of early colonial deforestation. Firewood shortages, drought and soil erosion were major problems that became more acute through the eighteenth century, despite attempts by the East India Company to reverse the environmental decline.

Major-General Alexander Beatson nonetheless prepared a memorandum on St Helena that was delivered to the government on 28 July.[83] Beatson was an officer in the East India Company who had served as governor of St Helena from 1808 to 1813. He was therefore intimately acquainted with the vagaries of the island's climate and the environmental problems it faced.[84] He insisted that the island was 'preeminently suitable to the purpose of confining a state prisoner'. It was small, inaccessible and remote and no one could approach it without being observed. No mention was made, however, of the climate.

The under secretary of state for war, Major-General Sir Henry Bunbury, arrived in Plymouth on the evening of 30 July to present Napoleon with the government's decision. The next morning, he had to force a passage through the boats full of onlookers that were already thronging around the *Bellerophon* by ten-thirty. People knew that Bunbury was in town and that his mission was most likely to inform Napoleon of his fate; they were anxious therefore to catch a glimpse before he was taken away.[85] Keith complained to Melville that the 'concourse of people is beyond all imagination ... they pressed so much on the ship as to touch the side in defiance of the Guard Boats'.[86] Keith accompanied Bunbury on board the *Bellerophon*, and was with him when he delivered his instructions to Napoleon in his cabin that morning, officially announcing the cabinet's decision to send him to St Helena. Since the letter was in

English, Bunbury read it out aloud in French. It is brief and to the point, callous even.[87]

There are two written descriptions of this event, both similar, upon which all historians have to date based their accounts, one by Keith and a more detailed one by Bunbury.[88] According to them, Napoleon listened throughout the translation without interrupting. When asked whether he wanted a written translation of the letter, he replied that he had understood everything perfectly. When handed the letter, he laid it on the table in front of him, paused for a moment and then began firing a volley of protestations at the way he had been treated. He wanted to know before what court of law he could appeal. He asserted that he was not a prisoner of war and that even if he were he still had to be treated according to the law of nations. He claimed he was England's guest and that Maitland had not indicated he was running such a risk before he had come on board, that if he had known he was going to be treated like this he would have remained behind at the head of an army. Being sent to St Helena, he claimed, was the equivalent of a death sentence (because it was in the tropics), and he demanded to be received as an English citizen. Napoleon put the question individually to both Keith and Bunbury, to which neither replied: 'What would you do under the circumstances? Go to St Helena – no! – no! I prefer death.' He reiterated that the climate of St Helena was too hot for him and repeated time and again that he would not go. 'Botany Bay is better than St Helena. If your government wishes to put me to death, they may kill me here.'[89]

When Keith and Bunbury had left, it was Maitland's turn to come in for a drubbing along the same lines, 'in jerky passionate tones', as Napoleon raged about the 'perfect horror' that was his fate, 'worse than Tamerlane's iron cage', how he would prefer to be handed over to the Bourbons, and how they might as well have signed his death warrant.[90] The length and breadth of the argument used suggest that Napoleon had been expecting this outcome – the English news-papers had certainly forewarned him – and that he had prepared a response to it.

Napoleon managed to control himself. After dinner, during which he was calm and even cheerful, he retired to his cabin and had the Comte de Montholon read to him Plutarch's account of Cato the Younger's death. Cato, a diehard republican opposed to Caesar, supposedly killed himself in the most gruesome way, which had inspired any number of artists and writers, by stabbing himself with his sword and, when that did not work, pulling out his intestines through the wound. It is impossible of course to know just what was going through Napoleon's mind. He may have been looking to consolation from history, he may have briefly considered putting an end to it all, or it may simply have been a performance. He had once before attempted suicide by swallowing poison after his first abdication in 1814 at Fontainebleau. The poison didn't have the desired effect because it was old.[91] Napoleon's doctor, Jean-Nicolas Corvisart, probably gave him a vial of poison just before leaving Malmaison, where Napoleon had lingered after Waterloo and before fleeing to the Atlantic coast.[92] The vial would have worked this time if taken. In a conversation with the Comte de Las Cases, he is supposed to have said, 'I sometimes feel like leaving you, and it would not be very difficult. It is only necessary to work oneself up a little, and I shall soon have escaped you, everything will be over, and you will then be able to quietly rejoin your families.'[93] A self-sacrificing thought, but it was suicidal ideation, and was never seriously considered.

THE CHOSEN FEW

It is doubtful that Napoleon ever remembered scribbling the words, 'St Helena, small island,' in a schoolbook at Brienne, but on receiving confirmation of his final destination, he would have felt little but dismay. His entourage were just as anxious about their own futures, some because they feared where they might end up, others because they were afraid of being left behind. 'The whole party seem to have formed the most dreadful idea of that island,' commented Bunbury.[94] In all, fifty-eight people had followed Napoleon into exile from France to England, including women and children,[95] the vast majority of them courtiers and servants, but the British government would allow only a restricted number to remain with him. Napoleon was consequently asked to draw up a list of no more than three officers, a doctor and twelve servants, including the servants of his companions (a thirteenth servant was smuggled on board the *Northumberland* but was discovered on reaching St Helena and immediately deported).[96]

For a while he declined, hoping the government might review its position; to draw up a list at this point would be to acquiesce in his exile.[97] The only person to refuse to attend Napoleon was his physician, Louis-Pierre Maingault, who had accompanied the party from France in the belief that their destination was America.[98] A substitute was found in Barry O'Meara, a twenty-nine-year-old Irish surgeon working on board the *Bellerophon*. O'Meara spoke both French and Italian; Napoleon found him 'sympathetic' and asked to have him appointed as his personal physician.[99] O'Meara, as we shall see, would also end up working for the Admiralty – a sort of inside man – reporting back everything that he heard and saw.

In the end, twenty-six people would accompany Napoleon to St Helena: Comte Bertrand, his wife and three children along with a female servant and her child; Montholon, his wife and child and a female servant; Gourgaud; Las Cases and his son; and eleven servants, including Marchand, Saint-Denis, Cipriani, Noverraz, the two brothers Archambault, Lepage, Rousseau and Gentilini. Nicolas-Louis Planat de La Faye was slotted to go instead of Gourgaud, but the latter was so upset by the decision that he urged Napoleon to reconsider; he did.[100] Even though exile was considered one of the worst experiences for those with strong personal ties at home, and even though, as we shall see, most of them did not want to go to St Helena, competition for a place was fierce. They were torn between loyalty to their master and fear of what the future might hold. That is why Montholon and Gourgaud were openly fighting with each other, while both of them had knives out for the upstart Emmanuel-Auguste-Dieudonné, Comte de Las Cases.

General Comte Henri-Gatien Bertrand was the most senior in rank of the party. Forty-two years old in 1815, described by one English observer as 'a small, plain-looking man, with lively eyes but mild expression and mild manner, not so French as most Frenchmen',[101] he had replaced Michel Duroc as grand marshal of the palace when Duroc was killed at the battle of Bautzen in 1813.[102] Balding and rather timid, Bertrand had been with Napoleon since Egypt. He had married a protégée of Josephine's, Fanny Dillon, daughter of a general who had been guillotined during the Terror. Described by one English officer as 'long and lanky, and sallow and shapeless', Fanny was nevertheless by all accounts a 'most engaging, fascinating woman', who did not play the part expected of her.[103] It is said that she married Bertrand, a mere count, out of lassitude and that she would have much preferred an Italian or German prince.[104] She nevertheless gave Bertrand four children, one of whom was born on St Helena.

General Charles Jean Tristan, Comte de Montholon, thirty-two years of age, had seen some fighting in his time but had supposedly left active service because of his health. He became Josephine's chamberlain, but fell out of favour with Napoleon after marrying Albine-Hélène de Vassal, who was separated but not yet divorced from a Swiss banker. Napoleon did not take kindly to the marriage and Montholon was ostracised from the court until 1814, when commanding officers were badly needed to fight in what was to become the Campaign of France.

Gourgaud, also thirty-two, had fought in every campaign since Austerlitz and had been wounded twice (once at Austerlitz in 1805 and again at Montmirail in 1814).[105] At one stage during the campaign for France, he helped fight off a small band of Cossacks who were riding furiously towards Napoleon. After Waterloo, he followed Napoleon to Rochefort out of loyalty, out of love.

Las Cases was the most curious of the men who accompanied Napoleon into exile.[106] Shorter than Napoleon at around five feet one inch, forty-eight years old, 'of a meagre form, and with a wrinkled forehead',[107] he was a former noble, a marquis of the *ancien régime*, who had emigrated during the Revolution. He took part in the disastrous Quiberon expedition of 1795, when the British supported a counter-revolutionary landing in Brittany to assist the Chouans revolt. He eked out a living in London as a private tutor, while he worked on an historical atlas that became a remarkable and immediate success when it was published in 1801.[108] He returned to France after the Peace of Amiens in 1802, taking advantage of the amnesty offered to émigrés by Bonaparte. He did not rally to the Empire, however, until 1806 when Napoleon had conquered central Europe. Like many *ralliés*, he worked for Napoleon with enthusiasm and was rewarded for his efforts with the Legion of Honour and the title of baron. He became a chamberlain in 1809 and may have developed a devotion to the man during this period. He fled France for England when the Bourbons first returned in 1814, but came back during the Hundred Days, the period after Napoleon's return from Elba, and accompanied

Napoleon to Rochefort and then into exile. He was not obliged to do so. His role during the Hundred Days was such that he could easily have continued to work for the Bourbons. But, for reasons that will always remain obscure – an innate sense of self-sacrifice, a desire to play the martyr, loyalty to Napoleon, a sense of history – he decided to forgo everything to accompany the ex-Emperor into exile. There is no doubt that he was of the faithful, but he was also an opportunist who (probably) planned to profit from his time and his close proximity to Napoleon by publishing his memoirs. Just who was using whom remains open to speculation, despite Las Cases later declaring that he had no ulterior motives and that he had completely given his life over to Napoleon.[109] Hitherto a relatively obscure personality, he was about to enter the pages of history. His role in the construction of the legend would be primordial.

Not everyone was so keen to follow Napoleon. Fanny Bertrand was particularly opposed to the idea of accompanying him. The daughter of an Irish refugee, the wife of Comte Bertrand, she had found her nerves fraying over the past days and weeks. At one stage on board the *Bellerophon*, she had shrieked at Maitland that 'the Emperor is a monster of egotism, and would see women and children perish without feeling a thing'.[110] On the evening of 31 July, she was walking on deck with her husband, pleading with him not to follow Napoleon. When that did not work, she dashed into Napoleon's cabin and threw herself at his feet, imploring him not to go to St Helena, and not to take her husband away.[111] Napoleon stood, immobile, looking down at her, perhaps a little perplexed by this performance. Receiving no answer from him, she rushed away into the wardroom where a number of officers and ladies had gathered for drinks. When Maitland invited her to join them, she muttered something incoherent and went off to her cabin. Montholon, who had noticed how distraught she was, followed her into the cabin just in time and caught her by the legs as she attempted to throw herself out of a quarter gallery window.[112] Her screams, along with Montholon's cries for help, brought a number of people jostling to get through a narrow door to confront the darkly comic sight of Mme Bertrand, her body half out of the window and her legs being desperately held by Montholon as she kicked and struggled to get free of him. The assembly was able collectively to drag her back in and carry her to bed, where she lay sobbing hysterically. It should be pointed out that Fanny's attempted escape or suicide, whether genuine or affected, did not sway her husband in the least; he was still determined to follow his master into exile. What must it have been like as husband and wife lay together that night in their cramped quarters?

What is not often mentioned is that most of the prominent personalities in Napoleon's entourage, as well as a number of domestics, wrote letters to the British authorities requesting permission to return to Europe, if they so chose, in six months' time.[113] It was a way out in case things proved to be worse then they feared. They included General Bertrand, Gourgaud, even though he had caused a scene to be with the Emperor, Napoleon's valet, the twenty-four-year-old Marchand, and Mme Montholon on behalf of her husband and child.[114] 'I am leaving with the Emperor for the island of St Helena,' wrote Bertrand, 'but I do not wish to stay there.'[115] O'Meara also asked to be allowed to resign as Napoleon's doctor and return to England when he saw fit. We do not know whether these requests were made with the knowledge and consent of Napoleon, but I suspect they were not. Captain Charles Frédéric Piontkowski was the only person to write imploring the British for permission to accompany his 'unfortunate sovereign'. 'I should be very happy to serve as one of the least of the domestic staff.'[116] It was the kind of loyalty Napoleon believed to be prevalent among the chosen few, but which was sadly lacking.

'I DO NOT VOLUNTARILY GO'

Napoleon was portrayed during this period as exhibiting 'great calm, without showing any emotion'.[117] This was interpreted by Marchand as a demonstration to the world of how a great man acts in the face of adversity,[118] but it would appear that in fact he fell into a deep depression, one that would never really leave him, or only ever intermittently. Maitland describes Napoleon as 'lethargic', sleeping about twelve hours a day (highly unlike him) and dozing on the sofa in his cabin during the day.[119] After Bunbury's visit, Napoleon rarely left his cabin, except to eat. Disappointing the crowds that still came out to see him, he did not appear on deck again while at Plymouth. When the *Bellerophon* was moved out of Plymouth Sound, he withdrew further still. He confined himself to his cabin and did not come out even for meals, his mood no doubt compounded by the change in weather – it had become overcast and rainy – and by his impending transfer to the vessel that would carry him to his place of exile.[120] He sat in his cabin, in his dressing gown, impassive, quiet, reflecting perhaps on what awaited him, on what might have been and on the two weeks that had passed since he first boarded the *Bellerophon*. That Napoleon had not been sighted for some time so worried the British authorities that Maitland ordered a midshipman to crawl out on a spanker boom to see if he could catch a glimpse of him through a cabin window.[121]

British fears, and rumours of Napoleon's escape, were groundless. During the night of 4 August, he composed a letter with the help of Bertrand and Las Cases which began, 'I solemnly protest, in the face of heaven and of men, against the violence that has been done me, against the violation of my most sacred rights, in disposing of my person and of my liberty by force'.[122] In it, Napoleon argued that he had come on board the *Bellerophon* of his own free will, and that once he had set foot on the vessel he was 'on the hearth of the British people'. This was Napoleon as tragic figure caught in the machinations of ruthless politicians. If the letter was directed at the British government, it was hardly likely to make much difference. But then the letter was much more about appealing to public opinion and was, in some respects, the first shot fired in the battle for history that would be played out over the course of Napoleon's imprisonment on St Helena. Keith forwarded the letter to Melville. The government waited two weeks before allowing it to be published in the press, but by that time Napoleon and his entourage were well out to sea.

On 4 August, the *Bellerophon*, accompanied by the *Tonnant*, an eighty-gun vessel with Lord Keith on board, was moved out of Plymouth towards Start Point, some forty kilometres to the south-west.[123] Napoleon, according to Keith, was 'very angry',[124] no doubt because his remonstrances till then had been in vain, and the moment was rapidly approaching when he would be transferred to the ship that would sail for St Helena. At nine o'clock the next morning, the *Northumberland*, a creaky old seventy-eight-gun warship, refitted for what was to be its last voyage along with its two escorting vessels, the *Bucephalus* and the *Ceylon*, sailed into view.

The crew of the *Northumberland* were in a foul mood.[125] They felt they had been unfairly treated. The war was over; the crew expected to be discharged and paid off, rather than sent halfway around the world to keep Napoleon prisoner, possibly to rot on St Helena with him. Twenty-four men had already deserted and the rest were bordering on mutiny. If Napoleon were to come on board and take advantage of a disaffected crew, anything could happen. Admiral Sir George Cockburn, chosen to lead the convoy to St Helena, and the man who would remain in charge of the island until the arrival of the new governor, went on board and looked through the roster. Anyone who was considered a risk or a suspect in the present unrest was laid off and replaced, seventy-six men in all. Volunteers from the *Tonnant* and the *Eurotas* took their place. The mood of the French on the *Bellerophon*, meanwhile, was one of profound gloom, for some had realised that they would be leaving Napoleon for ever, while those slated to serve him feared they might never return to Europe. Napoleon was still relatively young, only forty-six, so it could conceivably be another thirty-odd years before he died. To leave with him was in effect a life sentence; it was to cut off all ties with hearth and kin.

On the evening of 6 August, Napoleon was presented to Admiral Cockburn, who came across as civil but stiff and cold.[126] It was during this meeting, in the presence of Lord Keith, that Napoleon learnt of the conditions of his imprisonment on St Helena: he was forbidden to go beyond a certain perimeter without an escort; to enter into relations with the inhabitants of the island; to send or receive letters in secret; and to carry arms. In addition, no foreign vessels were allowed to anchor off the island.[127] Napoleon launched into a protest, 'in the most earnest manner', reiterating everything he had been complaining about for the last week. At the end, Cockburn deflected the attack by simply asking him what time they could expect him on board the *Northumberland* the next day – 'any hour he pleased after breakfast, which was generally at about ten o'clock'.[128] Napoleon was about to leave behind one phase of his life, in which he had ruled over most of western Europe, and enter another as an apostate and exile.

The next day, the little flotilla was anchored about a mile off Berry Head. Napoleon remained in his cabin with Bertrand for the better part of the morning, no doubt going over last-minute arrangements.

At one point, he told Keith, 'I do not voluntarily go either from this ship or from England; it is you, Admiral, who take me.' Keith is supposed to have replied, 'I hope, Sir, that you will not reduce an officer like me to do so disagreeable an act as to use force towards your person.' To which Napoleon answered, 'Oh no, you shall order me.'[129] It was a sort of face-saving exercise. Napoleon had repeated a number of times that he would not go to St Helena,[130] but it would be nothing short of humiliating if he were to be forced from the *Bellerophon*. He could, however, leave the ship of his own accord on the pretence that Keith had ordered him to.

The other members of his suite waited in the outer cabin, writing letters or fretting, pacing up and down. General Anne-Jean-Marie Savary, Duc de Rovigo, and General Charles-Frédéric-Antoine Lallemand, who had both fought at Waterloo and had both followed Napolen into exile, were particularly agitated because they did not know what their fate was going to be. As they had not been chosen to accompany Napoleon, they feared being sent back to France where they would have been arrested, tried and executed, like a number of their comrades in arms.[131] When Napoleon finally appeared before his entourage, it was time to say goodbye. Savary sobbed and threw himself at his feet; Napoleon bent down to help him back up and embraced him.[132] He then embraced the others in turn; some knelt to kiss his hand and wept, but he remained unmoved, at least outwardly.

It was the first time the crew had seen him in four days and they all remarked on his changed appearance: unshaven, pale, his features drawn, unkempt, possibly a little confused.[133] 'Had his execution been about to take place,' wrote George Home, 'there could not have prevailed a more dead silence – so much so, that had a pin fallen from one of the tops to the deck, I am convinced it would have been heard; and to anyone who has known the general buzz of one of our seventy-fours, even at the quietest hour, it is a proof of how deeply the attention of every man on board must have been riveted.'[134] The crew of the *Bellerophon* had become attached to Napoleon, to the extent that 'a horrid gloom hung over the ship'. Maitland later described his thoughts and feelings at that moment – a sense of pity, tinged with regret, for someone who had once occupied such a high position only to be reduced to this.[135] The men of the *Bellerophon* were reported to have said, 'if the people of England knew him [Napoleon] as well as we do, they would not hurt a hair on his head'.[136]

As Cockburn's barge pulled away from the *Bellerophon*, carrying Napoleon to the *Northumberland*, the former Emperor turned and, when he saw 'heads crowding out of every port', stood and 'lifted his hat and inclined his head to the ship's company'.[137] Also present on the barge were Bertrand and his wife, Montholon and his wife, Gourgaud and Las Cases. Napoleon told Keith to sit by him so they could talk. He spoke of St Helena, then laughed at the ladies being seasick.[138] Again on this occasion, a number of boats turned out to see him off, despite the drizzling rain. An accident occurred when the cutter *Nimble* smashed into and overturned a small boat containing a party of eight or nine people who had come from Torquay. Notwithstanding the rescue efforts, two young women drowned.[139] Their bodies were never recovered.

2

Golgotha

The commander of the *Northumberland*, Captain Charles Bayne Hodgson Ross, Cockburn's brother-in-law, thirty-seven years old, saw the barge approach with Napoleon sitting in it. The 'very nasty, priest-like looking fellow' who came on board disappointed him. 'He appears by no means that active man he is said to be. He is fat, rather what we call pot-bellied, and altho' his leg is well-shaped, it is rather clumsy, and his walk appears rather affected, something between a waddle and a swagger ... He is very sallow and [has] quite light *grey Eyes* rather thin, greasy-looking brown hair.'[1] No sooner had Napoleon come on board the *Northumberland* than Cockburn forced him into the presence of visitors – William Lyttelton, a relation of Cockburn, an MP by the name of Lord Lowther, and Colonel Sir George Bingham, who was to command the garrison at St Helena. Cockburn was making a point, that Napoleon would not be treated like a sovereign, but rather like any other senior officer on board. Left alone with Napoleon, the visitors were extremely uncomfortable, not quite knowing what to say. There were long moments of embarrassed silence, to the point where Bingham supposedly whispered to Lyttelton, 'For God's sake say something to him, if it be about a dog or a cat.'[2] They too found Napoleon's physique less than impressive, 'not at all giving an idea that he had been so great or was so extraordinary a man'.[3]

The context was, of course, very different from that of the *Bellerophon*. The descriptions from the men of that ship are generally flattering, since they had received an emperor. Whereas the men of the *Northumberland* were receiving a prisoner, and one who had let his appearance go somewhat; this may have influenced their impressions of him. It is possibly the reason why someone like John Glover, Cockburn's secretary, was able to write that 'Greatness of mind or character, in my opinion, he possesses not, very frequently acting the part of a spoilt child. Feeling I consider him devoid of.'[4]

English descriptions of Napoleon, many of which were published in newspapers over the years, provided the reader with the minutest details about his personal appearance, from the growth of his beard to the colour of his skin, hair and eyes, not to mention the manner in which he behaved or even held himself. In the process, an intimacy was created between the English reader and Napoleon that until then had not existed. He became human, and when the villain was seen in a new light, the public's opinion of him began to shift. At first it was barely perceptible, but as the audience became increasingly sympathetic to his plight, it grew in momentum so that within a short time the descriptions of Napoleon had radically altered. This was not only the case in Britain, where there was a free press, but in other parts of Europe as well, such as the German and Italian states. By contrast, in France any mention of Napoleon was banned, or at least any favourable mention. But we shall come back to this later.

Admiral Cockburn was a stickler for rules. Napoleon was to find a somewhat different reception under him from what he had experienced under Maitland. Cockburn had just returned from North America, where he had been dubbed 'The Ruffian', and where he had made a name for himself in August 1814 by burning Washington and the White House during what has become known as the War of 1812 between Britain and the United States.[5] Nor did Cockburn have any reason to admire Napoleon. His brother, Sir George Rumbold, the British envoy to Hamburg, had been kidnapped by French troops in 1804 before being forcibly returned to England.[6]

Although there was more room on board the *Northumberland* than there had been on the *Bellerophon*, the passengers, including

Napoleon, were less well accommodated; there were more than 1,000 people aboard.[7] It was in these cramped, unhealthy and promiscuous conditions that the men, women and children were going to live for the next two months, getting to know each other somewhat better than they might have liked, learning to appreciate or detest those with whom they were to spend their lives in exile. Preparations for the long voyage had had to be made in such a rush that the vessel was ill equipped for the voyage, so a short stop at Madeira for provisions was planned.

Cockburn was determined that the voyage would take place under the strictest conditions. Moreover, Cockburn emphasised that men were no longer required to stand in Napoleon's presence; they sat down, and kept their hats on.[8] After dinner on 9 August, for example, when they went up on deck for a walk, Cockburn had the effrontery to put his hat on in the presence of Napoleon. The Frenchman was 'piqued'.[9] Napoleon was, in Cockburn's words, 'still inclined to act the sovereign', something the admiral had no intention of allowing: 'the sooner therefore he becomes convinced it is not to be admitted the better'.[10] However much it may have irritated him there was little for the moment that Napoleon could do about it. It was to set a precedent for what followed on the island itself, where the newly appointed governor, Lieutenant-General Sir Hudson Lowe, would relentlessly implement the rules laid down by the War Office. This clash of wills, of different political expectations, of different ways of culturally being and seeing, would be resolved only with Napoleon's demise years later. Cockburn's attitude was not helped by his detestation of the French, and he anyway regarded Napoleon as little more than a 'common disturber'.[11] Napoleon in turn considered Cockburn to be a 'gendarme', a 'shark', even if his own behaviour during the voyage was for the most part surprisingly conciliatory and even somewhat affectionate towards him. There were to be occasions, for example, when Napoleon and the admiral would take walks on board the *Northumberland* and on St Helena, arm in arm.[12]

On the morning of 8 August, the *Northumberland* set sail in a fair wind, although twenty hours later they had made little headway and were still off Portsmouth. That changed on 9 August; it rained hard, obscuring the horizon, while the wind buffeted the sea. For the next

two days Napoleon nevertheless managed to appear on the bridge
in the early afternoon, and even ate dinner, although according to
Cockburn he was 'sulky'.[13] On 11 August, he did not appear on deck
all day, ill with seasickness.[14] The crossing was difficult, the living conditions cramped, the food as bad as one could expect on an early nineteenth-century British naval ship (although Cockburn complained
that Napoleon and the French drank too much for his liking)[15] and,
once the convoy had reached the tropics, the heat unbearable. And as
with most British naval vessels during this period, sailors either had
to run the gauntlet or were given the lash as punishment for infringe-
ments of one kind or another. 'I had no idea,' recalled Marchand, who
witnessed a flogging, 'this flagellation could be so barbaric.'[16]

During the voyage, Napoleon rarely appeared before twelve o'clock
according to some, three or four o'clock according to others, after having taken breakfast either in bed or in his cabin.[17] The poop deck had
been set up for him, and he occupied a room to the right, Cockburn a
room to the left. In between was the stateroom which was nominally
meant for Napoleon's use but of which he availed himself for only
part of the day. Marchand slept in the cabin with Napoleon, on a mat-
tress on the floor, while Mameluke Ali (Saint-Denis) slept outside the
cabin across the doorway. Since Cockburn was determined to treat his
prisoner as nothing more than a superior officer, he would not allow
Napoleon's personal chef to cook for him. Although by no means a
gourmet, Napoleon was less than appreciative of the food served by
the English, and found it unbearably difficult to while away the time
at table. The English regarded the meal as a ritual for relaxing, drinking and enjoying each other's company. Napoleon, on the other hand,
could not sit for long in a state of inactivity. As soon as he had downed
his coffee, he was up and away, impatient to leave the table. The first
time they dined together, the English were shocked that Napoleon got
up without so much as a by-your-leave, and was followed by all the
French officers. Cockburn expressed his disapproval, but was put in
his place by Mme Bertrand, who pointed out to him that he was dealing with a man who had been 'master of the world' and that the kings
of Europe had solicited the honour of being admitted to his table.
From then on, dinner was served more quickly, and when Napoleon
got up to leave, those present stood, only to sit down again after he
had left.

THE RECOLLECTIONS BEGIN

A few days into the voyage, Napoleon began to reminisce with the admiral about the past, usually after dinner.[18] Forced into a lengthy period of inactivity, he would eventually begin to 'write' his memoirs, in which he justified his decisions and his actions. He was supposedly prompted to do so by Las Cases, although the idea had taken some time to come to fruition. Las Cases asserts that Napoleon had at first been reluctant, and that he only came around to accepting the idea on 9 September, less than a month into the voyage, perhaps out of boredom.[19] Napoleon, who had always worked with an eye to posterity, may have been thinking about all the advantages he could gain from writing his memoirs. Now he had the time to reflect on how to massage his legacy and shape the way in which he was to be remembered. The memoirs, as we shall see, were to take the form of a daily dictation, a mixture of intimate recollections and inspired reflections about the greatness of his achievements.

Writing one's memoirs had become all the rage. During the Revolution, and in the decades following the French wars, the world saw more personal recollections, autobiographies and memoirs than had appeared in the previous four centuries. They were written by important political and military personalities, as well as – for the first time in large numbers – by ordinary men and women who understood that they had lived through extraordinary times and wanted to testify to what they had seen and what part they had played, however small, on the world stage.[20] Napoleon, without ever realising it, was caught up in this movement, one of thousands gripped by a desire to reflect on and justify their lives. The confinement he found himself in, first on the vessel and then on the island, would have provided ideal conditions for such an exercise. For a short while, he would exist only through his memories – nostalgic reimaginings of the past.[21] He was not entirely without the capacity for self-reflection. At the time of his coronation, for example, talking about power to Comte Pierre Louis Roederer, he told him that 'I have worked too hard at [its] conquest to allow anyone to take it away from me or even covet her. Although you say that power came to me of its own accord, I know what it has cost me – the sufferings, the sleepless nights, the scheming.'[22] We have an inkling that he may have looked squarely in the mirror and seen himself for what he really was – 'a tyrant, a murderer, a savage'.[23] Napoleon hoped that every day spent on the island would do away with that image.

They quickly got into a routine.[24] After lunch, and until about four o'clock, Napoleon dictated his life story while Las Cases took notes in a sort of shorthand. He began, not surprisingly, with the siege of Toulon, where his meteoric rise had started, followed by the first Italian campaign and then the expedition to Egypt. After four o'clock, Las Cases would retire to his cabin and with the help of his son put his notes in order, which he would present to Napoleon that evening or the next day for corrections. This went on regularly for the rest of the trip and was not without creating some jealousy among those in Napoleon's entourage who saw Las Cases as usurping the intimate role they, especially the military among them, had hoped to play. He was thus quickly dubbed the 'Jesuit' or the 'Rhetorician' or the 'Intriguer'.[25] Las Cases for his part was perfectly aware of these snide remarks, but rose to the challenge, and quickly became indispensable to Napoleon.

'THE FIRST LINK IN THE CHAIN'

St Helena came into view sixty-eight days after the *Northumberland* had left England. At about noon on 15 October, the ship cast anchor; 'it touched the bottom, and that was the first link in the chain that will nail the Modern Prometheus on his rock'.[26]

According to Greek legend, Prometheus brought fire to humanity. He was punished for it by the gods by being chained to a rock and having his liver eaten by an eagle, only to die and to be reborn again every day. It was the beginning of a narrative of suffering and torment, the beginning of Napoleon's Passion that would be cultivated and developed while he was on the island, and even beyond the grave. For Romantics, Prometheus came to represent the dignity of the individual pitted against a hostile and uncomprehending society,[27] a myth that Napoleon was easily able to exploit, even if the full potential of the literary trope was not reached until the 1820s and 1830s. The tale of the agony of Prometheus would become a central component of the 'history' of Napoleon; he and his acolytes made constant references to the myth, except that Napoleon was being punished for bringing freedom to humanity.

The Prometheus metaphor expressed a French as much as a British view of Napoleon's captivity.[28] The first to use it were French and British royalists who saw it as describing his just punishment.[29] Take for example George Cruikshank's 1814 print, *The Modern Prometheus, or Downfall of Tyranny*. It shows a vulture tearing at Napoleon's heart, with British Justice trampling the imperial eagle underfoot. It mocked the association of Napoleon and Prometheus and implied that the rock (and the much flaunted suffering that incensed Napoleon's British sympathisers) was where Napoleon deserved to be. Napoleon, however, used that image for his own ends. Rather than allowing himself to be portrayed as the criminal receiving his just deserts, he became the victim tormented by his jailers.

The British had hoped that by putting a vast distance between Napoleon and Europe he would soon be forgotten. Instead, Napoleon was to turn that distance into a weapon against his captors and to idealise and indeed romanticise his role in French and European history. But, as we shall see, by exiling Napoleon to this rock in the middle of the Atlantic, the British would unwittingly create the conditions that would transform him from ogre to martyr. If he had been kept captive in Britain, he would have become an ordinary, insignificant prisoner. In exile, far from Europe, he was going to be given a new lease of life.[30]

When Mme Bertrand, who would quickly learn to hate the island and all who lived on it, saw it emerge out of the sea, she described it in an eloquent if not particularly elegant turn of phrase as having been 'shat by the devil between two worlds'. 'Nothing could be more desolate or repulsive,' declared O'Meara, 'than the appearance of the exterior of the island.'[31] From Napoleon, however, who emerged from his cabin an hour after the ship had anchored, there was nothing, not a sound, not an utterance on what he may have felt or thought about the imposing geography that lay before his eyes. He remained on deck, staring out on to to this 'rocky catafalque' through a telescope, not the slightest hint of emotion in his face.[32] This silence is perplexing, disturbing even. What might have been going through Napoleon's mind? It is of course impossible to know whether his reaction was one of stoic resignation, whether he was overwhelmed by the enormity of this new reality or whether he had not yet comprehended the life that awaited him. He could not have known that this was the rock on which he was to pass the rest of his life; he may very well have thought that his stay there would be short, and that he would soon be back in Europe.

The German Romantic poet Heinrich Heine would later describe the island of St Helena as the Holy Sepulchre.[33] It rises more than 800 metres out of the sea, 'the ugliest and most dismal rock conceivable, an enormous black wart', whose cliffs are so steep that there is not even a harbour where ships can shelter.[34] The one town, Jamestown, sunk in a ravine and surrounded on both sides by steep mountains, consists of nothing more than a short street flanked on either side by a number of buildings.[35] St Helena is only about ten kilometres wide and sixteen or seventeen kilometres long, similar in size to Jersey in the English Channel, but much more mountainous. Because of its position, it had become a landing point for ships plying their trade between Europe and Asia so that hundreds of ships would drop anchor off the island in order to supplement their meagre rations. With a population in 1815 of 3,587, only about a third of whom were white (the rest were, in the majority, black slaves and emancipated slaves, as well as Chinese and Indians), the population would increase by more than half with the arrival of Napoleon and his retinue, and the British troops needed to guard them.[36] Given the inaccessibility of the island, the number of troops the British sent – along with a squadron of ten ships that constantly patrolled the surrounding waters – might today seem a little excessive, but is the measure of British paranoia about another possible escape. The garrison of more than 2,100 soldiers and 500 cannon was enough to hold off a concerted attack from a powerful force for a considerable length of time. And if that were not enough, Britain decided to annex the island of Ascension, 'another mere wart in the sea'[37] 1,120 kilometres to the north, as well as the island of Tristan da Cunha, 2,000 kilometres to the south. This was overegging the pudding, a sure sign that the British still feared Napoleon, or the potential harm that he could do if he escaped.

Napoleon went ashore on the evening of 16 October.[38] It was nearly dark as he stepped on to the landing. He proceeded down the main

street between Bertrand and Cockburn, troops lining the way, pushing back the crowd. The inhabitants had learnt only a few days before
the arrival of the *Northumberland* that Napoleon was on his way.
One can imagine the stir the news must have caused on what was otherwise a quiet way station. Just about the whole town had come out to
see him, and being stared at made him angry, as if he were a 'ferocious
animal'.[39] He spent the first evening not as a guest of the civilian governor of the island, Colonel Mark Wilks, in Plantation House,[40] which
was certainly big enough to accommodate him, but rather in Porteous
House adjacent to the public gardens at the foot of the main street
of Jamestown. It may have been a way of immediately marking him
out or there may have been some concern about having to give over
Porteous House to him. Whatever the reason, in a quirk of fate, the
house in which Napoleon stayed that first night was the same house
that Arthur Wellesley had slept in when he returned to Britain from
India in 1805.

THE BRIARS AS EARTHLY PARADISE

Napoleon's residence on the island was to be Longwood House, situ-
ated on a plain about 540 metres above sea level and about six kilometres from Jamestown. The lieutenant-governor, Colonel Skelton,
occupied it. Cockburn had visited the house and decided that it was
best placed to serve as Napoleon's residence; it was isolated, away
from the coast and surrounded by open flat ground that would be
easy to guard and observe.[41] While it was being prepared, and additions made to it, Napoleon settled into a pavilion at the Briars, a hill-
side house not far from Jamestown occupied by a purveyor to the
East India Company, William Balcombe, and his family. Napoleon
wanted to be away from town, and this was certainly a beautiful and
quiet spot, not far from a picturesque waterfall. But it is also possible that he decided on this stay because William had connections to
the Prince Regent through Sir Thomas Tyrwhitt, Usher of the Black
Rod and friend of the prince. Napoleon may have calculated that by
charming the Balcombes, who would have reported back to Tyrwhitt
everything their guest said and did, he might indirectly help shape the
prince's opinion of him.[42] Balcombe became the official purveyor to

Longwood, but he was either incompetent or dishonest for the provisions were below par. It was only when Balcombe was forced off
the island in 1818 that the quality of the food provided to those at
Longwood improved and complaints about it stopped.⁴³ Before that
though, for almost two months, Napoleon remained in the summer
pavilion that Balcombe had had built as a ballroom. He had been
offered the use of the main house at the Briars, and Balcombe had
been quite happy to rent it to him, but Napoleon declined, preferring
instead the use of the smaller pavilion. He slept, ate and worked in the
ground-floor room no bigger than six by four metres, while Las Cases
and his son occupied a small room in the garret.⁴⁴ A large marquee was
pitched on the lawn to add more space.

The stay at the Briars is portrayed as the happiest period of
Napoleon's exile, as a moment of 'paradisiacal peace' before the torment that was to be Longwood.⁴⁵ But then much of Napoleon's behaviour on St Helena has to be seen as 'performance', designed to arouse
the sympathies of the French and in particular of the British public,
that is, to attract support for his cause, which was to get off the island.
It is true that in the relative calm of his surroundings, troubled by little more than the occasional cries of children playing, the wind in the
trees and the noise of a few farm animals, Napoleon was able to relax,
perhaps for the first time in many years. There were only four people
in his entourage to hand during this period – two of his four valets,
Saint-Denis and Louis Marchand, Las Cases and his son – although
others would come and go throughout the day. After a few weeks,
Gourgaud would be allowed to pitch a tent in front of the pavilion.⁴⁶

It is here, at the Briars, that Napoleon took part in the Balcombes'
family life. He played with the Balcombe children, especially Elizabeth
(Betsy), took part in games like blind man's bluff,⁴⁷ good-naturedly
put up with their mimicry and acted the scary ogre to frighten Betsy's
friends. The relationship between Betsy and Napoleon might have
inspired novelists but does not merit all that much in the way of historical attention. Betsy was thirteen when she met Napoleon, and she
did not write her memoirs until she was in her early forties, almost
thirty years later.⁴⁸ There is no doubt Napoleon liked the Balcombe
children, and in particular Betsy, and that he put up with her cheeky
behaviour. It shows a human side to his character, one perhaps that

would have made his stay on St Helena far less miserable if he had
allowed himself to dispense with the trappings of monarchy and had
lived out his life as a simple citizen.⁴⁹

Samuel M. Slader, *The present residence of Buonaparte on the Island of St Helena.*
Date unknown.

At the Briars Napoleon continued to dictate his memoirs, although
now much more systematically, distributing Italy to Las Cases, Egypt
to Bertrand, the Empire to Montholon, Brumaire and the years 1814
and 1815 to Gourgaud, shaping and reshaping his past in the process.⁵⁰
He rarely left the pavilion before four o'clock when he went for a
walk for an hour or two in the garden. The only thing that appears to
have kept him going, for a while, was the thought that posterity had
reserved a special place for him and that he would go down in his-
tory.⁵¹ In order to convince posterity to treat him kindly, he set about
making sure that his version of events would be remembered. We shall
come back to the content of the memoirs in a later chapter, but for the

moment it is worth mentioning that the mental exercise involved in writing his memoirs was one way of overcoming the relative inactivity into which he had been plunged.

'DIGNITY OPPRESSED BY FORCE' – LONGWOOD

After Napoleon had spent about six weeks at the Briars, Longwood was ready to be inhabited, although there was a delay caused by concern over the paint fumes.[52] By this time, Napoleon was beginning to tire of the Briars.[53] Betsy was perhaps becoming a little annoying, the living space was restricted, there was no possibility of taking a bath and there was absolutely no privacy. Sentries surrounded him, and a guard tent was pitched in the garden so they constantly had Napoleon in view. These measures did not prevent strangers from accosting him. On one occasion, it was a peasant woman who had had too much to drink. On another, the captain of a merchant ship simply walked into his room without knocking.[54] It was time to put all of that in order. As it turned out, unwelcome sightseers would also accost Napoleon at Longwood. Sailors from visiting ships, for example, would brave formal interdictions and threats of floggings to catch a glimpse of him in the house and gardens.[55] Visitors felt no compunction about going up to his dressing-room window and pushing the curtains aside to peer in.[56]

One has to remember that unlike his time on Elba, where Napoleon had retained his imperial title and a certain freedom of movement, on St Helena he was a prisoner, albeit a privileged one, and was treated as such by his British captors.[57] Five hundred British troops were camped in sight of Longwood House on the plain called Deadwood, which became a small tent town. A low stone wall seven kilometres in circumference was built around Longwood, within which Napoleon could walk as he pleased, although at night sentries were posted along it within sight of each other and immediately surrounding the house: sixteen sentries were posted around Longwood during the day, another twenty-three around the stables, and another twenty-eight on the outer boundaries.[58] A second zone of twenty kilometres in circumference allowed him to move without an escort, but within which he might run into English patrols or troops. Beyond that, he was not allowed to travel without an English officer for company. An aerial telegraph (semaphores) made it possible to communicate with Plantation House, enabling messages to be sent by hoisting coloured flags, if the weather allowed. Among those were: General Buonaparte is well; He is sick; He asks permission to; He has left the limits of; He is absent for some time; He has escaped. It was even reported that Lowe wanted to erect a palisade around Longwood when he arrived, but that Cockburn laughed at the idea.

For the British, the task of building twenty-five rooms to accommodate Napoleon and his entourage in a relatively short period of time had been a mammoth one. Carpenters and seamen from the *Northumberland* had to cart the building material from Jamestown to Longwood, some six kilometres, most of it uphill. As a result, the construction was not of the highest standard, while furniture was taken from wherever it could be found.[59] It was still being built when Napoleon moved there, but the new premises – more than forty rooms after the extensions – were little better than wooden huts covered with roofing paper daubed with tar and grit, not waterproofed, and far from adequate. Needless to say, there were constant complaints from Napoleon and his entourage about their lodgings.

The complaints about Napoleon's living conditions also served a political purpose; they placed him in the position of the victim and made his jailers appear excessively harsh if not unjust.[60] They fed into the depiction of Napoleon as martyr, as someone who stoically put up with the mistreatment he was constantly subjected to by the British. That is why Las Cases was able to write that, after the Briars, Longwood marked the real beginning of their exile.[61] The complaints that emanated about Longwood also placed Napoleon on the moral high ground, in the process destroying the legitimacy of his exile.

One of the problems associated with Longwood, one which all witnesses to the unfolding drama liked to point out, was the presence of rats. Rats had always been a problem on the island since they were first introduced by visiting ships, probably after 1420, and were present in 'vast quantities' by the end of the seventeenth century.[62] The construction of buildings at Longwood simply exacerbated the problem; the rats found food and shelter there so they multiplied exponentially. All witnesses agreed that they were so bad, their numbers so enormous, that it was impossible to do anything about them. Marchand notes that they were sometimes so thick on the carpet that it appeared black.[63] That may have been an exaggeration, but one could not leave anything edible unattended for more than a few seconds otherwise it would be swarmed over by rats. Not only was the house infested with them, but it meant that they could not keep hens for eggs. The idea of enclosing the chickens in pens in the hope of fattening them up rather than leaving them to roam was short lived as they were all devoured by rats.[64] The dogs and cats employed to combat the rats were out-numbered. Poison was used, but not for long since 'the smell of their putrid carcasses [between the walls and under the floorboards] would render the rooms uninhabitable'.[65] Every now and then there would be a concerted attempt to eradicate them – on one occasion the whole household turned out to kill as many as they could with whatever sharp instruments were to hand – but the rats always won the day. Naturally, this did not look terribly good for the British government and an effort was made to rebut the rumours. John Wilson Croker, first secretary to the Admiralty, wrote an article which boldly proclaimed that the 'alleged plague of rats' was imaginary.[66]

In the British press of the day, conservatives and radicals attacked each other over Napoleon's supposed treatment, as indeed they had attacked each other as soon as news of his presence off the English coast had been reported. *The Times* was in a running battle with the *Morning Chronicle* to present Napoleon's life on St Helena in respectively the best and worst possible light. Both papers began to publish extracts of letters and reports coming from the island. The sources of these letters and reports are not always identifiable. Although there was no shortage of communications between the inhabitants of the island and England, some were no doubt inventions of imaginative journalists. On 18 October 1815, for example, the *Morning Chronicle* ran an article – 'Authentic Particulars of Bonaparte. [From an officer on board the *Northumberland*.]' – whose purpose seems to have been to flatter the English reader by giving an 'accurate' portrayal of Napoleon's character.[67] Part of this battle occurred over whether or not the island was proper for someone of Napoleon's stature. O'Meara told the readers of the *Morning Chronicle* that 'your imagination cannot form an idea of anything more dreary than the first aspect of this island'.[68] *The Times* countered by trying to diminish the stature of their prisoner – in one letter a tourist to the island concluded that there was nothing in Napoleon's 'appearance at all indicative of the great qualities he possesses'[69] – and by arguing that the extreme conditions were necessary to prevent his escape.

Despite the howling of the wind through the flimsy woodwork and the constant scurrying of the rats keeping the inhabitants awake at night, a new routine was quickly established. Napoleon would nominally arise between six and seven, often after a restless night. Just as he had suffered from insomnia when he was emperor, so would he continue to suffer from it at Longwood, often getting up at three or four o'clock in the morning, wearing nothing but his dressing gown, to work or simply read, 'remembering all the errors he had made and comparing his past position with his actual situation'.[70] As in the past, he would call people to him in the middle of the night to work or to keep him company. Napoleon's moods could swing from melancholy to upbeat from one day to the next. After a coffee and his ritual ablutions, he would, depending on the weather, go for a short stroll or a ride before breakfast, which was generally served at about ten and almost always taken alone. Then he would settle down to his papers, dictating, reading and correcting the texts of his memoirs that were put before him and which were copied by his valets Marchand and Saint-Denis.[71] When he dictated, he would walk up and down the room, head down and hands behind his back. He would dictate quickly and disliked being interrupted, no matter how incoherent his thoughts were.[72] This was the first draft, so to speak; everything would be put into some kind of order later. If the scribe didn't get it right, Napoleon would get impatient. Work was the only thing staving off the insipid monotony of the passing days, 'without character, without colour'.[73] Las Cases tried to teach Napoleon English during the first few months of their stay on the island, but Napoleon was terrible at languages and soon gave it up.[74]

Around two in the afternoon, he would take a long bath, sometimes reading, sometimes writing on a plank of wood laid across the bath that acted as a rest, sometimes receiving visitors. The daily ritual of the bath was a rather complicated affair given the lack of wood and fresh water on the island. One of Napoleon's valets, aided by the Chinese workers who had been recruited as servants, would spend over an hour preparing for it, heating the water which spiralled through an

antique system and which eventually found its way in a thin stream
into the copper bath. Napoleon liked his water hot, and would lie in
it up to his neck for at least two and up to four hours at a time.[75] Not
only did it help him relax and perhaps forget his surrounds for a while,
but he also considered it good for his health. It was a habit that supposedly exasperated the governor of the island, Hudson Lowe; British
troops had trouble finding enough fresh water to cook with, let alone
bathe.[76] For a long time, water had to be brought up to Longwood
in barrels pulled on carts by the Chinese servants.[77] It was only after
Lowe undertook to build a reservoir at Diana's Peak that conduits
brought water to Longwood and to the military camp at Deadwood.

Once dried off, rubbed down with eau-de-Cologne and dressed,
Napoleon would formally receive visitors in the parlour. Informally
he would often receive people like O'Meara in the bath, or sitting in a
chair opposite the fire, or lying on a sofa in what was referred to as a
morning gown with a madras (a sort of kerchief) around his head. The
formal visits were relatively numerous in the first months and into the
first two years of his captivity; they were generally British, obliged to
stop at St Helena on their voyage to or from India. They often later
published accounts of their meeting with Napoleon once they had
returned to Britain, either in newspapers or in order to spice up an
otherwise mundane travelogue (publishing travelogues had been in
vogue for some time). Napoleon used the visitors to some extent to
find out what was going on in the world, but he also hoped that they
would be able to tell the world about the conditions in which he lived.
This could work both ways; Cockburn tolerated, even facilitated,
many visitors in the belief that they would report favourably on the
conditions of Napoleon's detention.

Napoleon received his visitors according to a strict protocol. All
of them would first have to pass through Bertrand, that is, they had
to apply to and be approved by him. He thus continued to play the
role of grand marshal of the palace. Bertrand was also in charge of
security and took the same precautions as he had always done against
potential assassins and poisoning. The grand marshal would deliver
a pass allowing visitors to be received in audience; a servant in livery
would be waiting for them in the garden and would escort them to the
billiard room. There an officer would welcome them and announce
that His Majesty would receive them. The grand marshal would then

appear at the entrance to the salon and invite them in. Napoleon was still insisting that he be treated as an emperor.

Napoleon would remain standing in the presence of visitors, hat under his arm, thereby obliging men to do likewise (although female visitors were invited to sit). Ever since Cockburn had had the tactlessness to sit in his presence on one of these visits, Napoleon preferred to stay standing, using etiquette as a tool with which to browbeat the British into some kind of recognition, if not respect. Most visitors respected the imposed conditions of the ceremonies, standing, but not sitting. Of course the aura already surrounding Napoleon, and the fear that British propaganda had inspired over the last fifteen years, would normally be enough to overawe the most self-possessed visitor, but this courtly etiquette served the same purpose as it had at the Tuileries Palace, or any other court for that matter – namely, to place a distance between the ruler and the ruled, or in this instance between the conquered and the conquerors. Otherwise, visits would have deteriorated to the level of a tea party or an afternoon reception around cake and coffee.

After one of these visits, Lady Malcolm, the wife of Rear-Admiral Sir Pulteney Malcolm (Cockburn's successor, who arrived in June 1816), left the following description of Napoleon: 'He is neither like any picture or anybody I ever saw. The profiles are like those of some of the pictures, but not the full face, which is rather too fat and very pale. His eyes light blue or grey, with a pleasant expression. His neck is very short and he holds his head forward when he sits.'[78] The extent to which Napoleon became a tourist attraction for English visitors plying their way either to or from India is both remarkable and somewhat pathetic (in the true sense of the word). In some respects, he had been reduced to a curiosity, a sort of circus freak to be looked at and pointed at. Gourgaud described how visitors would arrive in groups of fifteen or twenty at a time.[79]

Behind this polite façade, tensions mounted as the exile wore on. There was little to do in that confined environment: receiving visitors, who arrived for the first couple of years, but stopped from August 1819; his memoirs, largely finished by May 1817, although he would continue to revise them over the years;[80] commentaries on various historical campaigns; reading; a couple of flirtations in the

early months with local girls whom he met while riding – Mary-Anne
Robinson (he visited the cottage where she lived twelve or fourteen
times, and twice in one day; rumours about an affair were rife within
the small community but utterly unsubstantiated), and then Charlotte
Knipe, the daughter of a farmer, but nothing ever came of it;[81] and
possibly something more than just a flirt with Esther (also known as
Henrietta) Vesey, a seventeen-year-old mulatto servant girl, who was
the Montholons' chambermaid. Napoleon may have got her pregnant – wagging tongues certainly asserted that Marchand was simply
deflecting rumours from his imperial master by claiming paternity –
but it seems highly unlikely. At the beginning of June 1817, Esther
gave birth to a boy, James-Octave, who was said by some to resemble
Napoleon.[82] The liaison between Marchand and Esther nevertheless
continued and she gave birth to a second son in April 1821, although
this time he did not claim paternity.

Certainly in this first phase of his captivity, Napoleon deliberately
pushed the boundaries to see what he could get away with. It was not
all that much, as it turned out. Whenever he managed to escape his
English observer, who was meant to keep on eye on him at all times,
there were consequences.[83] From the beginning of 1816, Napoleon
simply refused to go beyond the twenty-kilometre limit because he
could not accept being accompanied by an English officer. Given that
there were dozens of people living or serving at Longwood, tensions
must have been high at certain periods, especially since some of the
personalities involved could not bear the sight of each other. Jealousy,
intrigues, conceit and hatred were the order of the day (and not just
among the French, it should be underlined. The atmosphere among
those in the English community centring on the governor, Hudson
Lowe, was just as toxic). Mme Bertrand, for example, hated Mme
Montholon,[84] and Gourgaud was jealous of everyone whom Napoleon
looked on with favour. Gourgaud was conceited and a braggart – on
board the *Northumberland* he had boasted that he could have taken
Wellington prisoner during the battle of Waterloo – who became
entirely isolated in Longwood, frequenting only the Bertrands.[85]

Napoleon never considered forgoing ceremony or the recognition
of his title. It was the only way he could assert his claim to being
emperor in the face of the British insistence that he was a simple

general.[86] Much of his stay on St Helena was about constructing a space for himself in which he displayed his quality as an imperial sovereign. He maintained not so much court etiquette (a court as such no longer existed) as a number of ceremonies, a range of rituals through which he could still express his imperial authority.[87] His valets wore the imperial livery; his generals wore their uniforms in front of him; Bertrand was still called 'Monseigneur'; Montholon was regarded as the lord chamberlain; and Gourgaud acted as a kind of equerry, looking after a dozen or so horses. To renounce the title 'emperor' would have been to acknowledge how far he had fallen, something Napoleon could not admit to himself. To renounce ceremony was to renounce his past in ways that he was not capable of. On the contrary, the fact that he was dictating his memoirs meant that he had clearly turned to the past, reliving it and at the same time reconstructing it for the future.

The men in his entourage not only played the game, but also went well beyond what was expected of them. Part of this was born out of the competitive nature of being in such a small retinue and having to curry favour with Napoleon, but it was also a symbolic recognition of the importance that he, and his body, had taken on since his fall from grace. Paradoxically, his prestige was not diminished as a result of his fall, but somehow enhanced. An example can be found in an incident that occurred when Napoleon was taking a walk in the company of several members of his entourage. At one point, the buckle from his shoe came undone and everyone rushed to reattach it.[88] How does one interpret that gesture? As the behaviour of toadying courtiers, or as the reverence due to a sacred figure? A bit of both no doubt, but I lean towards the latter explanation. How else does one explain Las Cases' professed thoughts as he contemplated his master's sleeping face, 'that face on which Marengo, Austerlitz and a hundred other immortal actions are written. What were then, at that moment, my ideas and feelings!?'[89] How else does one explain the feelings of hurt and sadness aroused within these followers whenever they had not seen Napoleon all day or for only a few minutes?[90]

In terms of ritual, Longwood became the successor of the Tuileries.[91] At dinners, for example, the men wore ceremonial dress while the women did the best they could to imitate court life. But there is another probable reason Napoleon insisted on a strict ceremony in such a confined space, and that was as a way of managing the interaction between the various personalities in his household. It was difficult enough with some of those who chose exile, such as Gourgaud. Tall, thin and muscular, with fashionable sideburns, Gourgaud was intelligent but irascible beyond measure, a man who, as we shall see, had the temerity to talk back to Napoleon. It could have degenerated very quickly into a free-for-all if behaviour had not been strictly regulated. Napoleon had to retain the image of himself as the sun around which all other planets revolved. Once the ritual had been observed, though, he generally put his visitors at ease. He was after all anxious for news of the outside world. He would ask his interlocutors all sorts of questions or, with regular visitors like the Balcombes and the Malcolms, get into long conversations about anything from literature to history or farming. Every few months crates of books, and every three to four weeks a bundle of newspapers, would arrive from Europe, which 'aroused and excited' everyone at Longwood for several days as they devoured and dissected the news. Then they 'fell back once more, insensibly, into a depression'.[92]

Once the audience was over, Napoleon would retire and leave it to his officers to escort the visitors out. At around four o'clock, Gourgaud would hitch up the calash to six horses, and with either Fanny Bertrand or Albine de Montholon sitting next to Napoleon, and Bertrand or Las Cases across from him, they would go for a ride, with Gourgaud galloping alongside. Some afternoons, a walk around the property replaced the ride. Their conversations would feed the journals of Gourgaud, Bertrand and Las Cases. Napoleon knew they were keeping journals and may have for that very reason carried on talking about anything that came into his head.

Before dinner Napoleon would often play chess, sometimes bowls or billiards. Dinner time would vary but would be around seven, eight or nine o'clock over the course of the years. When they dined together, the protocol would always remain the same. Napoleon originally set out to do this every day but eventually abandoned that, so the common table was held only once a week, on a Sunday evening. During the week he would dine with those in his entourage he had invited. When he did not dine alone, dinner took place in full-dress uniform and never lasted more than forty minutes. At a given hour, the

doors of the dining room would open and his majordomo Franceschi
Cipriani, in livery, would bow and announce, 'Your Majesty's dinner
is served.' Those present would take up the same places for as long
as they remained on the island: Napoleon with his back to the chim-
ney, Albine de Montholon on his right, Las Cases on his left, except
when the Bertrands were present, when they took precedence over
the Montholons. This in itself caused tension, the result of an invis-
ible divide between the old and new nobility – that is, between those
whose nobility dated to before the Revolution, like the Montholons,
and those who had been ennobled by Napoleon, like the Bertrands.[93]
One's place at the dining table was particularly important, especially
for Gourgaud, who believed that he should take, but was never given,
precedence over Las Cases and the Montholons.[94] Two servants, Saint-
Denis and Cipriani, would stand respectively to the left and the right
behind Napoleon and would serve only him. Antoine Gentilini and
English sailors in livery would wait on the other guests.

The five-course meal was served on Sèvres porcelain as well as gold
and silver plate. A butler, Jean-Baptiste Pierron, would concoct mar-
vellous desserts (at least for as long as he remained on the island).
A bottle of claret and a decanter of water were placed by each plate.[95]
Dinner was not necessarily a pleasant experience for the English visitor. George Bingham, commander of the troops on the island, was
invited to dine at Longwood. The food and the serving ware, he
remarked, were all beautiful, but the dinner was 'stupid enough'. On
that occasion, 'the people who live with him scarcely spoke out of a
whisper, and he [Napoleon] was so much engaged in eating that he
barely said a word to anyone'. Moreover, he had so filled the 'room
with wax candles that it was as hot as any oven'.[96] Bingham was a snob
in a way that only the English upper classes could be, and was not particularly fond of Napoleon to boot. When Napoleon once received
him in his bathrobe, Bingham couldn't help but remark, 'a dirtier figure I never beheld'.[97]

After dinner came what for some was the most difficult part of the
day – the guests would retire to the salon for coffee in a Sèvres coffee set depicting scenes from Egypt. Evenings could be long. Albine
would play the piano and sing at the same time, or Napoleon would
read aloud – passages from Molière, Racine or Voltaire[98] – something
guests came to hate since he read badly and was incapable of keeping

the rhythm of the prose.[99] They might also play card games – reverse or piquet.[100] During these interminable evenings, Napoleon could also reminisce about his experiences or discourse about past political figures, generals, prefects, sovereigns, while his guests struggled to keep their eyes open, until he decided to retire around eleven or twelve o'clock.

The rhythm of Napoleon's existence would alter little over the years, with the exception of a few crises with the governor, or when the former Emperor was ill, or with the departure of some of the faithful. Communal dinners were held during the first two years at Longwood, but from about the second half of 1819, he more often than not dined alone or with Montholon.[101] From 1819, as his health deteriorated, his routine became less regular. One day he would be outside the house, the next shut up inside; there would be feverish activity for one or two weeks, and then there would be days when he did little other than lie on the couch and read; sometimes he got up and dressed very early, other days would be spent in his dressing gown.[102] Day and night could be turned on their heads; it was rare for him not to disturb one of his valets during the night, instructing him to prepare a bath, make tea, fetch hot towels, look for books and maps or take dictation, though it might be that he simply wanted someone to talk to. How depressing all of this must have been to a man who had once been master of Europe.

PASSION

1816–1821

3

Staging the Passion

Hudson Lowe arrived on the island to take up his posting on 14 April 1816. It was, according to Las Cases, the start of 'great suffering'.[1] Before continuing any further, let us examine Lowe's background and how he came to be governor. He was born in Ireland in 1769, a couple of weeks before Napoleon. In many respects his career has some strange intersections with that of his captive, at least in terms of geography. Like Napoleon, he too worked his way through the ranks after he had joined the army at the age of eighteen. He was stationed first in Gibraltar and then in Corsica during the British occupation of the island (1794–6), when he commandeered the Bonaparte house in Ajaccio. After the evacuation of Corsica, he was sent to Elba and then Minorca, where he was ordered to organise a Corsican militia – the Corsican Rangers – made up of royalists and émigrés.

At the head of this band, he was sent to Egypt, where he took part in the battle of Alexandria, and then to Malta, where he was stationed when the Treaty of Amiens was signed. With the renewal of war he took part in a number of operations with his Rangers in various parts of Europe, but especially the Kingdom of Naples, the Ionian Islands and northern Europe. He was at the battle of Bautzen in 1813 and saw Napoleon through his spyglass. It was, so to speak, his first encounter with his future prisoner. For the rest of the campaign in Germany and France he was on Blücher's staff, and accompanied him into Paris at the fall of the Empire. He was then stationed in the Netherlands

under the command of the Prince of Orange, in charge of organising the matériel and arranging the deployment of troops, responsible
for supplies, lodgings and armaments. He should therefore have been
present at the battle of Waterloo but his relations with Wellington,
who considered him a 'damned fool', were a little strained.[2] But then
Wellington had little time for officers who were not from the aris-
tocracy. We do not know whether Wellington organised a transfer,
or whether the War Office made the decision, or whether Lowe
requested it, but transferred he was – to Genoa. By the time he got
there, Waterloo had been decided.

The first person to be considered for the job of governor of St Helena
was a man by the name of Trevor, but a number of members of the cabinet found him to be too charitable or conciliatory.[3] General Bunbury,
who had made friends with Lowe when in Sicily, put his name forward
and it was accepted. We know that the secretary of state for war and the
colonies, Lord Bathurst, asked Lowe to return to London having concluded that Lowe was well suited to the task. He wrote to Wellington
to say in somewhat qualified terms, 'I do not believe we could have
found a fitter person of his rank in the army willing to accept a situation
of so much confinement, responsibility, and exclusion from society.'[4]
We're not entirely sure what Bathurst saw in Lowe, but it is possible
that he chose him because he knew that Lowe could be counted on
never to stray far from the rules. Others were a little more admiring
than Bathurst. On hearing of Lowe's appointment, Admiral Edward
Pellew, Viscount Exmouth, wrote to Bathurst, 'it will ever be a source
of pleasure to me to have served with him and it is justice to say that
I never felt greater pleasure in serving with anyone'.[5]

The praise was not entirely warranted. Bathurst impressed upon
Lowe that he was to conform to the government's directives regarding
Napoleon as captive, and warned him of the disaster that would befall
his career if Napoleon were ever to escape.[6] At the same time as these
directives reached him (12 September 1815), Lowe received a letter
from Bathurst underlining the government's support for whatever initiative he might be required to take and allowing him a certain degree
of flexibility in the interpretation of the regulations. If that flexibility
was rarely exercised it was, as we shall see, in part because of Lowe's
character, but also because of an abiding fear of Napoleon's ability to
escape.[7]

In fact, Lowe received much the same instructions as Cockburn and they can be reduced to four particular injunctions: Napoleon was always to be accompanied by a British officer appointed by Lowe; Napoleon and his entourage were to be confined to the boundaries of Longwood House while any ships were in sight of the shore, and during that time to have no contact with the locals; all letters to and from Napoleon and members of his entourage were first to be vetted by Lowe; and any representations made by Napoleon to the British government had to go through Lowe, who then had to append his comments to the letter.[8] It was these instructions, coupled with Lowe's intractable character, that brought about the change in Napoleon's exile from one of simple detention into one of punishment.[9] Historians have been quick to lay the blame for the severity of Napoleon's conditions on Lowe. Many of his contemporaries did so too, but Lowe was a scapegoat in some respects. He did nothing without the approval of the British government, and in particular of Bathurst, who hated Napoleon and the French. Lowe was constantly on the receiving end of the most detailed instructions on every possible issue, many of them excessively trivial.

Relatively tall and skinny, with an aquiline nose, thin lips, a ruddy, freckled complexion and a face framed by bushy eyebrows and strawberry-blond hair, Lowe was not a particularly attractive or kindly-looking man.[10] Although some considered him to be of a generous nature, there were at least two character traits that put him at a disadvantage in dealing with Napoleon. He was indecisive, and he was shy and socially awkward. He was unable, for example, to look his interlocutors in the eye.[11] As a prison warden, for that is what he was, he may have been considered suitable for the job, but history has not on the whole treated him well,[12] nor did most of those who knew him. There is no doubt that he was meticulous to the point of being officious, and that he was a prickly, thin-skinned character whose 'angry, rude, violent manner of speaking' repeatedly offended those under him.[13] He was, moreover, vain and inclined to preen himself. He could also be mocking, petty and ignorant to the point where one wonders if he deliberately exacerbated relations with the French or whether he really was just a fool. I suspect the latter. Many years later, reflecting on Lowe's governorship, Wellington pronounced him an 'imbecile' and 'stupid', someone who was not necessarily mean, but 'like all men who know nothing of the world, he was suspicious and jealous'.[14] Wellington's assessment seems to be the most accurate; Lowe was what today we would euphemistically call a difficult character, overwhelmed by the task before him, incapable of appreciating Napoleon and his achievements. To him, Napoleon was simply a 'villain' and a 'scoundrel', a 'curse to the world'.[15]

Lowe's suspicious temperament, combined with an obsession with the most minor detail – the 'shortest note' could take hours and sometimes days to compose[16] – resulted in his alienating even those who should have been his closest allies. Major Gideon Gorrequer, who played a significant role as Lowe's aide-de-camp and secretary, and who therefore had the opportunity to observe him at close quarters every day, left a devastating portrait of his commander in his secret diary. Composed in the course of his stay on the island from the middle of 1817 onwards, but not decoded and published until 1969, it gives an impression of Lowe as a thoroughly unpleasant man. The diary was no doubt written as a way of letting off steam, with code names for various characters – 'Nincumpoop' for Lowe's deputy Sir Thomas Reade, 'Old Frog' for the French commissioner the Marquis de Montchenu, 'Neighbour' for Napoleon, 'Mack' for Lowe, 'Sultana' for his wife, and so on – so that if anybody came across the diary, it would at least be partially inscrutable. Outwardly, Gorrequer acted as Lowe's confidant, displaying devotion and loyalty, but privately he was highly critical if not spiteful towards him. But then Gorrequer treated just about everyone on St Helena with equal amounts of disdain and contempt, and was particularly vicious in his appreciation of those around him. At the end of his stay on the island, after years of abuse from his superior, Gorrequer concluded that Lowe was 'gloomy, unsocial and ferocious' and that he was both 'unreasonable and unjust'.[17] With some circumspection, he added that if Lowe had had a different education, he might have had a different character and might have acted otherwise, but instead he was 'just what his nature and circumstances made him', a man 'satisfied to spread around him anguish and despair'.

It is quite possible that the task before Lowe brought out the worst in him. One observer on the ship that brought Lowe out from Europe to St Helena was Georg Wilhelm Janisch, whom Lowe had met in Germany in 1814 and subsequently invited to join him as secretary.

Janisch recorded Lowe's invitation in a letter to a cousin in April 1816. 'Will you bind your fate to mine?' Lowe had asked. 'Then you will become witness to great tragedy.' Janisch joined Lowe's staff at Plymouth and set sail on the *Phaeton*. 'It was a turbulent voyage in the first months of the year [1816]; the ship pitched heavily through the dashing waves. The Governor [Lowe] was taciturn and the folds of his face became more inflexible day by day, as if he were preparing himself for his hard sphere of duty as jailer, and this rigid coldness weighed on all his officials and on me. We were not going towards a too pleasant future.'[18]

THE ALLIED COMMISSIONERS

He was right to be pessimistic. On 17 June 1816, three allied commissioners arrived. They had been sent by their respective governments, in accordance with the Paris Convention of August 1815, to keep an eye on Napoleon, to assess Lowe's character and to report back on the conditions of Napoleon's detention. Their presence was meant to make it clear to the former Emperor that he was the prisoner of the allied powers, and not just of Britain. Soon after their arrival, however, they very quickly became entangled in the unpleasantness of the situation. The Austrian commissioner, Bartholomäus von Stürmer, aged twenty-nine, a former secretary to the Austrian legation in Florence – whose French wife was apparently an admirer of Napoleon – spoke of Lowe's 'system of dissimulation, reserve and distrust'.[19] The Russian commissioner, Alexandr Antonovich Ramsay, Count de Balmain, a descendant of a Scottish family that had emigrated to Russia a century before, complained to his own foreign minister, Count Nesselrode, that Lowe 'becomes alarmed at the slightest incident, puzzles his brain for hours over nothing, and does with vast trouble what any one else would do in a minute'.[20] Lowe was, according to Balmain, 'fussy and unreasonable beyond all expression. He gets along with no one and sees only betrayal and traitors.'[21] Lowe, on the other hand, thought Balmain a 'complete blackguard' and a 'mean dirty fellow'.[22] The French representative was the Marquis de Montchenu, an émigré who despised Napoleon, but even he fell under Lowe's suspicion for calling his prisoner 'Napoleon' rather than 'Bonaparte'.[23]

At one point, Lowe was so infuriated by the commissioners having conversations with the inhabitants of Longwood that he stopped
inviting them to dinner.²⁴ At least two arguments between Lowe and
Stürmer were documented. Lowe objected to Stürmer's (and Balmain's)
manner, and his attempts to seek out meetings with Napoleon and
his entourage.²⁵ Stürmer objected to being treated like a prisoner, to
Lowe's bad temper and to the high degree of suspicion with which the
governor treated the commissioners (they never had a meeting with
Lowe without witnesses being present). In the end, Lowe complained
to Bathurst, with the result that Stürmer was recalled in July 1818 and
given another diplomatic posting. Shortly before, Stürmer had penned
a letter to the Austrian foreign minister, Clemens von Metternich,
claiming that Lowe spared no one and made himself odious to everyone. 'The English fear and flee him, the French make fun of him,
the Commissioners complain of him, and everyone agrees in saying
he is unsound of mind.'²⁶ Balmain also found Lowe 'empty, muddled
and unbalanced'. He added, 'Lowe shows his narrow-mindedness in
everything, his responsibilities suffocate him, make him tremble, he is
frightened at the least thing and racks his brain over trifles.'²⁷

LETTERS FROM ST HELENA

The English public first became aware of Lowe's problematic character thanks to William Warden, a naval surgeon who had been on
board the *Northumberland* and who was stationed on the island until
June 1816. Warden published an account of his stay there when he
returned to Britain, *Letters Written on Board His Majesty's Ship the
Northumberland and at Saint Helena* – the first published account by
an Englishman of his interactions with Napoleon on St Helena, and
one that proved enormously popular.²⁸ It was the start of an English
literature that defended Napoleon and criticised his treatment, apparently with a view to bringing about his eventual repatriation to Europe.
Warden, a frequent visitor to Holland House, the unofficial centre of
the Whig opposition in England,²⁹ related in the form of letters to his
fiancée what had occurred on the *Northumberland*, as well as conversations he supposedly had had with people in Napoleon's entourage.
They showed Napoleon in a humane light and revealed much about

his private life and habits, while depicting Lowe less flatteringly. As we shall see, the similarities with Napoleon's utterances make it more than likely that the seeds of doubt in Warden's mind were deliberately planted by Napoleon himself.

When Napoleon received a copy of Warden's book in March 1817, he devoured it in a few hours. But it made an unfavourable impression on him. He called it 'conceited' and described it as 'a tissue of nonsense, of trifles' that no reasonable man would have published.[30] Napoleon's companions too were unhappy with the way in which they had been portrayed. Gourgaud was upset because he came across as a braggart. And then the penny seems to have dropped. Napoleon realised that despite the book's faults, or rather precisely because of them, it would work for rather than against his cause.[31] For the first time, a witness had published an account of the conditions in which he was being held, however inaccurate that account may have been. Napoleon nevertheless decided to publish a rejoinder in what was meant to be an anonymous pamphlet, supposedly written from the Cape. Entitled *Lettres du Cap de Bonne-Espérance* (Letters from the Cape of Good Hope), it appeared largely as a result of the help and complicity of Barry O'Meara, and rebutted most of the assertions made by Warden.[32] Despite being 'anonymous', everyone was perfectly aware of the author's identity. Despite the restrictions that had been placed on Napoleon and his entourage around communicating with the outside world, they always managed to find a way of getting letters and documents to Europe. They either bribed captains of British East India ships to carry letters back to England, or used the Chinese servants to make contact with Chinese vessels that landed on the island.[33] Almost everyone, it seems, was happy to receive bribes to this end.

Of course, every figure of authority has both supporters and detractors. Not all observers found Lowe to be the cold pedant so often depicted by others. When Thomas O'Connor, a resident of St Helena, returned to England in the summer of 1818, he was shocked to discover how much Lowe was denigrated in the newspapers, and how disparagingly he was spoken of in the coffee houses of London.[34] More telling, however, is the testimony of Captain Robert Spencer, whose ship the *Owen Glendower* landed in St Helena in October

1820. He arrived convinced that the stories circulating about Lowe were true, but went away believing the exact opposite.[35] Others too maintained that 'never was a character more maligned', and that Lowe was a kind, 'tender-hearted man' whose conversation was 'as agreeable as his manners'.[36] These were admittedly observations made in Lowe's later years, but the most revealing sign that, for some at least, he was not as bad as Napoleon and his supporters made out was when, in 1825, only four years after leaving the island, Lowe briefly stopped at St Helena on his way to a new posting in Ceylon. By one account, he received a genuinely warm and spontaneous reception from the island's people.[37]

These vastly different reports highlight one of the difficulties for the historian in cutting through the descriptions to arrive at a balanced appraisal, not only about Lowe's character but also about Napoleon's behaviour on St Helena. Napoleon's exile on St Helena was the subject of more writings and memoirs than possibly any other moment in his life. He had become more than an object of curiosity; he had become a subject of study. Every word, every gesture, every mannerism, his behaviour and state of mind, every detail was noted down no matter how trivial. Napoleon's exile has thus often been reduced to a struggle between himself and Lowe. It is true that an examination of this struggle is essential for understanding Napoleon during this period, and the cult that followed. According to one assessment of their difficult relationship, Napoleon argued with Lowe not because he was interested in obtaining better living conditions, but because he was using Lowe as a 'whipping boy' in order to create an 'incessant din'.[38] There is some truth in this. For Napoleon, Lowe was a constant reminder of just how far he had fallen, and it must have irked him terribly.

'THE FACE OF A HYENA CAUGHT IN A TRAP'

Given how much the two men despised each other, it may come as a surprise to learn that in the course of his stay on the island Lowe only met Napoleon six times, and that all the meetings took place in the first four months after the governor's arrival. Lowe's accounts of these meetings are first hand, in reports back to Bathurst. Napoleon later recounted the meetings to his acolytes, or on occasion they witnessed the meetings themselves. After the six encounters, despite the proximity of the two men on the island, and despite Lowe visiting Longwood on numerous occasions, they never met each other again and only on one other occasion did Lowe ever see Napoleon alive, from afar, when Napoleon was out riding in November 1820.

The first attempted meeting between the two men ended in miserable failure. On 16 April 1816, Lowe, Cockburn, Bingham and several other officers arrived in pouring rain before Longwood. Lowe, as governor, assumed he could simply turn up unannounced. Instead, he and the others were kept waiting in the library for half an hour, only to be told by Montholon that His Majesty was indisposed and could not receive.[39] Lowe left 'abashed, embarrassed and very angry'. We don't know whether Cockburn had warned Lowe that he had to arrange a time through Bertrand, or whether he had deliberately failed to brief him on protocol, as the French suspected. It seems a little odd that Cockburn should sabotage Lowe's first meeting in this way, but it is possible he was giving Lowe a lesson in what to expect from Napoleon. In any event, Lowe asked Captain Poppleton, the man tasked with verifying Napoleon's presence twice daily, to notify 'the general' that he would visit the next morning.[40]

An appointment was made for the next day at two o'clock. Etiquette required that Cockburn introduce Lowe to Napoleon as the new governor, but things didn't work out that way. According to O'Meara, when one of Napoleon's valet's, Jean-Abram Noverraz, opened the drawing-room doors and called for the 'governor', Lowe immediately got up and shot forward. Noverraz, however, barred the entrance to Cockburn, possibly believing that Napoleon had asked to have only Lowe admitted. According to Las Cases, when Napoleon learnt of this, he burst out laughing with the joy of a schoolboy; according to Montholon, Napoleon was upset.[41] We have here two very different reactions and two very different character portraits, the one boyish and playful, the other serious and statesmanlike. As with much of what took place on St Helena, it is impossible to know exactly what happened. The actual meeting itself lasted all of fifteen minutes; they spoke in Italian, although Napoleon did most of the talking. Lowe supposedly came out of the reception room 'pale' with 'hardened features'.[42]

The second meeting, on 30 April 1816, did not go particularly well either.[43] Napoleon received Lowe in his dressing gown, as he sometimes did, lying on the sofa in his bedroom, exclaiming that he was ill. That did not prevent him, however, from launching into a litany of complaints 'with the most perfect composure', according to Napoleon's own account, largely directed at the British government. We know that Napoleon took an immediate dislike to Lowe, later telling his entourage that the governor reminded him of a 'Sicilian thug',[44] and objected in particular to Lowe's face. 'This man has something so horrid, hangman like and repugnant in his crime committing countenance, that I cannot describe. It makes my teeth chatter to look at him.'[45] At one point he complained that Lowe had 'the face of a hyena caught in a trap'.[46] Napoleon considered himself a bit of a physiognomist,[47] and mentioned Lowe's face to others, looking for confirmation of what he asserted. 'Can you judge whether a man possesses talents from observing the features of his face?' he asked William Warden.[48] Physiognomy, or the idea that character could be gleaned through facial expressions or features and that the face was the mirror of the soul, was popular throughout the nineteenth century.[49] Napoleon, according to O'Meara, went on to describe Lowe as 'A man without education, without any politeness, and whose countenance, instead of inspiring any confidence to the beholder, imparted an idea of a man capable of committing any crime, and withal a *Coglione* [arsehole].' Certainly, Napoleon professed that he could not bear to look upon him. 'Nothing good can arise of our meeting and *son certi che se c'incontriamo ci sara une scena e potrebbe darsi che ci sarebbe un accidente* [I am sure that if we meet there will be a scene and there might be an accident]. The last time we met he put his hand upon his sword two or three times, and I seeing that, was ready to take hold of him by the throat. My blood boils when I see him, his manners are so abrupt, repulsive and forbidding that I cannot bear the sight of him.'[50] There is more than a touch of the melodramatic in all of this. It is curious too that, in St Helena of all places, Napoleon reverted to Italian (rather than the Corsican dialect) to express himself more than at any other time in the previous twenty years.

The third meeting (16 May) also ended in an argument when Lowe tried to get some idea of what Napoleon might be looking for in a new residence that was being purpose built for him. Napoleon again launched into a tirade about the conditions in which he lived with 'such rapidity, such intemperance, and so much warmth' that it was difficult for Lowe later to repeat every word he had used. This was the first but certainly not the last occasion when Napoleon accused the British (and Lowe) of wanting to kill him. 'Do they [the British government] want to kill me? Are you come here to be my executioner – my gaoler?'[51] It was an accusation that would be levelled regularly at either the British government or Lowe over the coming years, usually in regard to the restrictions placed on Napoleon's movements (his reasoning was that lack of exercise would kill him).[52] The accusation was nonsense and it is doubtful Napoleon ever meant it. He was venting his frustration: he had been on the island for months and there was no sign of either his conditions of detention being relaxed or of his being moved to a more hospitable place of detention.[53] He later admitted that he had behaved very badly towards Lowe, 'but my bad humour made it permissible'.[54] He was known on other occasions to be contrite, if only for short periods, once saying that he would not have treated a servant the way he had treated Lowe. He thought it was all right to behave in the manner in which he did because he was emperor, and Lowe's 'delicacy did not seem wounded by it. I should have liked, for his sake, to have seen him evince a little anger, or pull the door violently shut after him ... it would have shown that there was some spring and elasticity about him, but I found nothing of the kind.'[55]

'THE GREATEST GLUTTONS AND EPICURES I EVER SAW'

On the next occasions Napoleon and Lowe met (20 June and 16 July 1816), the two men quarrelled, or at least Napoleon shouted while Lowe apparently tried to keep calm. The final meeting, which took place in the gardens of Longwood on 18 August that year, was the worst. There were a number of French and British witnesses to what followed.[56] Lowe had already deeply offended Napoleon on a number of occasions, the most recent when he placed Bertrand and his wife under house arrest for refusing to discuss Longwood's household expenses.[57] It seemed a vindictive thing to do, and at the very least was impolitic. So when confronted with Lowe, Napoleon let

loose a stream of invective, but then apparently changed his mind and
addressed only Malcolm. Malcolm recounted the incident to his wife,
who wrote about it in her diary.[58] According to this account, Lowe is
supposed to have responded with something along the lines of 'Your
misconception of my character and the rudeness of your manners
excite my pity.'[59]

The sticking point on this occasion was the budget for the household. Too much was being spent on what was referred to in French as
'the ordinary', that is, daily comestibles. Bathurst had ordered Lowe to
reduce Napoleon's annual expenses from £12,000 to £8,000. Bathurst
had also instructed Lowe to expel four of Napoleon's attendants as
part of the cost-saving exercise.[60] If Napoleon did not want to modify
his lifestyle, he would have to make up the shortfall out of his own
pocket.[61] Lowe tried to raise the issue with Bertrand on a number of
occasions, but Bertrand simply passed him on to Montholon, who
then pleaded that it was beyond his remit.

This was a humiliating experience for Napoleon; to have to enter
into discussions about 'a bottle of wine or for a few chickens' was
mortifying. But it was just as humiliating for Lowe, insulted in front
of his own men. 'You do not know how to conduct yourself towards
men of honour,' railed Napoleon, 'your soul is too low. Why do you
not treat us like prisoners of war? You treat us like Botany Bay con-
victs.'[62] He refused to see Lowe again. For the next five years, Lowe
would only ever once catch that one distant glimpse of his prisoner.

The amount spent on Napoleon's household has to be put in
perspective. Despite initial instructions from London limiting the
annual budget for Longwood to £12,000, it quickly reached between
£16,000 and £18,000, an enormous sum of money for the period and
equivalent to well over one million pounds in today's terms. Lowe's
own salary as governor of the island was £12,000.[63] The thirty-odd
residents of Longwood certainly ate very well; two meals a day, one
at eleven or twelve o'clock and another at eight o'clock – 'to which
joints, roast and boiled with all their various mashes, ragouts, fric-
assees &c, are served up, with wine and liqueurs' – plus a smaller
(English-style) breakfast between eight and nine in the morning,
as well as a 'luncheon' with wine at four or five in the afternoon.
Even the sympathetic O'Meara remarked that, apart from Napoleon
who always ate and drank sparingly during this period, the French

were 'the greatest gluttons and epicures I ever saw'.[64] They were, moreover, well served. Not only were there Napoleon's personal servants – Marchand, Cipriani, Jean-Noël (Giovanni-Natale) Santini, Gentilini, Noverraz, Saint-Denis – but after Bertrand had complained to Cockburn about the inadequate number of servants, twelve English sailors from the *Northumberland*, who were sometimes obliged to don the imperial livery, were put at his disposal (at least until about May 1816). On top of this, up to fifty Chinese (the number varied) worked in the house and gardens, supervised by an English officer.

The level of alcohol consumption is interesting in this respect although it is impossible to verify who was drinking how much. The Comte de Montholon's 'list of wines to be brought up for daily consumption' included ten bottles of claret, one bottle of champagne, one and a half bottles of Madeira, three bottles of 'Vin de Grave', seven bottles of Tenerife, three bottles of malt liquor, three bottles of cider and thirty-one bottles of Cape wine (intended principally for the Chinese employed around Longwood).[65] For the month of October 1820, the French consumed a total of 1,859 bottles of alcohol. Similar figures exist for August 1820.[66] The actual Longwood household numbered twenty-eight, including the French domestic servants, in March 1816.[67] The household could also include the English sailors and the Chinese workers. But before we jump to the conclusion that the French were turning to the bottle for comfort, it is worth pointing out that men, women and children always drank wine during meals, that it was considered nutritious, that they drank much more than we would today, and that at a time when fresh, clean water was in short supply, alcoholic beverages were an acceptable substitute.[68] Even Napoleon, considered an 'extremely abstemious' drinker, could down half a litre a day.[69] Gourgaud may have remarked, 'We cannot possibly be drinking seventeen bottles of wine and eating ninety-eight pounds of meat and nine chickens per day' and 'They are going to take us for drunkards,' but this was a dig at Montholon, in charge of providing the food and drink to Longwood, an insinuation that he was being wasteful.[70] It is possible that Napoleon's servants were doing business on the side, selling food and wine to British soldiers, but if that is the case, Montholon's supervision of the servants would have been very lax.[71]

'THE LITTLE LUXURIES THAT WERE DENIED HIM'

Napoleon's response to the request to reduce his expenditure was, first, to compose a long letter of complaint, the 'Remonstrance of August 1816', which he worked on with his companions from 16 to 22 August. It was a protest against the principle of his detention, against Lowe's behaviour and against the recent changes to the conditions of his captivity. The letter was delivered to Plantation House on 24 August.[72] Soon the whole island knew of its content. Copies were made and discreetly circulated among the inhabitants. It was then smuggled off the island by Santini, a Corsican who had served as usher, handyman and hairdresser, and who was one of the four servants evicted in 1816 (about which more below).[73] He succeeded in getting it to a leading Whig politician, Henry Richard Vassall-Fox, Lord Holland, who then had it published. At about the same time, another pamphlet, supposedly written by Santini (but in fact written by a certain Colonel Maceroni, who had served under Marshal Murat during his years as king of Naples), lamented the conditions on St Helena. The Emperor, this pamphlet asserted, lived in a hovel infested with rats – 'When the Emperor is at dinner, the rats run about the apartment, and even creep between his feet' – and claimed that the exiles were so badly provisioned that Santini had to wake early in the morning to shoot pigeons, so that the Emperor could have some breakfast.[74] It was nonsense, but public opinion in Britain had already heard about the supposedly lamentable conditions in which Napoleon was held – recall, for example, Warden's book that brought to light Napoleon's 'condition' on St Helena. It prompted Lord Holland to insist in March 1817 on an inquest into Napoleon's treatment on the island. Bathurst felt obliged to respond in parliament, called Napoleon's complaints lies and pointed out that plans for a new residence were in place.[75]

Then Napoleon carried out what in today's terms could only be called a publicity stunt. In September 1816, he ordered that a silver dinner service should be sold locally, ostensibly to raise money to pay for food and provisions.[76] The silver service had been valued at £25,000, so its sale would supposedly allow him to procure for the next two years 'the little luxuries that were denied him'. This had still not taken place when a note from Lowe dated 19 October informed Longwood that the household budget had been exhausted and that the French would now have to make up the difference.[77] Napoleon retaliated in what on the surface appears to be an incomprehensible, self-defeating gesture, but which also shows that the issue was not really about money. Napoleon ordered his servant, Noverraz, to take a hatchet to the service to remove the imperial crest.[78] He had to reiterate the order before the stupefied servant obeyed. The next day, Cipriani, a man of 'strong, but uncultivated talents', was sent to Jamestown with twenty-seven kilos of mutilated silverware; all he could get for it was the sum of £1,046 or about 26,000 francs, a fraction of what it was worth.[79]

This gesture, born of anger and frustration, was hardly enough to cover the needs at Longwood, but it had an unintended consequence. British officers present when the silver was being weighed told of the story when they got back home, so that it looked as though Napoleon was forced to sell his plate in order to buy the basic necessities.[80] Napoleon did this on two other occasions, on 9 November and 30 December, when he sold off a further thirty-five and fifty-eight kilos of silver, also beaten up.[81] By that time, he had probably realised the political mileage to be gained from doing so. Similarly, his decision to smash up some of the furniture in Longwood in order to provide fuel was nothing more than a stunt designed to make him appear a great deal worse off than he was, and to discredit his English captors.[82] It was true that there was a lack of wood for fuel on the island, something Lowe had attempted to remedy by ordering more coal. Napoleon, however, disliked the smell of coal. Lowe, as far as we know, had not been aware of this dislike, and he later declared that if he had known he would have ordered more wood.[83] It is impossible to verify the sincerity of that assertion, but Napoleon's behaviour once again was less than open.

Napoleon's actions are understandable up to a point, and were no doubt born of the utter frustration and resentment provoked by his circumstances. His biggest grievance, something that he complained about time and again, was to have been sent as prisoner to a godforsaken island in the middle of nowhere. He hated the regulations that had been imposed on him, and he hated most of all being addressed as 'General Buonaparte' rather than by his imperial title, saying that it was like being slapped in the face.[84] The first time Bertrand referred to Napoleon as 'Emperor' in a letter to Cockburn, he replied, 'I have no cognisance of any Emperor being actually on the island, or of any person possessing such dignity having, as you stated, come hither with me in the *Northumberland*.'[85] But Napoleon still considered himself emperor and expected his captors to respect his social and political position. He even invoked the validity of the imperial unction with which he had been anointed during his coronation, which is ironic since at the time it had meant nothing to him.[86] The British, however, had always refused to recognise his French imperial title; at most they had condescended to refer to him in 1814 as 'Emperor and Sovereign of the island of Elba', but Napoleon forefeited that title when he fled the island.[87] Apart from that one instance, the British had always referred to him as 'General Buonaparte', and 'Sir' or 'Excellency'. That is why Lowe thought nothing of 'inviting' Napoleon to Plantation House dinner, as he did in May 1816, treating him as an equal, and why Napoleon found the invitation 'too stupid'.[88] A social inferior did not invite an emperor to dinner. For the British to recognise the imperial title now would have had all sorts of implications, not the least of which would be the question of the legality of detaining an emperor, or having to consider that his current residence at Longwood was hardly fitting.[89]

Lowe, with Bathurst's approval, reinforced the restrictions to the point where any Briton who referred to him as 'Napoleon', even inadvertently, was treated with enormous suspicion. At the same time, Lowe refused to allow Napoleon to assume the name of either 'Colonel Muiron', in honour of the aide-de-camp who had died for him in the first Italian campaign, or 'Baron Duroc', after his marshal of the palace and one of his closest companions in arms, Michel Duroc.[90] The idea had been suggested as a means of avoiding the difficulties that Napoleon's imperial title had caused, and of facilitating communications with Lowe. The pedantry with which the governor insisted on calling Napoleon 'general' is telling, especially since it was obvious that it served only to poison relations between the two men even further. A more intelligent, flexible man might have found a way around this while still keeping within the spirit of his instructions, but we are dealing here with two intractable characters, two tyrants in their own way, in two entirely different and entrenched positions. As the Russian commissioner to the island so aptly put it, 'he who only knows how to command is at the mercy of him who only knows how to obey'.[91] Lowe finally reached a compromise in October 1817, when he agreed to refer to his prisoner simply as 'Napoleon Bonaparte', but this was hardly likely to appease Napoleon.[92] It has to be said that Lowe took things to extremes by withholding even innocuous books sent to Napoleon by wellwishers because they had been inscribed with 'Imperator Napoleoni'.[93] Of course the French could be just as intractable, accepting letters addressed to the 'Emperor' but not those to 'Napoleon Bonaparte'.[94]

CROWN OF THORNS

There is another way of interpreting what on the surface appears to be petty squabbling. The three issues that fuelled the conflict between Napoleon and Lowe – the close guard maintained on Napoleon, the cost of keeping house at Longwood and the question of Napoleon's title, part of a larger question of etiquette[95] – were no more than pretexts used to portray Napoleon as the victim and Lowe as the 'executioner' (as Napoleon sometimes referred to him), all to garner support in Europe in the hope the British government would change its mind and bring him back from the island. Viewed through this lens, Lowe's character becomes irrelevant. What counts is that Napoleon was extraordinarily successful in portraying Lowe to the world as an unsympathetic, narrow-minded, mistrustful bureaucrat. Napoleonists in France believed it. Liberals throughout Europe and the world believed it. It is remarkable, for example, that despite the treatment he had received at the hands of Napoleon, Pius VII wrote to Tsar Alexander of Russia protesting about the conditions of Napoleon's detention on the island, a letter that was left without a response.[96] Many Britons eventually came to believe that Lowe had mistreated Napoleon. Napoleon had in effect successfully transformed Lowe from a governor into a loathsome jailer.

Regardless of character and intent, Lowe unwittingly provided the conditions that redeemed Napoleon in the eyes of many Europeans. Lowe played Pontius Pilate to Napoleon's Christ, and as such the island became a Golgotha on which Napoleon lived out his Passion.[97] Napoleon himself used the imagery, as is evident from a line quoted in Las Cases' later account *Le Mémorial de Sainte-Hélène* that is as astonishing for its insight as for its hubris. 'I made the torch blaze, founded principles, and today persecution has made me the Messiah.'[98] Napoleon portrayed himself as the Messiah of liberal values, the Saviour of humanity. Is it any wonder, then, that in the dining room of Longwood there was an engraving of Christ in agony? Napoleon identified with this figure, and he said as much to the diplomat Lord Amherst, who stopped off in St Helena in June 1817 on his way back from China. 'You have placed on my head, as it was with Jesus Christ, a crown of thorns, and by doing so, you have won me many partisans.'[99] He was perfectly conscious of the role that he was playing, calculated to elicit as much sympathy for him from a European public as possible. There was a part of him that truly believed he had been persecuted, either because he had come to believe his own rhetoric, or because he believed that the gods had conspired against him.

Christ aux outrages (Christ mocked). 1817. Crayon, charcoal, gouache. Image found in the dining room of Longwood.

It was exactly that suffering – and the constant portrayal of stoic endurance – that transformed the ogre into a martyr. In the early years of his political-military career, Bonaparte had portrayed himself as the Saviour who had come to put an end to the Revolution, and to war.[100] Both Waterloo and later St Helena became associated in Bonapartist literature with Golgotha. (I use the term 'Napoleonism' to describe support for the person of Napoleon, and the term 'Bonapartism' to denote political support for a return of the imperial regime.)[101] That association had to be made in the French mind-set before the resurrection of the people's Christ, Napoleon, could occur. In other words, without Napoleon's defeat and Passion there could be no martyrology. In a poem by the French Romantic, Charles Caillaux, *Arche de la Nouvelle-Alliance* (The ark of the new alliance), Napoleon is depicted as France and liberty, and Waterloo as the Calvary on which the world was to be saved.[102] The theme of the poem is that death and suffering lead to regeneration. Death is not the end, but rather the beginning of another, better life. If Christ was crucified on Golgotha before his resurrection, then Napoleon, that is France and the French, the people of God, were crucified at Waterloo (Mont Saint-Jean) before undergoing a regeneration. If Christ reconciled the world to God by dying on the cross, and his suffering was atonement, then Napoleon's suffering on St Helena was his atonement that reconciled the world to him.[103]

The Napoleonic Golgotha and the ensuing Passion were necessarily constructs – they had to be invented in order for Napoleon to accomplish the transformation from despot to an enlightened but misunderstood ruler.[104] In the minds of nineteenth-century Europeans, the truth about Napoleon's living conditions became inextricably entwined in the personal dispute that took place between him and Lowe so that it became impossible to disentangle fact from fiction. During his reign, he was sometimes ascribed divine features – recall the parallel with Christ in Antoine Gros' *Plague Victims of Jaffa* – and increasingly in exile and death he became associated with images of the Christ or the Christian saints.[105] The connection was all the more easily made because of the pagan and para-Christian practices that existed throughout France and Europe in the first half of the nineteenth century.[106] This veneration was religious as well as political, in that it reflected both belief in Napoleon's extraordinary, even miraculous powers and faith in his ability to provide what post-1815 governments could not. The media war that was being waged over the former emperor and the conditions of his detention were to have enormous consequence for the manner in which he was remembered in world public opinion.

Lowe was so anxious to prevent Napoleon from escaping as he had done from Elba that he made it difficult for his prisoner to receive visitors,[107] required that all correspondence to and from Longwood be inspected by him, and insisted on twice-daily sightings of Napoleon to make sure he was still there. In order to annoy Lowe, but also as a muted act of resistance, Napoleon would lock himself in his rooms and not allow the British officer on patrol in the grounds to set eyes on him. The difficulties that these orderly officers – between December 1815 and May 1821 they were in turn Thomas Poppleton, Henry Pierce Blakeney, Thomas Lyster, George Nicholls, Engelbert Lutyens and William Crokat – had in carrying out their task to verify his presence make for amusing reading. If Napoleon did not feel like co-operating, and he rarely did, the officer on duty was often left wandering around the grounds for hours on end trying to catch a glimpse of him through a window.[108]

The six officers didn't succeed as often as they would have liked. Nicholls was there for two weeks in 1815 before he set eyes on Napoleon, and then it was through the window of the billiard room from a distance of about twenty-seven metres.[109] It has been calculated that in the 421 days Nicholls was at Longwood, prowling around trying to catch sight of the man, from morning till night, in rain and shine, he reported Napoleon's presence only 68 per cent of the time.[110] Nicholls was often on his feet ten hours at a stretch trying to spot Napoleon, lurking around the house and the garden, in the process having to put up with the jibes of the French servants and the gardeners. When Lowe, or his deputy Reade, insisted that the orderly officer get close to the house and peep in through the windows, the officers obeyed unwillingly; they considered it ungentlemanly, a repulsive form of prying.[111] On one occasion, Reade was so frustrated at not being able to verify the presence of Napoleon that he turned up at Longwood and knocked on the doors of his apartments yelling, 'Come out, Napoleon Bonaparte. We want Napoleon Bonaparte.'[112] Napoleon's attempts at hiding himself in order to avoid being formally sighted only worked up to a point, though the longest he appears to have gone without being identified is eleven days.

In spite of the constraints they imposed, all the officers were well regarded at Longwood, except for Lieutenant Colonel Thomas Lyster, who replaced Blakeney for ten days in July 1818, described by Bertrand as a 'demented old fool' and by Napoleon as Lowe's 'creature'.[113] Lyster's personal habits were somewhat wanting – he used to blow his nose on the bed curtains at Plantation House – and he appears to have been overly sensitive. In the short time he was on duty at Longwood, he challenged Bertrand to a duel for some perceived slight, and when Bertrand did not reply threatened to horsewhip him.[114]

The constraints placed on Napoleon were about to get worse. Dispatches with new orders from Bathurst arrived on 29 September 1816.[115] The British had been worried by rumours of plots that were afoot in the Americas to liberate their prisoner (about which more below). One attempt was supposedly being planned with the complicity of people who were already on the island. None of the plots was credible, but the British government was taking no chances: sentries were now posted at sunset around Longwood (instead of at 9 p.m.), and the boundaries of his unrestricted freedom and movement were shortened for the next two months. Lowe was convinced that the island contained no fewer than twenty-three places where a boat could land in fine weather.[116] But given that the island was constantly patrolled by naval vessels and guarded by thousands of men, any attempted rescue or landing would have required a force of considerable strength. In any event, any ships approaching the island could be spotted a hundred kilometres out to sea.[117]

On 1 October and again the next day, Lowe tried to see Napoleon to talk to him personally about these measures, but was both times rebuffed. Napoleon did, however, accept a visit from Sir Thomas Reade, who managed to gain an audience on the 3rd or possibly the 4th.[118] During the interview, Reade announced a number of fresh restrictions: that the members of Napoleon's entourage would be obliged to sign a new declaration (one had previously been signed on Lowe's arrival); that four of them would be ejected from the island, including Captain Piontkowski; that the entourage would be obliged to renounce making any further disobliging remarks about the British government; and that they would not be allowed to see anyone else on the island without the presence of an English officer.

There followed interminable squabbles between Napoleon and his entourage and Lowe over signing a declaration that contained the words 'Napoleon Bonaparte' instead of 'Emperor Napoleon'.[119] 'I do not want anyone to sign Napoleon Bonaparte,' he declared to Bertrand. 'I prefer everyone to leave than to see you stay at this price. I do not even want one valet [to sign].'[120] On 15 October, Lowe made the trip to Hutt's Gate, the Bertrands' residence, where he addressed the French individually in the hope of persuading them to change their minds. That night, as the usual guests were gathered in the parlour of Longwood House, with Napoleon reading *Don Quichotte*, a note arrived from Lowe – it was presented to Bertrand by a domestic – insisting that anyone who had not signed the declaration by midnight would be ejected from the island and transported to the Cape. This was at ten o'clock.

The Bertrands looked uncomfortable (they possibly saw this as a means of getting off the island), Montholon and Las Cases bowed their heads, staring at the carpet, while Albine de Montholon burst into tears. It was Gourgaud who acted first. He stood and declared that he was going to sign. Without a word, everyone else, except Bertrand, followed (he signed the next day). Then Poppleton was woken and the declaration sent back to Lowe. It was a gesture that touched Napoleon, and made him almost happy.[121] The next day, Lowe named the three other servants who would have to leave – Santini, Joseph Archambault and Théodore Rousseau. Marchand relates how it left everyone wondering whether they too might be asked to leave the island.[122] Joseph was thus separated from his brother Achille – they had both accompanied Napoleon – who remained on the island 'overcome with sorrow'.[123]

4

'Longwood has Become Unbearable'

BONAPARTISTS AND PLOTS OF ESCAPE

Lowe's anxiety about his prisoner reflected the inordinate fear in some circles in Europe and in the United States that Napoleon would escape from St Helena, as he had escaped from Elba, and either return to Europe, there to reignite the flame of war, or make his way to America where he would lay claim to Louisiana, carve out another empire and then wage war on Europe.[1] The English newspapers were full of rumours about supposed escape plans or attempted escapes on the part of Napoleon, all of which appear to have been treated with excessive credibility by either the French or British government.[2] The *Morning Chronicle* believed that the rumours were being deliberately spread in order to increase public anxiety about Napoleon and to justify the conditions of his detention.[3] That was far fetched, but Bathurst admonished Lowe to place tighter restrictions on Napoleon, his entourage and those who visited Longwood.[4] Some of the rumours surrounding Napoleon's imminent escape were deliberately put about in France by Napoleonists to keep Napoleon's name alive. The threat posed by veterans of the Grande Armée, at least in the eyes of reactionary governments, was such that wherever they congregated in numbers it was assumed they were hatching some sort of plot to bring about their former leader's escape. With nothing to do, they would congregate in cafés, never hiding their views about Napoleon or the Bourbons.[5] Historians have gone so far as to argue that the biggest threat to the post-1815 monarchical regimes

were not republicans, or even the numerous secret political societies
that sprang up throughout Europe during this period, but what has
been described as Bonapartism.[6] At least that was the perception of
the Bourbons in France, a perception that was no doubt reinforced
by the knowledge that a significant proportion of the population was
made up of veterans.

In France, more than one million men had been discharged from
the army in 1814 and 1815. Most were pleased to be released from
duty, but many would have found it difficult to reintegrate into civilian life after the horrors of campaigning and the long absences from
their families and communities.[7] In addition, about 20,000 officers
were placed on inactive duty on half-pay (they were known as the
demi-soldes).[8] Despondent, proud, they would congregate in particular cafés in the major cities, like the Café de Mars in Paris along the
Quai Voltaire. They were often marginalised and humiliated if not
harassed by a regime suspicious of them. It is not difficult to understand why some veterans soon became 'high priests' of the Napoleonic
cult.[9] How much they may have contributed to propagating the cult
is, however, impossible to know, and has been called into question.[10]
They may have done little more than indoctrinate a few regulars at
village cabarets, supplying even more victims to an overzealous police
force. Besides, we know that the number of veterans who were politically active was relatively small, possibly between 500 and 1,000
men, but enough to cause the authorities a disproportionate amount
of anxiety.[11]

Attitudes toward the veteran varied, depending on the region in
which he lived and on his individual behaviour. However, the veteran's military exploits and nostalgia for the Empire meant that these
men eventually gained a certain reputation, and a certain amount of
social standing in their communities. As a result of the vast numbers
of men who had been conscripted to defend the fatherland during
the revolutionary and Napoleonic wars, the soldier went from being
reviled by society at large – signs at the entrance to public places reading 'No dogs, prostitutes or soldiers' were common enough before
the Revolution[12] – to earning respect for having sacrificed his wellbe-
ing in the service of the nation.[13] But this transformation took some
time and certainly had not occurred in 1815. Returning soldiers were
persecuted and even in some instances massacred by royalists after

the Hundred Days.[14] The assassinations of Marshal Brune at Avignon and of General Ramel at Toulouse were perhaps the most famous cases, but there were any number of other victims. Many were out of work, had their movements watched by the police and were generally poorly treated by the Bourbon regime, especially if they had fought during the Hundred Days.

Théodore Géricault, *Le factionnaire Suisse au Louvre* (The Swiss sentry at the Louvre). 1818. Lithograph. A mutilated veteran, stopped by a Swiss Guard, pulls back his coat to reveal a Legion of Honour.[15] The lithograph was based upon an article that appeared in the newspaper, *Le Constitutionnel*, which described the event in 1817.

That they hated the Bourbons was a given, but for these men the lack of a legitimate outlet for their political views – voting rights were restricted to a small minority of landowners – meant that their only recourse was opposition to the Bourbons. Some took it further and were bent on their violent overthrow. There were a number of conspiracies hatched during the Consulate and the Empire against Napoleon by royalists or republicans, but far more plots were carried out by disaffected Bonapartists, liberals and republicans against the Bourbons.[16] There was the so-called Didier affair at Grenoble in 1815, two 'patriotic' plots in the spring of 1816, another two in 1817 and one in August 1820.[17] There were at least nine badly conceived plots to overthrow the government, easily put down, between December 1821 and July 1822.[18] It was evident that liberals and Bonapartists alike were united in their opposition to the Bourbons, and that Bonapartists profoundly influenced the centre-left not only in France but in Europe.[19]

Other veterans decided to leave France, a country where many considered that there was no longer any 'salvation', 'honour' or 'patrie'.[20] Thousands of them fled to the Americas, some to become members of colonies in the United States. One was established near the Bay of Galveston in Texas, known as the Champ d'Asile, and another in Alabama known as the Vine and Olive Colony.[21] These Bonapartist colonies did not last long, but the leader of the Champ d'Asile, General Charles Lallemand, supposedly devised a daring plan to send a flotilla to liberate Napoleon.[22] When by coincidence, in the summer of 1816, a fleet of sixteen or seventeen ships set sail from Baltimore for an unknown destination, the French ambassador in the United States, Jean-Guillaume Hyde de Neuville, reported that while some believed the convoy was destined for St Helena, he believed it was heading for Mexico, where the émigrés on board were going to establish a new kingdom under Joseph Bonaparte, their former Emperor's elder brother.[23] The fear was that, if a Bonapartist monarchy were established in Central America, an expedition could be launched to free Napoleon. A year later, Hyde de Neuville reported, 'that an expedition for St Helena would find in every port in the Union intrepid auxiliaries, weapons, money, in a word more than the most devoted could offer'.[24] He went on to say that it was not the plots of one adventurer or another that one had to fear so much as trickery. Where force is in default, cunning and address can often succeed. It caused the French foreign minister, the Duc de Richelieu, to write to his counterpart in London in September 1817, asking that stricter security measures be implemented on St Helena.[25] One of the more bizarre plots to liberate Napoleon was supposedly concocted by the renegade British admiral Lord Thomas Cochrane, hired by the Chilean government in 1818 to command its fleet during the war of independence against Spain. He was to persuade Napoleon to become emperor of South America.[26] But these and other plots to rescue Napoleon, including of all things the use of a submarine, or one that involved 'a boat that will drift to the back of the island … in the shape of an old cask but so constructed that by pulling at both ends [it would] be seaworthy and both boat and sail which will be found inside will be painted to correspond to the colours of the sea', are complete fabrications.[27]

There was never any serious consideration given to an escape plan by Napoleon, but lack of news often gave free rein to the imaginations of those who most feared him. There were reports of a certain Captain Latapie, at the head of around thirty veterans, preparing an escape attempt from Brazil.[28] From Montholon, there were reports of an American captain offering his services to smuggle Napoleon to America for one million francs, and an English captain making a similar proposal, but Napoleon always refused even to consider such offers for the simple reason that if ever he were caught it would compromise his dignity.[29] His followers did not always agree; for Montholon at least it meant that Napoleon had given up on life, and had deliberately decided on the path to martyrdom, for it was only on Napoleon's death that his son, proclaimed Napoleon II in 1815, could return to France to continue the dynasty.[30]

RUMOURS AND SIGHTINGS

The months between December 1815 and the spring of 1817 saw one of the most intense periods of rumour in nineteenth-century France. Besides the stories circulating around Napoleon's return (as we shall see), a number of other rumours flourished about Louis XVIII's abdication, the proclamation of Napoleon II and the establishment of a regency under Marie-Louise, all of which whipped parts

of the French countryside into a frenzy.[31] If Napoleon had returned
once, some peasants reasoned, why would he not do so again?[32] The
rumours of Napoleon's return seemed to reach a peak in the month of
March 1816, the first anniversary of his landing from Elba; peasants
tended to think in cyclical terms and believed in the repetition of historical events.[33] It was to become a sort of tradition in France. From
1815 right up to the years after Napoleon's death, usually around the
anniversary of his return from Elba, there would be false proclamations (signed by the Emperor himself) and placards pasted on to the
walls of French towns, and even songs on the subject, all asserting that
Napoleon was on his way back.[34]

One historian has distinguished a number of different types of
rumour around Napoleon's appearance during this period. One group
of rumours centred on his arrival at the head of a Turkish army ready
to reconquer France. These seem to have been common from about
September 1815 through to January 1816. Another set had Napoleon
at the head of an African, Indian, Algerian, Persian, Chinese or
Barbarian army, or alleged that he had become king of Morocco.[35] Yet
another group of rumours involved American troops incorporated
into the ranks of the Turkish army. The American reference became
more frequent after the summer of 1816 and may have had something
to do with the fact that Napoleon had expressed a desire to find refuge
in the United States after Waterloo.[36] There were the rumours suggesting that Napoleon would be assisted by a European power or a com-
bination of European powers (including England). And then there
were the rumours resulting from harmless dares or wagers, such as
that of the tailor Denoyer, who in 1820 bet that George IV (the former
Prince Regent having just succeeded his father) had taken Napoleon
to America.[37]

In France, it has been argued the rumours were the work of an
'organised network of Napoleonic agents' travelling from one locale
to another,[38] deliberately spreading stories about Napoleon's impending return in the full knowledge that they were false. Royal authorities certainly believed that all the rumours were orchestrated and that
there even existed a rumour laboratory in the Aveyron in the guise of
a Society of Freemasons in the Rodez.[39] Various other 'secret commit-
tees' were also believed to be responsible for spreading rumours – in
Versailles, Villefranche (Rhone) and Vaudrémont (Haute-Marne).[40] It

is possible that individual Bonapartists disseminated rumours and distributed proclamations in an attempt to create a climate of uncertainty
and in order to destabilise the monarchy,[41] although there is not all
that much evidence to suggest a co-ordinated campaign. We know
that rumours relating to Napoleon touched more than a third of the
eighty-six departments in France. Some of these rumours spread from
regional centres into rural areas, or from the provinces up to Paris,
while others came from outside France.[42]

Why people believed these rumours is more difficult to explain
than the rumours themselves, but they certainly reveal the political
fissures in post-Napoleonic society, and were probably fuelled by the
complex political and social landscape after Waterloo, which included
a range of factors that helped destabilise the Bourbon regime: the rav-
ages caused by 150,000 allied occupation troops, which led to inci-
dents of looting and rape; the excesses committed by royalists against
republicans and Bonapartists in what has become known as the White
Terror; the resentment felt by many in the military, unable to come to
terms with defeat and harshly treated by the restored Bourbons; a king
that many believed was only in power because the allies – 'Cossacks
and Prussians' – had placed him back on the throne; a humiliating
indemnity of 700 million francs that had been imposed on France by
the allies; and the pursuit of Bonapartists in the administration – tens
of thousands were purged by the Bourbons.[43] All of this coincided
with an economic downturn and a subsistence crisis that lasted until
the middle of 1818, during which there were frequent grain riots and
revolts.[44] The Bourbons were often blamed for the country's woes,
and very quickly became hated by large sections of the population.[45]

Even more curious than the rumours about Napoleon's return was
the appearance of a number of fake Napoleons in the French countryside. 'Apparitions' or 'sightings' were commonplace in France in the
eighteenth and the early part of the nineteenth centuries. There were
also apparitions of Louis XVII and other pretenders to the throne
even while Louis XVIII was still alive.[46] Of interest here is not who
these fake Napoleons were so much as what reactions they elicited
from the people they encountered. Almost invariably these sightings
occurred in rural areas, although a few ventured as far as provincial
capitals such as Rouen or Lyons.

Sometimes they were conmen who so physically resembled Napoleon that they were able to pass for him. At least two 'Napoleons' claimed they had escaped from St Helena. One by the name of Ravier appeared in the rural areas of the Ain, Loire, Isère, Saône-et-Loire and Rhône, where he impersonated the Emperor in the summer and autumn of 1815. He was eventually arrested near Fontainebleau in February 1816. A fake Napoleon was arrested in a village in the Isère, and imprisoned in the town of Vienne.[47] The inhabitants of the village were certain he was Napoleon because they had all seen him when he passed through there on his way to Paris only seven months earlier. In July 1817, a man (whose name was later discovered to be Charney) introduced himself to the innkeeper of Saint-Paul-de-Varax in eastern France (between Bourg-en-Bresse and Lyons) and whispered into his ear, 'I am the Emperor.' He was given the best room in the inn. The news quickly spread that Napoleon had returned, and in order to convince those about him that he was the real deal, he revealed a red ribbon that he was wearing across his chest. He went on impersonating Napoleon in a number of other localities until the gendarmes caught up with him and put an end to his escapade. He was condemned to five years in prison by the correctional tribunal of Trévoux.[48] In 1819, in the region of Villefranche, an Irishman passed himself off as the Emperor with the help of a priest who was either his accomplice or his dupe.[49] In Troyes, a number of Bonapartists were taken in by another 'Napoleon', parading him around the town.[50] But there were other instances of Napoleon sightings that seem to have resulted from some sort of collective hysteria. In 1816, in the region around Avallon, a number of peasants swore they had seen the vanguard of Napoleon's army riding towards Paris; the local gendarmes set off in pursuit, giving an even greater degree of credibility to the rumour.[51]

Together, rumours of an impending return and the appearance of fake Napoleons mirrored the desire of some sections of the French population for a restoration of the Empire, and were confirmation of a persistent popular Bonapartism in the countryside where peasants were fundamentally and traditionally hostile towards the local notables. Their daily sufferings found political expression in a desire to see Napoleon back on the throne. It was in that respect above all a 'popular' phenomenon.

BARRY O'MEARA – 'BETWEEN THE ANVIL AND THE HAMMER'

Let's return now to St Helena, where the drama was still being played out on the island. One of the key figures in the events was Napoleon's doctor, Barry O'Meara. He was keeping up a lengthy correspondence with a friend, John Finlaison, who happened to be working as a clerk in the Admiralty in London. Finlaison passed the letters to John Wilson Croker,[52] first secretary to the Admiralty, who in turn passed them on to the first lord of the Admiralty, Lord Melville. Melville not only approved of the correspondence, but also appears to have shown the letters to the Prince Regent. The communication of the correspondence to senior figures at the Admiralty initially took place without Bathurst's knowledge. When he later found out about it, he argued with Lord Melville.[53] After all, it undermined Bathurst's authority. It was the army that was responsible for Napoleon's condition and treatment and Bathurst would hardly be favourable to the navy having an 'inside man' in Longwood. Lord Liverpool had to intervene in the dispute and had to weigh up the advantages of having an insider in Napoleon's entourage. He opted for the insider but ordered Melville to pass copies of O'Meara's letters to Bathurst.

Just how trustworthy a character O'Meara was is difficult to judge. According to Mme Bertrand, he was a 'troublesome man' and 'a mischief making man'.[54] The problem is that O'Meara was playing to both camps. He recounted Napoleon's conversations in his letters to Finlaison in great detail, as well as recording the state of Napoleon's (often poor) health, but also reported these things to Lowe without any prompting on his part. It is even possible that O'Meara had received permission from Napoleon to reveal parts of their conversations,[55] but when Napoleon eventually found out that O'Meara was writing to the Admiralty he was not at all happy about it.[56] On the other hand, as relations between O'Meara and Lowe deteriorated, the doctor became less willing to communicate everything that passed between himself and Napoleon. The more Lowe insisted that he report everything Napoleon said in conversation, the more obstinate O'Meara became. His justification for not telling the governor all the details of their conversations was that 'it could not produce any good purpose'.[57] O'Meara certainly seems to have been harassed and hounded by Lowe, who at one point in December 1818 supposedly threatened him with physical violence.[58] That may or may not have been the case, but Lowe certainly lost patience with him and took umbrage at his having any conversations with Napoleon that were not purely medical.[59]

At first, however, O'Meara acted as a kind of go-between, an intermediary between the French and the English, something made relatively easy since he got on well with Napoleon and most of those in Longwood House, where he took up residence a number of months after his arrival. He very quickly came to understand the somewhat invidious position in which he found himself, caught as he was in the struggle between Longwood and Plantation House for moral supremacy. Even Lowe accepted that O'Meara's position was 'delicate', although he expected the doctor to 'make a full and ample disclosure to him' of whatever conversations took place with Napoleon. As O'Meara later admitted, he was caught 'between the anvil and the hammer'.[60] Living in close proximity to the French inevitably meant that he was inclined to identify with their plight. And as we already know, Lowe was a difficult character, and he slowly but inexorably pushed O'Meara into the French camp.

Lowe did not suspect O'Meara of disloyalty until a number of months after his arrival (in July 1816), and only then because Bathurst wrote to him saying he believed O'Meara to be the author of an article that had appeared in a Portsmouth newspaper.[61] As a result, Bathurst ordered Lowe to deport O'Meara unless the doctor could provide a satisfactory explanation. O'Meara admitted that he had corresponded with Finlaison, although he denied being the author of the newspaper article. Confronted in this way, O'Meara offered to resign, but since he was the only doctor Napoleon could abide, Lowe had little choice but to keep him on, at least for the moment, although mistrust prevailed – how could it not after he had found out that O'Meara was writing to the Admiralty behind his back – and arguments between them were not uncommon.[62]

FORSAKEN

Las Cases' Betrayal
We will come back to O'Meara later in the story, but let's return to the tensions within the small French community, where the constant petty bickering inevitably began to take its toll. Within a year or so of

Sir Charles Lock Eastlake, *Napoleon Bonaparte on Board the 'Bellerophon' in Plymouth Sound.* 1815. Oil on canvas. Eastlake, who was living in Plymouth at the time, went out over a number of days to sketch a portrait of Napoleon from his boat.[1] It was meant to be a good likeness, although the end result is somewhat affected. Over Napoleon's left shoulder and facing away from the viewer is Comte Bertrand while Captain Piontkowski, a Polish officer who had accompanied Napoleon to Elba, looks at the viewer from over Napoleon's right shoulder. Piontkowski was initially refused permission to accompany Napoleon to St Helena, but was later allowed to follow him out.[2] Note that Napoleon's right elbow leans on a railing immediately below a Union flag underlining Britain's victory over him.

George Cruikshank, *A Scene at the London Museum Piccadilly, 1816* (etched). The inscription at the top reads: 'A Swarm of English Bees hiving in the Imperial Carriage!! – Who would have thought it !!! !!! !!!' It was no doubt a play on the Napoleonic emblem, the bee. At the bottom, the inscription reads: 'A Scene at the London Museum, Piccadilly – or a peep at the spoils of Ambition, taken at the Battle of Waterloo being a new tax on John Bull for 1816 &c &c'. The balloon texts read, from left to right, 'Look at the horses Tommy'; 'Oh! Mon dear Empreur dis is de shocking sights' (from the man looking at the bust of Napoleon); 'This is one of Napoleon's shirts Ladies'; 'You'r prime bang up!!'; 'Look at Zaboe Sashes'; and 'Oh! My Frill' (from the man being trampled by the crowd). The figure in the lower-right-hand corner is possibly a self-portrait of the artist.[3]

Thomas Rowlandson, *A Rare Acquisition to the Royal Menagerie: A Present from Waterloo by Marshalls Wellington & Blucher*. 28 July 1815. Etching, hand-coloured. Napoleon in a bird's cage drawn by two donkeys, with the fool's cap and ears, threatened by an angry woman with a pair of scissors, laughed at and jeered at by others. The balloon texts read: 'Just caught a Ferocious Animal never Exhibited before in this Country commonly call'd the Corsican Tyger or Man destroyer to be seen for a short time for Two Pence a Piece'; 'Mort de ma Vie [from Napoleon] – Dat be one Cossach in Petticoats. She will soon Skin and Bone me'; 'Once more My Dear Megg of Wapping, we have got him under the Hatches and shiver my Timbers the only way to secure him is to send him to Dock Head'; 'I'll Dock Head and Dock Tail him. I'll cut of his Ears I'll cut of his — — I'll make a Singing Bird of him'.

George Cruikshank, *The Modern Prometheus, or Downfall of Tyranny*. 1814. Hand-coloured etching. In this particular image, the eagle that tears at Napoleon's heart is more vulture-like. The eagle/vulture's neck is inscribed with the word 'Conscience'. A blindfolded Justice stands over him holding scales. From one scale falls a tricolour flag and what looks like a *bonnet rouge*; in the other is a crown and a Bourbon flag. In her right hand is a sword of fire, pointing down and to the left, into the abyss from which the rock rises. The flames are inscribed with the names of the five allied powers – England, Russia, Sweden, Prussia and Austria. To the left of Napoleon's bare, manacled foot is a broken crown and an imperial eagle, while to his right are small serpents that crawl towards him.

Anonymous, *Deux vues: la première est prise du chemin de Deadwood, la seconde est prise du jardin fleuriste 1820–1830* (View of the House of Longwood. 1820–30. Two views: the first is taken from the path to Deadwood; the second is taken from the flower garden).

Anonymous, *Proposition de Constitution aux Habitans de l'île de St Hélène par l'Ex Empereur et Roi* ('The Ex-Emperor and Ex-King Propose a Constitution to the Inhabitants of the Island of Saint Helena'). August 1815. Engraving. This is a satire of the constitution handed down by Napoleon on the Champ de Mai in 1815. Under God's watchful eye (in the top left-hand corner), Napoleon, depicted with the long nose of a liar and wearing a ridiculously plumed hat, asks his new subjects to swear allegiance to him. The owl to the right portends disaster. Rats are a constant feature in both the British and the French royalist caricatures of Napoleon on St Helena.

Karl Auguste von Steuben (better know as Charles de Steuben), *Mort de Napoléon Ier à Sainte-Hélène, le 5 mai 1821*. 1828. Oil on canvas. Steuben consulted with Bertrand about the placement of furniture and the position of the witnesses.[4] Bertrand made a sketch from memory. This is not a heroic death in the traditional military sense, or indeed an inspiring one, but rather it is about Napoleon's suffering.

Masque mortuaire de Napoléon (Mortuary mask of Napoleon). 1821. One of five made at St Helena, personal copy of Antommarchi, physician of the Emperor at St Helena. Plaster. There is some doubt about the authenticity of this mask.

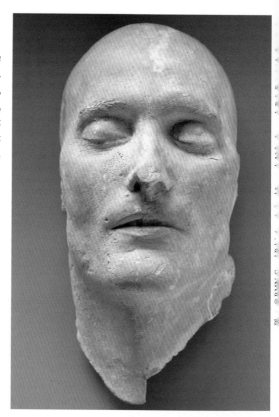

Reliquary put together by Las Cases – 'Souvenirs from St Helena'. 1840.

arriving, so frustrating and wearisome had life on the island become that people in Napoleon's entourage began to think of leaving him. The first acolyte to do so was Las Cases. He had largely been able to ignore the sarcasm, slights and insults directed at him, but he eventually reached breaking point. It came in November 1816, over the issue of his bedpan.

Lowe had dismissed Las Cases' servant, a local 'mulatto' by the name of James Scott, for attempting to enter into contact, at Las Cases' request, with the wife of the Austrian commissioner, Baroness von Stürmer. Lowe had offered to replace him with an English soldier, but Las Cases refused. Napoleon then intervened and put at his disposal his valet Gentilini. At that, a wave of indignation washed over the small French colony, as Gourgaud and Montholon in particular objected to a member of the Imperial Household having to 'empty the bedpan of that Jesuit', as they called Las Cases.[63] At that point, Las Cases decided he had had enough, and from that time on sought an occasion to leave. The fact that his son's health had deteriorated, and that his own eyesight was on the wane so that he could 'scarcely read or write', no doubt contributed to his decision.[64] The difficulty for the historian is understanding the complicated ruse by which he chose to leave. In reality, all Las Cases had to do was to ask either Napoleon or the governor for permission, but that would have looked like a betrayal of his master and would discredit him in the eyes of the faithful. Of course, Napoleon could have refused Las Cases permission, as he was later to do when Montholon asked to leave.[65] Instead, Las Cases engineered his own expulsion from the island.[66]

He did so by disobeying a direct order from the British and attempting to communicate with the outside world without the knowledge of the governor. Las Cases gave his former servant, James Scott, a number of missives, including two for Lucien Bonaparte, and another for an old friend, Lady Clavering, which were sewn into the lining of Scott's waistcoat.[67] There was nothing in the letters particularly revealing or compromising.[68] In fact, they could easily have been sent through the regular postal service. Scott was somehow meant to carry the letters to England. Instead, he showed them to his father, a slave who immediately took them to a farmer by the name of Richard Barker (we don't know what the connection was), who then brought the pair for questioning to Lowe, who decided to arrest Las Cases.[69] Napoleon was unable to account for 'such an act of folly', that is, to give letters to an

illiterate slave, who was somehow meant to smuggle them to England.
He is reported to have said that 'For a man of some talent like him
[Las Cases], to make an ambassador of a slave, who could neither read
nor write, to go on a six months' embassy to England, where he never
had been or knew nobody [sic] and who in fact unless the Governor
was a *Coglione* and a *Scioccone* [an arsehole and a blockhead], would
never be permitted to leave the island, is to me wholly incomprehensible unless a man had lost his senses.'[70]

It is one of the reasons historians have cast doubt on Las Cases'
motives. If he had wanted to communicate with the outside world in
secret, there were far better ways of doing so. By being expelled, on the
other hand, Las Cases was able to maintain the fiction that he, as a loyal
follower, had suffered an arbitrary punishment for simply trying to send
messages from St Helena. Even though some of those in Napoleon's
entourage saw through this charade,[71] it showed that Las Cases had perfectly understood what Napoleon had been attempting to do, that is,
portray himself as the victim. Now Las Cases was imitating his master: that he had been unjustly expelled from the island could be used to
manipulate public opinion and to highlight how poorly the French were
treated by Lowe and how much the governor persecuted Napoleon.

The other reason why contemporaries (and historians) were suspicious of Las Cases' motives was his apparent determination not to see
Napoleon before he left, as though he were ashamed of his behaviour.
According to O'Meara, Lowe wanted to prevent any contact between
Las Cases and Longwood, but it wasn't as simple as that.[72] When Lowe
offered to let Las Cases return to Longwood to reside there before
sailing for the Cape, supposedly so that Napoleon was not deprived of
a companion and so that his son could receive constant medical attention, Las Cases declined.[73] The pretext he used was that 'an extreme
susceptibility of honour' prevented him from accepting Lowe's offer.[74]
(In any case, Napoleon would not have agreed to see Las Cases under
the conditions stipulated by Lowe, that is, in the presence of a British
officer.)[75] More puzzling is that Las Cases would not even write to
Napoleon, although Lowe gave him permission to do so.

Las Cases stayed on the island for another five weeks (he left on
30 December) without seeing Napoleon again. Most of the French at
Longwood were delighted by Las Cases' arrest, but not Napoleon,
who missed him terribly as a companion and as the only person (apart

from Fanny Bertrand) who could speak English. 'I cannot now read an English newspaper,' he complained.[76] Napoleon is reported to have shut himself away and to have gone without shaving for days after Las Cases' arrest. When Bertrand and Gourgaud managed to meet Las Cases before his departure, he told them that he could better serve Napoleon by returning to Europe to publicise his plight.[77] That wasn't to happen immediately, however. Las Cases was imprisoned in the Cape from January to August 1817. Detention in the Cape is certainly something Las Cases should have expected. When Napoleon and his followers first arrived on the island, they were obliged to sign a declaration to the effect that they had decided to remain there voluntarily. If caught corresponding without Lowe's knowledge, they knew they risked deportation. This included being sent to the Cape, where they were to be detained for a few months before being allowed to return to Europe. The measure was designed to allow the governor time to write to London to explain why a particular person had been expelled.[78]

Las Cases' arrived in Brussels on 27 November 1817, but was expelled the very next day.[79] The return to Europe nevertheless gave him an opportunity to broadcast Napoleon's supposed plight, although without his notes and papers.[80] When Las Cases was arrested, they were confiscated. In particular, his voluminous journal – more than 900 pages in fifteen notebooks – was placed under seal awaiting instructions from Bathurst.[81] Nevertheless, over the coming months and years, Las Cases managed to portray himself in an heroic, self-sacrificing light, shunted from one country to the next by monarchical governments (he eventually settled in England, only returning to France after Napoleon's death in 1821), selflessly spreading the word about his master.[82]

Gourgaud as Jealous Lover

The second acolyte to leave Napoleon was Gourgaud. Words that appear frequently in his diaries are *ennui, grand ennui, mélancolie* and *tristesse*.[83] Of all the inhabitants of Longwood, Gourgaud best expresses the boredom of being stuck in a small space on a small island, going through the same gestures day in, day out. The terrible weather, the stifling ceremony the lack of news from France, the tedium of the evenings, almost always in the same company, and the lack of female companionship exacerbated the monotony. There had

been the beginnings of a flirtation with Laura Wilks, the daughter of
the civilian governor, and another with Amelia Churchill, returning to
England from India, but nothing seems to have come of either.[84] When
Montholon and Gourgaud fell out over a trivial matter in December
1816, shortly after Las Cases had been arrested, Gourgaud challenged
Montholon to a duel.[85] Napoleon had to intervene; the last thing he
needed was a public altercation between members of his entourage.
How much of this was planned as a means of getting Gourgaud off
the island in order for him to make representations to the Russian
Tsar, as some historians suggest,[86] and how much of it was genuine,
is anyone's guess. There is little doubt that Gourgaud was immensely

Georg Saal, Le général baron Gaspard Gourgaud, 1783–1852. 1844. Lithograph.

jealous of anyone Napoleon bestowed favour on. He hated Las Cases, for example, because he was able to insinuate himself into Napoleon's life and gain his trust. After Las Cases had left, his place was gradually taken by Montholon, who became Napoleon's most trusted confidant, once again inciting Gourgaud's jealousy.

There is a touch of the homoerotic in Gourgaud's attitudes and behaviour. He appears to have been utterly obsessed with and quite open about the degree of attention he required from Napoleon. His diary is littered with comments about Napoleon's mood and his behaviour towards him – 'The Emperor is angry with me,' 'The Emperor is feeling much better towards me,' 'The Emperor is friendly toward me' and so on.[87] He constantly underlined how much he had sacrificed everything to follow him, and stressed that he had followed him out of loyalty. At times, when he did not receive enough attention from Napoleon, he behaved like a jilted lover, succumbing to crying fits and bouts of jealousy, and hypersensitive to perceived slights.[88] Gourgaud was one of those faithful who would die for Napoleon, who would 'blow his brains out' for him. He must have felt crushed on Christmas Day 1816 when Napoleon told him, 'I suppose you imagined, when you came here, that you were my comrade, but I am no one's comrade ... You would like to be the focal point here, like the sun among the planets, but that position befits me alone.'[89] Napoleon then accused Gourgaud of being the cause of the 'vexations' that had plagued him since he arrived on the island and suggested that it would be better for him to leave. When the two men quarrelled, increasingly often as the months went by, Gourgaud would answer back in a manner that would never have been permitted had they been at the Tuileries. Napoleon would storm out of the room, slamming the door behind him.[90] 'I am not his wife,' he is said to have exclaimed after one of these bouts; 'After all, I cannot sleep with him.'[91] And yet at times his behaviour would appear (at least to the contemporary observer) intimate, if not bordering on the flirtatious. 'Would you like me to give you some of these macaronis?' Napoleon asked Gourgaud at a dinner in March 1817, spoon-feeding him two mouthfuls, then asking how he found them. 'Excellent, Sire, I have never tasted any as good.'[92] And he often affectionately called him 'My son', 'Gorgo' or 'Gorgotto'.[93] Gourgaud 'opened his heart' to Bertrand, who suggested that he should try to please Napoleon more, to which

Gourgaud somewhat crudely replied, 'Do I have an a[rse], a neck [that is, a bosom] that pleases?'[94] When Gourgaud finally did leave, Napoleon is reported to have said, 'I am three, four times, ten times happy that Gourgaud has left. How exhausting! Every day he wanted to b[ugger] me in spite of myself.'[95]

Tensions between the Montholons and Gourgaud had been simmering for many months.[96] Things came to a head in February 1818 when Gourgaud informed Napoleon that in the face of continuing insults from Montholon he had again challenged him to a duel. Napoleon flew into a rage, called him a bandit and a murderer, and threatened to put a curse on him.[97] Bertrand witnessed the scene, and stood by silent the whole time; there is not a word about it in his journal, *Cahiers de Sainte-Hélène*. Bertrand later ordered Gourgaud to ask for permission to leave the island, pleading ill-health. Gourgaud at first refused, but soon had a change of heart. He left Longwood on 13 February, not without bidding a tearful farewell to Napoleon. He had to wait another month for a vessel from the East India Company to take him directly to England without passing by the Cape. During that time he shared a cottage with Lieutenant Basil Jackson, who found him a 'foolish, vain fellow, without sense enough to conceal his weaknesses'.[98]

What followed was four weeks of Gourgaud spilling his guts out to all who cared to listen – and they cared to – telling the English what he thought of Montholon and Bertrand, and of the way he had been treated by Napoleon. He may have been lulled into a false sense of security by Lowe, the commissioners and the English officers treating him with more resepct than he had received at Longwood, or he may simply have vented his spleen after all the slights he had supposedly endured, but his version of what was going on at Longwood fed into Lowe's preconceptions.[99] Gourgaud insisted that everyone at Longwood had forgotten him and had left him 'to die like a dog', that Napoleon was not as sick as O'Meara had made out, that he was not short of money, that he carried on a secret correspondence with Europe, that he believed he would one day come back to power and that he could escape whenever he felt like it. Napoleon had not already done so, Gourgaud claimed, because he secretly enjoyed all the interest his exile generated in the European press and being the object of attention among the political elite. According to Gourgaud, Napoleon often said, 'I prefer to be a prisoner here than dwell as a free man in the United States.'[100] Gourgaud's assertions were all patently absurd, and were designed to ingratiate himself with the English and the Bourbons with whom he would inevitably have to deal on returning to mainland Europe.[101]

Gourgaud left the island on 14 March 1818, without having seen Bertrand or Napoleon again. He landed in England in May, and presented himself first to the under secretary for war and the colonies, Henry Goulburn.[102] In London, Gourgaud repeated the assertions he had made on St Helena about the 'real' state of affairs. We do not know whether Bathurst believed Gourgaud's assertions, but he nevertheless made two decisions: that O'Meara had to be sent away; and that the planned new residence for Napoleon – dubbed New Longwood House – would be built next to old Longwood House.[103] It did not end terribly well for Gourgaud though. When he realised that he wasn't going to be readmitted into the French army, he made an about-turn and published an open letter to Napoleon's Austrian wife, Marie-Louise, pleading with her to intercede personally with the crowned heads gathered at the Congress of Aix-la-Chapelle to allow Napoleon to return to Europe. The British government decided in November 1818 to deport him.[104]

The Servants

Everyone tried to leave St Helena at one stage or another, even the Bertrands, an indication of just how difficult and tense life on the island and at Longwood must have been, not least because of Napoleon's character.[105]

When Napoleon's cook, Michel Lepage, left the island in June 1818 and landed in Hamburg in August, he was interrogated at length by the French diplomat Baron de Marandet.[106] According to Lepage he had been sacked because Napoleon had found out that he had gone to Hudson Lowe to ask about leaving the island. He claimed that when he had boarded the *Bellerophon*, it was on the understanding that he would stay only one year, after which he would be repatriated. Lepage was by all accounts a morose character. He had indeed gone to Lowe to ask to leave but – again possibly in an attempt to ingratiate himself with the governor – could not help but add that he thought Napoleon's health was good and that the provisioning of Longwood could not be faulted, but that a lot of wastage occurred. When Napoleon found out about this interview that same evening – we do not know how – he told Lepage he no longer wanted to see him and that he had to leave immediately. Like that of the others who had left, Lepage's testimony may not be entirely reliable, but he asserted that life at Longwood had become 'unbearable', that Napoleon's bad moods were increasing in frequency and that 'all those in his service were exposed to the harshest of treatment'. Their position was all the more 'frightful' because they saw no end to their suffering. It was the monotony of it all, the sameness of the days, that reduced everyone to despondency.

By this stage, five of the twelve French servants who had accompanied Napoleon to the island (Santini, Rousseau, Archambault, Lepage and Bernard Hayman) had either become so dissatisfied with the conditions in which they worked that they had left or had been forced off the island. With the sudden death of Cipriani in February 1818 – he died of 'inflammation of the bowels', which might have been acute appendicitis or a perforated peptic ulcer[107] – only six servants remained. After Lepage had left, Chinese servants prepared the meals. At the least upset, Napoleon would run through the house with a billiard stick, which he often used as a walking aid, swearing and swinging at anyone who got in his way. When he was not angry, he was taciturn, and would spend a large part of the day lying down. According to Lepage, Napoleon was not the only one who got into bad moods. Those who remained behind fought terribly with each other, miserable and frustrated at the prospect of passing the rest of their lives there. It was reported that Mme Bertrand used to treat her servants abominably and that she beat her chambermaid.[108] Napoleon was not averse to lashing out when he was angry,[109] but Lepage is the only person who talks about him taking out his anger on those around him in such a manner. Both Las Cases and Marchand, determined to portray Napoleon in a flattering light, reported that the 'Emperor always exhibited great evenness of temper', and emphasised that he was 'kind, mirthful, [and] playful in his own quarters'.[110] He may have been, but at times he was moody and temperamental, he could fly off the handle and he was still capable of punching and kicking his servants.[111]

Albine

The Comtesse Albine de Montholon is suspected by some historians of having slept with Napoleon, possibly with the consent of her husband, who either did not care or was using his wife to get closer to the ex-Emperor. Albine was, by all accounts, a woman who loved men. She had been twice divorced before marrying Montholon, an extremely rare occurrence in the late eighteenth and early nineteenth century, and she appears to have been an incorrigible flirt.[112] While on St Helena, she had two children – Marie-Hélène-Charlotte-Napoléone, born on 18 June 1816, exactly one year after Waterloo, and Joséphine, born on 26 January 1818. Fanny suggested none too subtly that Joséphine was Napoleon's.[113] The evidence for a liaison with Napoleon is, however, circumstantial. O'Meara reported Napoleon as having spent more than two hours in the Montholons' rooms in July 1816. 'This will make Madame Bertrand as jealous as the deuce,' he told Thomas Reade.[114] We also know that, in December 1816, Gourgaud claims to have seen Napoleon receiving Albine in his dressing gown and that, when he reported to her husband where she was, he seemed embarrassed.[115] On another occasion, Napoleon received her while he was in the bath; that might appear a little odd but it was not all that unusual for him to receive in this way.[116] Familiarity, however, is not intimacy. The only other person to affirm Albine's place in Napoleon's heart was the Russian commissioner, Balmain, who declared that Napoleon was 'mad about her' and gave her 'expensive presents of dresses and jewels'.[117] We know that after Las Cases' departure Albine helped out as secretary. Napoleon thus saw her every day, often in the absence of her husband. It was a development that the ever-jealous Gourgaud could not tolerate. Albine, whom he had possibly once propositioned himself only to be rebuffed, had taken the place he coveted as the intimate of the Emperor.

Despite or possibly because of her proximity to Napoleon, Albine too tired of Longwood. She talked of one day returning to Europe to see her two children from a former marriage, left behind in France, or of going to look after her mother's estate, but it was something that she always spoke of as though it were far in the future. A request for a medical certificate from the British surgeons on the island in January 1819 attesting to the deplorable state of her health was rejected, although we are not quite sure why they wouldn't allow her to leave.[118] Unlike Fanny, who made a fuss and openly demanded of her husband that they leave, Albine was subtle.[119] She resorted to another, time-honoured method – she absconded with a British officer.

Albine became friends with Lieutenant Basil Jackson of the 20th Regiment of Foot a year or so after he had cohabited with Gorgaud. We do not know whether a liaison actually took place between Albine and Jackson, who was sixteen years younger. The correspondence between Montholon and his wife after she had left the island suggests it didn't, while Jackson later claimed that they were simply 'very good friends', although of course it is hardly likely that he could admit to much else in writing.[120] It may have grown into a sexual liaison only once they were both off the island. When Bertrand found out through Balmain that meetings between Albine and Jackson were taking place in the Montholon house late into the night, he told Napoleon. He was convinced that Jackson had been sent to spy on the French.[121] Napoleon confronted her in February 1819 only to be dismissed with 'he's just a friend'.[122] The upshot of it all was that Albine refused to stop seeing Jackson, meeting him while out walking. Napoleon intervened again the following month, ordering that all relations between the Montholons and Jackson had to stop. It was at this point that Albine sought permission to leave the island for health reasons. We are not quite sure why, but six months later she was given permission and she left on 2 July 1819. Jackson followed less than a week later – although it's unclear whether he did so of his own free will or was ordered to – eventually joining Albine in Brussels, where she found refuge.[123] We do not know if Montholon was aware of this or, if he was, what he thought of the situation.

We do know, however, that Napoleon was upset by Albine's departure. According to her husband, Napoleon openly cried when she left, perhaps for the first time in his life.[124] In his own words, Albine had 'sowed flowers' on his tomb.[125] Eventually Montholon too got sick of Napoleon and Longwood; he wrote to Albine after she had left to say, 'If you have not yet sent someone to replace me [in Napoleon's entourage] do not waste a moment, little does it matter who, provided it is one of his former officers, generals or friends. I think someone will be easy for you to find.'[126] His letters became more insistent. In response to her husband's growing reproaches, Albine assured him that she had made it known that she was looking for his successor, writing to Napoleon's sister Pauline in that vein, but she added that no one had presented themselves.[127] Eventually, she contacted Captain Nicolas-Louis Planat de La Faye, who had accompanied Napoleon on board the *Bellerophon* and had been prepared to follow him into exile. He agreed to go, but Napoleon died before he could leave.[128] Montholon had obviously spoken to Napoleon about leaving, because he reported a conversation in a letter to Albine that had Napoleon declaring, 'I understand your desire to join your wife and your children.' Montholon had moreover asked Lowe for permission to write to Lord Bathurst on the subject of his replacement (this was around September 1819).[129] About six months before Napoleon's death, Montholon was writing to his wife to say, 'It is only you I await, I cannot hope for any measures [to find a replacement] to be taken from here.'[130]

NAPOLEON'S DOCTORS AND LOWE'S PARANOIA

One of the most demoralising aspects of life at Longwood was the climate. The house itself is on a plateau with its own microclimate, so that the inhabitants speak of 'the Longwood weather'.[131] The locals had been surprised by the choice of Longwood for Napoleon's residence; the plateau is constantly exposed to the harsh wind – the *ventaccio* as Napoleon called it – and at 500 metres above sea level it is often enveloped in clouds or drenched in diluvian rains. And it rains a lot, even during summer. In fact, it rains between 224 and 288 days of the year.[132] In summer, the ground is so hot that the rain immediately transforms into steam, which wraps the plateau in fog; the humidity is above 80 per cent during the rainy season.

Some of the symptoms of ill-health that Napoleon manifested were already present before he came to the island. For example, in 1806, when the Emperor was in Warsaw, the Comte de Ségur, his grand master of ceremonies, noted that Napoleon suffered from 'convulsions of the stomach'. Similarly, after his return from Russia, and again on the first day of the Battle of Dresden, he experienced violent stomach pains.[133] His health significantly deteriorated from about the middle of 1817 onwards. Before that, there was little that was particularly worrying – a pain in the right side in July 1816, followed by colic in September and December, and a brief period of dysentery at the beginning of 1817.[134] On 17 January 1817, O'Meara reported that Napoleon had experienced another pain in the right side, this time accompanied by a loss of consciousness. Nevertheless, O'Meara did not start to worry about his patient's health until the middle of that year. His detailed medical reports give us a reasonably accurate description of Napoleon's physical deterioration, although the reports have to be tempered by knowledge of the doctor's personal conflict with Lowe. On 22 September, O'Meara recounted that the symptoms manifested were 'precursory to some serious dropsical affection by which indeed I am well convinced that his life will be sooner or later be terminated. There was an oedematous swelling of the feet and ankles which pitted upon pressure. His gums also presented a spongy appearance and bled upon the slightest touch. His appetite impaired, frequent headaches, want of rest at night, some difficulty of respiration and anxiety, painful affections of the cheek and teeth and lower extremities.' On 1 October, Napoleon complained of 'dull pains in the right side and other symptoms indicative of an attack of chronic hepatitis, which in this part of the world is a very prevalent complaint and in a subject like him, so averse to taking medicine, would probably ultimately prove fatal'.[135]

The principal cause of all of this was thought to be a lack of 'exercise on horseback'.[136] A general examination took place on 3 October. O'Meara reports that he 'examined the right side, and perceived that it felt firmer to the touch than the left. There was also a tumefaction evident to the sight, which when pressed hard gave a little pain. Napoleon said that this was observed about two months since. That he had thought nothing of it, and attributed it to obesity, but that now, from its being attended with pain, he imagined it might be connected with enlargement of the liver.'[137] Around the end of 1817, O'Meara concluded that Napoleon might not survive another two years on the island.[138] He was not, as it turns out, all that far off the mark.

The two diseases that appear to have been rife on St Helena were dysentery and what was referred to chronic hepatitis. Dr Archibald Arnott, the surgeon attached to the 20th Regiment of Foot on St Helena, found the two diseases everywhere; 'nothing escaped the influence of the climate', he concluded.[139] During the first twelve months following the arrival of the 66th Regiment, for example, 56 out of its 630 men died of dysentery.[140] Gourgaud too suffered a bout of dysentery that almost carried him to the grave.[141] In fact, the two terms 'hepatitis' and 'dysentery' were employed to describe a variety of conditions that do not necessarily correspond with current mean-ings.[142] 'Dysentery' was used in the eighteenth and early nineteenth centuries as a term to cover all diseases in which the predominant symptom was diarrhoea, but it covered a range of bowel disorders from food poisoning to some possible cases of typhoid.

Similarly, 'hepatitis' was associated with any disease of the liver, was linked to the prevailing climate and may have been connected at the time with constipation, from which Napoleon certainly suffered. Given the state of early nineteenth-century medicine, doctors were mostly reduced to describing symptoms without knowing the causes, and the cures were often worse than the illness. Calomel, a mercury compound, was often used as a purgative, while bleeding was still reg-ularly practised, as were what the French referred to as *lavements* or enemas. Napoleon received all of these treatments but to little avail; even if the diagnosis had been correct, there was little that could have been done to help him.[143]

The diagnosis of 'hepatitis' put Lowe and the British government in a difficult position because it had political implications. If O'Meara turned out to be correct, the British government could be accused of causing Napoleon's early death by banishing him to an environment with an unhealthy climate. Rather than get confirmation, Lowe's reac-tion was to accuse O'Meara of being in collusion with the French and forbade him to use the word 'hepatitis'. He even went to Longwood to see Bertrand, only to claim that O'Meara had reported Napoleon to be ill when he was in good health, and that 'everyone was trying to deceive him'.[144] It says much about the character of the man.

The situation was made even worse when Napoleon complained to O'Meara that the medical reports being sent to London referred to him as 'General Bonaparte' and that unless he used his correct title he would refuse to continue to see him. Lowe subsequently ordered O'Meara to discontinue writing the reports and to deliver them orally to the island's deputy inspector of hospitals, Alexander Baxter. Baxter, who had served once with Lowe in the Corsican Rangers, was now placed in a very awkward position. Without being allowed to examine Napoleon, he had to render an accurate translation of O'Meara's medical reports in a way that satisfied the governor. Did Baxter amend O'Meara's reports in order to placate Lowe? We are not entirely sure. O'Meara suggested that he did, but we also know

that Lowe himself was perfectly capable of altering and even making additions to O'Meara's bulletins.[145] Despite this, Lowe did not
want to concede that his prisoner was ill. The upshot is that the
British government was not getting a particularly accurate picture of
Napoleon's health.

There is little doubt that O'Meara contributed to the poisoning of relations between Napoleon and Lowe. He came to take Napoleon's side,
but above all he was probably used by Napoleon for his own purposes.
Here was a doctor who was sympathetic to him, who would exagger-
ate the poor conditions on St Helena to the point, it was hoped, that
the British would be obliged to repatriate him to England. Whether
O'Meara was consciously involved in this ploy is hard to say, but for
Lowe O'Meara's position and attitude were intolerable. He could not
have someone so close to Napoleon whom he could not entirely trust.

Given O'Meara's position as a secret informer inside Longwood,
however, Lowe could not have dismissed him without first receiving orders from Bathurst. Bathurst was clearly not disposed to giving such orders. At the beginning of May 1818, he wrote to Lowe
telling him to ignore any personal differences with O'Meara, pointing out the consequences if Napoleon's health were to decline rapidly.[146] Only two weeks later, however, he changed his mind, having
concluded that the doctor had been misleading everyone about
Napoleon's illness and that his accounts had been 'very fallacious'.[147]
He now considered O'Meara 'unfit to continue near the person of
General Buonaparte'.

This sudden shift in attitude coincided with the arrival in London of
Gourgaud, telling everyone who would listen that O'Meara was lying
and that Napoleon's health was good. The Irishman was subsequently
dismissed, on 25 July 1818, but the decision was not made easily. Even
though Lowe wanted to be rid of O'Meara, he was typically indecisive
and fearful of the consequences. 'For a long time', wrote Gorrequer,
his aide-de-camp, 'he cursed over the orders received from home to
pack him [O'Meara] off. He sometimes determined to do it, at others
seemed undecided. No decision took place for one and a half to two
hours.'[148] The pretext he found to be rid of O'Meara was his gift of a
silver snuffbox to an English chaplain, the Reverend Richard Boys, on
behalf of Napoleon. Boys had officiated at the funeral of Napoleon's

servant Cipriani.[149] Lowe had forbidden such an exchange of gifts and used this infraction as an excuse to dismiss the doctor.

What followed was a burlesque, highlighting the claustrophobic paranoia into which the island had descended as a result of Lowe's ineptitude. Reade ordered O'Meara to stay within the confines of Longwood until further notice.[150] Keeping him under house arrest was an odd thing for Reade and Lowe to do, but was born of the necessity of having a doctor in attendance on Napoleon. Napoleon's response was to refuse to see O'Meara in protest, which meant that he was indeed left without an attending physician. Lowe then ordered the 66th Regiment, with whose officers O'Meara sometimes dined, not to receive him as a guest. It was a petty gesture, and put some of the officers in a difficult position, since many of them liked him. Without wanting to go into the details of all that then transpired between Lowe and these officers, suffice it to say that at least one, Lieutenant Rodolphus Reardon, had his career destroyed for being too close to O'Meara.

And so O'Meara left the island on 3 August 1818.[151] When he arrived London in September, he wrote a long letter to the Admiralty, justifying his stance and largely condemning Lowe's behaviour. O'Meara crossed a line when he suggested that the governor had intimated to him 'the benefit which would result to Europe from the death of Napoleon'.[152] According to Walter Henry, assistant surgeon to the 66th Regiment, O'Meara insinuated that Lowe 'had suborned him to poison Buonaparte, or sounded him respecting such a crime'.[153] The suggestion was clear, that Lowe had spoken to O'Meara about doing away with Napoleon. On the other hand, the Board of the Admiralty told O'Meara that Lowe had reported to them that Napoleon's illness was imagined and that indeed O'Meara himself had once stated that Napoleon had the 'pain of a hypochondriac'. O'Meara insisted that this was not the case, and that in fact he had reported the pain was 'in the hypocondrium' (the liver is in the right hypochondrium).[154]

This accusation and counter-accusation necessarily placed the Board of the Admiralty in a difficult position; it was one man's word against another's.[155] For the Admiralty, there was no question of disowning Lowe, but in order to silence O'Meara he was supposedly offered the important post of consultant surgeon at the Chelsea and

Greenwich naval hospital. When O'Meara refused it, he was cash-iered from the navy and struck off the medical register. In order to make a living, he rented rooms on the ground floor of a building on the Edgware Road in the heart of London and started up as a dentist. He even hung Napoleon's wisdom tooth, which he had extracted in November 1817, in the window as a kind of advertisement.

After O'Meara had been forced off the island, there was no doc-tor in attendance on Napoleon for quite some time. As far as we are aware, however, the former Emperor's health during that period remained more or less stable.[156]

The story of Napoleon's doctors is as chaotic as it is theatrical. In all, he was attended by four different doctors while at Longwood: O'Meara from October 1815 to July 1818; the naval surgeon Dr John Stokoe, who paid five visits in 1818 and 1819; Francesco Antommarchi (about whom more below) from September 1819 to Napoleon's death on 5 May 1821; and the senior army surgeon, Arnott, who worked along-side Antommarchi from March 1821 to Napoleon's death. After the departure of O'Meara, Napoleon refused to receive his replacement, Dr James Roche Verling, but only because he had been imposed on him by Lowe.[157] Verling was an Irishman who had served in the Peninsular War and had risen to the rank of assistant surgeon in the Royal Artillery. He had been on board the *Northumberland* on the passage to the island and had had a chance to talk to both Napoleon and members of his entourage while on board. Verling was ordered by Lowe to take up residence at Longwood, where he lived for over two years, arriving early on the morning of 25 July 1818, shortly before O'Meara left the island. Verling is really only of interest to the his-torian because he kept a detailed journal of his time at Longwood, right up until his departure from the island in 1820.[158] It shows his close relationship with the Bertrands and the Montholons – who were happy for him to attend as their physician – and the insights he gleaned from their willingness to gossip. He never actually got to examine Napoleon, despite attempts by Bertrand and Montholon to persuade their master to relent. When Napoleon offered to pay him a salary so that he would become *his* man, Verling wanted nothing to do with the offer and shortly afterwards asked to leave the island.[159] The offer was enough to arouse the suspicions of Lowe, who began to regard Verling as untrustworthy.[160]

Napoleon's refusal to see Verling meant that there was no attending doctor when he fell seriously ill in January 1819, complaining of 'great uneasiness in his side and shoulder, of restlessness and anxiety, but above all, of severe pain in the head and giddiness (vertigo), which for a short time amounted to a state of insensibility [loss of consciousness]'.[161] Dr John Stokoe, surgeon on HMS *Conqueror*, which was anchored in harbour, was called upon. Napoleon agreed to see Stokoe as he had met him on a previous occasion in O'Meara's company. They had conversed in Italian, and Napoleon had warmed to him. This had been enough to once again arouse the ire and the suspicion of Lowe. Stokoe had, therefore, been reluctant to see Napoleon as physician, realising just how impossible the situation would be under Lowe's scrutiny. He had to be ordered on 16 January, when Napoleon suffered a particularly bad night, to attend to him.[162] Over the coming days, Stokoe visited Napoleon on five occasions and delivered the same diagnosis as O'Meara – chronic hepatitis.[163] 'The more alarming symptom,' reported Stokoe, 'is that which was experienced on the night of 16th [January, namely, the loss of consciousness], a recurrence of which may soon prove fatal, particularly if medical assistance is not at hand.'[164]

That both O'Meara and Stokoe had come to the same conclusions about Napoleon's health did nothing to reduce Lowe's suspicions. Exactly what kind of conspiracy Lowe imagined was being cooked up he never said, but an assortment of allegations was levelled at Stokoe. Stokoe is reported to have said to Balmain, 'They will not believe he is ill until they find him dead in his bed.'[165] Lowe probably mistrusted Stokoe because, as Napoleon had been asserting all along, he claimed that the climate on St Helena had adversely affected the prisoner's health. It was the type of news the government feared, and that might be used by the British public to demand Napoleon's return to live out the rest of his life in England. Both Lowe and his commanding officer, Admiral Plampin, acted so appallingly towards Stokoe that he decided to resign from his post and return to Britain.

The manner in which he was subsequently treated was shameful. On arriving in England, he was ordered back to the island to face a court martial. We can pass over the details, but the 'charges' included referring to Napoleon as 'the patient' and 'receiving communications' from the French 'not at all connected with medical advice'.[166]

Stokoe was unable to find anyone to defend him; no one, it would appear, was courageous or foolhardy enough to come forward. A veteran of Trafalgar with twenty-five years' service, he was found guilty, stripped of his rank and drummed out of the navy. It is an illustration, if ever one were needed, of Lowe's utter vindictiveness, but also of the British government's determination to maintain Napoleon on the island till the end of his days.

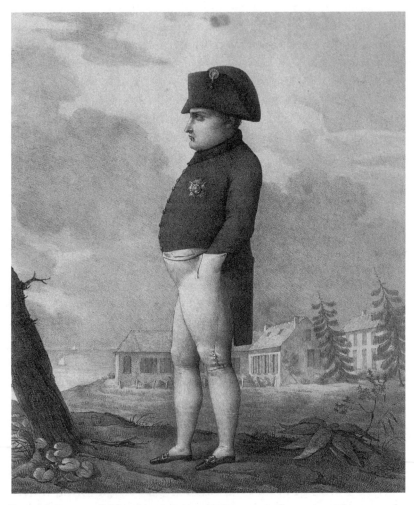

Gaspard Gourgaud, *Napoléon à Sainte-Hélène*. 1818. Engraving. This somewhat unflattering sketch was carried out in January, a few weeks before Gourgaud left the island to return to Europe.

DEATH

1821

5

The Last Stations of the Cross

The difficulties the British authorities experienced with Napoleon's physicians were symptomatic of a much larger problem: the increasingly fraught relations between Napoleon and everyone with whom he came into contact. The year 1819 was possibly the worst. If the desertion of his closest companions had left Napoleon bereft, the arrival of news from Europe left him stunned.

The allied powers had been meeting at Aix-la-Chapelle since late September 1818.[1] It was the first time they had met since the Congress of Vienna in 1815; they were there to discuss, among other things, whether to put a term to the allied occupation of France. The British treatment of Napoleon was also discussed, but it was never more than a side issue. British reports, as well as personal appeals to the sovereigns of Europe by Napoleon's mother, Letizia, Las Cases, Gourgaud and Napoleon's son-in-law, Prince Eugène, all pleading for Napoleon's release, were delivered to the allied ministers.[2] They were unlikely to sway these men. Fear that Napoleon might yet escape prevailed. To the allies, Napoleon represented the 'power of revolution concentrated in one individual' who had become, as a consequence, the 'prisoner of Europe'.[3] At the end of November, they issued a proclamation supporting the British government. The crowned heads of Europe, who had once been dominated by Napoleon, had sealed his fate.

Napoleon learnt officially of the allies' resolution at Aix-la-Chapelle never to allow him to leave the island at the beginning of

March 1819.[4] This was a terrible blow for him. Until that time, he had believed that he would eventually return to Europe. He sometimes fantasised that he would be able to join his brother, Joseph, in America (while, as we have seen, at other times he declared that he would 'prefer to be a prisoner' on St Helena 'than dwell as a free man in the United States').[5] Indeed, Admiral Cockburn had intimated in April 1816 that Napoleon would be on the island for only two or three years.[6] There were rumours that he would be transferred to Malta; Napoleon himself appears convinced that he would get off the island.[7] Once news of the Congress reached him, the shock plunged him into a deep depression, and he increasingly displayed what one English observer described as a 'strong disposition towards seclusion'.[8] There were days, quite early on during his stay on St Helena, when he would lock himself in his room and not see anyone. Those periods seemed to increase in the course of his stay at Longwood, from about one week in April–May 1816 to a period of about five weeks in October and November 1817, when he dined completely alone and cut himself off from everyone around him.[9] For a period of nearly six weeks in June and July 1818, Napoleon barely left his room.[10]

News from the Congress meant that Napoleon had lost his ultimate battle with the English. From that day on, his disputes with Lowe ceased,[11] lending credence to the view that they had been nothing more than a weapon in his armoury to get off the island. Increasingly over the coming months, he withdrew from the outside world, as well as retreating deeper and deeper into himself. What had started as a cat and mouse game, for example, that he had played with Lowe to foil the governor's attempts to verify his presence, began to take on more alarming overtones. Napoleon hid in the house and refused to come out; he cut holes in the shutters and curtains so that he could peer out with his telescope from within darkened rooms,[12] and he would spend weeks on end alone in his rooms. Napoleon thus adopted what Las Cases called an attitude of 'dignity oppressed by force', erecting around his person a 'moral barricade' to defend himself against the insults of his persecutors.[13]

At the same time as the English were physically isolating Napoleon on the island by installing him in Longwood House, Lowe further isolated all the French on the island by making it increasingly difficult both for locals to talk to them and for visitors to go to Longwood.[14] We know, for example, that on 5 June 1820 Lowe refused a passenger on the ship *Mellish*, a Mr Maitland, who was stopping off at the island, permission to call at Longwood.[15] There were a number of other cases like this. On 2 April 1819, Napoleon had received Charles Milner Ricketts, a cousin of the British prime minister, Lord Liverpool, and in the service of the East India Company. Napoleon was already in poor health and asked Ricketts to arrange for him to be delivered from Lowe and to end his days in some comfort in England.[16] This was the last time Napoleon would receive any visitors, but if he hoped that Ricketts's relations might help him, he was wrong. Ricketts thought that he was feigning ill-health and that the whole interview was a sort of performance put on by Napoleon in order to try and influence his interlocutor. When Ricketts got back to England, he simply confirmed Bathurst's belief that Napoleon's poor health was a fabrication.

In September 1819, three people chosen by Napoleon's mother Letizia and his uncle, Cardinal Fesch, arrived on the island to replace some of those who had left. There were two priests, the Abbé Antonio Buonavita, whom Montholon characterised as 'quite moribund', and the Abbé Angelo Vignali, a small, thickset young man described by Montholon as someone 'whose education has not altered his savage and brutal exterior'.[17] Buonavita, a sixty-five-year-old who had suffered at least one stroke, and who as a result was partially paralysed and had difficulty speaking, had served as Letizia's chaplain on Elba but he was already 'broken', according to Napoleon, by the years he had spent as a missionary in South America.[18] He did not in any event see things out; he was to leave in March 1821, a couple of months before Napoleon's death. Napoleon wanted nothing to do with Vignali, a semi-literate Corsican of low birth. He played little or no role in the events that were to unfold, except to conduct Napoleon's funeral service. Vignali died seven years later in a blood feud on Corsica.

Also among the arrivals was a doctor by the name of Francesco Antommarchi. On first meeting him Napoleon complained that he was 'young and presumptuous', a little ironic considering that the former Emperor had possessed the same character trait at the same age. It is possible that Antommarchi was suffering from some kind of mental disorder,[19] but at the very least he was a difficult character who found it impossible to get on with anyone, not to mention the fact that he had little experience as a physician. He was an anatomist and a pathologist. The only decent new arrival appears to have been Jacques Chandelier, a cook recommended by Pauline.

The choice of personnel made by Napoleon's mother and uncle was poor to say the least. They all had one thing in common – they were Corsican – but the selection can in part be explained by the belief that Napoleon had escaped from St Helena. It seems that a professional swindler, a German clairvoyant, had told Letizia that the Virgin Mary had appeared before her to say that Napoleon was no longer on the island; angels had transported him to a better place.[20] Since Letizia was a devout Catholic, she bought the story, despite the howls of protest from Napoleon's siblings Pauline and Louis, living in Rome at the time.[21] To Letizia and Fesch, there-fore, it made no sense to send good men to the island. Napoleon immediately realised that the newcomers were either inexperienced or incompetent, if not both. Antommarchi's admission to him that 'Hitherto I have only ever had to deal with dead bodies' would not have helped much.[22] Napoleon never placed much faith in the doc-tor, although he did allow himself to be examined by him, and even offered an explanation for his symptoms: 'I am attacked by chronic hepatitis, a disorder endemic in this horrible climate. I must fall prey to it.'[23] Antommarchi was only too willing to come to the same con-clusion – he had read Stokoe's reports before coming to the island – later writing to the Chevalier Colonna, chamberlain to Letizia in Italy, exculpating himself from all blame for his condition by insist-ing that 'the disease under which the Emperor is labouring is an effect of the nature of the climate'.[24]

DECLINE

Isolation may have been one of the defining characteristics of this phase of Napoleon's life – although there were moments when he made an effort to interact with others – but the other defining char-acteristic was the beginning of a serious physical decline. The lack of a competent doctor did not help. On the days he could he walked,

dressed in civilian clothes – Napoleon had stopped wearing his uniform while at the Briars – usually white, but inevitably wearing his
iconic hat. Also, in late 1819 and early 1820, there was an unusual rush
of activity as he decided to redo the garden completely, getting everyone involved in the process. Dressed in a nankeen jacket and trousers,
and a wide-brimmed straw hat, he directed the workers to plant here
and dig there.[25] 'Longwood had never been so animated,' declared
Saint-Denis, 'than during the garden works.' This did not, could not,
last. From July 1820 onwards, his stomach pains grew worse, resulting in constant nausea and frequent vomiting so that he spent most of
his time in bed, his 'place of luxury' as he called it.[26] These symptoms
were different to the complaints of previous years; Bertrand recognised this even if Antommarchi did not.[27]

On 4 October 1820, Napoleon planned an excursion to Sandy
Bay, on the south coast of the island, involving all the members
of his staff. Picnic baskets were packed full of food and wine, and
everyone set off early in the morning. They got no further than
Mount Pleasant. Sir William Doveton, the owner of the house at
that spot, saw the party riding past and invited everyone in. Tables
and chairs were spread on the lawn where they ate breakfast. The
picnic included cold pie, potted meat, cold turkey, curried fowl,
ham, coffee, dates, almonds, oranges and champagne (Napoleon
poured himself a tumbler).[28] Sir William's daughter, Mrs Greentree,
brought out fresh butter, jelly, eggs and watercress and some home-
made 'Orange Shrub' water to add to the picnic table. Napoleon
appears to have been in a jovial mood, possibly because it was
the first time he had eaten outside Longwood since moving there
from the Briars.[29] Napoleon tired very quickly though, to the point
where on the return journey near Hutt's Gate he had to dismount
from his horse and transfer to a carriage. By the time he got back to
Longwood at around two in the afternoon, he was so exhausted and
weak he had to be helped to bed.

This seems to be the turning point in Napoleon's health. After that,
the symptoms worsened in frequency and intensity – vomiting, stomach pains and an inability to eat. There were periods of respite over the
following months – the end of November seems to have been a period
of slight remission – when he was able to sit in the garden or go for
walks. Riding was no longer possible and it was with great difficulty

that he ever got into the calèche. The only exercise he appears capable
of taking during the last months of his life was playing on a seesaw. He
had one built and installed in the billiard room, pretending at first that
it was for the children at Longwood, but then admitting that he had
had it built for his own use. He planned to use it for a quarter of an
hour or so every day, but the sessions only ever ended in fatigue and
physical discomfort. Bertrand paints a rather sad portrait of a portly
Napoleon, the one-time ruler of Europe, reduced to playing seesaw
with his companions, while Fanny looked on laughing.[30] Montholon
wrote to his wife at the end of 1820 to say that 'he cannot perform
any vital activity without experiencing an extreme fatigue and often
loses consciousness, his stomach has kept nothing down for several
days and he feeds himself with very light things that we make him
take every 6 hours, he always remains lying down, either in bed or on
a couch and is constantly drowsy … I employ all my efforts to make
him take some air every day.'[31]

After July 1820, Napoleon hardly ever left his room, complaining that the light hurt his eyes. Any physical activity exhausted him,
so that he spent days bedridden or hours in his bath. Even shaving
became an arduous task, although he always insisted on doing it himself.[32] He hardly dressed any more and often remained in his dressing
gown, when he wasn't bedridden.

Then came news of the death of his sister, Elisa, the former Grand
Duchess of Tuscany. She had been living in exile at Trieste and had
died of an undefined illness in August 1820. Napoleon did not learn of
her death until the following December. She was young – only forty-
three – and while he was not particularly fond of her, the news seems
to have hit him hard. It is possible that from this time on, he understood that he too was going to die and that in accepting this he had
given up on life.[33] His mind wandered back to his father and the cause
of his death, stomach cancer, and he no doubt suspected, even if he
never admitted it, that he would meet the same fate.

On 17 March 1821, Napoleon went for a carriage ride and returned
utterly exhausted. It was the last time he left the house. In fact, it was
the last time he left his bed except for short periods when it was necessary to change the sheets, which could be as many as six or seven times
in a night because they were drenched in sweat, or when he was given
an enema.[34] From about this time on he had trouble eating and could

not swallow meat; his diet was restricted to toasted bread that had been dipped in syrup, soup, jelly or a biscuit with Malaga wine.[35] As a result, he lost a considerable amount of weight. A group of Italian scientists measured twelve pairs of trousers worn by Napoleon between 1800 and 1820, during which time they calculated that his weight increased from sixty-seven to ninety kilos. In the last six months of his life, however, Napoleon lost anywhere between ten and fifteen kilos.[36] And yet Reade and Lowe still refused to believe that anything serious was taking place, largely because Dr Archibald Arnott persuaded them that 'Bonaparte will be out again very soon; and that his complaint is nothing more than a fit of *Bile*, brought on by the Declaration of the Allied Sovereigns'.[37]

'I WOULD LIKE TO DIE: I AM NOT AFRAID OF DEATH'

Towards the end of 1820, Bertrand seriously considered taking leave of absence to escort his wife and children back to Europe. He had of course talked about leaving before, but now Fanny was at her wits' end and could no longer take it.[38] Napoleon was shocked by the suggestion and never gave his consent. Fearful that he would be left alone, he could not agree to it. Eventually Bertrand, loyal to a fault, dropped the whole idea. Even when Napoleon later insulted him – calling him a 'simpleton' and a 'pig' – or abused Fanny to her face, telling her how badly she was dressed, or calling her a chambermaid or a strumpet, accusing her of sleeping with Antommarchi of all people, Bertrand bit his lip, bowed his head and continued to serve.[39] It was not the first time that Bertrand had had to put up with this kind of abuse; Napoleon had accused Fanny once before of sleeping with a Captain Hamilton.[40]

Montholon too was desperate to leave, as his letters to Albine suggest.[41] But the husband-and-wife team was much more calculating than the Bertrands. They had agreed that Montholon would leave only with the approval of Napoleon, or when he decided that he could no longer keep Montholon by his side, so as not to endanger any chance of a financial reward on his death.[42] The façade of an amiable companion always ready with a smile belied what Montholon truly felt. He was nevertheless the only person who was constantly by Napoleon's side. He was there at about eight-thirty in the morning, at which time Montholon took a few notes; he generally ate with Napoleon in the morning.[43] He left about midday or one o'clock when Bertrand would make an appearance but would be back again at around three, when he attempted to coax Napoleon into getting dressed and going out a bit. He would then often dine with Napoleon and spend his evenings with him, which could last until ten o'clock, if he was not required to read to him.

Montholon did not have to wait much longer. All the eyewitnesses attest to the pain in the upper part of the stomach that Napoleon suffered, as well as the nausea, vomiting, hiccups, dysuria, lethargy, spikes of fever, diarrhoea alternating with constipation, abdominal cramps, heavy perspiration and circulatory problems.[44] By this stage, Napoleon was insisting that all the blinds and shutters stay closed so that anyone entering the room had to feel their way around it.[45] In a letter to his wife dated January 1821, Montholon described Napoleon's state of health as one of constant deterioration: 'Every day [his] moral and physical weakness increases.'[46] He believed that Napoleon was waiting for the end with impatience. 'The Emperor's malady yields to no cure, it advances constantly though fortunately slowly. He cannot at all walk, even in his room without being supported, so weak is he. Today he is a corpse animated by a breath of life.'[47] Montholon was convinced that Napoleon couldn't live much longer, and yet Lowe still believed that Napoleon was trying to make himself look ill, that it was 'his last game'.

At the end of March, Montholon persuaded Napoleon to seek a second opinion from the surgeon of the 20th Regiment of Foot, Archibald Arnott. After Napoleon had initially refused to see him, Arnott was admitted into his presence late in the evening on 1 April.[48] In what can only be a reflection of Napoleon's state of mind, he insisted the consultation take place in virtual darkness; the room was barely lit by a covered lamp in an adjoining room. However, a second examination took place the next morning, this time with a little more light, during which Napoleon complained of an acute pain that cut him 'like a razor' in the stomach, constant nausea and repeated vomiting.

For most of April, that is for the last month or so of Napoleon's life, Arnott, accompanied by Antommarchi, paid regular visits to

Napoleon, once or twice a day, and made regular reports updating Lowe on the condition of the 'patient', as Arnott called Napoleon (but, unlike Stokoe, he did not incur Lowe's wrath for this). None of Arnott's reports come across as particularly alarming.[49] On the contrary, Lowe's disbelief in the seriousness of Napoleon's illness was reinforced by Arnott, who reported to Reade on 6 April, only a month before Napoleon died, that he was 'not affected with any serious complaint', and that it was 'probably more mental' than anything.[50] Lowe is supposed to have added, 'If a person were to go in there [Napoleon's apartments] and make a great clamour, it would be the most likely thing to revive him. Depend upon it.'[51] Arnott, who couldn't abide Lowe or his wife, was telling the governor what he wanted to hear, no doubt fearful of the consequences if he told the truth, with the fate of Stokoe at the back of his mind. We know this because Arnott's written records diverge significantly from what he was reporting to Lowe, and because Gorrequer reported a conversation in which Lady Lowe declared that Arnott would present Napoleon's health 'as much better than it really was', 'because he knew it would please'.[52]

By the middle of April, Arnott was finding it difficult to reconcile Napoleon's somewhat corpulent body with the fact that he had eaten so little over such a long period of time coupled with the constant vomiting.[53] He was struck by the 'almost cadaverous appearance' of his face. Nevertheless, he continued to report that his patient's symptoms were due to hypochondria, and that there were 'no symptoms of immediate danger about him'.[54] This is a diagnosis that Arnott continued to proffer to Plantation House right up until the last week of Napoleon's life. Years later, Reade tellingly accused Arnott of having been 'much too civil' to Napoleon's entourage.[55]

Antommarchi, on the other hand, reported to Bertrand and Montholon as early as 6 April that the end was near. His two most loyal followers both spoke to Napoleon about their concerns, but the former Emperor already had an inkling that death was imminent. Back in February, he had remarked that he did not think he would see out the year, and kept on repeating a line from Voltaire's play, Zaïre: 'But, to see Paris again, I can no longer pretend.'[56] By the end of March he was confessing that he would like to die, that he was not afraid of death and that he would be happy if he could die within the next fortnight.[57] When it was suggested that he might be more at ease in New Longwood House, he replied that it was too late.[58] Bertrand and Montholon did, however, convince him to write his will, which he began on the evening of 13 April, partly writing it in his own hand and partly dictating it, when he could, to Montholon, who became the executor as well as the principal beneficiary.[59] It was two weeks before it was finished.

There are in fact two wills. The first is a long document that, according to Montholon, took between eight and ten days to write.[60] It was obvious that Napoleon was perfectly aware of the impact, both emotionally and politically, that his last will and testament would have on the public at large.[61] It was above all a political testament, but it was also suggestive, an emotional plea, in which, determined to hammer home right to the very last minute of his life the carefully constructed image of martyrdom, he included the following passage: 'I die prematurely, murdered by the English oligarchy and its hired assassin.' The 'hired assassin' (*sicarian*) referred to was of course Lowe. In the will, he thanked his family, explained his defeat, defended the assassination of the Duc d'Enghien and proceeded to parcel out his fortune to no fewer than ninety-seven legatees.[62] We see Napoleon underlining his insistence that he had only ever acted for the people of France, but we also see just how unforgiving he could be. A man by the name of Cantillon, who had tried to assassinate Wellington in Paris in May 1819, was left 10,000 francs because 'he had as much right to assassinate the oligarch [Wellington] as he did to send me to the rock of St Helena'.[63] With a touch of black humour, he left the sum of twenty francs to Antommarchi, so that he could buy a rope to hang himself with.[64] Bertrand paid the price of not living in close proximity with Napoleon and was left significantly less than Montholon. Finally, Napoleon asked to be buried 'on the banks of the Seine among that French people whom I have loved so much'. The language tells us that he did not entirely identify with the French, as though he still considered himself a foreigner, an outsider, even after all those years. As we shall see, when news of it got out in France – the will was an immediate publishing success that went through ten editions between 1822 and 1833[65] – it produced a public outcry demanding that Napoleon's last wishes be fulfilled.

The second 'will', written a day or two after the first, was in the form of a letter to his son that doubled as a political programme for the nineteenth century.[66] It starts with the words, 'My son should not think of avenging my death; he should profit from it.' Again, it was in effect a declaration that he had been murdered. The important thing for Bonapartists was that Napoleon predicted that the Bourbons would not last, and that his son would come to power after a period of unrest in France. The rest is a litany of advice given by a ruler to a future heir, but which also serves as a justification for his own past behaviour ('my dictatorship was necessary'). This was as much meant for his son as it was a political love letter to his followers back home.

DELIVERANCE

He had been dreaming of Josephine, but in the fever that had taken hold of his mind he believed that he had just seen her. 'I just saw my good Josephine,' he told Montholon, 'but she didn't want to kiss me; she ran away the moment I wanted to take her in my arms. She was sitting there; it was like I had only seen her the day before; she hasn't changed, always the same.'[67] Montholon didn't have the heart to tell him it was only a dream. On 27 April, there was more vomiting in the presence of the two doctors, including a 'dark coloured fluid resembling coffee-grounds, and very offensive', an indication, we now know, that there was internal bleeding. Napoleon had become wracked with pain – to the point where he sometimes cried out.[68] It was only the next day, on 28 April, one week before Napoleon's demise, that Arnott finally admitted to Lowe that the situation was indeed serious.[69]

As for Lowe, attempts to see Napoleon were fobbed off by Bertrand and Montholon. The last thing Napoleon would have wanted was to lay eyes on the man he most hated and whom he held responsible for his condition. By that stage, he had hardly left his bed for weeks. Now, he shifted in and out of delirium. Arnott and Antommarchi were joined by two other doctors sent by Lowe, Charles Mitchel, a surgeon on the *Vigo*, and Thomas Shortt, the chief medical officer on the island since December 1820 and probably the best medical doctor to come into contact with Napoleon on St Helena.[70] Neither of them actually saw Napoleon; they only discussed his case with Arnott and Antommarchi, although Shortt recommended applying what was referred to as a large 'blister' on the stomach, 'one of the most efficacious remedies to be applied'.[71] The remaining reports are long, detailed lists of the symptoms.[72]

A few weeks before Napoleon's death, a comet appeared in the sky above St Helena, visible only in the evening between seven and eight o'clock. It had come, Napoleon believed in an astonishing show of hubris, to mark the end of his career. 'When I die, each of you will have the consolation of returning to Europe. Some will see your parents, others your friends. I on the other hand will meet my brave soldiers on the Elysian Fields. All will come to see me.'[73] On the 28 April, following a horrible night in which he was overcome with nausea, his bed was transported into the living room. After taking some of the sedative potion that had been prescribed for him, he fell into a restless sleep, emitting moans now and then. That night, unable to sleep, he dictated what were referred to as the 'reveries'. The first took two hours and concerned imaginary plans for the Château de Versailles. The second concerned the reorganisation of the National Guard. Neither of the texts survived, probably destroyed by Montholon (or another), no doubt owing to their rambling nature.[74]

Little by little, Napoleon was losing touch with reality, lapsing in and out of consciousness and delirium. He insisted that he had gone for a walk in the garden, when he patently had not. He asked whether the oranges from the Cape were sweet, and when he was told he had eaten some that morning, he insisted he had not. In fact, they were sour and he had thrown them back up. His once sharp mind was now fading; he kept on asking questions which people had already answered. He asked for some coffee but was refused by his entourage. He insisted, but they did not give way. It was enough to bring Bertrand to tears, to see this man who had once inspired such fear, 'who commanded so proudly, in so absolute a manner, beg for a spoonful of coffee, solicit permission, and not getting it, asking again and again and always without success'. The great Napoleon, miserable, feeble, humble.[75] At times he sent his doctors packing, then he was as docile as a child.

He was so weak he could not even get up to urinate, and he had to relieve himself in a pot. Twice the servants were obliged to change the sheets when he tipped his pot over, not that he was aware of what he had done.

On 1 May, Napoleon was overcome with a fainting fit. It was possibly then that he dreamt about a battle on a bridge. Was it Arcole that he was dreaming of, or the unconscious telling him that he would soon have another bridge to cross, this one much more terrible, more daunting than Arcole?[76] That day, in a lucid moment, he declared, 'I know I am dying.'[77] The doctors fussed over him, trying to relieve the pain as best they could in the days leading up to his relapse into a delirious state, placing mustard plasters on his feet, vesicants on his chest and calf, a bottle of boiling water on his stomach, nostrums which caused him even more discomfort, and which he would sometimes tear off despite the entreaties of Marchand. On the afternoon of 3 May, he was given the last rites by the Abbé Vignali, although he could not receive communion as he could not keep anything down.[78] He allowed Vignali to administer extreme unction not because he was devout or because he was hedging his bets, but because, as monarch, he believed it his duty to die expressing his attachment to the religion of his people.[79] Napoleon's attitude towards religion was ambiguous, and could change from one day to the next. We know that a chapel had been set up in the living room around September 1819 after the arrival of Vignali, but this appears to have been more for the inhabitants of Longwood than for Napoleon. Despite the discussions about God dotted through the memoirs later written by members of his entourage, Napoleon did not turn to Christianity during his final years.[80]

Death would come two days later. At one point he tried to get out of his bed and was caught too late by Montholon; both ended up on the floor.[81] He spent a painful, restless last night propped up on a pillow, moaning. Around four in the morning he said a few words that might have been 'qui recule' (who pulls back) and 'à la tête d'armée' (at the head of the army).[82] They were his final words. After his death, his last words, authentic or not, were avidly sought by a public wanting to know every intimate detail of his dying moments.[83] From the few details of the deathbed scene that had filtered through, the English, French and German press constructed and reconstructed multiple versions of his death. For royalists in France, the final words 'à la tête d'armée' revealed his obsession with war and power. For the opponents of the restored Bourbon monarchy, somehow the words 'Mon Dieu!... Nation française!' or 'Armée ... Nation française' or 'Dieu! Protège la France' miraculously emanated from Napoleon's lips in order to demonstrate that his dying thoughts were given over to France.[84]

The curtains were opened that morning, his last. The morning brought him calm, his body was perfectly immobile, and the only sign of life was the occasional eye movement. His eyes were fixed and three-quarters closed. Every half-hour or so he would emit a sigh or a groan, or rather a whistling sound that seemed to come from the lower abdomen. His right hand was under the covers; the left hand had been placed under his buttocks. He looked like a cadaver. His vest was covered in bloodstained spittle. Sixteen people were present to witness his last moments. His death was a very public act. Several times, the British doctor felt for a pulse on Napoleon's neck.

As he was dying, Napoleon may have thought of the thrashing he had received as a boy at the hands of his mother in Ajaccio, after she tricked him into taking off his pants; the ice in his plate at Brienne where he was a cadet; walking through the courtyard of the Tuileries Palace looking at the aftermath of that horrible massacre in 1792; seeing Paoli for the first time; the officer standing next to him at the siege of Toulon cut in two by a cannonball; that first night with Josephine; their wedding night when Josephine's dog bit him on the leg while he was on top of his mistress, enough to make him bleed; standing on the bridge at Lodi; almost fainting before the Council of Five Hundred on that fateful day at Saint-Cloud amid the shouts of 'Outlaw!'; placing the crown on his beloved, in the cathedral of Notre Dame; the mist over the fields at Austerlitz; in a carriage, the first time he set eyes on Maria Walewska; the time he deflowered Marie-Louise at Compiègne; his forty-second birthday in the throne room of the Tuileries Palace, and the dressing-down he gave the Russian ambassador, the sweat pouring down poor Kurakin's face, his mouth opening to reply but, unable to get a word in edgeways, looking like a fish gasping for air; his meeting with Balashov in Vilnius in which he threatened to throw the barbarians back into their icy wastes; standing on the banks of the Berezina, watching while the bridge was being built, and while some of the men building it were swept away; at the crossroads at Villia, on a hill overlooking a wide stretch of snow-covered road,

Mort de l'empereur Napoléon, le 5 mai 1821. Etched engraving. Date unknown but probably 1821. In the absence of any verifiable or definitive information about what had happened on St Helena, illustrators created the drama of the moment by capturing the actors around his deathbed. Many more representations of Napoleon's death were made than of the actual burial, contributing to the cult of the martyr. There was, moreover, a certain fascination with the space in which he died, the living room at Longwood. The fact that Napoleon was reduced in some respects to one room, which served at one and the same time as bedroom and dying room, and that he was laid out on his campaign bed, tells us a great deal about how he wanted to be perceived by the world, but also about what people wanted to read into the situation: someone who was simple and frugal, but also someone who had been reduced to a humiliating position. The death scene thus defines the space in which artists imagined Napoleon's final hours. Various personalities were selected to underline the veracity of the historical moment, as though it were an accurate portrayal of his dying moments, even if it had nothing to do with the reality. Napoleon was always portrayed in a placid, if not supine state, in part because he was falling in and out of consciousness in the last few days of his life, but it may also have been a metaphor for the supine state of the French body politic.

surrounded by his bodyguard, watching the survivors of his Grande Armée struggle past; riding his horse over a smoking howitzer shell at Arcis-sur-Aube only to have it explode and kill the horse, but leaving him untouched; gulping down a vial of poison at Fontainebleau the first time he abdicated; the welcome he received at Lyons on his way back to Paris; the plains of Waterloo, an empire lost as he tried to enter the last square; the crowds cheering him from the boats in Plymouth Sound; smashing up the silver at Longwood – that will teach Hudson Lowe a lesson.

He died in the evening, at 5.49, just as the sun was setting.[85] The clocks were stopped throughout the house. Not only did this accurately record the actual time of death, but it also held a deeper, spiritual significance. Stopping the clocks at death and restarting them after the burial was meant to symbolise the end of one period of life and the beginning of another.[86] It was also usual to cover the mirrors, although this was a superstitious custom: some believed that if the mirrors weren't covered the first person to look into one would be the next to die; others believed that the spirit of the deceased would enter the mirror, or see its reflection and refuse to leave. One of the servants covered Napoleon's face to protect it from the flies that were now buzzing around.

By coincidence, thirty-two years previously to the day, the meeting of the Estates-General had taken place at Versailles in 1789 to resolve the country's financial crisis, a crisis that began a series of events that would lead to the French Revolution, and that would enable someone like Napoleon to make his mark on the world. As a twenty-year-old, when Bonaparte entered an essay competition on the theme of happiness organised by the Academy of Lyons, he wrote the following lines: 'The ambition which overturns whole States and individual fortunes, which is nourished on blood and crimes ... is, like all disorderly passions, a violent and unreflective madness which ceases only with life itself: like a fire that, driven on by a pitiless wind, ends only when it has consumed everything.'[87] Napoleon's fire had been finally extinguished.

THE BODY MADE PUBLIC

About eighteenth months later, in a letter to Lowe, Reade rather pointedly described having seen Mme Bertrand that night or the following one. 'I am sure that she did not appear to me at all like one who had lost a friend, but on the contrary seemed in good spirits and cheerful.'[88] He suggested there was no sorrow in any of Napoleon's followers and claimed that the only person to have shed a tear was Archambault the groom.

In fact, there is little to convey the mood of those who witnessed his death, a mixture no doubt of 'cruel emotions' and relief that they would at last be returning to France. Napoleon's servants were probably exhausted after having kept watch over him for the past forty-odd days, and yet, wrote Saint-Denis, sleep was unable to overtake them.[89] They were possibly at a loss now that they had nothing to do and no one to order them about. Saint-Denis, Marchand, Noverraz and Pierron prepared the body at midnight and washed it with a mixture of cologne and water. Noverraz shaved him, keeping the bristles for souvenirs. Napoleon was then dressed in a clean shirt and laid to rest with a sheet covering all but his face. Candles were placed to the left and the right of him, while a silver cross was placed on his chest. Then commenced the vigil, shared during the night by Bertrand, Montholon, Marchand and Vignali. Lowe arrived in the morning around six or seven o'clock with a large party of officers to pay their respects. The autopsy was performed around two o'clock. Later in the day, between four and six o'clock in the evening, 'respectable people' were allowed to file past to witness the lying-in-state. After six o'clock, soldiers of the 20th Regiment were allowed to file past.[90] A number of them remarked on how Napoleon's countenance 'gave one an idea of everything serene and placid' and noted how his face was 'really beautiful'.[91] The next day restrictions were lifted and at this point the public, including all the troops, sailors and civilians on the island, was finally allowed to pay its respects, filing past the body, often touching Napoleon's hand or pressing their lips to his cloak, making remarks like 'he is the greatest man in the world'.[92] At least six sketches were made of Napoleon on his deathbed, including those of Marchand and Arnott (the other four were by Denzil Ibbetson, Frederick Marryat, William Crokat and E. E. Vidal). The body had lain in state for only a short while, but had begun to smell so badly that preparations for burial were hurried along.[93]

Frederik Marryat, *Sketch of Bonaparte. As laid on his Austerlitz Camp Bed, taken by Captn. Marryat R.N., 14 hours after his Decease, at the request of Sir Hudson Lowe, Governor of St. Helena, & with the permission of Count Montholon & General Bertrand.* 1821. Lithograph, paper. Marryat was a British naval officer on guardship duty in St Helena at the time of Napoleon's death. The publication of these deathbed scenes, mostly coming out of London, was also designed to refute rumours that Napoleon was alive.[94]

The autopsy was carried out by Antommarchi, in the company of sixteen witnesses, including three British officers and seven doctors.[95] Napoleon had specifically asked for an autopsy to be carried out; he wanted it to be known whether he had suffered from the same disease as his father, or whether he had indeed had hepatitis. His naked body was placed on a plank covered by a white sheet and supported by trestles in the middle of the billiard room.[96] If the report showed that he had succumbed to the same illness as his own father, Napoleon's son was to be informed. An autopsy undertaken in the first half of the nineteenth century was generally speaking a mark of honour, shared by many famous men, even when they had not died a suspicious or violent death.[97] The autopsies carried out on kings or princes always remained private. Napoleon's autopsy, on the other hand, was made very public, not only through the publication of official reports, but more particularly through the publication of opinions surrounding the autopsy in the months that followed. His body was laid out and opened up before all the world both literally and metaphorically, exposing the nineteenth-century reader to the 'inner' details of Napoleon and his life, which included his prolonged pain and suffering. The godlike figure of Napoleon was thus rendered human, reduced to a body like any other.

The autopsy was also important politically. If it showed that the cause of Napoleon's death had indeed been hepatitis, the French could claim that the climate on the island had killed him. However, the post-mortem, which took about two hours to complete, concluded that he had died of a cancer of the stomach.[98] Some doubt has been cast on this diagnosis, since there was disagreement about whether death was caused by a tumour found where the stomach joins the duodenum, or by stomach perforations resulting from an ulcer.[99] In a recent study, a number of Italian pathologists have concluded that the *immediate* cause of Napoleon's death was a massive gastric haemorrhage that had occurred in or around a gastric tumour. He is likely to have had a long-standing infection (Helicobacter pylori), which might have led to the development of a prepyloric ulcer, and in turn have brought about the beginnings of a gastric adenocarcinoma.[100] In other words, it was not cancer that killed Napoleon, although it would have killed him eventually.

After the autopsy, the British doctors who had witnessed it drew up the minutes of what they had observed, and gave the document to Antommarchi to sign. As the doctor who had performed the autopsy, he refused; Bertrand supposedly told him not to because the document did not refer to the 'Emperor Napoleon'. It was up to him to draw up his own report, a copy of which he would give to them, but (at least according to Antommarchi) the British doctors did not accept it.[101] The political significance of the autopsy is one of the reasons why we have five different post-mortem reports, three contemporary and two written at a later date. Shortt, as the senior doctor who had overseen the autopsy (while Walter Henry took notes), wrote the official report. Lowe amended Shortt's report, as was his wont, to eliminate any

mention of an enlarged liver, so as not to give any hint of 'hepatitis'.[102]
Antommarchi wrote his report on 8 May, but published a much more
detailed version of it in his memoirs in 1825. Thomas Reade also wrote
a report to Lowe a few hours after the autopsy. Finally, after a request
from Lowe, Walter Henry, who did not sign the official report, wrote
his own report in 1823, based on notes taken during the autopsy. The
reports, and the subsequent pamphlets that were based on them, had
different political agendas and were used to illustrate particular viewpoints. Their purpose, therefore, was to expose the body and to make a
claim for either sympathy or disapproval.[103] For want of a better term,
this was the political exploitation of his death.

For the English, the reports were used to belittle the man and
to quash any arguments about the climate as the cause of death. In
Reade's report to Lowe, for example, there are striking remarks about
the 'extraordinary quantity of fat which covered almost every part of
the interior, under the chest, but particularly about the heart, which
was literally enveloped in fat'.[104] For the English doctors present
at the autopsy, there was no ambiguity about the cause of death; it
was the 'diseased state of the stomach'. The stomach was taken out;
two-thirds of it 'appeared in a horrible state covered with cancerous
substances and at a short distance from the Pylorus, there was a hole
sufficient to admit a little finger through it'. There was disagreement,
however, over whether the liver was 'enlarged' or not. Shortt believed
it was, but the other doctors present did not think there was anything
extraordinary about it.

This last point was underlined in the French royalist newspapers,
such as *La Quotidienne*, which maintained that the doctors performing the autopsy had concluded that Napoleon's liver was healthy and
that cancer was the cause of his death.[105] There was instead an insistence on portraying Napoleon's death as the result not of the climate
but of an hereditary sickness. The French royalist press also portrayed
Napoleon's body in a relatively ignominious light, describing 'a thick
layer of fat on the sides; it was even greater on the lower parts of the
body'.[106] The royalist focus was therefore on how little Napoleon had
suffered, how his death was the result of family history, and how therefore it was inevitable.[107] In the process, they denied Bonapartists and
liberals any reason to 'feel' Napoleon's pain and suffering, and thereby
legitimised the decision to send him to St Helena in the first place.

For Napoleonists and liberals, on the other hand, the autopsy explicated the history of Napoleon's suffering; it became a narrative that proved the veracity of the overarching claim that had been made first by Napoleon himself and then by his followers, namely, that his death had been precipitated by the unhealthy conditions on St Helena. The most important element to all this is that the reader was asked to sympathise with Napoleon, and even perhaps to feel his pain vicariously through the detailed description of the sick body. All of this was, of course, an indirect way of criticising both the Bourbon regime and the government of Britain. In the process of detailing the pain and suffering experienced by Napoleon, there was an evident attempt to lay claim to the sympathy of the reader.[108]

After the autopsy, Napoleon's head was shaved and locks of hair were distributed, in accordance with his wishes, to members of his family and those close to him, and were in due course circulated throughout Europe. Las Cases, Bertrand, Marchand and Montholon later gave little reliquaries – sometimes bejewelled – containing locks of Napoleon's hair to friends and relatives.[109] We will come back to the creation of reliquaries. For the moment, Napoleon's heart was removed and put in a vessel until the English doctors should receive further instructions; Montholon was so insistent that it be removed that they acceded to his demand.[110] Napoleon had requested that his heart be given to his estranged wife, the Empress Marie-Louise, as a relic, a gift, a sentimental reminder of the love they had once shared.[111] In the seventeenth century, aristocrats took it for granted that the heart would be buried separately. By the beginning of the nineteenth century, however, it was a custom that had fallen into disuse, except among royals.[112] Bertrand and Montholon attempted to carry out their master's wishes, but the English insisted that both the heart and the intestines be buried with the body for fear of a sort of cult of the Sacred Heart developing around it.[113] Reade later wrote a detailed account in which he stated that Napoleon's body was closed up, dressed and remained attended while lying in state.

There is some speculation that Antommarchi cut off Napoleon's penis during the autopsy and gave it to Vignali, who took it back to Corsica, but this seems highly fanciful.[114] Saint-Denis claims that Antommarchi took 'two small pieces' from the rib during the autopsy and gave them to Vignali and Jacques Coursot (who had arrived on the island with Antommarchi).[115] Body parts of the deceased were no longer collected, as had once been the case with saints. Nevertheless, objects that had been worn by Napoleon, or that had been in contact with the tomb, could still take on mystical if not magical qualities.[116] Anything that had once belonged to or had come into contact with Napoleon was now considered if not sacred, then at least valuable. Some of these objects were simply used to remind the owner of Napoleon's life, a memento perhaps of the connection between the owner and the Emperor. The collecting of relics – locks of hair, traces of blood in the case of violent death (as with Louis XVI's execution) or scraps of fabric – was not an unusual practice in the late eighteenth and early nineteenth centuries and is connected on one level with religious practices and on another with the Romantic Movement.[117] Any number of examples could be given, including the venerated remains of the royal couple Louis XVI and Marie-Antoinette, as well as the collection of memorabilia associated with the martyrs of the Revolution, and the relic-collecting that developed around the cult of Queen Luise of Prussia (locks of hair, dress fragments, everyday utensils).[118]

The most precious of the Napoleonic relics was the former Emperor's death mask. Two days after his death, Bertrand asked Antommarchi to make a cast of Napoleon's head so that he could present it to the family. It was not unusual for death masks to grace the living rooms of the well-to-do in the early nineteenth century.[119] But Antommarchi failed in his attempts. Instead, he turned to the British surgeon, Francis Burton, who made a plaster (or possibly wax) mortuary mask, assisted by Antommarchi. It was Mme Bertrand who took the mask from Burton, or at least the front half, and allowed Antommarchi to produce a plaster mould of it from which he later made copies, in both bronze and plaster.[120] Napoleon's death mask became fashionable among the Parisian elites in the 1820s and grew into a sort of object of pilgrimage among fervent admirers of the Emperor; they would travel to Antommarchi's apartments in Paris, in the rue de Rivoli, to see it 'locked in a small box lined with velvet'. The mask thus took on political and even semi-religious overtones. The sculptor David d'Angers went with the Irish novelist Sydney, Lady Morgan to see the mask in 1828 and was deeply moved by the effect it had on him. 'I said goodbye to this piece of plaster, with as much clenching of the heart as the last man will experience when the world is snuffed out.'[121] Even in death, Napoleon could elicit a strong emotional response from his admirers.

Other relics included bloodstained pieces of linen and cloth used during the autopsy, and even twigs and leaves from the weeping willows around the tomb (eventually these trees would be so badly stripped by visitors that they themselves died), as well as rocks, earth, water and flowers, anything that surrounded the grave.[122] They circulated in great numbers among Napoleonists in the decade following the former Emperor's death. And as with relics of the 'true cross', a small industry developed around the fabrication of fake Napoleonic relics, such as meshes of hair that were not his and wood from the trees surrounding his tomb that did not come from St Helena. The Bonapartist and republican Agricol Perdiguier described a scene which took place in July 1826. An innkeeper in a village a few leagues from Royan was given a leaf from a weeping willow near Napoleon's tomb by a sailor who had stopped off there. The innkeeper was overwhelmed: 'He wept with tenderness and joy!... He no longer controlled himself.'[123] The collection of relics was a personal, deeply private exercise and says a good deal about the place of the relic in the mind of the collector, as well as about the collector's political beliefs.[124] These relics were meant to embody the essence of Napoleon, acting thereby as a locus of his power.

What is particularly significant is that people collected memorabilia belonging to Napoleon while he was still alive, in much the same way that people today collect memorabilia associated with their favourite celebrities. When the Emperor stopped off outside Kaunas (Kovno), in Lithuania, on his retreat from Russia in December 1812 and had a wash and changed his clothes, the cast-off shirt and stockings were seized on by the locals and cut into strips to be preserved, in the words of Napoleon's Mameluke servant Roustam Raza, as 'holy relics'.[125] Vivant Denon, the former director of the Musée Napoléon, had a private reliquary of secular saints that included body parts (hair, teeth, pieces of bone) and clothing from historical figures throughout the ages. The collection encompassed effects belonging to Napoleon that Denon had gathered throughout Napoleon's life, among them hair and clothing, as well as a leaf from one of the weeping willows that hung over the gravesite at St Helena.[126]

BURIAL

There was every expectation on the part of the French on the island that Napoleon's body would be returned to France.[127] Lowe had not communicated to the French the orders he had received, dated February 1820, to bury his prisoner on the island. The funeral took place four days after his death, on Wednesday 9 May, in a small chapel that had been set up in Longwood for that purpose.[128] A funeral chariot was drawn by four of Napoleon's carriage horses and was accompanied by British Grenadiers. Napoleon's own horse was decked out and followed in the rear, and as had become customary black riding boots were reversed in the stirrups to represent a fallen leader looking back on his troops for the last time. Napoleon's sword and his greatcoat were placed on the coffin. The funeral chariot was followed by his entourage as well as by the island's English civil and military dignitaries. Several bands played a dirge until the procession had passed. The route itself was lined by 2,000 British soldiers and sailors who fell in silently behind the coffin as it went past. The funeral procession was an exclusively masculine affair, as was the convention in the first half of the nineteenth century.[129] Women were permitted to attend the mass, but they were not present at the actual burial.

Napoleon was buried in the Valley of the Geraniums, a site he had chosen, where the shade of two weeping willows fell across his grave, close to a small fountain in the middle of the ravine. A barrier was later built around the site and an English functionary kept watch over it for the next twenty-odd years.[130] The French wanted the simple inscription 'Napoleon' placed over the tomb, but Lowe preferred 'Napoleon Bonaparte'.[131] As a result of this disagreement, the tomb remained without an inscription. Lowe's insistence was seen by Napoleon's supporters as the last, spiteful act of a petty man.[132] It was certainly the act of an intractable pedant. Down to the last, Lowe had been obsessed with observing regulations to the point where he would not permit the dying Napoleon to bequeath a two-volume work on the life of Marlborough to Captain Lutyens because the inside cover of the first volume had been inscribed with the words 'L'Empereur Napoleon'. Lutyens was ordered to return the volumes; at first he objected, but acquiesced when threatened with a court martial. He vented his feelings to Bertrand, exclaiming, 'What a cowardly business! The wretch [referring to Lowe]! To rebuff a dying man in that fashion.'[133]

There is something profoundly poignant about Napoleon on St Helena, not because of his fall from power but because of what he made of his life there. Another man might have used this time to reflect upon his life, his mistakes and his place in the world, and possibly in the process come to know himself a little better. Napoleon did none of these things. Instead, he entered into a battle against the English he could not possibly hope to win; he found refuge in lies; he perpetuated the myth that he had created in the belief that posterity would ultimately see him as he wanted to be seen. He was not entirely wrong. His admirers, right up to the present day, prefer to see in him a man capable of tremendous feats and innumerable victories, rather than a man incapable of acknowledging the consequences of his actions.

St Helena became a pathetic spectacle of daily bullying on the one hand and the fantasy-filled dreams that Napoleon thought up on the other. They could be as imaginative as wanting to make Paris the 'capital of the Christian world', where he was meant to play the role of a Constantine or Charlemagne, to creating a federated Europe.[134] It is perhaps ironic that he was portrayed and indeed remembered as divine or saintly given that over the years the descriptions of his character by French men and women he encountered portrayed him as all too human: he griped about his coffee; he pulled people's ears and slapped their cheeks (usually affectionately); he played practical jokes on those around him; he whistled and he sang; he got headaches and was moody; he asked for food to be simply handed to him by hand, that is, without 'ceremony'; he (supposedly) grabbed a plough and helped draw a furrow; and his symptoms during his prolonged illness all brought him down to the level of the common mortal.[135] As we shall see, it was the revelation of this human dimension that made his followers love him even more.

THE EXILES DEPART

Six days after Napoleon's death, Lowe inspected Longwood and went through his personal belongings, as well as leafing through any correspondence and documents he found there, looking for evidence that might incriminate people on the island.[136] With his usual lack of tact, he forced open boxes and chests that had been sealed, including three small boxes destined for Napoleon's son, which he was to be given on his sixteenth birthday and which contained small personal items and jewellery Napoleon had worn during his lifetime. Lady Lowe also went through the house, choosing furniture.[137]

If Lowe expected a promotion or congratulations from his superiors for having carried out such an arduous task, he was mistaken. When he returned to London (Lowe and his wife left the island on on 25 July), he was presented to George IV on 14 November.[138] However, he found that society shut its doors on him; he was ostracised by an establishment that found it convenient to scapegoat one of its own, although admittedly it was his behaviour and a certain amount of bad publicity that had turned the tide of public opinion against him. Less than a year after his return, O'Meara published *A Voice from St. Helena*, which portrayed Lowe in a very poor light. He eventually received another posting, but as no more than deputy governor of Ceylon, and that only briefly. He ended his life in 1844 at the age of seventy-five in disgrace and poverty. It is hard to feel much sympathy for a man who had callously destroyed so many careers – those of Reardon and Stokoe come to mind – while he was governor of St Helena, simply because they had incurred his displeasure. A mean-spirited man, Lowe died in mean circumstances.

On 26 May, a few weeks after Napoleon died, Bertrand and his family, Montholon, Marchand and Saint-Denis among others left the island on the storeship *Camel*. During the remainder of their stay on the island, they made a pilgrimage to Napoleon's grave once a day.[139] Marchand tells of kneeling before the grave on the day of his departure 'giving free rein to [his] tears'. Everyone was on deck as the vessel sailed away so that they could assure Napoleon that their 'thoughts would be with him each day'. They set sail at about three o'clock. On board, they watched the island where they had spent the last six years recede until, with the setting of the sun, the island merged with the shadows.

They disembarked at Portsmouth on 31 July.[140] Bertrand went to London with Charles de Montholon to deliver, among other things, a snuff box from Napoleon to Lady Holland.[141] While there, they sent a letter to George IV with a request for the repatriation of Napoleon's body. The British government replied that it considered itself the custodian of 'General Bonaparte's' remains, but that a formal request would have to come from the French government. That was unlikely to happen. The Bourbons had no desire to see Napoleon, even in a coffin, return to France. Bertrand eventually retired to his family's estate in Châteauroux. Montholon, since he had inherited the bulk of Napoleon's fortune, was able to lead the high life, without Albine, with a residence in Paris and a château in the country, until he declared himself bankrupt in 1829. He was not, it seems, a particularly astute businessman. Marchand married two years later, in 1823, leading a rather peaceful life that was really only interrupted, as we shall see, in 1840, when he again went back to St Helena. Since the Bourbons did not look favourably on the prospect of works written by Napoleon's companions in exile, the police kept a close watch on them.[142]

6

Mourning from Afar

'HE IS NOT DEAD'

By the time the exiles reached Europe, news of Napoleon's death had preceded them. The news arrived in Portsmouth, over 7,400 kilometres from St Helena, on 4 July 1821. The reports in the British papers were a mixture of acknowledgement of his greatness (even his genius) with a condemnation of the consequences of his ambition. By this time, the intense hatred felt for Napoleon in some quarters of British society had been attenuated, with the result that anger had been replaced by pity, while the underlying fascination for the man remained. For a few Britishers of a radical bent, the passing of Napoleon was deeply saddening, especially since his death more or less coincided with the coronation of George IV (on 19 July).[1] The new English monarch, portly, debauched and slightly ridiculous, inspired little hope among people like Byron. Thomas Noon Talfourd, later a judge, author and friend of Dickens, went into mourning over Napoleon's death for a month. 'I am fully persuaded,' Talfourd wrote, 'that Bonaparte was not only a splendid warrior & politician; but a very kind-hearted man.'[2] The poet and radical journalist Leigh Hunt edited a special issue of the *Examiner* on 8 July with 'Death of Napoleon Bonaparte' in bold on the front page – 'The age has lost its greatest name' – framed by a black border.[3] Those who had been critical of the conditions in which Napoleon had been kept on St Helena felt vindicated on hearing of his death.[4]

There was little patience for this kind of reaction among most Whigs, let alone among Tories. The *Annual Register* reported that the death of Napoleon, a man who had long been the scourge of Europe, was regarded with indifference.⁵ The *Morning Post*, a newspaper that supported the Castlereagh–Liverpool government, acknowledged that he was 'one of the greatest conquerors this world ever produced, but not a great and noble character'.⁶ *The Times*'s obituary was more scathing. 'Buonaparte will go down to posterity as a man who, having more good at his disposal than any other potentate of any former age, had actually applied his immense means to the production of a greater share of mischief and misery to his fellow creatures – one who carried on a series of aggressions against foreign States, to divert the minds of his own subjects from the sense of their domestic slavery.'⁷ The *Edinburgh Magazine* described him as 'selfish, perfidious, bloody. He had no value for any life but his own … He crushed the hope of freedom in France and would have crushed it throughout the world. He was a tyrant in the darkest sense of the name … he was an adulterer and an apostate. He was felt to be an enemy of mankind, whom no faith could bind … He was declared an outlaw by the hearts of all nations … and after having run the career of a villain, he died the death of a slave.'⁸

In Paris, on 5 July, Louis XVIII was one of the first to learn of Napoleon's death. The news was officially announced in the papers two days later.⁹ As he had in life, his death elicited enormously polarised responses, from those who openly mourned his passing to those who openly castigated his memory. In Paris, crowds gathered around engravings sold in the streets – the *Convoi* and the *Tombeau d'un brave* appear to have been particularly popular, but were seized by the police as soon as they appeared¹⁰ – while pamphlets commenting on the death sold faster than they could be printed.¹¹ A couple of weeks after the news first broke, people were tearing copies of newspapers out of each other's hands for fear of missing out, although a few street arrests by the police seemed to calm people's enthusiasm.¹² There were discussions, arguments, fights, men and women crying in public.¹³ According to one historian, a newspaper vendor was beaten for having announced the death of Napoleon, although we are not sure if royalists carried out the beating because the vendor dared mention the name 'Napoleon' or if it was perpetrated by Bonapartists who refused to accept his death.¹⁴ The police seized a mass of pamphlets and illustrations dealing with the death,¹⁵ but more were produced to fill the void. For royalists, his death would have been a relief; for Bonapartists, all hope of his return was forever at an end.[16]

And yet descriptions of the popular reaction to news of Napoleon's death, at least among a certain class of people, are generally muted. The Comtesse de Boigne, who could be described as a moderate royalist, heard the hawkers spread the news in the streets of Paris – 'the death of Napoleon for two sols [a small copper coin], his speech to General Bertrand for two sols, Madam Bertrand's despair for two sols' – without it having any more impact, she remarked, than if the announcement of a lost dog had been made.[17] The lack of emotion displayed in response to the news surprised a number of other observers.[18] 'Life goes on,' noted the liberal deputy and former Napoleonic general Maximilien-Sébastien Foy, a supporter of the Emperor. 'Everything passes, and everything passes without it barely being noticed.'[19] Charles-Maurice de Talleyrand, Napoleon's former foreign minister, was at a certain Mme Crawford's when news of the death of Napoleon was announced. 'Ah! My God, what an event!' Mme Crawford declared. Talleyrand is supposed to have quipped with his usual laconic wit, 'It is no longer an event, it's just a piece of news,' or something along those lines.[20] Similarly, police reports point to the lack of reaction and the seeming indifference of the people. 'Rumour of the death of Bonaparte that spread yesterday at the Stock Exchange, and which has been confirmed this morning by all the newspapers, has not produced a great sensation, and did not affect the court of public opinion.'[21]

Beyond Paris, the police reported very little public reaction, even in Bonapartist strongholds. In Chartres, Nantes, Orleans and Lyons, the news was supposedly greeted with indifference, proving in the words of the police that Napoleon 'had been dead to the public for a long time'.[22] At Lyons, 'the prestige with which this extraordinary man was surrounded has disappeared', reported the prefect, 'even among his most pronounced supporters. Feelings were more noticeable among the inhabitants of the countryside and among former soldiers.'[23] The prefect of the department of the Eure-et-Loir expressed his 'profound surprise' at the indifference with which the news was greeted.[24] At Marseilles, there was not much of an impact either.[25] In the little town of Saint-Brieuc in Brittany, groups of workers danced in a ring on one

of the promenades, singing the refrain 'Ioumi is no longer.'[26] 'Ioumi'
was what royalist peasants in Brittany used to call Napoleon.

How do we explain this supposed indifference? For a start, the
police reports are not entirely reliable. Servants tend to tell their mas-
ters what they want to hear, and in this case the police were probably
doing just that. One should also remember that the Bourbon regime
was politically repressive. The policy of moderation adopted by the
monarchy post-1815 in an attempt to unite the country around the
throne was abandoned after a Bonapartist named Pierre Louvel assassinated Charles Ferdinand, Duc de Berry, in February 1820 outside
the Opera in Paris.[27] Berry was the son of the king's brother Charles,
presumptive heir to the throne. The assassination was, in the words
of Louvel, an attempt to extinguish the Bourbon line of succession. It
profoundly destabilised politics in France. In the atmosphere of moral
panic and fear of sedition that followed, the new ultra-royalist government did three things that alienated public opinion even further: it
suspended habeas corpus; it tightened press censorship (for a while at
least; it appears to have lapsed again after 1822);[28] and it amended the
electoral laws, restricting even further the eligibility to vote. However,
far from being a period in which politics diminished, it expanded dra-
matically as people found ways in which to express their ideas in
public arenas such as the town or village square, the cafés, theatres
and *guinguettes* (cabarets) on the outskirts of Paris (the *banlieues*),
through songs, placards, pamphlets, illegal memorabilia, bric-a-brac
and objets d'art. The simple acts of crying out 'Vive Napoléon' or
wearing a tricolour cockade were considered seditious and liable to be
punished by imprisonment. In the town of Sedan in the Ardennes, a
twenty-seven-year-old man was sentenced to three months in prison
for shouting in the street 'Vive l'Empereur', while in in the Vosges
Jacques-Philippe Hurst was jailed for a month and fined 150 francs
for a similar offence.[29] People who publicly excited hatred against the
king could also be sent to prison and fined up to 5,000 francs.[30] Back
in June 1817, twenty-three people had been condemned to death and
another thirty-three deported for a putative plot against the monarchy in Lyons that appears to have been a conspiracy fabricated by
the local authorities.[31] One of the condemned men, a former officer
by the name of Dumont, supposedly pointed a pistol at a priest and
ordered him to cry 'Vive Napoléon.' Many more were imprisoned

for expressing their political views.[32] Is it any wonder then that public displays of mourning for Napoleon were muted?

Finally, it is possible that it simply took time for the reality, once confirmed, to sink in, and even that news of his death was often simply not believed.[33] There had been so many rumours over the years about Napoleon's death, not to mention the number of false sightings of him, that at first the news may not have been taken very seriously.[34] According to one police report written towards the end of July, 'The rumour vaguely circulated among the lowest class of people that everything the newspapers contained on the subject was false, and that Buonaparte was at Lyons.'[35] 'The lower classes do not believe,' declared General Foy, 'and this only serves to switch their attention on to this extraordinary man.'[36] The refusal to believe in Napoleon's death was especially widespread in the countryside where he was commonly venerated.[37] 'Vive Napoléon,' cried one veteran from Gers. 'He is a brave man. They say he is dead, but I do not believe it. I pray for him every day.' A navvy from the Vendée was accused of saying, 'Vive l'Empereur Napoléon ... Vive Bonaparte. He is not dead. He has good soldiers. He is himself a good soldier. He was my sovereign. I loved him. I will always love him.'[38] An individual at Nemours declared in a cabaret on 8 July that he wanted to see Bonaparte return (despite news of his death), and then proceeded to insult the royal family.[39] A day labourer from the Deux-Sèvres declared, 'The Emperor is not dead, he will awaken soon,' a refrain that would be taken up and used in the works of both Victor Hugo and Honoré de Balzac.[40] In 1822, at Saint-Jean-d'Angély, a Belgian deserter was arrested for telling people he had just seen the Emperor and that he would arrive in the village in a few hours' time.[41] In April that same year, a bookseller was caught with a pamphlet entitled *Miraculous Event*, which contained the following passage: 'Soon we will see a very big change across the four corners of the world, but mainly in Europe; the genius of Napoleon I, our worthy Emperor, will soon make us forget all the misfortunes we have been witness to, and we will soon enjoy the perfect tranquillity the people desire so much. You will see that commerce will resume better than ever, as well as public works ...'[42] The writer Paul-Louis Courier claimed that in 1823 there wasn't a peasant in the whole of France who did not say that Napoleon would return. 'They don't all believe it, but they say it.' It was a kind of cipher designed to taunt the Bourbon government, which the peasants hated.[43]

One can see here the beginnings of a millennialism that was born of, and fed into, the cult. For these people, the bravado was a means of denying the unbearable reality. When the reality sank in, and it had become obvious that the news was no longer rumour and that their idol was never coming back, the faithful – they themselves used the term *fidèle*, which has religious connotations – were often obliged to mourn in private. If Colonel Perraton is to be believed, 'I retired to my room to be alone with my pain. I put on my old uniform and raised to my lips the Cross of the Legion of Honour that the Emperor himself had given me, and I looked at his portrait, crying. I needed to shut myself off to think only of him. I was devastated.'[44]

'ONLY DEATH PROVED THAT HE WAS MORTAL'

There was, therefore, an apparent slow burn as Napoleonists came to grips with the significance of the news. Ten days after the announcement, the prefect of police in Paris noted an increase in 'public attention' around the death of Napoleon, something that was also apparent in the provinces.[45] The Duchesse de Broglie, a royalist, later admitted in a letter to Prosper de Barante, who had once been a prefect under Napoleon, that 'The impact that this death has had on the people is much stronger than I led you at first to believe.'[46] It took time, but some sections of Paris society eventually went into a sort of veiled mourning, veiled because the name of Napoleon and images of the defunct Emperor were forbidden by a regime that considered any representation of the man, even in death, to be a threat.[47] The Palais Royal supposedly began to attract 'great crowds' of people dressed in black, although no mention of this can be found in the police reports of the day.[48] One English observer also noted the crowds, which the police reported as a few 'liberals', who donned black and went to salute the Vendôme Column on the night when news of Napoleon's death reached Paris.[49] Wreaths were laid at the foot of the Column. The same English observer reported that:

> The account of his [Napoleon's] interment has compelled many to believe, and the effect is certainly terrible for the reigning house. I asked one of the [Royal] Guard, whom I know – he is related

to one of my domestics – what his comrades said? 'They will not believe,' said he. 'Why?' 'Because they dare not: they fear the effect upon themselves. Ah!' continued he, 'I served him in Russia too, and, if I could see him again, I would follow him to the end of the world – 'tis too cruel to be dragged from his wife, his mother, his family, and his son and to be carried to a hole by grenadiers, foreigners, and gaolers.' The tears ran down his cheeks, and the drops hung on his mustachios – but not a muscle was distorted.'[50]

Students too started wearing black crepe on their hats or around their arms, or sometimes violets painted black in the buttonhole of their coats as a public sign of mourning.[51] The violet was adopted by Bonapartists as early as 1815 as an emblem of hope, in contrast to the fleur de lys, symbol of the Bourbon monarchy. To sport it was thus also a means of expressing opposition to the Bourbons, but the regime soon put to a stop to it.

On 28 July, the police prefect of Paris systematically pursued anyone wearing black on the streets and boulevards, especially around the Palais Royal.[52] Interestingly, these students had never known the wars, had grown up under the Empire and had reached adulthood around the time of Napoleon's death.[53] For fifteen years, to paraphrase Alfred de Musset, they had dreamt of the campaigns conducted in faraway lands, and associated the word 'glory' with the name of Napoleon.[54]

Among the faithful, the news was rather earth-shattering. On 12 July, General Fantin des Odoards wrote from Strasbourg:

The end of the Emperor came as a thunderbolt for those who like me had in their fanaticism made a demi-god of the hero who had carried the glory of the French name so far and so high. It seemed to us that Napoleon was above humanity, and that he could not die, his body had to be as imperishable as its name; and he is dead! That the King of Kings sleeps in his coffin! His eyes will launch no more lightning bolts; his presence and his voice will no more electrify armies; a movement of the Modern Jupiter's eyebrows will no longer rock the world.[55]

Similarly, Nicolas-Louis Planat de La Faye, a devout follower who had attempted to join Napoleon on St Helena, confessed that his heart

broke on hearing the news: 'Everything is over for me, I have lost all
that made me strong, everything that made my existence worthy …
I feel as though I have been skinned alive, anyone who touches me
makes me cry out; when they try to console me, I become furious.'[56]
Veterans devoted to their Emperor felt the same way. Colonel Brack
irrupted into Horace Vernet's studio in the rue des Martyrs, announcing between sobs that Napoleon had died. Everyone there immediately became emotional, while Vernet lit his studio and put a bust
of Napoleon on a table along with two candles that burnt all night.
General Bro, witness to the event, had some sort of vision: 'I felt dizzy
… they helped me to a seat and I thought I saw, in my confusion, the
Emperor on horseback in front of his Guard, the Guard to which
I had once belonged!'[57]

Maurice Persat, in exile in London, recounted that the news of
Napoleon's death had struck like a thunderbolt and that he had cried;
he hated the Bourbons and the English even more after that.[58] When
the Comtesse de Kielmannsegge, who had been a lady-in-waiting
to Queen Hortense, heard of Napoleon's death she is supposed to
have said, 'Only death proved that he was mortal.'[59] She steadfastly
remained in mourning for the rest of her years (she died in 1863 at
the age of eighty-five).[60] Ernest Legouvé believed that no one was left
indifferent, not even those who had been implacable enemies, like the
poet and playwright Népomucène Lemercier, who broke down in
tears, or Chateaubriand, who felt moved.[61] Colonel Perraton 'had not
thought the death of the Emperor could occur: such a spirit animated
this prodigious being':

> He was so much a part of my life, our Life, to us, his faithful, his
> former soldiers who never forgot him and who, in order not to
> repudiate him, left everything, even the army to which we were
> so attached! He was our pride, our leader, our 'protector'. He had
> become our memory, our hope! We had followed him for so many
> years, we had had him before our us, in our hearts and in our minds!
> He had so much lived his life, burnt with his fever. We had thought
> of nothing other than him … We had lived only for him, bewitched
> by him as all were who approached him … He personified for us the
> *patrie*. He owned our hearts because he was our Emperor, but also
> because he was for us the heart of France.[62]

When news reached individual members of the Bonaparte family, here too the reactions were as varied as in the rest of Europe. Letizia, living in exile in Rome surrounded by some of her children and grandchildren, is supposed to have cried out loud enough for the whole palace to hear, to have thrown her arms around a bust of her son, and then to have fainted. She remained prostrate for another two weeks.[63] This sounds like the kind of thing that would have been written about her, but we do not know for sure whether she really behaved in that way. In any event, she was to outlive her son by fifteen years and, like him, in the final years of her life she became a semi-recluse in her *palazzo*. Jérôme wrote to his mother on 21 July 1821 to say that 'the enormous loss we have just experienced of him who was always a father to us is irreparable!!!'[64] Jérôme's wife, Catherine, supposedly cried for four days. The news did not reach America until August of that year. Joseph, it is often reported, fell into a deep depression, although there does not seem to be much evidence of this.[65] On the contrary, he wrote that his brother's death was 'more the end of a long martyrdom, than an inconsolable loss'.[66]

When Captain Jean-Baptiste Foresti, preceptor to Napoleon's son, announced his death to him, he was a little surprised at the quantity of tears that flowed from a boy who had never really known his father.[67] The Comte de Neipperg reported that Marie-Louise was 'very affected' by reading the news on 17 July in the *Gazette de Piémont* (she was Duchesse of Parma and wasn't officially notified of her former husband's death until 20 July by the Austrian ambassador to Paris).[68] On 19 July, Marie-Louise wrote to a friend, the Comtesse de Crenneville:

> Although I never entertained any strong sentiment of any kind for him [she appears to have forgotten her love for him and the tears that came to her eyes every time she thought of the proof of love he had given her][69] I cannot forget that he is the father of my son, and far from treating me badly, as most people believe, he always manifested the deepest regard for me, the only thing one can expect in a political marriage. I was then very distressed, and although I ought to be pleased that he has ended his unfortunate existence in a Christian manner, I could have wished for him many years of happiness and life – as long as it would have been far from me.[70]

A funeral service was held on 31 July in the chapel in Parma's Palace of Sala (destroyed during the Second World War).[71] There were no ornaments or emblems that may have recalled Napoleon's imperial past.

'NAPOLEON HAS DIED OF POISON'

Within weeks if not days of the news of his demise reaching Europe, rumours of his having been poisoned very quickly caught the public's imagination, spread in part by hawkers whose cry – 'Napoleon has died of poison' – seemed to confirm the allegation, unfounded as it was.[72] For many Napoleonists, it was the only possible explanation for the death of such a great man so early in life. Between 27 July and 14 August, seven pamphlets appeared with a combined print run of around 6,500 confirming this thesis and rebutting the diagnosis of cancer.[73] How could Napoleon die of cancer in forty days, it was argued, when it was well known that his father had taken four years to die?[74] The refusal of the English to allow Napoleon's heart and intestines to travel to France was seen as part of the cover-up.[75] For these people, the autopsy was nothing more than a 'tissue of lies'.[76] To them, it was obvious that in the interests of the 'tranquillity' of the Bourbon regime, and of the cabinets of Europe, the British had decided to get rid of him.[77] These rumours persisted for years, and were believed in some circles as late as 1829.[78]

The poisoning thesis says a great deal more about contemporary preoccupations and anxieties than it does about historical reality. It was born of a desire to explain what to many was an incomprehensible death, and was reinforced by a deep-seated mistrust of the authorities. There is no direct evidence linking anyone with his supposed poisoning,[79] despite the theory being resurrected and perpetuated by many well-intentioned but misinformed twentieth-century amateur historians.[80] In 1961, a number of strands of Napoleon's hair were submitted to the Harwell Nuclear Research Laboratory and to the Federal Bureau of Investigation laboratories for forensic examination. The results found high levels of arsenic, which led amateur historians to the conclusion that Napoleon had been deliberately poisoned either by the British or by Montholon, desperate to finish it all and get off the island.[81]

The thesis is implausible. Like all conspiracy theories, it is based on a fundamental misreading of history, on a failure to contextualise, on spurious connections and on an inability to accept reality. The traces of arsenic that were later found in locks of Napoleon's hair – the smoking gun according to the poison theorists – mean only that arsenic was commonly used in everyday products in the eighteenth and nineteenth centuries. We know, for example, that it was contained in the hair cream Napoleon used. Moreover, tests carried out on locks of Josephine's hair as well as on his son's have also found high levels of arsenic.[82]

Nor does arsenic explain why Napoleon's body was so well preserved when it was exhumed a little less than twenty years later. Mummification can occur naturally, especially in dry environments where the body is protected from insects.[83] St Helena was not a dry climate, but one plausible reason for the preserved state of Napoleon's remains is the manner in which he was buried. The body was placed in a sarcophagus constructed by a local, Andrew Darling, made of four coffins: an inner coffin of tin (soldered shut); a traditional coffin of mahogany; another coffin of lead (soldered shut); all of which were put into a final coffin of mahogany. The burial site – 3.4 metres by 2.4 metres wide and 2.4 metres deep – was lined with masonry (0.6 metres thick at the bottom, the walls almost half a metre thick), in order to prevent moisture from reaching the casket.[84] Then the tomb was lined with a stone slab and the hole was covered in cement. These measures were put in place not just to keep Napoleon's resting place dry, but to ensure that his body could not be easily disturbed.

Talleyrand, and those like him who considered the death of Napoleon to be of no importance, got it wrong. On the contrary, Napoleon's death had a profound impact on the development of the cult and on the manner in which he was remembered. It sparked off a renewed contestation in the press around his image and legacy that had not been seen since his reign, when pro- and anti-Napoleonic imagery counterposed each other. In the last week of July 1821, thirty-four pamphlets appeared with a combined print run of about 28,000 copies, on the subject of Napoleon's death.[85] Between July and November of that year, there were another 130 pamphlets with a print run of 134,000 copies, alongside dozens of engravings from across the political spectrum, not to mention the innumerable newspaper articles.

Napoleon's name had lost none of its potency, and was still able to elicit strong emotions years after his fall from grace. Royalists attacked him in much the same manner as they had attacked him in the latter years of the Empire – as an ogre, a despot, a dictator, an Attila, a Nero, a barbarian responsible for the deaths of millions of Frenchmen.[86] The inexpungible stain that was the execution of the Duc d'Enghien was brought up (again and again).[87] A number of anti-Napoleon pamphlets repeated the themes that had been around since at least 1814: Napoleon was a coward, he hated the French, he was a sexual pervert, he was a despot, and so on.[88] Some of the pamphleteers took it a step further and questioned whether Napoleon was even French; he was a foreigner who hated the French,[89] a Buonaparte born in 1767 before Corsica had been welcomed into the French empire (Napoleon was born in 1769, one year after Corsica became French), and what is more a bastard since he 'did not commonly pass for the son of his father'.[90] One author even went so far as to suggest that Napoleon had never existed in the first place, that he was a nineteenth-century myth, the personification of the sun.[91] For those unable to come to terms with the legacy of Napoleon, unmoved by the pathos constructed around his exile, he deserved all the punishment he had been dealt.

The criticisms of Napoleon came as much from liberals as from royalists. André Carrion-Nisas, for example, in a work titled *Bonaparte et Napoléon, parallèle* was willing to accept Bonaparte because he had restored order and introduced the Civil Code, but rejected Napoleon because he had brought back the monarchy.[92] He argued that two people had died on 5 May 1821: Bonaparte, the greatest captain of the century, who became Napoleon when he was crowned emperor, as a result of which he compromised the Revolution.[93] Staunch republicans were therefore caught in a bit of a bind. They were prepared to recognise that Napoleon had brought glory to France through his military victories, and that as such his passing should be mourned, all the more so since he died an 'exiled hero, banished from the country he had defended for twenty years'.[94] But they did not want to weep for the death of 'the most formidable enemy of liberty', for that is what they saw him to be.

Others pointed to the folly that was Napoleon's foreign policy, including the invasion of Spain.[95] Even his death was ignominious;

rather than having the courage to die in battle, he chose to end his days 'two thousand leagues from the world that had trembled before him'.[96] In *La Quotidienne*, one author reminded his readers that neither Francis I nor Louis XV had let foreign troops invade their capital, and that he was 'more tempted to feel sorry for the fate of his [Napoleon's] victims than for his courtiers and his servants who largely enjoy his bounty'. In another piece one can read, 'He would have been a *great man* ... but he lacked the noble thoughts and great sentiments that make the greatest men.'[97] The *Drapeau blanc* was scathing, and asserted that 'Buonaparte' did not know how to die well.[98]

For the faithful, however, Napoleon's death was the ultimate stage in his deification.[99] The opposition press, as well as a considerable pamphlet literature, hailed the Emperor as the 'the most prodigious genius who ever appeared on the world stage'.[100] The usual themes were dredged up to hammer home the point: he was the saviour of Brumaire; the conqueror; the new Alexander or Caesar; the great legislator; the restorer of religion and social order, and so on.[101] For Bonapartists, mourning transmogrified Napoleon into a protest: a protest against the Bourbons; against the violations of the constitution (the Charter); against the excesses committed during the White Terror. The figure of Napoleon became a political affirmation of liberal principles against the royalist reaction that had followed the assassination of the king's nephew, the Duc de Berry, only eighteen months previously.[102] The black legend that had been so prominent in the early years of the Bourbon regime slowly dissolved under the reality of their rule. Besides, the Bourbons were more interested in rallying the country around the throne than in criticising the man and the regime that had preceded it. By 1818, the struggle for Napoleon's memory had more or less played itself out as the idea of a liberal, democratic Napoleon started to take root. Nevertheless, there would always be those who disliked or even hated him; for them there was no mourning his death.[103]

THE POEM AND THE IMAGE

The revived political sentiment surrounding Napoleon was fed by two other types of media, one which could be called 'mourning poetry'[104] and the other a series of popular engravings, many of them adapting Christian iconography to the Napoleonic legend.[105]

One of the better-known poems of the period, now forgotten, was written by an Italian, Alessandro Manzoni, called *Il 5 Maggio* (The 5 May).[106] Manzoni believed Napoleon to be the moderniser of Italy. He had learnt of his death in the *Gazzetta di Milano* on 16 July 1821, and within a few days had composed an ode that would make him the most important literary proponent of Napoleon in Italy.[107] The censors wouldn't allow the poem to be published in Florence, but it was translated into French, English and German. Goethe, Lamartine and Hugo all approved and even imitated the poem. Indeed, a string of poets from just about every European country felt compelled to lament and to reflect on Napoleon's passing – Byron and Shelley in England; Franz Grillparzer in Austria; August Lamey and Adelbert von Chamisso in Germany; Esaias Tegnér and Karl August Nicander in Sweden; Adam Mickiewicz in Poland; Manzoni (as we have seen) in Italy; and Alexander Pushkin and Mikhail Lermontov in Russia.[108]

Napoleon's demise also spawned what can best be described as a spate of death images, or images of the late Emperor ascending into the heavens.[109] In the engraving by the anonymous artist illustrated overleaf, soldiers of the Grande Armée imitate the religious iconography of the apostles before the crucifixion, as Napoleon, Christ-like, ascends into the heavens where Alexander the Great and Ceasar are awaiting him.

The French representations (lithographs, engravings, paintings) were at first considerably more subtle – 'mystical' was one word used to describe them – because of the censorship laws in place.[110] Contemporaries, however, easily recognised them in the form of images entitled 'Man' (*l'Homme*) or simply 'Him' (*Lui*), or images of his son entitled 'the son of Man' (*le fils de l'Homme*).[111] This is not something the Bourbon regime particularly appreciated. In 1829, for example, Auguste Barthélemy was imprisoned and fined 1,000 francs for publishing his *Fils de l'homme* (The Son of Man), a poem about Napoleon's son, the Duc de Reichstadt.[112] Throughout the post-1815 period, according to the German poet Heinrich Heine, Napoleonists rarely mentioned Napoleon by name, almost as though to do so would be to take his name in vain – rather, referring to him simply as 'l'Homme' or 'Lui'.[113] Veterans transformed into beggars asked for alms not in the name of God, but in the name of Napoleon. Napoleon was their god,

Ger[ville], *Alexandre [et] César le reçoivent dans les Cieux* (Alexander [and] Ceasar receive him into heaven). September 1830. Engraving.

their religion. There was not a working-class woman in Paris incapable of singing one of the popular songs about Napoleon. And it was towards the Vendôme Column that the thoughts of the people turned. The memory of Napoleon, it would appear, was omnipresent.

One of the more notable portrayals of Napoleon's death from this period, which was widely copied and sold as an engraving, is a painting by Horace Vernet. It has two titles in French, *Le Songe de Bertrand* (Bertrand's dream) and *L'Apothéose de Napoléon* (Napoleon's apotheosis), and in English is commonly known as *Napoleon's Tomb*.[114]

Regarded as one of the turning points in the popular representation of the Emperor, Vernet's painting depicts Napoleon's Passion and Transfiguration before he is welcomed into the Imperial Valhalla by a number of dead generals, including Lannes, Desaix and Berthier.[115] Even before the painting had been completed, Vernet's studio and house in the Chaussée d'Antin quarter, already known as a Bonapartist haunt, became a site of pilgrimage where people came to admire a small sketch of the larger work in progress, eliciting emotional responses from veterans of the Grande Armée.[116] The painting

Simonau, *L'Obre [sic] de Napoléon visitant son tombeau* (The shadow of Napoleon visiting his tomb). Date unknown. Lithograph. 17.8cm × 23.1cm. Allegory of a woman in mourning holding a crown of laurels sitting next to the tomb of Napoleon, guarded by an eagle. Napoleon's silhouette can be seen between the two weeping willows.

was submitted to the Salon of 1822, but was refused entry and was really only made public in 1830.

Other images were more subtle – little more than the image of Napoleon's grave on St Helena – especially in the years before the Revolution of 1830. Or again, Napoleon's image could be hidden among the shadows, as in the lithograph by an artist called Simonau.

'HE WILL RETURN WHEN HE LIKES'

In August 1821, only weeks after the announcement of his death, a rumour did the rounds in the salons of Paris that Napoleon was alive and well and fighting the Turk in Greece.[117] In 1823, two years after his death, prefects were reporting the Emperor's return to France.[118]

Given that the vast majority of French people were aware of the death of the Emperor, it is extraordinary that these rumours were still in circulation, let alone believed. They parallel, in some respects, the survival myths surrounding Hitler after the Second World War, or even those relating to Elvis Presley after his death in 1975.[119] It would appear that some people simply refused to believe he had died, even years after the fact.[120] 'He will return when he likes,' asserted an individual in the department of Doubs, an attitude found not only among simple peasants. The poet and songwriter Pierre-Jean de Béranger exploited the theme, perhaps cynically, in a song written in 1829: 'My God, isn't it true that he is not dead?'[121] The news of his death, according to the true believers, was nothing more than a political manoeuvre on the part of the restored monarchy to discourage the faithful.

And as with the rumours during Napoleon's years in exile, so too did the appearance of fake Napoleons continue after his death, although admittedly not as often. An incident occurred in April 1821, just before his death, when a former tailor by the name of Jean-Pierre Leclerc, who had been condemned to eight years in prison for theft and released in March of that year, was mistaken for Napoleon's brother Louis in the department of Aube.[122] In the interrogation that followed his arrest, Leclerc admitted that while he had been in a cabaret in the town of Provins a soldier had come up to him, tapped him on the shoulder and said, 'Either I am mistaken or you are Napoleon.'[123] Leclerc supposedly replied, 'You're an idiot.

I'm nothing more than a poor traveller.' It was enough to get the rest of the patrons going. His neighbour piped up, 'If you are not Napoleon, then certainly you are Louis Bonaparte.' They became so insistent that Leclerc finally succumbed, declaring, 'All right, yes, I am Napoleon, I am Louis Bonaparte, I am anyone you would like.' This dismissive remark was all it took to start a rumour, and a lot of peasants came to the cabaret to see for themselves. They examined him, but said nothing. Leclerc said nothing in return. But during the conversations that took place around him he overheard someone say, 'Would to God that he was Bonaparte. Commerce was much better in his time.' Everywhere he went he heard the same thing repeated. Leclerc, who confessed to being an ardent supporter of the monarchy, was probably guilty of nothing more than playing along to the crowd's expectations, without thinking of the consequences. He was arrested, but the tribunal at Troyes later decided there was no reason to pursue the matter further.

Others remained firm in their conviction that either Napoleon was not dead – return stories circulated throughout 1822 and 1823 – and that the body buried at St Helena was not his, or he was immortal.[124] Napoleon was frequently confused with a General Malmort, a character who did not exist except in the popular imagination, but who was believed to be in command of the French forces that intervened in Spain in 1822, and who was said to be Napoleon in disguise (the fictitious name, Malmort, made up of two words *mal* and *mort*, could conceivably be understood as 'wrongly dead').[125] This may reflect the pervasiveness of Christian doctrine throughout the countryside, and the belief in the resurrection of the 'just'.[126] In 1822, in the Lozère, witnesses claimed to have seen Napoleon not far from Mende, where he was supposed to be in hiding under the name of Father Hilarion, wrapped in a monk's cowl, leading a life of profound humility and repenting of his former misdeeds. It was reported that with a few other brothers he had bought a château in ruins and that together they helped the mentally ill. The rumour was taken seriously enough for the prefect and his entourage to pay a visit to this monk. To their stupefaction, they found 'the Emperor, the Emperor at 32 or 35 years of age – the age of the coronation – as millions of images had fixed in the popular imagination'.[127] In October 1826 Gabriel Fauqué from Avignon was caught shouting, 'The Emperor will soon return; he will sort you all out properly; at least he will give us bread to eat.'[128] This was a belief reflected in a novel published by Honoré de Balzac in 1833, *The Country Doctor*. One of its characters, an old veteran by the name of Goguelot, is heard saying,

> A lot of them say that he is dead! Dead? Oh! yes, very likely. They do not know him, that is plain! They go on telling that fib to deceive the people, and to keep things quiet for their tumble-down government. Listen; this is the whole truth of the matter. His friends have left him alone in the desert to fulfil a prophecy that was made about him, for I forgot to tell you that his name Napoleon really means the LION OF THE DESERT. And that is gospel truth.[129]

In 1828, some preferred to believe that Napoleon had somehow found his way to Vienna to be with his son, disguised as a priest.[130] As late as 1829, people went on believing he was still alive in some regions of France, like the Vosges,[131] and it was even rumoured that his silhouette had been seen among the crowds rioting in Paris in 1830. It may have been one of the students of the Ecole Polytechnique who, according to the English novelist Frances Trollope, all walked and dressed like Napoleon.[132] But sightings of the Emperor became increasingly rare and died out entirely, after a final brief flurry, in 1848 with the arrival of Napoleon's nephew, Louis-Napoleon, on the political scene.[133] These anecdotes nevertheless clearly show the enduring influence of Napoleon and his memory over the passage of time, to the point where the myth was stronger in the minds of some people than the reality. As we shall see in the coming chapters, the death of Napoleon was going to drive a resurgence of his cult as people found ways to express both their admiration for him and their opposition to the Bourbon monarchy.

REDEMPTION

1821–1840

7

Voices from Beyond the Grave

Napoleon's death, the media sensation that it caused and the return of his acolytes to Europe created an atmosphere of expectation among an informed public only too willing to buy the memoirs of those who had been closest to Napoleon on St Helena.

As we have already seen, Napoleon spent the first months and years on the island dictating his 'memoirs' to Las Cases, Gourgaud, Bertrand and Montholon.[1] At the same time, his acolytes often kept their own private journals and memoirs: Las Cases' memoirs, by far the most detailed, cover the period from June 1815 to his departure in December 1816 (Napoleon certainly knew of their existence);[2] Gourgaud kept a diary from July 1815 until his departure in March 1818; Bertrand did so from April 1816 to the very end; O'Meara and Marchand had been taking copious notes of their interactions with Napoleon; Montholon had been maintaining his own records, although as it turned out in a much more muddled manner.[3] Las Cases, Gourgaud, Bertrand and Montholon have been referred to as the 'Evangelists', for they spread the word – the gospel of Napoleon – rewriting history in His name and according to His will. Napoleon placed his trust entirely in their hands – they were also known as the 'Apostles' – in the firm belief that they would faithfully convey his version of events.[4] And they did. Time and again they highlighted the difference between the treatment the Emperor had received at the hands of Lowe and the former power and glory the name Napoleon had once represented; between the accusations of despotism levelled at the man and the humble image his life in exile now conveyed; between Napoleon the conqueror and Napoleon the liberal who had consolidated the foundations of the Revolution.

Napoleon's own 'memoirs' were an attempt directly to manipulate the public's opinion of him, to create a character in and for history, to control the ways in which people would remember him. 'Look at France,' Napoleon is supposed to have said; 'from here, on my rock, does it not seem as if I still reigned there?'[5] In this light, Las Cases' *Mémorial* can be seen as a continuation of the myth-making Napoleon had started in 1796, further shaping his own place in history by moulding the reality to fit with his own version of it. 'History,' he is said to have pronounced, 'is nothing more than what men repeat.'[6] In other words, Napoleon played with reality and moulded it in much the same way as an artist moulds and kneads a lump of clay into a desired form. The telling of his story was not then about accurately recording history or setting the record straight – it was about reconstructing a past that would be imposed on and influence the future.

But this was a double-edged sword. Napoleon's (re)interpretation of the past could just as easily be countered by other histories.[7] Uppermost in his mind would have been the matter of whose version of events would triumph.[8] His version of the past distorted reality so that it was made to fit his own vision of what he had done and what his place was in universal history. There were various aspects of his temperament that contributed to this rewriting of history: his inability to admit past mistakes; an ingrained habit of presenting events to his advantage (what today we would call propaganda or spin); and a desire, whether unconscious or conscious, to forget painful elements of the past. This is what historians would today refer to as the 'silences' of history, a category that falls somewhere between remembering and forgetting, an attempt to cancel one memory of the past and to replace it with another.[9]

In France, Napoleon's much publicised conversion to a liberal regime during the Hundred Days, despite its brevity, made a powerful impact on his followers well beyond the collapse of the regime in 1815, and indeed beyond his own life.[10] The ascendancy of this 'liberal image' while he was in exile was in part a reaction to the oppressiveness of the Bourbon regime, during which Napoleon's memory and exploits were increasingly romanticised. How do we understand this dramatic turnaround?

The first reason has to do with forgetfulness. Such is the peculiarity of the human mind that despite all the grief and sorrow inflicted on Europe by the wars, despite all the criticism and venom poured on Napoleon during the latter years of his reign, people soon forgot what his regime had been like – conscription, never-ending wars, the deaths of millions, dictatorship, police spies – and began to fall into the trap of comparing him with the Bourbon regime they were living under. The fact that Bonapartists, republicans and liberals found common cause was in part a reaction to what they perceived to be a new alliance between throne and altar, between the monarchy and the Catholic Church.[11] As we have seen, censorship laws did not prevent clandestine poems and pamphlets from being printed and sold illegally. In the space of a few years, Napoleon had been transformed from an oppressor into a protector of the weak against the strong, the poor against the rich.

The second reason is that the cult became associated with the political aspirations of a frustrated social class that had been explicitly excluded from politics during this period. This was Bonapartism, mixed with large doses of liberalism and republicanism. The press of the day was harnessed, albeit unwittingly, to do Napoleon's bidding as his political message was distributed throughout France. However, one should also note that this worked both ways, and that at the same time the liberal press throughout Europe exploited Napoleon for their own political ends. It is somewhat ironic that liberals were now holding up an authoritarian monarch as a political model.

It is difficult to explain why Napoleonism and Bonapartism became so popular after the fall of the Empire. It may simply have been because thousands upon thousands of veterans looked back with a certain nostalgia on the glory days of their youth, recounting epic tales of their adventures, and of the countries and peoples they had once ruled. This retelling of the past, which for the most part seemed to gloss over the immense suffering the Empire had caused, kept the revolutionary and Napoleonic wars very much alive during a period when the restored Bourbons were doing their best to forget them. The dictator was thus transformed into the Emperor of the people, the liberal democrat, the Citizen Emperor. The willingness of the French public (in particular) to accept Napoleon's version of events has been underscored by historians: the disillusionment with the Bourbon regime, especially on the foreign political front; Napoleon's success in building up his revolutionary heritage during the Hundred Days; his self-portrayal as martyr on St Helena; and his appeal to Romantics.[12] Throughout his exile, Napoleon exploited his own legend in order to construct a mythified past. Through his Evangelists, he in effect rewrote history, and in a manner that reflected kindly on his achievements and glossed over his failings.

This was to be Napoleon's ultimate victory, a long ode to himself as fallen hero, one that would have enormous implications for how he was to be perceived by contemporaries. And yet it was to take some time for those words to take effect. None of the Evangelists' works appeared in Napoleon's lifetime, and only two did so in the years immediately after his death. O'Meara's and Las Cases' works, which both became hugely popular, were published in 1822.[13] These writings significantly influenced both the French and the English publics (they were written in one language and translated into the other). In France alone, Las Cases' *Mémorial*, dubbed the bible of the nineteenth century, went through sixteen editions before the end of the century, while O'Meara's *A Voice from St. Helena* went through a dozen.[14] In 1823, Gourgaud and Montholon published Napoleon's 'memoirs' covering the same period and events, at the same time with the same title, the *Mémoires pour servir à l'histoire de France sous Napoléon* (Memoirs of the history of France under Napoleon) respectively in two volumes and in six volumes.[15] On the other hand, Gourgaud's St Helena journal – *Sainte-Hélène, journal inédit de 1815 à 1818* – which was written in code and never meant to be made public, did not appear until 1899. Bertrand's *Cahiers de Sainte-Hélène* were not published until 1949. It is worth dwelling on the two most important memoirs from St Helena in some detail.

O'MEARA'S NAPOLEON

O'Meara became one of the most comprehensive chroniclers of the conditions on the island, and possibly one of the most unreliable. He had planned to publish something on his return to Britain after he realised what a success William Warden's *Letters* had been, going through sixteen editions in 1816 and 1817 (pp. 56–7). O'Meara's first attempt was *An Exposition of Some of the Transactions that Have Taken Place at St Helena*, published in 1819. It was ostensibly a reply to a book by Thomas Hook, a scurrilous character who spent a few weeks on St Helena on his way to England to face charges of embezzlement while employed on the island of Mauritius. Once in England, he understood he could cash in on the interest in Napoleon and published a pamphlet, *Facts Illustrative of the Treatment of Napoleon Bonaparte.*[16] In it he portrayed Napoleon and his companions as intensely difficult to deal with. O'Meara countered by describing the 'real nature of the St Helena transactions'.[17] It was as much a defence of his own actions and behaviour as an attack on the English establishment.

However, it was only in 1822 with the publication of *Napoleon in Exile; or, A Voice from St. Helena*, that O'Meara hit upon the right formula. It was the first of the proper memoirs to come out of St Helena. In a letter he later wrote to Joseph Bonaparte's wife Julie, he declared that the main reason for writing the book 'was to defend the reputation of the late emperor ... and to refute the frightful calumnies with which our ministers and their paid agents tried to sully his memory and also to give a picture of this great man, full of noble courage, expiring under the talons of that monster, half monkey, half tiger whom they chose to be his jailer'.[18] On the morning of the book's release, the publisher in Ludgate Hill was mobbed by so many people trying to get a copy that the police had to be brought in to control the crowds.[19] Thomas Creevey, a Whig MP, wrote to a friend, 'Well, I wonder whether you will be anything like as much interested by O'Meara and Buonaparte as I have been and am still. I can think of nothing else ... I am perfectly satisfied Buonaparte said all that O'Meara puts into his mouth. Whether *that* is all true is another thing ...'[20]

O'Meara portrayed a situation in which Napoleon was the object of Lowe's petty harassment, consistent with the image of a Promethean Napoleon. Take, for example, the time Lowe ordered four servants to leave the island in October 1816. When Lowe included one of the Archambault brothers among the four, Napoleon objected that 'it would be great cruelty to separate two brothers'.[21] He suggested that Lowe instead take either Gentilini or Santini. The reply came back that Lowe had been ordered to expel 'Frenchmen', and that Gentilini was Italian and Santini a Corsican. Lowe, who had served in Corsica, knew that it was part of the French empire. To call Santini a Corsican and not French was virtually to accuse Napoleon of the same thing.

O'Meara's Napoleon was a simple man who had devoted his life to the nation. It was this quality that distinguished him from the other sovereigns of Europe; it made him a monarch who was of the people, little different from the Napoleon that was being cultivated in France at the time by poets and writers. One of the insights we get from O'Meara's accounts of his conversations is Napoleon's interpretation of his own history, particularly the battle of Waterloo, which he came back to time and again. Thus the English army 'would have been destroyed' at Waterloo if the Prussians hadn't arrived, or if Marshal Grouchy had arrived.[22] 'Had it not been for the imbecility of Grouchy, I should have gained that day,' Napoleon declared. The utter destruction of the 'flower of [English] youth' at Waterloo would immediately have produced a change of ministry and England would have sued for peace. He also gave Wellington a lesson in how to conduct a battle and pointed to all the ways in which Wellington had fought Waterloo badly.[23] Similarly, the Russian expedition had failed because of the 'premature cold, and the burning of Moscow'. 'Had it not been for that fire at Moscow, I should have succeeded … I would have proclaimed liberty to all the slaves in Russia, and abolished vassalage and nobility.'[24] If he had succeeded in defeating Alexander, he would have obliged him to join the blockade of Britain known as the Continental System, and thereby forced Britain to make peace. He would also have formed Poland into a separate and independent kingdom.[25] He could have won in 1814 if it had not been for the treachery of Marshal Marmont.[26]

Napoleon's musings are replete with far-fetched claims: he had always been willing to conclude peace with the British – 'there is nothing that I would not have sacrificed to have been in friendship with them'; after a general peace he would have massively reduced the size of the European armies;[27] he would have proclaimed a republic after the invasion of England and he would have abolished the nobility and the House of Peers; he rose to an 'astonishing height of power' without committing a single crime (not counting the massacre at Jaffa, which he later attempted to justify on the grounds that 'to have done otherwise ... would probably have caused the destruction of my whole army'); if Tsar Paul of Russia had lived (he was assassinated in 1801), the French and the Russians would have combined forces to invade India; it had always been up to the allies to make peace; if he had not been 'induced' to sign a cessation of arms in 1813, after the battles of Lützen and Bautzen, he would have won the campaign.[28]

It was all fanciful nonsense, the kind of stuff that makes one doubt whether Napoleon did indeed have a great mind or whether these were simply the ramblings of a man who was thinking out loud, imagining what could have been but never was, or a man who was deluding himself.

THE BONAPARTIST BIBLE – LAS CASES' *MÉMORIAL*

By far the most successful of the works to come out of St Helena was the *Mémorial de Sainte-Hélène* by Las Cases, often touted as one of the greatest publishing success stories of the nineteenth century.[29] There were other works that were more successful in terms of sales, but the *Mémorial* was probably the most widely read political text of its time, and it was certainly the most popular Napoleonic memoir ever written.[30] The novelist Stendhal had one of his characters, Julien Sorel, refer to it as his Koran.[31] In effect, it more or less became the nineteenth-century Bonapartist bible, which does not mean to say that everyone accepted it at face value. One of Thomas Creevey's correspondents described it as 'the most delicious effusion of a sentimental old French twaddle that ever was read'.[32] But it was accepted as authentic, which is why it caused a sensation and sold out when it appeared, going through six editions between 1823 and 1842. Another 44,000 copies were printed between 1840 and 1850.[33] It was translated almost immediately into English and German. A Spanish version appeared in 1825, a Polish one in 1841, and an Italian in 1842. That same year, the first illustrated French edition appeared, with more than 1,800 vignettes drawn by one of the most famous Napoleonic illustrators, Nicolas-Toussaint Charlet.[34]

The success of the work is a remarkable story, considering that the *Mémorial* does not follow a classic structure and is an odd mixture of styles. Moreover, Las Cases was possibly the person least likely to accomplish this feat. For a start, he had spent only eighteen months on the island. It is true that he was the most conscientious at capturing Napoleon's words, even inventing a personal shorthand to that end, but he is also guilty of inserting himself into the text – not to mention plugging his own historical atlas whenever he could – so that it is sometimes impossible to distinguish between what came from the mouth of Las Cases and what came from Napoleon's. When Las Cases was finally reunited with his notes in September 1822 – the British had confiscated them when he left the island in 1816 – he undertook an editing process that significantly changed the content, rearranging conversations, suppressing passages and imbuing Napoleon with a rhetorical flair he never possessed. The work was written quickly while Las Cases was residing in Passy outside Paris, in a house that became a magnet for Bonapartists – Lazare Carnot, Eugène Ney (Marshal Ney's son) and General Lamarque – who read and corrected the chapters.[35] Moreover, the text was changed, sometimes significantly, over the years with the publication of new editions between 1823 and 1842.

The *Mémorial* conferred on Napoleon a human dimension that was largely lacking from previous works. It is full of passages that highlight the mundane aspects of his life, as well as his sensitivity, his grief, his boredom and his suffering at the hands of the British.[36] It is a complex interplay of conversations, anecdotes, gossip, emotional insights and political reflections. It allowed Napoleon's 'voice' to become public, and not only influenced the manner in which veterans remembered the Emperor, but also had a profound effect on shaping European points of view.[37] The political, the military and the everyday were all grist for the mill, so that one day Las Cases would relate a conversation around a battle, on another Napoleon's ideas and dreams, and on yet another the trivial details of life in exile.[38] The man we see through Las Cases' eyes is the Napoleon of the legend, not the Napoleon of history. Again and again, Las Cases' narrative underscores the myths surrounding Napoleon's ascent to power – his 'purity' and his 'integrity'[39] – and highlights the stark contrast between his exile and what his life had once been.

Like many memoirists of the day, Las Cases considered his work to be a reflection of truth and history.[40] In order to achieve this he unthinkingly and uncritically accepted everything Napoleon told him, at the same time documenting his gestures and habits, describing the way he talked and the way he walked – head down, hands clasped behind his back, snuffbox at the ready. No other person in the world, declared Las Cases, knew the private Napoleon as well as he did.[41] He reveals his stance on Napoleon at the beginning of the book by describing him as a fallen hero, who through mistreatment and humiliation became the victim. Like the other Evangelists, and indeed like a number of British converts, he recounted the torment the Emperor had to endure, as well as the personal and material deprivations from having to live so far from civilisation. Part of that suffering was his forced separation from his family, and especially his son and heir.[42] The stoicism with which Napoleon supposedly endured these affronts was meant to conjure the image in Las Cases' readers of the suffering of Christ.[43] Chapter headings such as 'Nouvelle méchanceté du gouverneur' (translated in the English edition as 'Fresh Instance of the Governor's Malignity') contributed to this impression.[44] Moreover, Las Cases underlined the extent to which 'days were without character and without colour'.[45] In portraying the boredom, the physical discomfort and the despair that often overcame the residents of Longwood, he was able astutely to link Napoleon's physical decline with the landscape, and with his struggle to be recognised by his official title.[46] But Las Cases, more than any of the other Evangelists, helped lay the foundations of the legend: Napoleon as Saviour of the Revolution; as champion of nationalism in Italy, Germany, Switzerland and Poland; as a peaceful man; as a family man; and as a French patriot. Let me elaborate on a two of the main themes that stand out in Las Cases' *Mémorial*.

The Saviour of the Revolution

Napoleon's 'suffering' was well known in Europe even while he was alive, but Las Cases' *Mémorial* was proof to many of the appalling way the English had treated him. In the eyes of his French followers, Napoleon's suffering was inextricably intertwined with that of the nation, which he had come to symbolise during the Empire.[47] Both had had to endure defeat and indignity.[48] 'I am the *patrie*,' he declared to Las Cases, and by 'wounding' him, that is, sending him to St Helena, the English had wounded the nation.[49] Moreover, in his narrative to Las Cases, Napoleon portrayed himself as a liberal-democratic character that he simply had never been when in power. Liberal ideas were, according to Las Cases, 'in his heart, in his principles, in his logic'.[50] If Napoleon had been obliged to adopt authoritarian policies (when they were mentioned at all), it was in order to preserve the French Revolution. Las Cases also portrayed Napoleon as a liberator of oppressed peoples, as someone who had always desired peace and who went to war to defend freedom, as the man who had brought the political factions together after the upheaval of the French Revolution. His republican tendencies, at least in his early years, were beyond doubt,[51] but it was the disorder of the Revolution, and the atrocities commited by the republicans, that curbed his republican zeal. Once in power Napoleon consolidated the principles of the Revolution; they were cemented in the 'blood of battles, decorated with the laurels of victory, [and] welcomed by the acclamations of the people'.[52] His role in consolidating the gains of the Revolution was accentuated time and again: the Civil Code did France more good than all the other laws that preceded it;[53] he had used men from every class and political faction, regardless of their past, as long as they worked towards the common goal – the good and the glory of all.[54] The upshot of all that was that France during the Empire had never been more strong, more prosperous, better administered or happier.[55]

The Supreme Commander

Much of Napoleon's time on St Helena was spent reimagining the past so that he came across not as warlike, but as a peaceful man who had been forced into war, and who was consequently generous to his enemies: he could have made Alexander I a prisoner after Austerlitz but did not; he could have destroyed the Prussian monarchy after Jena but did not; and he could have partitioned the Austrian Empire after Wagram but did not.[56] His mistake was being too magnanimous and not carrying through any of those designs. Napoleon claimed that he wanted not only to free the peoples of Europe but to unite them in a kind of multi-national confederation.[57] We can thus read passages in Las Cases about how, if peace had been concluded at Moscow, Napoleon would have wound up the expedition and would have been able to lay the foundations of a European system. Indeed, his conquests would have come to an end, the only task being to organise this new system.[58] As we have seen, of all the battles Napoleon

fought over in his mind, Waterloo stands out. He never really understood why he had lost – 'incomprehensible' is the word he used – and
even wondered whether he had been betrayed. If he had turned the
enemy's right flank, he asserted, instead of trying to force the centre,
he would easily have won the battle.[59]

According to Napoleon's rhetoric of self-justification, every campaign, every battle was fought in order to defend France from the
ancien régime monarchies that wanted to overturn the Revolution.
He had always wished for peace with England and had never disputed
Britain's mastery of the high seas. He had simply wanted Britain to
respect the French flag.[60] Thus all his wars had been defensive wars,
especially against Britain.[61] We saw in the previous volume that he
had been accused of striving after a Universal Monarchy and that he
himself had been ambivalent on that subject.[62] On St Helena, however, there was never any question about his motives in striving after
universal hegemony; he did so only in reaction to Britain and in spite
of himself.[63] Besides, the events of the Hundred Days put paid to that;
he returned to create a liberal empire and explicitly refused to save his
throne after Waterloo by becoming 'a tyrant'.[64]

NAPOLEON ON THE COUCH

Napoleon's memoirs thus reveal a great deal about his state of mind.
They are by no means a 'confession' in the Rousseauian sense of the
word – on the contrary, personal reflection is almost entirely lacking – but Napoleon exposes himself nonetheless. Of course, his
words have been interpreted and rearranged by the Four Evangelists,
but they nevertheless provide important insights into his feelings and
beliefs. They occupied the same position as psychoanalysts would
in the modern era: the analyst listens and notes while the analysand
(the person undergoing psychoanalysis) talks and reveals. There are
of course all sorts of ways of reading and interpreting what the analysand has to say, and this is why it is worthwhile reading the texts from
St Helena in a different way. They are of course at once a rewriting
of history, a stream of consciousness and a wish list of what he would
have liked to have done were he to have had the opportunity to do it
all over again.

So what do these memoirs reveal about Napoleon? There are three features that stand out, all of them characteristic of a narcissistic personality. The first is that Napoleon was not in the least bit sorry for all the pain and suffering, or the enormous loss of life, that had resulted from the wars. But then again this is typical of eighteenth- and early nineteenth-century rulers, and to expect compassion or remorse would be projecting our own preoccupations on to the past. The idea that an individual could accept responsibility for what had been done in the name of the Revolution, the Empire or France would never have occurred to anyone in a position of power. We have witnessed Napoleon's lack of feeling for others on innumerable occasions, but on St Helena he admitted it to himself. 'I care only for people who are useful to me,' he remarked to Gourgaud, 'and so long as they are useful.'[65]

Second, Napoleon thought he was the most important person in the world; he was convinced of it when he told his companions, 'The universe is watching us! We are the martyrs of an immortal cause! Millions of men grieve for us, the fatherland yearns for us, and glory is in mourning!'[66] 'Twelve hundred years hence my name will be mentioned with respect, while those of my oppressors will be unknown, or only known by being loaded with infamy and opprobrium.'[67] 'Had I died at Moscow, I should have left behind me a reputation as conqueror, without a parallel in history.'[68] 'The great works and monuments that I executed, and the code of laws that I formed, will go down to the most distant ages, and future historians will revenge the wrongs done to me by my contemporaries.'[69] These kinds of utterances in an everyday person would clearly indicate a grandiose sense of self. This is hardly the case, however, for a man like Napoleon given the prodigious feats he had performed. It does nevertheless demonstrate an astonishing degree of hubris.

The third feature is that Napoleon had a tendency to blame his failures, defeats and mistakes on those closest to him – his ministers, his generals, his family, even those lower down in the hierarchy who did not fulfil or carry out his wishes – or if not on people then on nature, or fate, or destiny – words that he used interchangeably.[70] He thus attributed his ultimate failure to create a united Europe and his military defeat on the whims of nature – the desert sands of Egypt, the English Channel, the snows of Russia.[71] The decision to go to war was never called into question; it was simply regrettable that the campaigns did not always end in victory.

Napoleon thereby absolved himself of all the decisions he had made that had turned out to be wrong or that had turned out badly by laying the blame on others. Thus, looking back on his decision to send an expedition to Saint-Domingue, he insisted that it was the 'various demands of the colonists, the merchants, and the speculators' that more or less forced him into taking action against Toussaint Louverture, the black general who led the slave revolt on Saint-Domingue.[72] Similarly, the execution of the Duc d'Enghien was not his doing, but the doing of his ministers Savary and Talleyrand.[73] Regarding the decision to invade Spain in 1808, he reflected that it would have been better to have left Ferdinand on the throne and to have married him off to a French princess. But, he rationalised, the war itself was entirely legitimate, its purpose to drag a backward country and its superstitious people into the modern era.[74]

WRITING NAPOLEON

Las Cases' *Mémorial* fell on fertile ground and had an impact well beyond France. The anti-Napoleonic literature that formed part of the black legend had already begun to wane a few years before Napoleon's demise, but the *Mémorial* was a turning point. Las Cases created an intimacy between Napoleon and the reading public that had not really existed before.[75] For the French, especially in Paris, read with an avidity that surprised foreign visitors. 'In every hand there is now to be found a book!' wrote Lady Morgan. 'Enter into the rudest porter's lodge of the simplest hotel, in the remotest quarter and you will find cheap editions of the best authors, which are beyond the means only of the very lowest indigence.'[76] Moreover, Napoleon's death and the advent of Las Cases' *Mémorial* coincided with a time when more serious attempts at writing the life of Napoleon, works that incorporated new trends in history writing, were starting to appear.

One of the first histories of Napoleon and the Empire to be published after his death was Antoine Vincent Arnault's *Vie politique et militaire de Napoléon* (Political and military life of Napoleon), the first volume of which was published in 1822. Arnault had rallied to

Napoleon during the Hundred Days and was as a result banished from France. This lavish, two-volume, leather-bound history containing 120 full-page illustrations was written in response to Napoleon's testamentary request to Arnault to write his life story.[77] Issued in instalments, the work was organised into 136 brief tableaux or sections. Each tableau was accompanied by an illustration; these were executed by a number of different artists, including Théodore Géricault and Horace Vernet. Ostensibly an objective approach to Napoleon's life – but then, every biography professed the same objectivity – Arnault's biography was overwhelmingly hagiographic, often repeating the myths associated with Napoleon's early life.[78] Other histories followed, often much cheaper because illustrated with wood engravings rather than lithographs, although still unaffordable for most peasants and workers.[79] There were several editions of works like Léonard Gallois' *Histoire de Napoléon d'après lui-même* (The history of Napoleon by himself).[80] Gallois was an ardent Bonapartist, so his biography was replete with many of the myths which helped shape the nineteenth-century legend and which were unthinkingly repeated by later generations of biographers. Many of these histories do little more than reprise the type of propaganda the French had been fed since the first Italian campaign, the gist of which was that Napoleon was a great general who had revolutionised 'manners, conduct and language'.[81] In 1828, in a book written by Auguste de Chambure and illustrated by Nicolas-Toussaint Charlet, one can find the whole repertory of anecdotes about Napoleon – some real, some fictional – and in particular his supposed encounters with the common people.[82] All of these anecdotes helped cast Napoleon in a democratic mould that had never existed while he was in power.

THE MELANCHOLY HERO

A number of competing images surrounding Napoleon vied for dominance in the years up to his death. There was the anti-cult fostered by diehard royalists, who hated him for what he stood for (war, death, the imprisonment of the pope, the overthrow of monarchs); there was the idealised Napoleon – the Saviour or Messiah – whose memory was fostered by those who suffered most under the Bourbon regime (loyal

Bonapartists, veterans of the Grande Armée who had lost everything with his overthrow, republicans and even radical revolutionaries); and there was the liberal Napoleon, embraced and cultivated by the political left in France, Italy, Germany and Poland, disillusioned with the repressive regimes that had returned after his fall.[83] The invective and vitriol characteristic of the anti-cult largely (if not entirely) disappeared after Napoleon's death in 1821.

The transformation from despot to liberal was further aided by some of the imagery that appeared around Napoleon on St Helena. Even before his death, and mainly as a result of his own efforts to portray himself as an isolated, persecuted figure, images started to appear that showed him alone, sometimes contemplating the sea. These images, which also evoke a longing to return, have since become iconic.[84] The misunderstood hero is a poignant hybrid of solitude and suffering: alone with nature, his happiness is as distant as the horizon is beyond him. To our knowledge, Napoleon never actually stood alone and gazed out to sea during his time on the island. However, it is what these depictions of solitude and suffering represent, both textually and visually, that is interesting. This solitude is highlighted in a number of contemporary works: in the pamphlet literature that emerged soon after Napoleon's death; in Alfred de Vigny's poem *Moïse* (Moses) published in 1823; and in Vigny's novel *Servitude et grandeur militaires* (Servitude and grandeur of arms), which appeared in 1835.[85] These texts contain images of solitude that acquired political significance, as if the geographical and physical isolation of Napoleon somehow represented French geopolitical isolation.

There are two aspects of this image that are worth underlining. The first is that the concept of 'loneliness' in the sense that we understand it, as a painful *feeling* of inner emptiness, as opposed to the physical state of being on one's own, was first used in the English-speaking world in about 1814 in a poem by Wordsworth – *The Excursion: Being a Portion of 'The Recluse'*.[86] 'Loneliness' has come to mean a sense of emotional pain, while 'solitude' describes a rather selfish joy at being on one's own. In France, however, the terms *seule* (alone) and *solitude* have a somewhat different meaning and a different history.[87] By the end of the revolutionary era and with the rise of the Romantic Movement, solitude was synonymous with an affirmation of individuality born of the Declaration of the Rights of Man (both American and French) in which freedom of expression, and hence the freedom to be unique, emerged for the first time on to the world scene.[88] In this new world, society was made to serve the individual; the individual was not made to serve society.[89]

Napoleon's solitude was more complex. It was both imposed by others, that is, the British had sent him to one of the most isolated spots in the world – where he was physically isolated even further by the governor – and, as exile and illness progressed, intensified by Napoleon himself, when he sought further solitude and isolation by shutting himself away in his room, which he did for increasing lengths of time. This was not the loneliness of the self-reflective; this was the loneliness of melancholia. Napoleon, like many exiles, was convinced of his own 'misfortune', recognisable as 'the melancholy of nostalgia'.[90]

Melancholy is the second trait worth emphasising. In the first half of the nineteenth century, melancholia was characterised in some respects by a Romantic sensibility, and was linked to the cult of the individual so prominent in early nineteenth-century art and literature. It was also considered to be a sign of genius and of ambition, typified by the contemplative pose in an outdoor setting, combined with a melancholy expression.[91] It is also possible that melancholy and loneliness became a form of political display, reflecting on a broader scale the disillusionment that revolutionaries, liberals and Bonapartists felt with the Bourbons. Napoleon's body, ill, tired, confined, served as a symbol of French national suffering.

Regardless of what today we might think of Napoleon, people like Las Cases helped complete his political transformation from tyrant to liberal idol, from defeated dictator into a sublime, heroic figure. After Napoleon's death, during the 1820s and 1830s, at the height of the Romantic Movement, his 'good' reputation grew as people forgot how much his reign had cost France, and how his abdication had been greeted with a European-wide sigh of relief. By attacking the black legend so prevalent in the years after the fall of the Empire, Las Cases helped inspire the flurry of war memoirs that appeared during the 1820s and 1830s, their authors no doubt hoping to imitate the *Mémorial*'s success. It was in the 1820s and 1830s, as we shall see in the following chapter, that the cult really started to take off.

8

Contextualising the Cult

The fascination with Napoleon and St Helena continued well beyond his death, was often used to subvert the Bourbon regime and led to the development of what has been referred to as the cult of Napoleon.[1] In the following pages, two different types of cult are explored. The first is the popular cult, which came from below, promoted by a rich assortment of memorabilia, songs and iconography, largely secretive until 1830 due to the repressive nature of the Bourbon regime. The second is what might be called the official cult, which emerged after 1830, which was promoted by a new king, Louis-Philippe, and which brought Napoleon back into the public domain as the new monarch attempted to co-opt the late Emperor's memory for his own political ends. Of course the two different types of cult were not clearly defined, and certainly the popular cult continued to thrive after 1830, but it helps to simplify here what became an incredibly complex phenomenon. We start with the development of the popular cult after 1815.

A FRANCE DIVIDED

Most scholars agree that the return of the Bourbons in 1815, restored to the throne for a second time, reopened old wounds, in part because the regime was never entirely accepted by the French people, and in part because it was never entirely successful as a government.[2] The period of Bourbon rule (1815–30) saw a bitter struggle between liberals, republicans and Bonapartists on the one hand – ideologies that were closely intertwined[3] – and royalists, many of them Ultras, on the other, a feud about contemporary politics that was deeply embedded in the recent past.[4] This was particularly the case in the first few years of Bourbon rule when the new regime did everything it could to suppress the memory of the revolutionary and imperial past. All emblems and symbols that represented either the Revolution or Napoleon – such as the tricolour flag, imperial eagles and busts of the Emperor – were banned and removed from public buildings, to be replaced by the statues of former French kings that had been toppled during the Revolution.[5] In a number of towns, busts, paintings, books and engravings with the image of Napoleon on them were publicly burned in a ceremony on the main square.[6] This occurred in Orleans in February 1816 and in Carcassonne in July in the same year. In Paris, all the grand Napoleonic paintings that had been commissioned during the Empire were removed from the Louvre, with one exception – Girodet's *Revolt of Cairo* – so as not to remind people of Napoleon.[7] Any mention of the great revolutionary and Napoleonic battles, such as Marengo or Austerlitz, was forbidden.

Bourbon policy was based on two misguided notions: first, that it was possible to restore the sacred nature of monarchy; and, second, that in order to bring people together around the throne – 'union and forgetting' (*union et oubli*) was the expression used – the past had to be buried.[8] This policy, however, had the opposite effect. Rather than obliterating the memory of the Revolution and Napoleon, it exacerbated divisions in the French polity. Tensions between various sections of French society and the monarchy played out in a series of demonstrations, political protests and acts of sedition that included an immense array of politically subversive plays, songs, pamphlets, placards, engravings and objets d'art.[9] Between August and November 1815, for example, there were over 1,000 reported cases of the Bourbon white flag being torn down in villages throughout the country.[10] The vast majority of subversive acts committed during this period were carried out by Bonapartists; these individuals were often tied to local communities but their acts had national import for they were not just nostalgic for empire,[11] they also incorporated liberal and republican thinking into their mind-set.

Many of these seditious practices followed a sort of national political calendar dating from the Revolution and the Empire.[12] Thus, in some communities, people celebrated the anniversary of the storming of the Bastille on 14 July by quietly toasting 'liberty'. One can find similar celebrations on 14 March (commemorating the Hundred Days), or on 5 May (the anniversary of Napoleon's death), or on 15 August (Napoleon's birthday, celebrated during the Empire as the St Napoleon). On 6 July, veterans and students in Grenoble commemorated the defence of that city against an Austrian army after Waterloo, something that became an annual event celebrated by a banquet.[13] On these occasions, tricolour flags – which recalled both the Revolution and the Empire – were planted on the squares of villages, on the houses of royalists (as a provocation) and on church steeples,[14] acts punishable by a hefty fine and a prison sentence.

On other occasions, commemorations organised by the Bourbon regime, such as the anniversaries of the executions of Louis XVI and Marie-Antoinette (21 January and 16 October), the feast day of St Louis (25 August) and the feast day of St Charles (4 November) – all seen as provocations by liberals, republicans and Bonapartists – were treated as invitations to arrange what have been called *anti-fêtes* or counter-celebrations in opposition to the regime.[15] Thus, on 20 January 1816, the eve of the anniversary of the execution of Louis XVI, Napoleonic veterans in the Lot-et-Garonne organised a ball attended by all the prominent locals opposed to the Bourbons.[16]

SITES OF CONTESTATION

There were three main public sites where oppositional politics could play out: cafés, cabarets and theatres, and marketplaces. Markets in particular, where everyone from near and far would gather regularly on appointed days, offered opportunities for placards and other subversive material to be posted or distributed.[17] Napoleonist objets d'art, often imported from outside France, were secretly sold here and brought back into the private sphere. Here too peddlers would go from market to market hawking their Napoleonic wares.

We will come back to the sale of Napoleonic objects in a moment, but market days and cafés were also places where a lot of drinking could take place, often leading to drunken outbursts against the regime. There was no clearer means of marking one's opposition to the regime than by uttering the words 'Vive Napoléon' or 'Vive l'Empereur'. Shouting out certain, often insulting words directed at no one in particular was a way in which anyone from a radical student to an illiterate peasant could express their discontent with the general state of affairs.[18] Reports from royal prosecutors to the Chancellery are replete with a surprising number of examples of 'seditious cries' uttered by men and women, or of people invoking the name of the 'usurper', as Napoleon was called by legitimists, that could lead to prison terms of anywhere from several months to two years, as well as heavy fines.[19] We know that thousands of 'politicals' were brought before the courts under the Bourbons.[20] However, this was probably only the tip of the iceberg. Many arrests and convictions would have gone unrecorded, especially if carried out by 'illegal' military courts, while a good number of offences would have been ignored depending on how zealous the local authorities were. It would nevertheless seem that the vast majority if not all of those arrested for 'seditious cries' were Bonapartists.[21] As late as 1828, seven years after Napoleon's death, one could read on the walls of the working-class districts of Paris the slogan 'Vive Napoléon. Civil War and Death to Charles X and to the priests who want to starve us to death'.[22] Workers could be seen gathered around the placard applauding as someone read it out. Of course it was a time of unemployment in France, and in hard times people turn to the past or look to new heroes to save them from hunger. That is why many still embraced Napoleon, even after death, as the providential man who could – would – resolve their problems.

THE COMMERCIALISATION OF MEMORY

Let us now come back to the Napoleonic objets d'art sold in secret around the country, often by veterans of the Grande Armée transformed into travelling salesmen.[23] These might be anything from a bust, which could be either small or large, to knives and forks with an image of Napoleon (or his son) on it, to jugs, pipes, canes, an inkwell in the shape of Napoleon's hat, plates, good-luck charms, hats with Napoleonic images inside them, tie pins, rings, fans, tobacco cases, snuff boxes and boxes of sweets with images of Napoleon on either the inside or outside, crockery, cake slicers, tweezers, irons, hammers, tongs, decks of cards, spades, plates, cups, mugs and candlesticks.[24]

These everyday objects were an evident political statement, but were also a personal expression of intimate feelings towards Napoleon. Other objects hid a double meaning, such as an image of Louis XVIII hiding an image of Napoleon. A Russian traveller in France noticed an illustrated sign outside a cabaret in Domrémy that seemed to be of Joan of Arc, but which on closer inspection masked an image of Napoleon.[25] This was a veritable 'domestic cult' in which Napoleon became a 'household deity'.[26] Small businesses in Paris, more or less clandestine, specialised in particular objects: Laforge, rue Saint Martin, specialised in canes; Visement, rue de Roule, in wooden egg-cups; Couesnon, rue aux Fèves, in bronze busts; Martineau, rue du Faubourg Saint-Denis, in small replicas of the Vendôme Column, and so on.[27] The authorities were able to find and destroy many objects,[28] but for every item they managed to remove from circulation, many more found their way into the homes of Napoleon's supporters, nostalgic for his reign.

Many of these objects were manufactured outside France and smuggled in, but they were also popular in those countries where the material was freely produced. Between 1815 and 1830, hundreds of thousands of busts, small statues, coins, medallions and images of Napoleon were manufactured and sold all over Britain.[29] During the 1840s and into the 1850s, the production of busts continued, so that more were made of Napoleon than of Queen Victoria.[30] Some of these figures were exported to France, but the majority of them were made for the British market.[31] Even Wellington was an avid collector of Napoleon memorabilia, as well as of portraits, china and silverware with Napoleonic themes. Canova's towering nude statue of Napoleon dominated the entrance to Wellington's residence, Apsley House (Napoleon never displayed the statue, embarrassed at being portrayed nude in the classical style; the statue was sold to the British government which then presented it to the Duke).[32]

How does one interpret this demand for Napoleonic artefacts? One reason for it was that the public bought Napoleoniana simply because it was forbidden.[33] A merchant arrested and tried for selling busts of Napoleon aptly illustrates this fad for the illicit. At his trial, he revealed that he had sold busts of Louis XVIII during the

Hundred Days.[34] 'The public only seeks these stupidities when they are forbidden,' he explained. In other words, we should not assume that those who bought Napoleonic imagery and objects were either Napoleonists or Bonapartists; the buyers may simply have been interested in history, nostalgic for the past or titillated by the illegality of the goods in question.

Another reason was that the artefacts were part of a broader culture of celebrity, as well as part of the nineteenth century's growing consumer culture.[35] To own one of these objects no doubt held a certain novelty value, tied to a respectful admiration for Napoleon. But it was more than that, of course. Possession of one of these objects can be interpreted differently either as an expression of the owner's personal sentiments or as a political view. In some households, he would have represented a desire, possibly nostalgic, to see a return to the past. In this respect, these objects represented different aspects of Napoleon's memory. Of course this profusion of memorabilia, this commodification of Napoleon, had political undertones, but it could have occurred only with the changes in the production and dissemination of goods that were taking place in Europe in the first half of the nineteenth century. One of the inevitable consequences of the increasing industrialisation of Europe was the commodification of public figures and of public events.[36] The commercialisation of Napoleon appears to have come about as a result of a conjuncture between the needs of a commodity culture and the desire for a national hero who reflected the potential glory of France.

Despite a seemingly relentless, if somewhat underground, presence, the proliferation of Napoleonic artefacts does not mean that there was an overwhelming acceptance of Napoleon, even as an historical figure. Individuals were free to accept, reject, revere, revile or simply ignore these objects and the man they portrayed. There is no doubting, however, that Napoleon remained an overarching and even intimate figure in France and many parts of Europe throughout the first half of the nineteenth century. Moreover, the cult was taking on mystical, semi-religious connotations. For example, in 1827 or 1828 the Comtesse de Boigne claims to have seen a little girl of around two years of age with brilliantly azure blue eyes. When one looked closely, one could read the words 'Napoléon Empereur' in them.[37] Maxime du Camp recounted a childhood memory of dining at the house of his uncle

General Decaen. After dinner, the family gathered to sing 'The Old Corporal' by Béranger, and as they sang the chorus his uncle pushed him down and said, 'On your knees, child, this is a sacred song.' They raised their arms to the heavens as if the song was about to sound 'the hour of deliverance'.[38]

SINGING NAPOLEON

A religion has to have hymns that move the heart and the mind. Songs and singing, one of the easiest ways to get a political message across, played an important role in harnessing opposition, and could have a 'profound impact' on the people listening to or singing them.[39] It is difficult today to comprehend the power and the popularity of the large number of amateur singing societies catering to all classes of society in France in the nineteenth century.[40] Singing associations with names like 'The Friends of Glory' would meet in cabarets – by 1836 there were over 500 in Paris alone – to sing songs whose political content was obvious to all even if covert. If they sang about 'the little corporal', for example, everyone knew whom they were referring to. Local songs compared Napoleon's suffering and death on St Helena with the Passion of Christ.[41]

Singing not only brought joy to those who listened, but it could also be a politically subversive act. It could be something as recognisable as 'La Marseillaise', or songs that had been popular during the Revolution or the Empire; the words of a popular drinking song could even be changed to become a political parody. A collection of songs by Béranger published in 1821 sold over 11,000 copies in just one week.[42] Between 1826 and 1830, Béranger's songs, which could be bought for as little as fifty centimes, were bestsellers, and not only in France, but also (translated) in Germany and as far afield as Russia.[43] Moreover, they were often illustrated, bringing to life Napoleonic scenes imagined in the songs.[44] Béranger was prosecuted three times and imprisoned twice for songs he wrote mocking royalist officials, once after the assassination of the Duc de Berry, when censorship laws were tightened, and again in 1828 when he was sentenced to nine months in prison and fined 10,000 francs.[45] The prison sentences made him a martyr of the liberal cause and were even used as a strategy on his part to sell more songs. When there was a change of government in August 1829, the new prefect of police, Claude Mangin, ordered street singers to stop glorifying the name of Napoleon.[46]

Such measures made little difference at the time. There was safety in numbers. When a crowd of people started singing Bonapartist songs in a café, often with the approval of patrons who would sit listening attentively to them, there was not much the authorities could do about it. It was a different matter of course when an individual, drunk and in a public space like a café, happened to toast Napoleon or insult the royal family; he could be prosecuted by the police, although sentences tended to be lighter when the perpetrator was drunk.[47] Local authorities were encouraged to pursue travelling singers and the hawkers of these songs, but they always had trouble doing so.[48]

The upshot was that the authorities could not control people, no matter how much they tried. This does not mean to say that French society was riddled with either Napoleonists or Bonapartists. The key motivation here may not have been so much love of the Emperor as hatred of the Bourbons,[49] an expression of their belief not so much in a political system as in a man. Nor should one underestimate the extent to which certain sections of the French population were nostalgic for Napoleon and the Empire. The flip side to that was the desire to see the Bourbons gone.

THE THREE GLORIOUS DAYS

Neither the Bourbons nor the émigrés had ever really reconciled themselves to the past, an attitude that seemingly grew and hardened with the death of Louis XVIII in 1824, and the ascent to the throne of his much more conservative brother, the Comte d'Artois, crowned Charles X. Charles was sixty-seven when he came to the throne, a man described by one veteran as 'used by the debauchery of youth, Jesuit, sanctimonious and mean'.[50] The ascent of Charlot, as he was nicknamed by Bonapartists, meant that Ultras, the extreme right of the royalist party, now had a sympathetic ear, and it did not bode well for the social and political reconciliation needed for the longevity of the monarchy. Charles was not popular, and his character was largely to blame. François Guizot, who would go on to become an important minister, described Charles as a 'loyal émigré and a docile devotee', whose government 'wafted from contradiction to contradiction and from inconsistency to inconsistency, until, restored to his true faith and his true desire, he made the mistake that cost him the throne'.[51]

The mistakes made by the Bourbons had dramatic consequences. In elections that took place in June 1830, only 145 out of the 428 deputies elected could be called royalist or pro-government.[52] When Charles X refused to appoint a ministry responsible to the legislature and issued what were called the July Ordinances – suspending freedom of the press, dissolving the Chamber of Deputies and calling new elections with an even more limited franchise – violence erupted in the streets of Paris on 27 July, and during the three days of street fighting that ensued there were anywhere between 700 and 2,200 deaths. Paving stones laid in some of the streets were dug up to help form more than 4,000 barricades, behind which the crowds were able to confront the army. This short revolution, known as the Three Glorious Days, resulted in the overthrow of the Bourbons; Charles and his family went into exile in Britain. That the Bourbons collapsed after only three days of street fighting in Paris shows just how little support there was for the monarchy. A new reigning house, the House of Orleans, and a new king, Louis-Philippe, Charles X's cousin, came to power in a brilliantly orchestrated political manoeuvre – he deserved the throne because he did not want it.[53]

In some respects, Louis-Philippe was thrust into a political vacuum in 1830. There was a republican presence, but republicans were more feared than admired, not only by the political elite but also by many in the working classes.[54] They certainly made a bid for power but were outmanoeuvred.[55] On the other hand, there were probably more cries of 'Vive Napoléon II' than for any other political character during the 1830 Revolution.[56] Hundreds of veterans of the revolutionary and Napoleonic wars took part in the street fighting, and represented two-thirds of those wounded.[57] Some historians have gone so far as to argue that the Revolution of 1830 came very close to being a Bonapartist revolution.[58] Adolphe Thiers, who would twice become prime minister under the new king, later recounted that each time his carriage was stopped on his journey to Neuilly on the outskirts of Paris to urge Louis-Philippe to act he was greeted with cries of 'Vive l'Empereur', leading him to believe that Bonapartists were in the ascendant.[59] The people who had imbibed the cult under the Bourbons – 'behind the closed doors of secret societies, in family reunions, in the *guinguettes* around Paris' – were now, with their overthrow, finally able to come out into the open.[60]

Bonapartism was not so much a political movement as a focus of political discontent. Besides, there were no prominent figures in France prepared to espouse the Bonapartists' cause: the Duc de Reichstadt, or the 'little eagle' as Napoleon's son was often called, was far away in Vienna; the Bonaparte family was still banned from entering France; and the movement was far too diffuse to result in any sort of concrete Bonapartist political outcome. Given the Bonapartist character of much of the Parisian Revolution,[61] it is likely that Napoleon II would have been offered the throne if he had been present. But the ill-defined movement was unprepared to take power, and was easily outflanked by those with more political nous. The House of Orleans seemed like the only viable alternative to those making and unmaking thrones. It had been touted before as a likely replacement for the Bourbons in 1815, but the allies had decided against it.[62] This time, the Duc d'Orléans more or less fell on to the throne. The new regime became known as the July Monarchy, named after the Revolution of July.

STAGING NAPOLEON

One need look no further than the theatre to understand the connection between popular Bonapartist political sentiment and the Revolution.[63]

It is difficult today to comprehend both the popularity and the impact of the theatre, and the extraordinary role it played in French public life in the nineteenth century.[64] It was far more popular and influential than the press. As a consequence, it was particularly feared by the authorities, who tried to keep a tight rein on it by obliging owners to announce well in advance what plays they were going to put on and prohibiting them from spontaneously performing a play at the behest of an audience or allowing actors to add lines that might incite the audience to respond. Despite these attempts to control the theatre, it was a public space where audiences directly and often vociferously contested politics by interacting with the actors. They booed and hissed, they shouted out political slogans, they distributed leaflets, they posted placards, they threw fruit and vegetables to demonstrate their discontent, they demanded that particular lines be repeated in the course of a play, they insisted that a play be performed – one that had usually been banned – other than the one scheduled, and often they got their way.[65] When that did not happen, crowds could disrupt performances by reading one play in the stalls while an entirely different play was being enacted on stage. Of course, the owners of the fourteen regular theatres in Paris had to be careful. Even an indirect reference to Napoleon during a play could see the theatre closed down, while an actor caught mimicking Napoleon could be jailed and heavily fined.[66]

In 1817, for example, Antoine Vincent Arnault was living in Brussels with other exiles when a play that he had written, *Germanicus*, was performed at the Théâtre-Français in Paris. There was nothing at all offensive about the play – it had indeed been read and approved by the king – except that Arnault was a supporter of Napoleon. On opening night, the play was watched respectfully by the spectators; things descended into chaos only after the curtain came down and Bonapartists in the crowd shouted for the author to be named. François-Joseph Talma, one of the most recognised actors of his age, and a personal friend of Arnault, came on stage and shouted his name above the uproar.[67] There were two camps in the theatre, each recognisable to the other by their dress. Royalists had come wearing black waistcoats and white ties; Bonapartists were attired in white waistcoats and black ties. As soon as Talma had pronounced the name of the playwright, the game was on for young and old. The battle between the two camps spilled out of the theatre into the streets and came to an end only when the police intervened.

It was rare for Bonapartists and royalists to clash in the streets in this manner. However, it was common for supporters of either camp to disrupt performances by whatever means they could. Bonapartists would shout down actors or throw objects at them to prevent plays from being performed.[68] If an actor were hamfisted enough to mock Napoleon on stage, working-class spectators would violently express their disapproval. The poet Théodore de Banville witnessed one such scene. The actor in question, in a working-class theatre called the Petit-Lazari, was

pelted with everything from apples to sausages for assuming the gestures of the Emperor.[69] The uproar continued until a squad of municipal
guards stormed the theatre, sabres drawn, and then evacuated it. These
reciprocal attacks were part of an ongoing struggle for control of the
public space. But with the fall of the Bourbon monarchy in 1830, and
the relaxation of censorship laws, that battle more or less came to an end;
Napoleon invaded the theatre with an explosion of plays.[70]

On 31 August 1830, a seemingly never-ending series of Napoleon
plays began at the Cirque-Olympique with *The Crossing of Mount
St Bernard*, but there were many, many others – 'occasional plays' as
they were called – written quickly with little or no literary value.[71]
The number of Napoleon plays really reached an apogee in the twelve
months from August 1830.[72] In 1831, twenty-nine new plays about
Napoleon and the Empire opened. During the July Monarchy (about
which more below), more than 120 plays about Napoleon and the
Empire were performed. In all, the nineteenth century saw over 600
plays performed about Napoleon, and that is not taking into account
plays that contained Napoleonic characters or street theatre.[73] The
output coincided with the development of new staging and acting
techniques that allowed the actor's abilities to be truly recognised.[74]
The most famous actor to portray Napoleon was a man by the name
of Gobert, who consulted with Napoleon's former valet, Louis-
Constant Wairy, on how best to imitate him. Gobert's rendition of
Napoleon could make someone like Mlle George cry her heart out, or
cause a veteran's heart to beat fast or even make him faint.[75] And then
there was the actor Edmond, not as good as Gobert but considered to
bear most resemblance to Napoleon.[76] Heinrich Heine, who went to
Paris in April 1831, noted that the working classes in particular were
deeply moved by any reference to Napoleon or the Empire, at a time
when it was normal to cry in public.[77] If Napoleon was the hero in
these plays, Hudson Lowe was the villain. Actors playing him had to
be escorted home for fear they would be set upon by Bonapartists.

It was almost enough for a play to have the words 'Napoleon'
or 'Bonaparte' in the title for success to be guaranteed. Some of the
authors were hack writers, in the tradition of Grub Street, hoping to
cash in on Napoleon's name; some published anonymously or under
pseudonyms; some signed with their initials; others were well known
in literary circles in Paris, and may have read each other's work and

even borrowed from each other.[78] For a while, the Empire and the July Monarchy somehow found common ground on the street and on the stage.[79] 'People are becoming authors just to write about Bonaparte,' complained one writer. 'Those who have never thought before of taking up the pen now do so instinctively as though they had been inspired.'[80] It was almost as though the authorities allowed these plays to be put on in the hope of diminishing the intensity of Napoleon as a political force; if it were no longer illegal, the drama around his person would somehow be attenuated.

The Napoleon that one most often comes across in these works is a Napoleon of the people – simple, humble, accessible to the common man, surrounded by his family in the Tuileries, quickly eating a frugal meal, sharing a campfire with his *grognards* or crossing the threshold of a cottage to talk to some peasants.[81] It was a theme that was also reflected in many of the paintings submitted to the Salons throughout the 1830s that portrayed Napoleon not as a military hero, but rather as a man of the people who understood their plight.[82] They were all popular clichés that conformed to the legend that was now firmly woven into the French cultural fabric. Here too we find the martyr of St Helena. In one play performed in Paris in 1830, Napoleon addresses a spy who is trying to convince him to flee the island: 'Jesus Christ would not have been able to found a belief if he had not had his forty days of passion ... My passion ... my cross, is St Helena.'[83] Contemporaries, in other words, had come to understand and to accept the legend constructed by Napoleon on St Helena.

PICTURING NAPOLEON

The Napoleonic legend was further promoted and disseminated by the distribution of cheap prints. The French, and Europeans in general, were still a largely semi-literate people. The image, much more so than print media, was therefore an accessible medium through which political ideas and messages could be easily transmitted. In France, cheap woodblock prints and broadsides that sold for one sou helped develop a 'graphic biography' that contributed to the propagation and development of the popular legend.[84] The most famous of these printing houses – Pellerin, from a town called Epinal in north-eastern France – developed a series

of fifty-nine poster-size woodblock illustrations that had print runs of
up to 5,000 copies per poster, although the images of Epinal, as they are
called, did not reach a broader public until the July Monarchy (between
1830 and 1848), when 100,000 copies at a time could be printed.[85]

Many of the popular prints conceived by Pellerin's chief artist,
François Georgin, portrayed Napoleon as simple, virtuous, compas-
sionate and a friend of the common people – a republican emperor –
helping overturn the negative impressions he had left after his second
abdication in 1815.[86] These prints, as with every other Napoleonic
image, have to be read as cultural and political texts. The vast majority of images after his death point unambiguously towards Napoleon
as martyr, but even within that dominant image other themes can
be discerned. In particular, they celebrate Napoleon's achievements
as military leader. In the top left-hand corner of the engraving by
Jean-Baptiste Thiébault, for example, one can see the Pyramids as
well as the Vendôme Column, an obvious reference to Egypt and to
Austerlitz. Recognisable too were the symbols traditionally associated with Napoleon's image – his hat, a sword, sometimes a bust that
vaguely resembled him.

But there is also what has been called a 'portrayal of powerless-
ness',[87] which depicted Napoleon as exposed and vulnerable. The
most famous image of this is the painting (often copied) by Charles de
Steuben of Napoleon dictating his memoirs to Gourgaud. He is portrayed in slippers and sleeping bonnet, clad in trousers and shirt but
also wearing what appears to be a morning gown, and looks somewhat dishevelled.

It is impossible to know what impact these images had on those
who bought them. In fact, we have no exact figures for their distribution or any indication of where they may have been bought. We
do know, however, that the Bourbon regime pursued merchants who
stocked Napoleonist imagery, and cleared out their stores whenever
they were found. In their place, Bourbon images – especially the
fleur de lys and the white flag, and the reinauguration of the statue
of Henry IV on the Pont Neuf[88] – were used to represent the monarchy in public and, like Napoleonic objets d'art, came to to deco-
rate everyday items like playing cards and crockery. However, every
Napoleonic object that appeared, every book, pamphlet and engraving, was testimony to the failure of the regime's attempts to obliterate

the past and return to a time when only one ideology had existed, that of the monarchy.[89]

LOUIS-PHILIPPE AND THE OFFICIAL CULT

The July Monarchy was much more liberal than the Bourbons had been. From the beginning, people were able to express their views more openly as the new king promised to chart a course between ideological extremes.[90] Napoleon was no longer perceived as a great political threat, although his son, the Duc de Reichstadt, was a little more worrying for a new regime and a new royal house that had yet to establish itself. Nevertheless, it was no longer considered seditious to cry out 'Vive Napoléon'. Civil servants who had been banished for going over to Napoleon during the Hundred Days were allowed to return. Those who had for years adhered to the cult in secret were now able to openly speak of their affection for the Emperor. A number of Bonapartist clubs for women – the Club des Culottes de Peau and the Cotillons – were founded in the 1830s.[91] The system of preventative censorship that had operated under the Bourbons fell away, allowing plays that celebrated Napoleon – several of which incorporated an actual coat or hat worn by him – to see the light of day.[92] Journals dedicated to his memory were also allowed, although most of them seem to have been short-lived ventures.[93]

A change of regime did not mean that the political divisions in France ceased all of a sudden. On the contrary, they continued to be played out, often violently, although now there was a concerted effort on the part of Louis-Philippe to invent new traditions and to place his dynasty within a national historical framework that acknowledged France's revolutionary and imperial past.[94] In doing so, he not only distanced himself entirely from the Bourbons' policy of forgetting, he not only broke ranks with all the other monarchical regimes in Europe determined to forget the past, but he also capitalised on the vibrant popularity of the cult. Indeed, not only did Louis-Philippe not ignore the Napoleonic heritage, but he was anxious to use it to his own advantage. When he was crowned on 9 August 1830, for example, the very simple coronation ceremony took place under the tricolour, as much an emblem of the Empire as it was of the Revolution. In addition, four prominent Napoleonic generals played a key role in the ceremony: Marshal Macdonald presented Louis-Philippe with the crown, Marshal Oudinot the sceptre, Marshal Mortier the sword and General Molitor the hand of justice. Only Oudinot was decidedly anti-Bonapartist. Napoleonists rallied to Louis-Philippe in numbers: the Chamber of Peers is said to have included four ministers, six marshals, fifty-six generals, fourteen councillors of state, nineteen prefects, seven ambassadors and twenty-one chamberlains from the Empire.[95]

By allowing Napoleon back into the public domain – recall that mention of him had been banished by the Bourbons – the new regime attempted to celebrate the Napoleonic legacy, and at the same time incorporate it into a larger narrative of French history. In that way, it hoped to diffuse any political threat represented by Bonapartists. That threat was present in the background until the death of the Duc de Reichstadt in July 1832. At that point, Orleanists hoped that Bonapartists would come to support the monarchy.[96] This never really happened, which is possibly one of the reasons Louis-Philippe had what could best be described as an ambivalent attitude towards Napoleon, or at least towards his memory. He may have used Napoleon's past military glory for his own political ends, but he was wary of being eclipsed by it.[97]

A PARTICULAR VISION OF NAPOLEON

The manipulation of Napoleon by the Orleans regime was part of a larger cultural undertaking by Louis-Philippe to exploit art for political purposes. It was hoped that by associating Napoleon with the new regime, some of the imperial glory and the popularity of the Emperor himself would rub off on the king. There are three sites in particular revivified by the July Monarchy in order to capitalise on the memory and prestige of Napoleon. First, in 1833, Louis-Philippe granted permission for the statue of Napoleon to be reinstated on the top of the Vendôme Column. Second, in 1836, the Arc de Triomphe was completed and inaugurated almost thirty years after Napoleon had laid the foundation stone. Third, in 1837, a vast new Museum of the History of France was opened at Versailles. A key focus of the museum was a series of new monumental paintings commissioned by Louis-Philippe, five of which depicted the military victories of the Napoleonic era. It is worth examining each of these sites in more detail.

The Vendôme Column

The Column of Austerlitz, as it was originally called when construction got under way in 1806, was not completed and inaugurated until 15 August 1810 (Napoleon's birthday), in a relatively low-key ceremony, a discretion prompted largely by Napoleon's recent marriage to Marie-Louise of Austria.[98] It seemed impolitic to celebrate a victory over the Habsburgs after just having married the Emperor Francis II's daughter. That is probably the reason it was renamed later that year the Column of the Grande Armée.

Modelled on Trajan's Column in Rome, it was a monumental piece of work, more than forty-three metres high, with over 200 metres of bas-reliefs, a sort of sculptural history of the campaign of 1805, constructed of bronze obtained by melting down the 1,250 enemy cannon that had been captured from the Russians and Austrians at Austerlitz. On top of the Column was a statue of the Emperor in Roman clothing by Antoine-Denis Chaudet; he was portrayed holding a globe in one hand, leaning on a sheathed sword with the other, and wreathed in laurel. Napoleon was not entirely happy with it; in fact he does not appear to have liked statues of himself at all, arguing that he did not want 'idols'.[99]

After the collapse of the Empire in 1814, the Column became the focal point of Bonapartists and anti-Bonapartists alike, a contested symbol – a beacon of social order for some, a war memorial for others, an emblem of political despotism for yet others again.[100] It was a reflection of what the memory of Napoleon had become as each political grouping attached to it its own meaning and interpretation of the past. The statue was taken down in April 1814,[101] in the presence of Russian and Prussian troops and a large crowd of Parisians, who remained silent during the whole operation, although whether out of prudence or disapproval it is impossible to say.

Chaudet's Napoleon – melted down in 1818 to help create a new statue of Henry IV – was supposed to have been replaced by a statue of Peace, but in its stead was erected a large flag bearing the white fleur de lys, the symbol of the Bourbons.[102] When Napoleon returned during the Hundred Days, the white flag was replaced with the tricolour. There was no attempt made, however, to replace the Chaudet statue, although in the political context of the day there was some talk about a statue to the 'French People'. When the Bourbons returned a second time in 1815, the tricolour was again replaced by the white fleur de lys, which would continue to fly over the Column until July 1830. Soon after the death of Napoleon in 1821, those loyal to the Bourbons insisted that the Column be 'bourbonised' by replacing the flag with a statue of Louis XVIII.[103] Nothing came of it.

After the Revolution of 1830, the July Monarchy began to see all public monuments as part of the French cultural heritage.[104] Now allowed to express openly their sentiments for the man, veterans of the Grande Armée regularly met at the foot of the Column on 15 August and 5 May (the anniversary of his birth and death) to commemorate Napoleon and the Empire.[105] On 5 May 1831, for example, on the tenth anniversary of Napoleon's death, thousands of wreaths, busts and engravings were placed at the foot of the Column, even though the police removed them as soon as they could.[106] There was also an attempt by a group of young men to place a wooden statue of Napoleon on top of the Column, only for the statue to be confiscated: the police were always on the look-out for 'agitators' on the occasion of anniversaries of this sort.[107] Republicans distributed portraits of the Duc de Reichstadt and sang 'sinister songs mingled with the most hostile cries'.[108] Riots broke out at the foot of the Column over the following days. The crowd had to be dispersed by cavalry, and then the fire brigade turned their hoses on the crowd, although the authorities played down the seriousness of the affair. On the anniversary the following year, fights broke out between republicans and police that led to the death of a republican demonstrator.[109] During the July Monarchy, the Column became an obligatory stopping-off point whenever a popular demonstration took place, as though the demonstrators felt obliged to render homage to Napoleon.[110] The Column also became a place of pilgrimage (as did many other Napoleonic sites after 1830).[111] It was one of the reasons Louis-Philippe agreed to restore Napoleon's statue to its spot in 1833, holding a contest for its commission.

The statue was unveiled by the king on 28 July 1833, the anniversary of the Three Glorious Days that had brought Louis-Philippe to

The installation of the statue of Napoleon by Charles Emile Seurre (1798–1858) in the Cour d'Honneur at the Invalides; photograph taken in March 1911. The statue, cast from sixteen cannon captured in 1805, was removed to Courbevoie on the outskirts of Paris in 1863 and replaced by a replica of Chaudet's original statue. Seurre's statue was thrown into the Seine in October 1870, on the orders of the minister of the interior, Léon Gambetta. It was fished out of the river in 1876 and placed in the Cour d'Honneur of the Invalides in 1911, where it can be seen today.[112]

power, in a ceremony in front of a large crowd of spectators. Cries of 'Vive l'Empereur!' were interspersed with cries of 'Vive le Roi!', although some squadrons of the National Guard refused to shout the latter.[113] During the July Monarchy, the 'little corporal' had emerged as the preferred Napoleonic figure among opponents of the regime; the grey greatcoat and simple hat made him seem a man of the people.[114] Louis-Philippe did not want a repeat of Chaudet's Caesarist representation of Napoleon, but something much more toned down. That is why he finally decided in favour of a Napoleon of the people – in a coat and hat, hand in waistcoat, the image most commonly associated with Napoleon – by the artist Charles-Emile Seurre. The choice was deliberate and entirely political; the government wanted to evoke the military man but not the Emperor.[115] In the process, the regime had appropriated what was supposedly a dangerous image and completely disarmed it by incorporating it into the lexicon of official art.[116]

Bonapartists and republicans alike found it distasteful and saw it as an attempt to play down Napoleon's grandeur.[117] By 1840, the gatherings of veterans at the foot of the Column began to epitomise the political tensions that existed between Bonapartists and the Orleanist government, which consequently took the decision to prohibit veterans from wearing their old uniforms in public. It provoked an outcry in the republican press of the day.[118] Well before the Orleanist regime came to an end in 1848, the Vendôme Column remained a contested site, a place where opponents of the regime would gather to express their discontent.[119]

The Arc de Triomphe
Perhaps the greatest Napoleonic monument, as well as the greatest building project during the July Monarchy, was the Arc de Triomphe. Napoleon ordered the building of an arch dedicated to the glory of the army in 1806. It was designed to be the largest arch ever built, but his empire collapsed before it could be completed. The construction was consequently abandoned between the years 1814 and 1823, an uncompleted reminder of what once had been. There was even some discussion about demolishing it, or transforming it into some kind of a utilitarian building.[120] If the structure was left as a ruin, however, it might serve as a reminder of an interrupted and uncompleted imperial

enterprise, a shrine to the martyr Napoleon, a remnant of the glory of French arms. It was only in 1823, after the death of Napoleon and the success of the French military intervention in Spain the previous year, that Louis XVIII was persuaded to resume the construction of the Arc.[121] This time, it was destined to fulfil a counter-revolutionary purpose, to commemorate the Bourbon dynasty. In short, rather than demolish it entirely, the regime eventually decided to try and put it to some use in the cause of the House of Bourbon. It was in keeping with a number of arches built in major cities in the post-1815 period by the powers that had defeated Napoleon – Moscow, St Petersburg, Madrid, Milan, London (Marble Arch) and Munich.

It was still unfinished in 1830 when Louis-Philippe came to power. In 1832, the king decided to resume construction and quite naturally modified its ideological purpose again. It would now be dedicated to the military victories of both the Revolution and Napoleon.[122] That is why we can see today four sculptural high-reliefs at the base of the Arc, two facing the Champs-Elysées – François Rude's *The Departure of the Volunteers of 1792*, dubbed the *Marseillaise*, along with Jean-Pierre Cortot's *Triumph of Napoleon* – and two facing the Avenue de la Grande Armée – *Resistance* (1814) and *Peace* (1815), both by Antoine Etex.[123] When Adolphe Thiers, minister of public works, approached Etex about creating a high-relief on the theme of 1814, the sculptor was perplexed; it was after all a year of defeat. Thiers is supposed to have replied, 'It doesn't matter. I insist on it. I need 1814 as a date.' Etex wasn't convinced and wasn't moved either by an offer of 300,000 francs (although we may suspect the artist was being a little disingenuous). The penny eventually dropped for him. 'What could have been more beautiful in 1814, I asked myself, if it was not the defence of the country's soil?'[124] The counterpart to 1814, on the other side of the Arc, is 1815, a return to normalcy and the monarchy. That is, two of the four high-reliefs show the end result of the Napoleonic wars, defeat for France and the return of peace, or the return of the Bourbons, depending on how one looks at it. The other two high-reliefs celebrate the citizen's army of 1792, hence the Republic, and Napoleon's defeat over the Habsburgs, both highlighting the military prowess of France.

As with the reinauguration of the Vendôme Column, the anniversary of the Three Glorious Days – 28 July 1836 – was chosen for

the opening of the Arc. This time the king did not appear for fear of
an assassination attempt; one had been made against him less than a
month before that had only narrowly failed.[125] Instead, the ceremony
was a rather drab affair, with two ministers, Thiers and the Comte
d'Argout, unveiling the high-reliefs at seven in the morning before a
platform for dignitaries that, according to some, was virtually empty.
No speeches were made and no parades were held.[126] It was, however, an opportunity for veterans of the wars to gather around the Arc
to shout themselves hoarse acclaiming Napoleon. The public turned
out in numbers just to see the celebratory fireworks on the Champs-
Elysées that evening.[127]

The Museum of the History of France

Finally, the third site of commemoration was an entirely new project. In June 1837, Louis-Philippe inaugurated the Museum of the
History of France in the Château of Versailles. The inscription which
still graces the façade of the building visible as one enters through the
main gates of Versailles – *A toutes les gloires de la France* (To all the
glories of France) – encapsulates the purpose of the transformation
of the château into a public monument to the history of France.[128] It
was a project close to the king's heart; he made 398 visits to Versailles
to check on the progress of the renovations.[129] He ordered more than
3,000 artworks for his museum, every one of which, it is claimed,
he initiated and meticulously examined.[130] It was also a conspicuous
and very expensive public statement that Louis-Philippe was willing to embrace the whole of French history leading up to the July
Revolution, demonstrating a desire to reconcile the different factions
that had made political life in France so difficult since the Revolution,
and in the process consolidate his own dynasty. This was of course
something that Napoleon had attempted and ultimately failed to do.

   The two wings of the château were entirely renovated, and much
of the original décor removed in the process. The north wing contained the Gallery of the History of France, with scenes from the
reign of Clovis through to the July Monarchy. On the first floor of
the south wing was the Gallery of Battles, 120 metres long and illustrated by thirty-three paintings of key moments in French history,
from the Battle of Tolbiac in AD 496 to the battle of Wagram in 1809.
Vernet and Paul Philippoteaux were commissioned to do a number

of paintings, including *Napoléon à Rivoli* (1837), *Iéna, Wagram* and *Friedland* (all 1836). François Gérard's *Austerlitz* was also on display. Directly underneath on the ground floor was the Salle du Sacre or the Coronation Room, dedicated to Napoleon and the Empire, which included some of the monumental paintings that had been commissioned by him. Jacques-Louis David's *Coronation of Josephine* and *The Distribution of the Eagles*, as well as Antoine-Jean Gros' *Battle of Aboukir*, all personally chosen by the king, were taken from the Louvre to adorn the gallery's walls. Antoine-François Callet's allegory of the coup of Brumaire can be seen on the ceiling of the Salle du Sacre.

These paintings represented an image of Napoleon that was largely, if not entirely military. His military exploits were historical facts that could be easily evoked, but in the process there was a deliberate and conscious decision to avoid any reflection on his civilian achievements. Moreover, by fixing on Napoleon as general – alone – directing the battle, the portrayal deliberately ran counter to the popular image of Napoleon as man of the people. He is exalted not only as military leader, but also as emperor, and it was exactly this that the regime wanted to highlight. In other words, in stark contrast to the popular engravings of the day, Louis-Philippe's 'Napoleon' was not a man of the people; he was above the people.

As with Seurre's statue on top of the Vendôme Column, not all Bonapartists were happy with the way in which the regime depicted Napoleon and his battles. Other contemporaries criticised the paintings for being far too featureless. One art critic described Vernet's *Iéna* and *Friedland* as 'vulgar and trivial'.[131] 'All the characters are immobile and frozen, and resemble more shadows than men.' They were not representations of historically specific acts or episodes. Indeed, it has been said that the titles of the paintings could be interchanged without making much difference. The Museum building too was not without its critics. The *Gazette de France*, for example, described the reconstruction of the château as a 'defacement', while the artwork was described as a 'jumble of picturesque daubs'.[132]

The failure of the paintings and the gallery to impress was symptomatic of the regime's failure fully to capitalise on the reputation of Napoleon. Every attempt made by the July Monarchy throughout the decade after 1830 to recuperate the past for its own ends appears to have handed the enemies of the regime a means of attacking it.[133] The regime's attempts were further stymied by a series of seemingly insurmountable difficulties: a number of short-lived governments; continued political unrest resulting in further revolts that were harshly repressed (in 1831 and 1834), along with frequent political demonstrations and rioting, often violent, that led to hundreds killed and wounded; a number of assassination attempts against the king; and an underlying economic crisis that exacerbated all these political tensions. Furthermore, the regime's foreign policy, considered by many to be timid and humiliating, alienated large numbers of people.[134] A grand gesture was needed to bring the people of France together around the throne. It was not long before someone came up with one.

THE RETURN

1840

9

Resurrection

By March 1840, ten years after the founding of the new regime, despite attempts to create new political traditions and to place the dynasty within a national historical framework – and despite attempts to reconcile the country through an astute use of political symbolism – France was still bitterly divided.[1] The recently appointed president of the council of ministers and foreign minister, Adolphe Thiers, did his best to present his government as above factions. To that end, he began looking for some sort of public manifestation, an integrating ritual that would help bring the country together, and fell upon the idea of bringing Napoleon's remains back to France.[2]

Thiers' motives for this particular public gesture were complex. The author of a successful history of the French Revolution, a former journalist and founder of the liberal newspaper *Le National*, he was a somewhat conceited political opportunist. Once described by a Russian diplomat as having 'the head of an owl on the body of a boy',[3] he had been a schoolboy in Marseilles at the height of the Napoleonic wars, and had been obsessed by the Emperor since childhood. He had signed a contract with the publishers Paulin for a large advance of around 500,000 francs to write a twenty-volume *Histoire du Consulat et de l'Empire*, which he spent most of the 1840s writing.[4] Gossips believed that he acted to return Napoleon's remains in order to enhance the sale of his own books, but there is little credibility in the rumours.[5] It was far more likely that he was looking for a spectacular public gesture that would flatter France's national amour propre and maintain his own political reputation, as well as make his mark on history. Such a gesture would also serve to distract public opinion from political manoeuvrings in the Chamber of Deputies, and to alleviate popular discontent with the government.[6] As in the past, the gesture meant capitalising on Napoleon's extraordinary popularity in France and appropriating the legend for the regime's own purposes.[7] Contemporaries could be forgiven for thinking Thiers' decision was little more than a publicity stunt.[8]

Whatever his motives, Thiers had to overcome the reluctance of Louis-Philippe, who did not have any particular fondness for him and whose initial reaction was to reject the proposal. Thiers then broached the subject with the king's eldest son and the heir to the throne, Ferdinand-Philippe, Duc d'Orléans. It took more than a month to persuade his father. Louis-Philippe supposedly agreed to the idea, albeit grudgingly, on 1 May 1840, his birthday, although he later took full credit for it.[9] It was to be his gift to the nation and was in a sense a kind of closing act with his own courtship of the legend.[10] The king announced to the ministers who had gathered at the Tuileries to present him with the wishes of the nation that he would send his third son, François Ferdinand, Prince de Joinville, to St Helena to bring back Napoleon's remains. Playing the undertaker, which was how Joinville described his mission, made the prince less than enthusiastic about the whole affair, but he too could see the political mileage to be gained from this public act of national reconciliation.[11] It was a risky business. Napoleon back on French soil had the potential to reignite old conflicts between pro- and anti-Bonapartists, as well as adding fuel to conflicts between revolutionaries and monarchists.

There had been a long history of attempts to get Britain to return Napoleon's body to France, dating back to 1821. The first petition to the British government was formulated by General Gourgaud and Colonel Charles Fabvier, a former aide-de-camp to Marmont (who would later become involved in a number of secret conspiracies), and transmitted to the Bourbon monarchy by the Marquis de Lafayette shortly after the demise of the Emperor.[12] On returning to France, Gourgaud wrote letters to Napoleon's mother and to his niece, Stéphanie de Beauharnais, Grand Duchess of Baden, lamenting his passing. 'He is no more!... This man who was more than man, our

Louis-Adolphe Thiers. 1885. Prime minister, 1 March–29 October 1840.

benefactor, our friend, our father … We have lost everything.'[13] He then suggested that their last duty was to 'snatch' his mortal remains from his unworthy enemies, and bring his body back to Rome. 'It is there, in that soil trodden by so many heroes, that the great Napoleon can find repose.' Stéphanie's cousin Eugène de Beauharnais was also supposed to have written to the sovereigns of Europe asking for the return of his stepfather's body.[14] In the summer of 1821, the year of Napoleon's death, any number of pamphlets called for the repatriation of his remains, in the name of 'martial piety' and French national pride.[15] Most of them were addressed to Louis XVIII, and appealed either to his sense of honour or to his clemency. On 15 August 1821, which would have been her son's fifty-second birthday, Letizia wrote (through Bertrand) to Castlereagh, then British foreign secretary, with the same request. She did not receive a response.[16] Montholon and Bertrand, who were in London at the time, also presented a joint request to the prime minister, Lord Liverpool, in September 1821, and again in 1830, when a number of discussions took place in the Chamber of Deputies.[17] By now, it was obvious that the Bourbons would never consider repatriating Napoleon's body. It would have been the equivalent, Louis XVIII is reported to have said, of another landing at Fréjus, a reference to Napoleon's return after the Egyptian campaign, a return that launched his political career.[18]

The question lay dormant for the duration of the Bourbon monarchy, and resurfaced with the advent of the July Monarchy: a new petition in October 1830; another in September 1831 (it ironically met with resistance from Lafayette, the very man who had petitioned to have the body brought back in 1822); three in 1832; six in 1834; four in 1835; six in 1836; four in 1837; two in 1838; and three in 1839.[19] The only year not to see any petitions was 1833. Most of them were debated, if only briefly, in the Chamber and most originated from associations or municipal councils in either Corsica or the Paris region, suggesting that Bonapartist associations were behind them. The rest were from individuals. Many of the petitions suggested that the foot of the Vendôme Column would be an appropriate resting place for Napoleon.[20] The petitions were never seriously considered, although they were treated a little more favourably after the death of Napoleon's son, the Duc de Reichstadt, in July 1832.[21] Even then, they were simply sent to the Council of Ministers, where they became lost in the paperwork.

Apart from the petitions, there was a stream of references to repatriation in prints and novels, plucking at the patriotic heartstrings of Napoleonists throughout Europe.

'BLOWING ON THE SPARKS'

And then Thiers happened along. We can pass over the diplomatic negotiations with Britain to gain access to St Helena.[22] It is worth keeping in mind, however, that the return of Napoleon's remains could not have been carried out without the consent of Britain, and that the diplomatic details were arranged within three days of an official request being made, incredibly fast by any standards. The

British foreign secretary, Lord Palmerston, may have quipped that it was 'a typically French request', but the fact is that the British government was somewhat relieved to have this responsibility taken off its hands.

The news of the British acceptance of the French request allowed the minister of the interior, Charles de Rémusat, to interrupt a debate in the Chamber of Deputies on 12 May 1840 to ask the house for the means to receive Napoleon's remains with dignity on French soil. 'Napoleon was emperor and king; he was the legitimate sovereign of our country ... Napoleon does not however deserve an ordinary king's sepulchre. He needs to reign and exercise command over an enclosure where the soldiers of the *patrie* will be laid to rest, and where those called upon to defend the country will always go to be inspired.'[23] The initial reaction in the Chamber was all that Thiers could have hoped for. 'Our announcement', Thiers wrote to Guizot, 'produced an enormous effect.'[24] One deputy declared that Napoleon's defence of the nation had cost him his crown in 1814 and 1815, and that he was 'national ... right down to his guts'.[25] Dissenting voices did eventually make themselves heard. The poet and writer Alphonse de Lamartine, for example, who was a member of the Chamber and a supporter of the July Monarchy, questioned the decision to remove Napoleon's remains, fearful that time had not calmed the passions that his memory evoked.[26] He concluded that the inscription on the tomb should read simply, 'To Napoleon'. He was attempting to dissociate the cult of Napoleon from Bonapartism.[27] He concluded in a letter to a friend that 'Napoleon's ashes are not extinguished, and they are blowing on the sparks.'[28]

The announcement of the return was greeted with widespread public approval,[29] and generated a plethora of pamphlets, poems, plays, novels, popular prints and engravings with hugely varying political messages that occupied a central place in public discourse for the rest of the year. Some celebrated the cult of Napoleon, while others represented the July Monarchy as the successor to Napoleon.[30] Not surprisingly, between the departure of the *Belle-Poule*, the frigate sent to bring back Napoleon's remains, from Toulon in July 1840 and the transfer of Napoleon's coffin to the chapel of St Jérôme at the Invalides in February 1841, an immense amount of Napoleoniana was produced and distributed. The event even seems to have resulted in an upsurge of the cult in Germany.[31]

The debates generated by this gesture in the press of the day were evidence that the government could not control Napoleon's memory, nor the uses to which it was put.[32] Reactions necessarily varied according to the newspaper's political leanings. At first, the reaction seems to have been so critical that Louis-Philippe is supposed to have had second thoughts.[33] There was, however, a shift in thinking between Rémusat's announcement of the king's decision to bring back Napoleon's remains to the Chamber of Deputies in May and the actual funeral ceremony in December 1840.[34] The newspaper with the largest circulation, the left-wing Le Siècle, declared that there was nothing to fear from the return of Napoleon's remains, that it was not a question of glorifying the imperial regime, which history would have to judge without 'favour or hatred', and that an expression of admiration for the man would honour the French people.[35] The liberal opposition's newspaper, the National, edited by Armand Carrel, objected to the violation of a tomb, and wondered whether the awakening of Napoleon's memory would be seen as 'a bloody accusation' against those in power. 'And so, here is the political significance of this event,' declared the National: 'within, to flatter the national sentiment in order to forget ten years of baseness, without, to tighten the bonds of counter-revolution by pardoning it for all its past.'[36]

The conservative press also had mixed reactions. The Journal des débats, which had been hostile to Napoleon in 1815, objected to Rémusat calling Napoleon a 'legitimate sovereign of France'.[37] The legitimist newspapers railed against Napoleon. The Gazette de France was particularly sarcastic: 'Who will you invite to this festival? If you do invite men who remained loyal to the Emperor, it will be a short list. But it will be long if we invite all those who betrayed him.'[38] It condemned Napoleon, a man it considered to be a 'tyrant' and a 'usurper', and published anti-Napoleonic texts written by Louis-Philippe in 1810, as well as by Chateaubriand and Mme de Staël. Even the Orleanist press found the whole thing 'comical'.[39] By the time Napoleon's remains had reached French soil, however, conservatives had realised his significance for the people and had begun to change tack. They now interpreted him as the incarnation of the national spirit and no longer as a dangerous revolutionary.[40]

E. F.

Mon cher Monsieur, ça ne vous va pas. Napoléon avait la tête carrée et vous l'avez pointue.

Caricature of Louis-Philippe by E.F. trying the hat of Napoleon with the
caption, 'Mon cher Monsieur, ça ne vous va pas. Napoléon avait la tête carrée
et vous l'avez pointue' (My dear Sir, it does not suit you. Napoleon had a
square head while yours is pointy). Note the pear-shaped reflection of Louis-
Philippe in the mirror. The king was often portrayed as a pear king, because
of a caricature made famous by Charles Philipon as early as 1831. Philipon's
caricature of the royal face quickly evolved into a caricature of the entire body.
It reflected the lack of respect felt for the king among large sections of the
public from the outset of his reign.[41]

THE FINAL RESTING PLACE

If certain members of the political elite and the press had reservations about, or were hostile to, the idea of resurrecting Napoleon, this was certainly not how the 'people' welcomed the news that his remains were to be brought back to France. It seems that the enthusiasm for the scheme was widespread. Even regions like Normandy, the site of the bloodiest revolt during the Revolution and hardly keen to express attachment to Napoleon during the Empire, appear to have welcomed the return of Napoleon's remains with enthusiasm.[42] The Chamber of Deputies as well as the ministry of the interior received a number of petitions from both individuals and municipal authorities relating to the return of Napoleon's body. The municipal council of Toulouse asked permission to send a deputation to Paris so that the town would be represented during the ceremonies.[43] A retired non-commissioned officer from Marseilles proposed that the remains of Napoleon should arrive in France at the port of Toulon, so that they could be carried overland to Paris, accompanied by a detachment of veterans from the Egyptian campaign.[44] The town of Saint-Denis asked that Napoleon be interred in the cathedral there, along with the other legitimate sovereigns of France.[45] A certain M. Lisse suggested that Napoleon should be buried on top of the Arc de Triomphe. 'The remains of the man who belongs not to France but to the world should have a shrine outside the usual forms.'[46] M. Estienne proposed the Champ de Mars, 'a site so rich in patriotic memories'. Others preferred the Vendôme Column,[47] the Panthéon,[48] the Place de la Bastille,[49] the Arc de Triomphe,[50] what is today the Place du Trocadéro,[51] the island of Louviers in the middle of the Seine, or the Church of the Madeleine 'amid the people he loved so much'.[52] And of course the Invalides, a retirement home and hospital for veterans.[53]

The decision on the final resting place was important politically. It was a statement about how central Napoleon was to the history of France. It had to be conspicuous, but not so conspicuous that it would become a site of protest. Lamartine, at the behest of the government, headed a parliamentary commission to examine a number of possibilities.[54] The Vendôme Column and the Madeleine were rejected for fear that they would act as a magnet for public demonstrations. Placing

Napoleon in the cathedral at St Denis, the traditional burying ground of the kings and queens of France, would be seen as legitimising the reign. The Arc de Triomphe was too problematic because Napoleon's presence would invariably colour any future military parades. After much debate, the commission finally decided on the Invalides. A conspicuous and prestigious monument, it fulfilled a number of criteria: it had been Napoleon's dying wish to be buried on the banks of the River Seine; the Church of the Invalides was already the home of one of the greatest marshals of France, Henri de la Tour d'Auvergne, Vicomte de Turenne, interred there by Napoleon; and, just as importantly, at that time in the history of Paris the location was relatively unpopulated. Bonapartists were, however, less than enthusiastic. They would have preferred to see the Place Vendôme or the Arc de Triomphe chosen, and thought the Invalides inappropriate.

If petitions to the government can be taken as a sort of nineteenth-century opinion poll,[55] what is the historian supposed to make of them? Are they a measure of the depth and breadth of Bonapartism and its growing popularity? This is possibly the case for individual petitions, but what of those from various communal authorities? Are they simply an expression of a desire to take part in a 'national' commemoration? Napoleon in 1840 was certainly considered a 'national hero' by all but the most extreme legitimists and diehard republicans (which does not mean to say that republicans could not have an ambivalent attitude towards him).[56] By 1840, Bonapartism, liberalism and republicanism had become so blurred it was difficult to make a clear distinction between what had effectively become complementary political ideologies (although by 1834 republicanism had become more focused on what is referred to as the 'social question', the demands of the poor, artisans and an emerging proletariat).[57] As we know, the meaning of Napoleon was intertwined with the legacy of the Hundred Days when he presented himself as a revolutionary in the republican tradition, resulting in what has been dubbed 'philonapoleonism'.[58] A distinction, nevertheless, has to be made between official and popular memories of Napoleon. The official memory, constructed by the Orleanist regime and found in the political rhetoric and in the state-commissioned representations of Napoleon, was devoid of revolutionary significance, a bland, uninspiring version of the man as political reformer. This is in direct contrast with the way in which he evolved in popular memory in opposition to both the Bourbon and Orleanist monarchies.[59] It is evident that the French public did not always accept the image foisted on to them by their political elites.

'AS IF HE WERE ASLEEP': EXHUMATION

The *Belle-Poule* left Toulon on 7 July 1840 and arrived before Jamestown on 7 October.[60] Accompanying the Prince de Joinville were a number of the old faithful, still alive, and all chosen by Thiers: Bertrand, now sixty-seven; Gourgaud, now fifty-seven and just as tetchy about precedence as he ever was; Las Cases' son (now a deputy); and five members of the domestic staff – Saint-Denis, Noverraz, Pierron, Achille Archambault and Coursot. On another corvette was Marchand. Also on board the *Belle-Poule* were the chaplain of the French navy, Abbé Félix Coquereau, Bertrand's young son Arthur and Philippe de Rohan-Chabot, an attaché to the French ambassador to Britain.

The degree to which Napoleonic propaganda had influenced contemporary perceptions can be seen in the way in which the Abbé Coquereau looked upon the island as the *Belle-Poule* weighed anchor. Overcome with sadness he later recalled, 'To us, who were only going there for a few days, to us, who had sought out the island as another promised land, to us, the island seemed horrible; how must it have appeared to him for whom it was a final resting place?'[61] He described with eloquence 'That blackish mass, immobile, whose arrested lines blend into the uniformity of the shadows, the white froth of the waves, surrounding its contours, white ornaments sown on the black marble of the sepulchre; that dry and brittle sound, like the sound of broken bones, pebbles rolled by the waves, the roaring of the sea as grave and monotonous as the voice of the last prayers; all this spoke a funereal language to the soul: it is the revelation of the supreme moment.'[62]

It was as though they had arrived in the Holy Land; they certainly treated the sites of legend with a similar degree of reverence. For Joinville, on the other hand, Jamestown was a 'miserable village'.[63] They walked for about two hours from the town to the valley where

Napoleon was buried; 'we trod the ground on which we could justly engrave the words: Sta viator, heroem calcas [Halt, traveller, beneath lies a hero]'.[64] Joinville uncovered his head, while the abbé took himself off and knelt under a cypress tree to say a prayer. They were all silent for a moment. Bertrand was unable to hide his emotions; his eyes filled with tears, he was breathing heavily and sobs shook his whole body. Bertrand's son, Arthur, appeared to be on the point of fainting. The young Las Cases was also beside himself with grief, 'suffocated by tears'.[65] Gourgaud hid his emotions in an exaggeratedly rigid military posture, although apparently he too could not prevent the tears from spilling down his cheeks. They stood around the grave in silence, and then in a gesture that anyone who has visited a holy site would recognise, they went and gathered whatever souvenirs they could lay their hands on – some grass, a stone, a root, a few leaves from the surrounding trees.[66] Over the next few days, trophy hunters devastated the area, filling bottles with water from the nearby source, taking nothing of true value, but laying bare the weeping willows, wrecking the greenery around the tomb and demolishing the woodwork around the windows at Longwood where Napoleon might have leant against them.[67] They also removed the stonework surrounding the tomb, pieces of the exterior coffin, the flag with which the coffin was covered, even fragments of the solder used on the tin coffin, all divided into a multitude of fragments and distributed as relics.[68]

There were Visitors' Books kept by the French guardian at the tomb, 'full of names and nonsense' written by the thousands of tourists in almost every European language who came to see the grave every year.[69] One can find in these books a mixture of silly remarks, bad rhymes, worse rhymes – 'Captain Tweadie and his party / Came to the Tomb of Bonapart-e' – and plenty of bitter invective against England and the English. How many of those visitors would have bent down to kiss the tombstone, and how many would have spat on it, is impossible to say. The French in Joinville's party, however, were in reverent mood. From the tomb they went on to Longwood and were shocked to discover the dilapidated state into which it had fallen. The gardens had long since gone and the house was being used as a stable. The interior walls were covered with graffiti, most of them anti-English, written by some of the French who had made the pilgrimage to the island since Napoleon's death.[70] In what had once served as the billiard room, someone had written on the wall a line from a 1759 poem by the Bishop of Chester and London, Beilby Porteus, 'One murder makes a villain, millions a hero.' And underneath it someone (probably French) had scrawled, 'You lie – you goddam Englishmans.'[71] Coquereau noted other examples: 'I loved you terribly when you were alive, I love you even more now that you're dead. Courtois, of the 27th'; or this, 'After being grenadier of the Guard, Michel Robert became a sailor on "The Amelia" in order to salute the last dwelling place of his little corporal. Adieu!'[72]

The impression they received on reaching the room in which Napoleon had spent most of his time, however, shocked them even more. Marchand opened a door and said, ' "Here is the bedroom and the study of Napoleon." We quickly entered and were stupefied: we were in the stables ... yes, the stables with their mangers and their muck; the muck lay where it had dropped; there stood the manger where he wrote and dictated about his campaigns in Italy and Egypt.' In their minds, of course, Longwood was something that should have been preserved, 'like a precious remnant ... a legacy transmitted for ever to the sons of the nation, as the most glorious trophy of his annals'.[73]

Preparations for the exhumation went ahead and were carried out on the night of 14–15 October, so that the coffin would be ready for opening by morning, exactly twenty-five years after Napoleon had arrived on the island. At midnight all the interested parties were huddled around the iron railing in their long overcoats, the fog pierced by a pale light thrown out by oil lamps.[74] It took the rest of the night to dig away the earth; it took another few hours to uncover the slab and the cement that had been placed over the coffin.

As the moment approached when the coffin would be revealed, a few of the workers got carried away and started to speak loudly among themselves. They were called to order by the commander of the Royal Engineers, Captain Alexander, who reminded them that only six inches remained between them and the coffin of Napoleon. By the time the slab had been lifted off with ropes and pulleys, it was 9.30 in the morning. Another hour, and the coffin itself was lifted out of the tomb and, in the pouring rain, was carried by twelve

British soldiers to a nearby marquee that had been set up to receive it. After some difficulty opening the 'secret' lock to the coffin made of ebony, they could now proceed with revealing Napoleon's remains to the world. 'The most profound silence reigned within the enclosure where alone those who had been designated were present. And as the work progressed, it took on a more serious and more religious character.'[75] It was by now a quarter past twelve. They had been there for twelve hours; three of the caskets had been taken off so that the fourth and final one was about to be revealed.

'All eyes were fixed on the coffin, everyone was holding their breath. Only those who were present at this scene, for whom the Emperor was everything, can imagine the bearing of the assistants and the extraordinary effect produced on the faces awaiting the moment when the Emperor would be uncovered.'[76] Once the final lid had been removed, a white covering was seen to cover the length of the body. Initially attached to the underside of the lid, the light cushion in white satin was carefully removed, beginning at the feet. 'Eyes filled with tears, hearts beat, breathing was hurried. The moment was sublime.'[77] Napoleon was there, recognisable, in his uniform with his decorations, 'as if he were asleep'.[78] A doctor present, Rémy Guillard, later described how he had 'uncovered the body of Napoleon, which [he] immediately recognised, so well was it preserved, so much did his head have truth in its expression … The hands left nothing to be desired; not the slightest alteration. If the joints had lost their movement, the skin appeared to have retained the particular colour that belongs only to life.'[79] Gourgaud too later told of the moment when Napoleon's shroud was pulled to one side. 'Everything appeared perfectly preserved … His hat reposed on his thighs. The doctor touched the hands, which appeared very good, although a little swollen … The head, with the exception of the nose, which seems to have been compressed by the coffin, was in perfect condition … The doctor lightly felt the skin on his head and declared that he had been mummified.'[80]

The only irregular feature was the slight indent that had been made on the nose, compressed somewhat by the coffin's inner lining, although the Abbé Coquereau also reported that his nails were elongated.[81] Several sobbed openly 'in a convulsive manner'. Others were sombre. Tears streamed down the faces of all those present.[82] Gourgaud insisted that this was not an experience that could be shared by all. In a rather solipsistic declaration, he claimed, 'One had to have loved the emperor like me to understand all that occurred in my soul when Dr. Guillard let us see, through floods of tears, the mortal remains of our hero.'[83] There was talk of taking the body out of its coffin in order to examine it. It was at that moment that Gourgaud got angry, according to his own account, and insisted that to leave the coffin open any longer was to show a lack of respect for Napoleon's remains and that each minute the coffin remained exposed to the air risked destroying what had been conserved.[84]

An unblemished corpse – an intact body – was the stuff of miracles,[85] and must have been an eerie sight to those who witnessed it. In the popular imagination, Napoleon's body was thus placed on the same level as certain Catholic saints whose bodies had supposedly been preserved from decomposition. Napoleon's disinterred and intact body helped complete his transformation into a kind of secular saint, and that is how he was portrayed in the iconography of the day.[86] In death as in life his body came to have a power of its own. In his *Memoirs from Beyond the Grave*, Chateaubriand cited the Abbé Coquereau at some length.[87] Bonapartists were quick to make political capital of it. Popular prints of the event resembled more a resurrection than an exhumation.

At the time, the fact that Napoleon's body was intact was for many proof of his moral probity,[88] although it was only revealed very briefly before the coffin was closed up again. When news of the intact body reached Paris months later, it resulted in an outpouring of imagery, textual and visual, as people came to grips with the event.[89]

How do we get from Napoleon's death in 1821 to his (metaphorical) resurrection in 1840? The connection is by no means linear. There was an obvious gap between these images, with their evident Messianic quality, and those who believed Napoleon to have mystic powers.[90] Admittedly, this kind of belief was the exception to the rule, but it evolved out of the imagery of Napoleon as Saviour.[91] There is nothing terribly unusual in this. Many political figures in French history – from Louis XIV to Marat, the list is long – have been associated with Christ. Indeed, there was a tradition of Christian reverence for saints and martyrs that was part of the cult of the great man in eighteenth-century France.[92]

People consequently projected Christ-like qualities on to Napoleon. Claire de Rémusat, a close friend of Josephine's, remarked that some believed Napoleon had only to plan a hunt or a military review for the sun to appear on that day. Every time it happened, people made a fuss about it, forgetting about the days when it rained or when the weather was otherwise bad.[93] During the Empire, stories circulated about how Napoleon had miraculously escaped being killed in combat,[94] stories that were embroidered and elaborated on under the Bourbons.[95] Under the Bourbons, those analogies continued, especially after the death of Napoleon, so that, for Bonapartists at least, the former Emperor came to incarnate a spiritual and divine being.[96]

Jean-Dominique-Etienne Canu, *Violettes du 20 mars 1815.* 1815. Coloured engraving. If one looks hard enough, one can make out in the blank spaces next to the flowers the supposed profiles of Napoleon, Marie-Louise and the King of Rome. Napoleon's supporters wore the violet not only as a sign of loyalty to the Emperor, but in opposition to the Bourbon fleur de lys. The period saw not just a struggle between different flags, but also a struggle between different floral emblems that continued well into the 1820s and 1830s.[5]

Horace Vernet, *Napoleon's Tomb.* 1821. Oil on canvas. His wife and children embrace a distraught Bertrand. Montholon stands over him, covering his face in grief. On the grave are placed Napoleon's hat and sword, while chains lie broken beside it, no doubt representing Napoleon–Prometheus finding freedom in death. To the right and in the background stand the ghosts of some of the officers and men who fought with him. The remains of a shipwreck – possibly symbolizing the French state, or Napoleon's ship of fate dashed against the rocks – are in the foreground and on a plank are inscribed his most important battles ('Rivoli, Piramides [sic], Marengo, Austerlitz, Jena, Wagram, Moskova, Montmirail, Ligny, Wat…'). The anchor, also in the foreground, is a traditional symbol of hope and resurrection.

François Joseph Sandmann, *Napoléon à Sainte-Hélène*. 1820. Watercolour. Such portraits show a man condemned to inaction, introspection and endless gazing out to the sea, something that Napoleon never did but which became an iconic image of his captivity and which can be found in some of the pamphlet literature of the day.[6] It coincided with the Romantic notion of the solitary figure, misunderstood, pitted against society. It also corresponded to the biblical notion of exile and return. Napoleon is always portrayed wearing a uniform, usually the green and white uniform of a colonel of the Chasseurs à cheval, which he habitually wore during the Empire. On St Helena, however, once ensconced in Longwood, he renounced wearing the uniform for civilian clothes.

Napoléon Ier en planteur à Sainte-Hélène (Napoleon I as cultivator on St Helena). 1825. Lithograph. An example of the contemplative pose in an outdoor setting that was meant to signify genius and ambition.

Pipe depicting Napoleon. Date unknown. Porcelain, bone and horn. 182cm long.

Cane with ivory head. Date unknown. Wood, metal and ivory. 900cm long. The head of the cane is meant to represent Napoleon in profile. This kind of object was recognized among Napoleonists.

Gisant de Napoléon Ier (Napoleon I Recumbent). Snuff box. According to one Napoleonist belief, on 5 May, the anniversary of Napoleon's death, and again on 15 August, the anniversary of his birth, the sun would appear through the axis of the Arc de Triomphe, as illustrated on this snuff box made in 1840, at the time of the return of Napoleon's remains to France.[7]

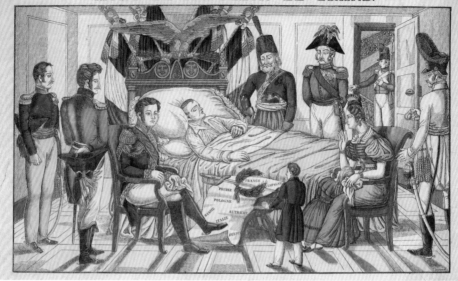

François Georgin, *Mort de Napoleon-le-Grand*. 1833. Coloured woodblock print. Military representatives of all the countries of Europe pay homage to Napoleon – there is even what looks like a Cossack – and call for the erection of a monument to his memory, the Vendôme Column.

Engraving by Jean-Baptiste Thiébault after a drawing by François Georgin, *Apothéose de Napoléon* (Apotheosis of Napoleon). 1835. Coloured woodblock print. Napoleon is being recognized as *the* greatest commander, welcomed into the heavens by the likes of Alexander the Great, Caesar and Frederick the Great on the right, and revolutionary generals like Hoche, Kléber and Desaix on the left. The 'apotheosis' was a trope often used in the pamphlet literature of the day, especially around the time of Napoleon's death in 1821,[8] which imbued him with a sacred character (not for the first time), as well as rendering a definitive historical assessment.

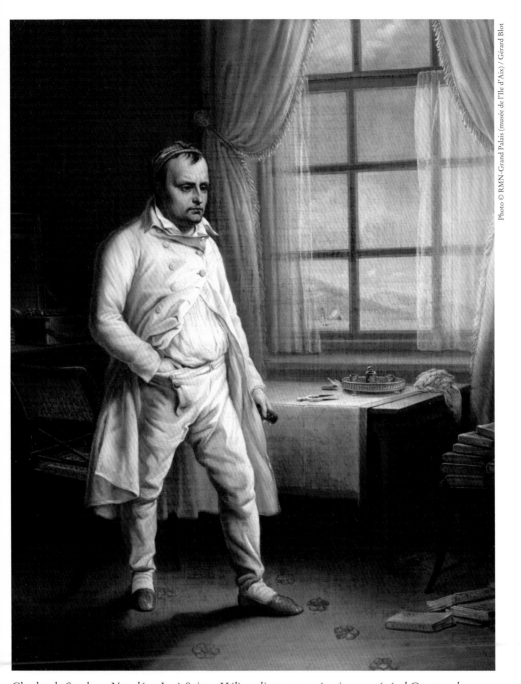

Charles de Steuben, *Napoléon Ier à Sainte-Hélène dictant ses mémoires au général Gourgaud*. Between 1825 and 1830. Oil on canvas. This is a study for a larger painting that was meant to portray General Gourgaud taking dictation for Napoleon. In later engravings of the study, Gourgaud is placed to the right, sitting at the desk taking notes. It is probably the most famous depiction of the creation of the Napoleonic gospels.

Petite boîte contenant un morceau du cercueil de l'empereur Napoléon Ier (Small box containing a piece of the Emperor Napoleon's coffin). 1840. Brought back from St Helena by General Bertrand.

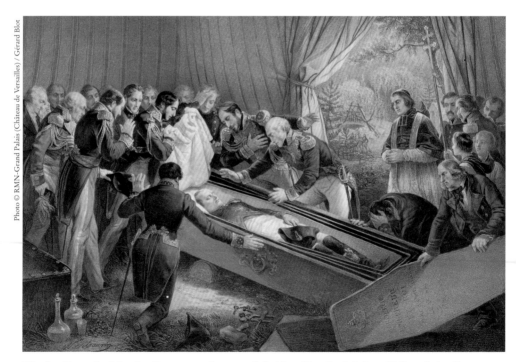

Nicolas-Eustache Maurin, *Ouverture du cercueil de Napoléon Ier à Sainte-Hélène, le jeudi 15 Octobre 1840* (Opening of Napoleon 1's coffin on St Helena, Thursday 15 October 1840). Coloured lithograph.

Jean Pierre Marie Jazet, after Horace Vernet, *Napoléon sortant de son tombeau* (Napoleon emerging from his tomb). 1840. Aquatint. The painting by Vernet has been lost. Note the laurel around his head, as well as the aura behind it, which transforms him into a saint-like, if not Christ-like, figure rising from the tomb, as his hand lightly pushes aside his own tombstone. The supernatural moment is marked by the wind whipping though the willow trees.[9] Note, too, that he is holding what appears to be an olive branch, the universal symbol of peace, which may be intended to evoke a comparison with Christ as peacemaker. Another parallel may be that a resurrected Napoleon represents the promise of a resurrected nation.

Translation des cendres de l'Empereur Napoléon aux Invalides (Transfer of the remains of the Emperor Napoleon to the Invalides). 1840. Engraving.

Louis Tullius Joachim Visconti, *Tombeau de l'empereur Napoléon Ier.*

The Second Coming

THE RETURN OF THE MESSIAH

In 1840, the year of the return of Napoleon's remains to France, thirteen or fourteen 'Napoleons' were admitted to the insane asylum at Bicêtre in the south of Paris.[1] One can imagine that each of them considered the others to be mad. Of course, there had been people suffering from this kind of delusion even while he was still alive. In 1818, at least five people were admitted to Charenton hospital believing they were Napoleon.[2] Now, however, Napoleon was being caricatured, right down to his temperament — 'imperial', proud, haughty, abrupt, tyrannical, capricious, choleric.[3] The men (and one woman that we know of) who believed they were Napoleon always fit the same profile: they took themselves seriously, they gave orders and they demanded loyalty; in return they treated people with disdain.

The 'Napoleons' of Bicêtre, in a world of their own, probably did not react to the arrival of Napoleon's remains in France. On 30 November 1840, the *Belle-Poule* cast anchor in the roads of Cherbourg harbour. The political climate it had left behind on its departure in July was very different from the one that greeted it on its return. Two events in particular – a diplomatic crisis in the Middle East and a thwarted coup by Napoleon's nephew, Louis-Napoleon Bonaparte – had resulted in a dramatic change in public opinion. There was much more belligerence towards Britain, and much more sympathy for the memory of Napoleon as conqueror who had withstood the coalition forces.[4]

Relations between France and Britain had deteriorated over events in the Middle East to such an extent that the two countries looked like going to war. The British foreign secretary, Lord Palmerston, had organised a treaty between Britain, Russia, Prussia and Austria to threaten France's ally in Egypt, Pasha Mehemet Ali. It smacked of the coalition that had toppled Napoleon in 1814 and 1815, and reawakened the country's Anglophobia, already fuelled by memories of Napoleon and the regime's decision to bring back his body.[5] Thiers' brand of confrontational diplomacy – he threatened to go to war with Britain – displeased Louis-Philippe, but it found widespread support across the political spectrum. Hundreds of thousands of reserves were called up to active duty, an emergency war credit was established, and work began on fortifications around Paris.[6] This sabre-rattling led to what can only be described as a sort of war fever taking hold of public opinion in France. The crisis came to a head when Louis-Philippe, fearful that the country was headed towards war, manipulated Thiers' resignation in October and replaced his government with a more moderate ministry headed by Marshal Nicolas Soult and François Guizot.

On top of this, Louis-Napoleon attempted another (his second) coup against the government when he landed at Boulogne-sur-Mer in northern France on 6 August with a band of followers, including the Comte de Montholon.[7] The coup, a rather pathetic imitation of his uncle's landing in the south of France in 1814, was soon foiled – the police had advance knowledge of it – and Louis-Napoleon was imprisoned for life in the fortress of Ham. It made Louis-Philippe less inclined than ever to make Napoleon's funeral the occasion for a national celebration, afraid as he was that it would become the occasion for a pro-Bonapartist demonstration. The new government was now faced with the problem of organising a funeral in such a way that Napoleon could be laid to rest without exacerbating the already heightened militarism of the Parisian crowds.[8] It was no longer a matter of using the event so that Napoleon's glory would shine on the monarchy; rather it had become imperative to keep things low key so as not to inflame pro-war emotions and rhetoric. That is probably why some cynics saw the decision to bring back Napoleon's remains as an attempt to bury him once and for all, metaphorically as well as literally, in order to efface his memory.[9]

LIMITING POPULAR PARTICIPATION

From the start, then, there was bound to be a disjuncture between the Napoleon the July Monarchy wanted to present to the French people and the multiple popular imaginings of him. The July Monarchy certainly did its best to downplay the event and minimise public participation as much as possible – probably motivated by fear of the crowd and its potential to turn violent – and discouraged any initiatives by municipalities to arrange ceremonies around the coffin.[10] If the river was chosen to transport the coffin from Cherbourg to Paris – although Cherbourg too had to petition to be designated the port of arrival[11] – it was because it was the fastest route to Paris and would, it was hoped, discourage public demonstrations of enthusiasm.[12] Instructions sent to prefects and municipal authorities made it clear that there was to be no communication of any kind between the inhabitants of the region and the fluvial convoy. The minister of the interior, Tanneguy Duchâtel, wrote to the prefect of the Eure: 'Care must be taken that this great event, which awakens memories and excites the passions, is not the cause or pretext of any criminal demonstration.'[13] When the convoy anchored for the night – at the towns of Havre, Val-de-la-Haye, Pont de l'Arche, La Roche-Guyon, Vernon, Mantes and Maisons – measures were taken to ensure that the barge was inaccessible to the public. No boats were allowed to leave their moorings to follow the catafalque, or to approach it. The firing of guns was prohibited, and no one was allowed to walk in front of the National Guard forming the guard of honour along the river.[14] Some local authorities were not even forewarned of the arrival of the convoy or were caught unawares as the boat sped ahead of schedule and passed through villages up to a day earlier than expected. This was the case for Meulan. The mayor vented his displeasure in a letter addressed to the prefect and published in the newspaper *Le Siècle*.[15] What reason, he asked, would the government have in treating people so poorly who had waited so long to see the convoy pass. 'That is what people ask, and I respond, "I do not know."' He resigned his position.

It was obvious to most authorities in localities in the path of the convoy that it would attract large numbers of people. For the sub-prefects, caught between their hierarchical superiors and the local populations, it became a question not of discouraging but rather of controlling these crowds so that they did not get out of hand. That was made more difficult in that no precise governmental instructions were given regarding the containment of crowds, or indeed on how the passing of the convoy was to be marked by the local authorities. It was left to individual prefects, sub-prefects and mayors to deal with the event as best they could. It speaks volumes about the naivety of the government or its unwillingness to admit to itself the extent of the popular enthusiasm surrounding the return of the remains. As a result, the authorities were time and again forced to give way in the face of the enthusiasm to organise, if not a ceremony, then at least decorations.

At Cherbourg, for example, the coffin was kept on board the ship until 3 December. It was only three days after landing that the local population was allowed to file past the coffin, but even then visiting times were restricted to three hours a day (between one and four o'clock), and individuals were admitted on board only if they were dressed in either a uniform or a frock coat. The municipality of Cherbourg issued 30,000 authorisations,[16] but the number of people who viewed the coffin over a six-day period was estimated at 60,000–80,000.[17] At the foot of the coffin they laid funeral wreaths, bouquets of flowers and more than 5,000 inscriptions. The crowds came from all the surrounding departments, and were prepared to wait hours in the cold weather for the privilege of gaining access to the *Belle-Poule*. And on 8 December, when the coffin was transferred from the *Belle-Poule* to the steamship *Normandie* to take it to the River Seine and part of the way to Paris, thousands of people witnessed the scene.

From Rouen, the coffin was to be towed to Courbevoie just outside Paris, on a funeral barge made for the occasion. During the trip upriver, crowds gathered along the banks of the Seine – people who had come from as far as thirty kilometres away[18] – including veterans of the Grande Armée who had donned their old uniforms for the occasion. This in itself was an act of defiance against the regime, since it was forbidden to display what were considered to be seditious or prohibited emblems. Women along the banks recited the rosary, old men knelt and prayed, while children ran along the bank trying to keep up with the convoy.[19] In the rest of the region, 'patriots' took the initiative and arranged ceremonies to celebrate the return without permission from the authorities. This was done in the village of Coutron, near Nantes, where a banquet was held for around forty people, presided over by a life-size statue of Napoleon.[20] Jean Eraud, a veteran of the Old Guard, was reportedly so moved on seeing the statue that he fainted. Similarly, the inhabitants of Bailly-en-Rivière, near Dieppe, celebrated a funeral service and then organised a banquet where 'La Marseillaise' and 'other songs in honour of Napoleon' were sung. Interestingly, when someone suggested singing 'La Parisienne', composed in 1830 in homage to the July Revolution, the request was greeted with silence.[21] The closer the coffin got to Paris, the larger the crowds seemed to get. In the meantime, an enormous crowd gathered to witness a dress rehearsal of the funeral procession in Paris on Thursday 10 December.[22]

The coffin was transferred from the *Normandie* to the steamboat *Dorade* at Val-de-la-Haye, a dozen or so kilometres from Rouen, where the municipal authorities were frustrated to find that they could not change the name of the central square, Place Royale, back to its original name, Place Napoléon – banned under the Bourbons.[23] Nor could they obtain permission for the convoy to stop at their town, despite a petition with more than 4,000 signatures.[24] The only compromise they managed to extract from the authorities, perhaps worried that things could turn ugly, was that the *Dorade* would remain immobile for about two hours in the heart of the town, although it did not weigh anchor.[25] Obliged to accept this offer, the city authorities attempted to make up for their disappointment by organising a ceremony and constructing a triumphal arch more than twenty-seven metres high on the bridge for the convoy to pass under.

It is possible that the government was anxious to reserve the honour of welcoming Napoleon's remains for the capital and its sovereign, but, as already suggested, it is much more likely that it was afraid that the enthusiasm such a ceremony might engender could get out of hand.[26] One need only look at some of the emotive and in some cases impassioned articles in the local press to realise how easily this could have happened. If most of the crowd at Rouen 'pensive and collected involuntarily maintained a solemn and religious silence', students of the Royal College of Rouen cried out 'Vive l'Empereur!'[27] As the flotilla passed by, some people used the occasion to express their feelings towards the House of Orleans. The reactions varied enormously, from those who refused to acknowledge the boat carrying the Prince de Joinville, which followed behind the *Dorade*, to others crying out 'Vive le Roi!' or 'Vive la famille royale!', sentiments that were hardly surprising given the region that the flotilla was passing through.[28] As one mayor put it, 'One could not be more royalist, even before the remains of the Emperor.'[29]

READING THE CROWD

In Paris too the funeral procession was strictly controlled and highly choreographed, but the government could not prevent a large show of spectators turning out, even though it chose to hold the procession on a Tuesday (Sunday was avoided in an attempt to reduce the numbers attending) and refused to declare it a public holiday. For the last week the people of Paris had been following the progress of the convoy along the Seine in their newspapers, as they had the voyage of the *Belle-Poule* from St Helena. Two weeks before the procession, reports had reached Paris of the opening of Napoleon's tomb on St Helena, and the remarkable news that his body was still intact.[30] It fed into a climate of expectation and excitement, especially among Bonapartists, for whom Napoleon's body now took on a mystical quality and itself became a sacred relic. A couple of days before the funeral procession, the *Journal des débats* expressed the hope that 'the spirit of faction ... would retreat before the reproach that would cover it in the eyes of the French people by trying to make the coffin an instrument of disorder and division'.[31] It was wishful thinking; the exact opposite was to transpire.

On the morning of the funeral procession, horse-drawn buses called *chocolats* or *béarnaises* according to their colour, and carrying placards announcing the 'Funérailles de Napoléon aux Invalides', transported thousands of people from the *banlieues* into the centre of Paris.[32] The new railway of Saint-Germain carried more than 20,000 people into the city, beginning as early as the eve of the procession, Monday 14 December.[33] Others walked several kilometres to take up a place along the route in order to see Napoleon's coffin pass by. The procession was to run from Courbevoie on the banks of the Seine, where a vast Greco-Roman temple had been temporarily built to house the coffin overnight, down the Avenue de Neuilly, across the bridge at Neuilly to the Arc de Triomphe and down the Avenue des Champs-Elysées. From there it would cross the Place de la Concorde, over the bridge and along the Quai d'Orsay, and then down the esplanade, where seating was by ticket only, until it reached the Invalides. Some had gathered along the route the preceding evening, in spite of temperatures of minus 14 degrees centigrade and snow completely covering the ground.[34]

When the coffin containing the remains of Napoleon arrived in Courbevoie on the morning of 14 December 1840, hundreds of survivors of the Grand Armée were there to greet its arrival (hundreds of thousands of the old soldiers were still alive in 1840), dressed in their fading uniforms, wrapped in their cloaks and gathered around fires on this cold winter's day. They most likely reminisced about the times they had once stood around their bivouacs in just the same poses. Surviving dignitaries of the Empire came to pay their respects, including Marshal Soult who, it was reported, expressed a 'painful emotion'.[35]

The coffin was to be transported to its final resting place at the Church of the Invalides by a massive chariot that had been built especially for the occasion. Ten metres long and just as high (about three storeys), five metres wide and covered with allegorical figures, it looked more like a monument on wheels than a funeral carriage. Fourteen plaster figures symbolising imperial victories held aloft a shield on which lay an empty coffin. The coffin containing Napoleon's remains was on the bottom level of the funeral chariot, out of sight. Admittedly, it was probably too heavy to be placed on top, but the fact that the coffin was hidden from view led people like Victor Hugo to speculate that the reason was the July Monarchy's ambivalent attitude towards Napoleon and the return of his remains.[36]

At the stroke of midday on Tuesday 15 December, a twenty-one-cannon salute signalled the departure of the procession. The funeral chariot was draped in black crepe and violet velour adorned with golden bees, the emblem of the Empire. The monument was drawn by sixteen horses, also caparisoned in violet, and held by valets dressed in the gold and green of the imperial livery. The cortège was preceded by a battle horse with the saddle and harness Napoleon had used at Marengo. Curiously, according to press reports, many in the crowd believed it to be Napoleon's horse, Marengo, who had died of old age in 1831.[37] Eighty-seven officers on horseback carried flags inscribed with the names of the eighty-six French departments, plus Algeria. The 400 sailors of the *Belle-Poule* flanked the chariot in ranks of two, followed by former aides-de-camp and civil and military officers from the Emperor's Household.

Who was allowed to march in Napoleon's shadow, and who was not, was a decision the government had carefully thought through. The people were never encouraged to do anything other than look on from a distance. They were not permitted to follow the funeral chariot, as would have been the case if it had been a civil funeral. The July Monarchy no doubt desired the unanimity of the people, but only on condition that they did not encroach on the representational space Napoleon and the procession had been accorded. A number of corporate bodies had petitioned to take part in the procession, but they had all been refused, as had former veterans and dignitaries of the Empire. Imperial veterans, moreover, were excluded from the official procession, indicating the ambivalence of the July Monarchy towards them.[38] Nevertheless, various groups attempted to force their way into the procession; these included veterans, for what might be called spiritual reasons, and a group of workers, for political reasons. The veterans of the Grande Armée who had bivouacked at Courbevoie, around 400 in all, successfully infiltrated the procession, although their passage was blocked once they reached the gates of the Invalides.[39] According to reports, the crowd's responses to the veterans ranged from mockery to veneration.[40] The Duchesse de Dino, Charles-Maurice de Talleyrand's lover and companion, believed that the only thing the ceremony proved was that there were no Bonapartists in France.[41]

Although they had instigated the whole affair, the only member of the House of Orleans to participate in the ceremony was the Prince de Joinville. There were no government officials or ministers, no members of either the Chamber of Peers or the Chamber of Deputies, or any other government institution. There were a number of possible reasons for this: perhaps the government realised how unpopular it was and did not want to risk exposing itself to popular ire, but at the same time it was trying both to exploit and to distance itself from the memory of Napoleon.[42] This is probably why no surviving members of the Bonaparte family had been invited. Nor was the army present in the procession in any great numbers. The National Guard, a sort of middle-class militia, replaced the army, although the government weaned out individuals it feared might engineer some sort of 'patriotic demonstration'.[43]

Between 700,000 and a million people turned out for the occasion,[44] many of whom may have had to sacrifice a day's wage and perhaps disobey their employers to attend. The reasons for their attendance were no doubt as varied as the individuals in the crowd. Of course, some people wanted to be seen in public, others fancied taking a day off and having some fun, and others again were keen to seize the opportunity to express their political views. In this respect, the crowds that belonged to this, the largest funeral procession in nineteenth-century France (until it was surpassed, in sheer numbers, by Victor Hugo's in 1885), were not just onlookers. They were also agents of political discourse that found expression in how they behaved and what they said.

Gauging the mood of the crowd on that day, however, is no easy thing, not least because the secret police reports for this period no longer exist. Historians usually associate the destruction of these documents with the burning of the prefecture of police during the Commune in 1871, but that is only partially correct. During the Second Empire of 1852–70 many archives were simply thrown out by bureaucrats indifferent to their potential historical value.[45] In order to understand how the funeral procession was received and interpreted by contemporaries, it is therefore necessary to rely on other sources: newspaper accounts, pamphlets, brochures and memoirs.

One need only consider the types of things that people cried out as the funeral procession passed by to understand just how contested and ambiguous was this ceremony. At Courbevoie, as soon as the coffin had been placed on the triumphal chariot by sailors from

the *Belle-Poule*, students started to sing 'La Marseillaise', taken up
by the crowd. (The song that is now the national anthem had been
banned under the Bourbons but was allowed again in 1830. If singing 'La Marseillaise' was no longer seditious, it was still considered a radical act. In the second half of 1840, as the foreign political
situation deteriorated, 'La Marseillaise' made a comeback and was
sung by 'patriots' all over France.)[46] Shouts of 'Vive l'Empereur!'
could be heard along most of the route, as could shouts of 'A bas
Guizot! Mort aux hommes de Gand!' ('Down with Guizot! Death
to the men of Ghent' – a reference to those who fled to Ghent with
Louis XVIII during the Hundred Days), and 'A bas le complice
de Dumouriez!' ('Down with the accomplice of Dumouriez' – a
pointed reference to the king who, along with General Charles-
François Dumouriez, fled France in 1793 during the Revolution).[47]
Criticism of the government became more vociferous at certain
points of the procession, particularly near imperial or revolutionary monuments. By the time the funeral chariot had passed through
the Arc de Triomphe, the Napoleonic monument par excellence, the
atmosphere in the crowd had become decidedly hostile. Here, cries
of 'A bas Guizot!,' 'A bas les Anglais!,' 'A bas les étrangers!' and 'A
bas les ministres!' could be heard. There were a few shouts of 'Vive
le Roi!', but when they did occur they unleashed renewed vitriol
against the government.[48] One newspaper asserted that eight out
of the twelve regiments of the National Guard had manifested dis-
tinctly pro-Bonapartist sentiments.[49] On the Place de la Concorde,
a revolutionary site – for it was there that the guillotine had been
erected during the Terror – fifty or so workers in smocks attempted
to force their way into the procession singing 'La Marseillaise' and
shouting 'A bas Guizot!', but they were soon ejected by troops
forming the guard of honour.[50] After the procession, as Victor Hugo
walked back up the Champs-Elysées, he was passed by people from
the working classes shouting, 'Vive mon grand Napoléon! Vive mon
vieux Napoléon!' (Long live the great Napoleon! Long live my old
Napoleon).[51]

Towards the end of the procession, as it neared the Invalides,
the chariot moved through the esplanade lined with seating that
was accessible by ticket only; there are no reports of political cries

Victor Adam, *Entrée du convoi de Napoléon à Paris, sous l'Arc de Triomphe de l'Etoile, le 15 Décembre 1840* (Entry of Napoleon's convoy into Paris, under the Arc de Triomphe). Lithograph. The top of the Arc was adorned with a huge Napoleon in coronation robes, flanked with allegorical figures. Victor Hugo somewhat scathingly remarked that 'It's a genuine stage set: from the Neuilly side the Emperor, the Glories, the Renowns are nothing more than roughly cut-out scenery flats.'[52] The crowd at this particular point of the procession is portrayed as an amorphous, anonymous mass.

coming from this part of the procession. Not surprisingly, people with connections, or people who wanted to be seen, avidly sought these seats.[53] The government supposedly received 500,000 requests for admittance to the interior of the Invalides.[54] The avenue was lined with thirty-two statues, each of them five metres high made of plaster, papier-mâché and wood, representing a selection of figures from French history.[55] Among them were Clovis, Charles Martel, Charlemagne, Philippe Auguste, Joan of Arc, Louis XIV and Henry IV, along with a number of Napoleonic marshals and generals such as Desaix, Kléber, Masséna and Mortier (who had died in an assassination attempt against Louis-Philippe five years previously). There was, interestingly, also a statue of the Duc d'Enghien whom Napoleon had executed in 1804.[56] Between the statues were columns on which were inscribed the names of victorious Napoleonic battles. The intention was clear: to assimilate Napoleonic history into the history of France, to normalise it in some respects, to position Napoleon as one in a long line of distinguished figures dating back to pre-medieval times.[57]

THE MEANING OF THE PROCESSION

From the moment it began its long procession towards the Invalides, the funeral chariot was transformed into a slow-moving commemorative site, the focal point for the crowds.[58] As with most rituals of this nature,[59] the whole point of the funeral as commemoration, along with the later construction of a permanent mausoleum to Napoleon, was to preserve the country's social and political cohesion, and in this particular instance to demonstrate that Napoleon was no longer a threat to the political order. For the vast majority of onlookers, however, this transient commemorative site elicited multiple meanings: it was a site of mourning for those who had loved Napoleon and for those who had fought for him; it was a site of national commemoration for those who bought into the regime's exploitation of his memory; and it was a site of contesting political ideologies for those who used the occasion to express discontent with the government and its policies. In any event, the presence of a vast crowd did not so much legitimate the July Monarchy as legitimate Napoleon's memory.[60]

The newspapers of the day reported the event according to their own political leanings. It is nevertheless interesting to note that a number of newspapers, like *Le Siècle*, attempted to downplay the opposition by pointing out that it was directed against the government and not the House of Orleans.[61] The *Gazette de France* remarked that 'no hope can come out of a tomb', and that while cries of 'Vive l'Empereur' might have been heard at Neuilly, the rest of the Parisian populace remained silent.[62] The newspaper *Le Constitutionnel*, which was close to Thiers, reported that large numbers of the National Guard were heard shouting 'A bas les traîtres! A bas les lâches! A bas les traîtres de 1815!' (Down with the traitors! Down with the cowards! Down with the traitors of 1815!).[63] On the other hand, the *Journal des débats*, close to the government, claimed that calm had reigned among the crowds during the procession, apart from 'a small number of powerless voices obeying the provocations of anarchist broadsheets'.[64] Louis-Philippe, the newspaper concluded, should be lauded for taking the initiative in bringing about 'this great act of national reparation'. The legitimist *La Presse* made no mention of dissenting voices at all, and claimed that the 'violent efforts of false patriots' had come to naught.[65] The *Quotidienne*, which referred to the 'double physiognomy' of the people and power, argued that the government was as incapable of receiving Napoleon as it was of understanding him.[66] An article in the *Atelier*, a working-class newspaper, likened the procession to a 'prisoner of war' being escorted, and accused the regime of a 'hypocritical homage'.[67]

The procession was not only an occasion for current political tensions to be played out, it was also one for individuals to recall and reflect on what Napoleon meant for them. That is no doubt why the *Journal de Rouen* invited its readers to 'withdraw into themselves' and to 'meditate on the emotions' they had felt as the coffin passed by.[68] It is, however, impossible to know with any degree of accuracy what proportion of the crowd was hostile to the government, how many were touched by the sight of the coffin and the memory of Napoleon – the theatricality of the procession no doubt lent itself to a certain emotional response – or how many were simply indifferent. Of course it is possible that individuals experienced a mixture of all of these feelings. Eyewitness accounts describe the emotion of the 'common people'.[69] At least one witness saw part of the crowd 'breaking down and sob' when the funeral chariot approached, while women made the sign of the cross 'as if God had come down from Calvary and was about to be resurrected before them'.[70] It is unfortunate that these accounts do not tell us who these people were or how old they were, in a crowd in which two-thirds would have been too young to have experienced Napoleon and the Empire. For those old enough, they may have reviled the name in 1814 or in 1815, but they had now forgotten how much they had once hated him.

The 'common people' were not the only ones to be moved by the spectacle. Heine, who was living in Paris at the time, wrote in 'Germany: A Winter's Tale', 'I wept that day. I could not keep / the tears in my eyes from welling / to hear the lost cry of Vive l'Empereur! / pathetically swelling.'[71] Heine wrote of the younger generation, who looked on the procession with a 'sad and tender filial piety', with 'more silent tears than loud cries'.[72] Veterans in their old uniforms tottered behind the funeral chariot as though they were grieving parents, although this sentiment does not appear to have been widespread among those old enough to have lived through the Empire.

One thing that does stand out, however, was the complete disjuncture in the emotional responses to the ceremony between the political elite inside the Invalides and the people of Paris outside on the boulevards. The Duchesse de Dino believed the ceremony to be 'incoherent, contradictory and ridiculous'. The Emperor's constant warring had simply been forgotten and replaced only by the memory of his military victories.[73] The Comtesse de Nesselrode came away with the impression that 'not the least emotion' was felt during the whole ceremony, and that there was nothing other than the curious to be found among the crowd. According to her, the procession was a 'comedy' from beginning to end.[74] The Comte Apponyi, attached to the Austrian embassy, wrote that 'never has a ceremony ever been less touching'.[75] William Makepeace Thackeray, who came from London to witness what he called the second funeral of Napoleon, decried the nationalist outpouring the ceremony had incited, and declared (probably quite accurately) that ennui was the only sentiment he could see among the dignitaries he was seated with.[76] The same detachment was observed among the members of the court who found themselves in the Invalides, waiting to receive Napoleon's remains. 'The memory of the Emperor was in the thoughts of no one,' wrote Mme Mollien. 'People talked of everything except him.'[77] Saint-Denis complained that 'People are quieter and more attentive to the representation of an opera than they were in the Invalides on that fifteenth of December.'[78]

TRANSMOGRIFICATION

The lying-in-state in the chapel of the Invalides was the setting for further displays of emotion. At the end of the religious ceremony at the Invalides, after the last blessings and the departure of the king, there was a rush of old veterans – including some amputees – to touch the Emperor's coffin. The carpet on which the coffin had been placed was torn into pieces by those wanting to keep a relic.[79] Eventually, the troops managed to push the intruders back out of the Invalides, but over the next two weeks between 80,000 and 120,000 people per day, including foreign tourists, would line up for hours in the cold to file past Napoleon's coffin.[80] Victor Hugo admitted to a 'profound emotion' standing before it.[81] Old soldiers would kneel for a minute of reflection before the coffin, and some would openly weep. Only those wearing the frock coat (*habit*) were admitted. A Rumanian visitor noted that a group of peasants were refused entry because they were not decently dressed. Only one of them was wearing something that resembled the coat tails of a black *habit*. He came out with teary eyes. He then passed on his 'rag' to his comrades so that they too could enter one by one to see the coffin. All apparently came away from the experience cursing a regime 'that doesn't care about the poor and then asks them to dress in the *habit*'.[82] The newspapers of the day recounted various anecdotes about the extremes to which some people went to enter the Invalides without having to queue for hours, or what happened while they waited – torn clothes, lost shoes, fainting women, straying children, people trampled.[83] The coffin was later removed to the chapel in the dome dedicated to St Jérôme, where it would remain for another twenty years while a final resting place was built.

There is a feature common among eighteenth- and nineteenth-century political funerals that is notably lacking from Napoleon's funeral procession, and that is violence. Violence might seem out of place in a funeral procession but was, according to Guizot, what the authorities were expecting.[84] About 100,000 troops were deployed in and around Paris in case there was any trouble. There had been occasions in the not too distant past when funeral processions had turned into riots.[85] Between 1820 and 1834, there were at least twenty-eight public political funeral processions, ranging from the unknown student demonstrator named Lallemand, shot in the back during the riots of June 1820, to the funeral of General Lafayette in 1834.[86] In May 1832, General Jean-Maximin Lamarque, a former Napoleonic commander who had refused to accept the defeat of 1815, fell victim to the cholera epidemic sweeping through France. The epidemic claimed over 18,000 lives in Paris alone (although the number may have been higher). Lamarque's funeral on 5 June became the scene of a riot.[87] The funeral procession

François Joseph Aimé de Lemud, *Le Retour en France* (The return to France).
1841. Lithograph on paper. In stark contrast with the actual funeral procession,
this fantastical image of six soldiers carrying Napoleon's coffin personalises
the moment. To the left are cheering onlookers, again in stark contrast to
many of the images around the procession, in which the crowd is a
non-distinct mass. Phantoms of the Grande Armée occupy the right and the top
of the composition, including a trumpeter of the hussars and a Polish lancer.
Underneath is an inscription, an extract from Hugo's poem 'A la Colonne',
which reads, 'Oh! go! We will make you a beautiful funeral! We will also
perhaps have our battles, We will shade your respected coffin!'

was hijacked by Bonapartists and redirected towards the Vendôme Column, around which the cortège circled three times so that the body could bid a symbolic farewell to Napoleon. Republicans and Bonapartists were temporarily allied in their opposition to the regime, indeed in their attempts to topple the Orleanist monarchy.[88] The two days of street fighting that ensued resulted in over 800 casualties.

The largest funerals attracted crowds in their tens of thousands. When violence did occur, during about a quarter of these processions, it was largely contained on the margins, expressed in verbal abuse between mourners and the police, and at worst never involved anything more than fists and canes. On the occasion of Napoleon's funeral too it is notable that despite the evident hostility towards the government, the tensions were largely contained. Certainly there were a few kerfuffles both before and after the procession, but violence was largely absent.[89] The police noted that republicans appeared to have experienced considerable disappointment and 'dejection' for not having caused as much trouble as they thought they might.[90]

What did accompany the funeral proceedings was a sustained output in different media. Around 350 pamphlets, poems, brochures and books, not to mention dozens of newspaper articles and hundreds of graphic images, appeared throughout 1840 and 1841 discussing both the meaning of the funeral procession and the importance of Napoleon for French history. No matter how 'impartial' this literature claimed to be,[91] it was all, in its way, an emotional appeal to readers, a conscious effort to pull at their patriotic heartstrings. Leaving aside the many gauche, overblown poems, let us instead focus on the brochures and pamphlets, most of them panegyrics, as well as on some of the histories of Napoleon that began to appear during the July Monarchy, in order to identify some common tropes.[92]

The first thing worth noting is that Napoleon is portrayed as both saint and martyr, as a victim who had suffered horribly on St Helena, often referred to as the modern Golgotha[93] – a theme that, as we have seen, goes back to Napoleon's days on the island – but whose 'noble and generous soul' had ascended to Eternity, and whose dying breath had been for France.[94] Now that his remains had been returned, he was to become the palladium of the fatherland. The portrayal of an unjustly exiled Napoleon who had suffered for France was the justification for bringing back his remains. That suffering also imbued him with a semi-sacred quality, and a nobility of character that he had so evidently lacked as emperor.[95] Much was made of the unexpected discovery of Napoleon's body, still intact and undecomposed. Descriptions of the exhumation began to appear by the end of 1840, some very detailed, usually in the form of eyewitness accounts or official minutes, so that there could be no doubting their veracity.[96] The focus was not only on the state of Napoleon's body, but also on the emotions that overcame all those who witnessed its unveiling. 'It was indeed Napoleon, Napoleon deprived of life, but not destroyed! It seemed as though it were still the last day of his labours and life ... the first day of eternity!'[97] The reporting of the body's lifelike appearance is an important development that would certainly have lent renewed impetus to the cult. To his followers, Napoleon was already sacred, even in Corsica where after his death his bust was paraded in quasi-religious processions and housed among the saints in a church in Ajaccio.[98] The discovery of the intact body twenty years later only reinforced the impression of sanctity, and would have done much to overturn the negative impressions people would have derived from the reports of his death in 1821. It was as though death did not dare put its mark on his body.[99]

The second theme running through the literature is the place of Napoleon in French and European history. Put simply, pamphleteers asserted that, despite his faults, Napoleon had brought 'honour and glory' to France, and for that reason alone his memory should be venerated.[100] There was an aura of nostalgia surrounding the position of dominance France had once enjoyed, and a criticism (implicit or otherwise) of the lacklustre foreign policy of the July Monarchy. An essayist by the name of Théodore Fadeville declared that one of the homages that would most please Napoleon would be to see his country regain the recognition it deserved as a great power.[101] He had been placed on St Helena and betrayed by those in his entourage, because he represented a dangerous ideal – liberty and the emancipation of the peoples of Europe.[102] According to Fadeville, the laws and democratic institutions that had transformed France were 'a constant source of light which would finally generate happiness and freedom for all those peoples still languishing in ignorance, servitude and degradation'.[103] A citizen of Europe, Napoleon accomplished more in fifteen years than the Bourbons had accomplished in eight centuries.

After the intact body of Napoleon had been uncovered, biographies predominantly focused on the positive aspects of his character, even when this had no foundation in reality. We can thus read in the work by François-Gilbert de Coston that Napoleon the artillery officer at Auxonne made his younger brother Louis take Holy Communion, taught him his catechism and went to the chapel at the Ursuline convent every day around two o'clock, where he prayed to the Virgin Mother (that explained his later devotion to 15 August, the Feast of the Assumption).[104] Or we can read a series of anecdotes about Napoleon's early life that underscore mythic events and character traits that were seen as necessary precursors of greatness.[105] A little-known author by the name of Joseph Ottavi concluded his short biographical piece on Napoleon by expounding on the reasons why Napoleon was so popular:

> Know this, if the people admire Napoleon, it is because they remember Arcola and the Pyramids.
>
> If the people admire Napoleon, it is because they see in the great man the legislator who carved into the Civil Code the eternal principle of equality.
>
> If the people admire Napoleon, it is because they pass under the shadow of that bronze epic, the [Vendôme] Column, and under the Arc de Triomphe, that archive in stone to the national glory, filled with the name of the Emperor.
>
> If the people admire Napoleon, it is because while his marshals and the great institutions of the state betrayed him, they defended the national territory at Montmirail and Waterloo under the orders of the victor of Austerlitz.
>
> Believe me, if the people admire Napoleon, it is because the people admire glory, genius and misfortune nobly borne.[106]

And, continued Ottavi, in modern civilisations, the voice of the people is the voice of God, and the heart of the people is the sanctuary in which the memory of Napoleon was kept. As far as explanations go, this is as good a summary as one can find of the populist view of Napoleon and his place in the hearts and minds of French men and women. In celebrating Napoleon, the French were in fact celebrating themselves.[107]

THE GHOST OF NAPOLEON

The day after the funeral procession, a veteran of the Grande Armée, Jean-Pons-Guillaume Viennent, came across two men standing before a statue of Desaix in Paris who could barely contain their joy. 'It's a good day for the prisoner of Ham,' they exclaimed, a reference to Louis-Napoleon, prisoner in the fortress of Ham for trying to overthrow the monarchy.[108] And therein lay the problem; Louis-Philippe was unable to capitalise on the memory of Napoleon, or certainly not to the extent that he wished. The return of Napoleon's remains and the procession in Paris marked a generation of French men and women and became a milestone in the political history of the nineteenth century. It was possibly *the* decisive moment in the development of Bonapartism and its translation from legend to political reality. For years afterwards, it remained a reference point for those French citizens grappling with their own political identities as well as those of France.

The funeral procession revealed just how fractured French society was, as different political groups interpreted the return of the remains in distinct ways. Conservatives, including those sympathetic to the Orleans regime, legitimists, Bonapartists, veterans of the Grande Armée, the military, liberals and republicans all reacted differently to what they saw and what they perceived to be the regime's intent. Those differing visions were attested to by the proliferation of Napoleonic objets d'art, as well as the contested interpretations of history found in the pamphlets, memoirs and histories of the day. The public ritual that was the funeral procession can be seen as an attempt by the July Monarchy at crystallising public memory in a particular way, at reconstructing the national community, or at least at projecting national unity, and in the process rendering innocuous the memory of Napoleon.

But it never happened. There had never been any guarantee the public was going to experience the funeral procession in the way the regime had intended. The monarchy certainly attempted to channel the crowds' emotions by subordinating the onlookers to an official agenda, but just as other orchestrated funeral processions in the early part of the nineteenth century had failed to align monarchy, nation and people,[109] so too the July Monarchy failed in its bid to rally the country around the throne. Rather than celebrate the monarchy, the nation and the hero it had produced, the political ghost of Napoleon came back to haunt the regime. Rather than put him to rest, the July Monarchy seems inadvertently to have revivified the idea of Napoleon, forcing the regime to reject any further use for the man – no new paintings of him were ordered by the monarchy after 1840, for example – obliging it to be more conservative in the process. The sympathy displayed by the crowds towards the memory of the former Emperor does not mean to say that Bonapartism had made great inroads, only that these same people would be more open to the arrival of Louis-Napoleon on the scene some years later.

For that is what transpired. Louis-Philippe never succeeded in reconciling the political divisions that existed in France and never managed to persuade the opposition groups to support him. It was not really in their interests to do so; liberals, Bonapartists, republicans and legitimists chipped away at the regime's edifice, attacking its domestic and foreign political failings, until it collapsed.[110] When eventually the July Monarchy was overthrown in another revolution in 1848, and replaced with the Second Republic (the first had occurred during the Revolution from 1792 to 1804), the popular cult of Napoleon found political expression in the person of Louis-Napoleon, elected president of the Republic in December of that year. He was forty years of age.

The July Monarchy had been unable to convince the public that it was performing adequately. Despite a number of economic successes, it simply could not overcome its perceived political fragility in the public eye; it was too obviously the regime of the rich, it was studded with scandals, it had had a number of foreign policy failures, and in 1848 its troops opened fire on demonstrators at a time of acute harvest failure and unemployment. Like his predecessor – and indeed like his successor – Louis-Philippe fled to England to live his remaining years in exile. The introduction of universal male suffrage later that year gave a huge fillip to Bonapartists. In December 1848, seven and a half million voters went to the polls, and of those five and a half million voted for Napoleon's nephew, Louis-Napoleon, as president of the Second Republic.[111] Louis-Napoleon had succeeded where Louis-Philippe had failed – despite the sophistication of the July Monarchy's propaganda techniques – in garnering massive popular support. Of course, one has to take into account the possibility that peasants voted for the nephew by virtue of his name, believing that he was the son of Napoleon, or that he was the real Napoleon come back from the dead.[112] Four years later, in a coup on 2 December 1852, Louis-Napoleon overthrew the Republic and in the process proclaimed himself Napoleon III at the head of what became known as the Second Empire.

Epilogue

'THAT BUGGER BONAPARTE THE FIRST'

During the early years of Napoleon III's reign, the Place Vendôme was officially used as a site to celebrate the return of the French army from Italy in 1859.[1] But by the end of the imperial regime, the meaning of the site had shifted again. Napoleon III's monumental reconstruction of Paris under Baron Haussmann had hardly enamoured him to the working classes, who were ruthlessly pushed north and east of the city. It was one of the reasons, in the latter years of Napoleon III's reign, why he lost a good deal of popular support. In 1863, a replica of Chaudet's original statue was commissioned from an artist by the name of Auguste-Alexandre Dumont. The image of Napoleon had been brought back to its original representation in Roman dress; the coat and hat of the Seurre statue were considered too simple for the imperial tastes of the Second Empire.[2] The unveiling of the Chaudet replica took place without any ceremony; 'they simply took down the little fellow and hoisted up another in his place, and that was that'.[3] Napoleon III's attempts to maintain his popularity by publicly drawing parallels between his own imperial aims and those of his deceased uncle meant that the two men became indissolubly associated in popular memory, along with the Vendôme Column. Bonapartism and Bonapartists, once embraced by liberal-thinking people, were increasingly reviled during the last years of Napoleon III's reign.

It should come as no surprise then that, after the defeat of the French army by the Prussians at Sedan in September 1870 when Napoleon III was captured, republicans, who had been gaining support during the

1860s and filled the political vacuum left by the fall of the imperial regime, vented their ire on Bonapartist symbols throughout the country in what one contemporary described as an 'explosion of hatred'.[4] 'If ever a man has landed us in the shit,' wrote an outraged French journalist in 1871, 'then it was that bugger Bonaparte the First. Not only by war, when he had so many people massacred, but by a host of tricks that stopped the Revolution and strengthened tyranny.'[5] In the south of France, in Golfe-Juan, a column erected to mark the landing of Napoleon on his return from exile on Elba in March 1815 was destroyed.[6] The insurrectionary Commune, which modelled itself on the Revolutionary Commune of 1792 and seized power in Paris in 1871, went about systematically destroying any symbol or building that reminded its members of the imperial dynasty. Naturally, one of the most prominent of these was the Column in the Place Vendôme, which was then also the headquarters of the revolutionary National

Bruno Braquehais, *Colonne Vendôme à terre: la Commune de Paris* (The Vendome Column on the ground: the Commune of Paris). 1871. Photograph. The Column was rebuilt during the Third Republic and completed by 28 December 1875, but there was no official inauguration.

Guard. These soldiers could hardly tolerate an imperial symbol right outside their door. The Column had become an emblem of all that the people of Paris detested in Napoleon III.[7] On 16 May 1871, after a number of delays encountered by the engineers in charge of the demolition, the Column was brought down.

The cult of Napoleon quickly revived after the fall of his nephew, as a counterpoint to the humiliating defeat of France by the Germans at Sedan in 1870. A Bonapartist party thrived in France for another twenty years or so.[8] It was during the Third Republic and before the advent of the First World War that the majority of veterans' memoirs were 'discovered' and published, again a nostalgic look at the glory days of Empire and a stark reminder that France had once ruled Europe.[9] Since 1840, there have been countless histories, novels, paintings, illustrations and eventually films (in which Napoleon was played by some of the greats, including Marlin Brando and Rod Steiger)[10] that have reflected on or represented every imaginable aspect of Napoleon's life and reign. But I have decided that my Napoleon will end with the return of his remains, well before the advent of his nephew in 1848 and the establishment of the Second Empire in 1852. Napoleon III saw the triumph of Bonapartism, but added little that was new to the legend.

The spectacular new tomb for Napoleon in the Invalides, designed by Louis Visconti, was completed only in April 1861, more than twenty years after the funeral procession (and eight years after Visconti's death).[11] The enormous porphyry sarcophagus into which Napoleon's remains were finally laid to rest is in a crypt below the main floor, directly under the cupola of the church attached to the Invalides. One of the first things you notice on entering the church is the simple stone balustrade encircling an opening in the floor. As you approach the opening, the sarcophagus and the sculptures surrounding it come into view. Standing at the balustrade, you look down on an impressive sarcophagus, half-crypt, half-monument. It is an ambivalent position for anyone to be in.[12]

On the centenary of Napoleon's death in May 1921, Marshal Ferdinand Foch, the Supreme Allied Commander during the last year of the First World War, stood in the chapel of the Invalides and gave a speech recognising Napoleon's military genius. One week after the fall of France, on 23 June 1940, during a visit to Paris, Hitler looked down on the tomb in a display of power that was meant to remind the French where they sat within the new European pecking order. Later that year, in a ceremony conducted on a bitterly cold winter's day in December, on the hundredth anniversary of the return of his father's remains, the Germans attempted to bolster the French collaborationist Vichy regime by returning Napoleon II from his crypt in Vienna.[13] Since then, thousands upon thousands of visitors have looked down on the tomb, or sat before it, or walked around its perimeter, impressed, in awe or indifferent according to their nature. At the time of its construction, it was a suitably impressive monument to Napoleon's achievements and his memory, a fusion of the cult of Napoleon and national sentiment. And it remains an impressive sight, although in today's political climate it seems to be as good an example of patriotic vainglory as one can find anywhere in the world.

THE CHRIST OF MODERN TIMES

On hearing of Napoleon's death in 1821, Chateaubriand astutely predicted what the consequences would be. 'After the despotism of his person,' he wrote, 'we will yet have to suffer the despotism of his memory. This despotism is more domineering than the first, for if we fought Napoleon on the throne, there is a universal acceptance of the irons that, dead, he has cast on us.'[14] It was evident to contemporary observers that the regimes that succeeded Napoleon would have to contend with his legacy and his memory. If anything is indicative of the emotional appeal that Napoleon still had twenty-five years after his fall from power and almost twenty years after his death, then it is the hundreds of thousands of people who turned out to see his coffin pass by, and who then lined up for hours to walk past his remains in the Invalides.

The Napoleon that the modern reader is so familiar with was created before the nephew came on the scene, and conforms to the nineteenth-century mould of the 'great man' in history: an overpowering force of nature; the providential man; an individual genius recognised as such by contemporaries; a man consumed by his own ambition; a man of action, who transcended the limits of ordinary men.[15] In many respects, he was the epitome of that ideal, which is why he still strikes a chord with modern readers. Many still identify with the narrative of the rise and fall of the 'great man'. His story resonates with many modern individualists, capitalist entrepreneurs and would-be autocrats. They may possess the 'soul of Mephistopheles' – to paraphrase the description of a character by Pushkin who resembled Napoleon – but the poetic fantasy is often missing.[16] In the preface to his 1836 *Napoléon*, the French writer Edgar Quinet wrote that Napoleon represented the development of individuality in modern times. Chateaubriand put his finger on it many years ago when he wrote, 'The truth about Napoleon is that he is already a character and no longer a personality.'

Modern-day historians have a tendency to compare Napoleon, if they compare him to anyone, to Alexander or Caesar – for Napoleon too was a great conqueror – or to Hitler, Mussolini and Stalin, ascribing to Napoleon the traits of the modern dictator.[17] If Napoleon is to be compared to any historical figure then it should really be Louis XIV, in the way that they both deliberately constructed an image around their person for political purposes, in the way that they both wanted to be at the centre of French society and politics, around which everything revolved, and in the way that they both obsessed about the glory of France and the throne.[18] Just as Europe was on the cusp of the modern age, Napoleon wanted to turn back the political clock one hundred years.

More compellingly, however, a case can be made for comparing Napoleon to Jesus Christ. The comparison between Napoleon and Christ is less far-fetched than it might sound, if only because contemporaries often made it. Chateaubriand compared Napoleon to God, and Heine was constantly representing Napoleon as a God-like or Christ-like figure.[19] On the occasion of the centenary of Napoleon's death in 1921, a French art historian by the name of Elie Faure wrote a short book that would later go on to inspire the silent filmmaker Abel Gance.[20] Faure portrayed Napoleon as an artist and a poet of action, and boldly stated that the person he could best be compared to was Christ. According to Faure, there was a wealth of similarities between the two. Christ suffered and died for his sins on Golgotha, so too did Napoleon on St Helena (his Golgotha). The apostles disseminated Christ's word, so too did Napoleon's Evangelists disseminate his word. Christ was a Saviour, so too Napoleon. Christ was both human and divine, so too Napoleon. Christ rose from the dead, so did Napoleon. Both were Mediterranean, both were heroes 'marching with their whole being to meet God'. Both were 'immoral' in the sense that they overthrew social customs and prejudices, dispersed families and precipitated the whole world towards war, glory, misery and illusion. Both were possessed of the same atrocious indifference which, without their being aware or even conscious of it, made the heavens gravitate around them. Both were obliged endlessly to conquer, to endure, to live and to die in the way they had lived and died. Both drowned the earth in blood so that the harvest it contained could sprout forth. Both excited love in their followers, but neither had friends. Like Christ, Napoleon acted on his dreams, rather than dreamt about his actions.

NAPOLEON THE GREAT?

And yet Napoleon is often credited with dragging Europe into the modern era, leaving an overall positive legacy for France. Historians usually trot out the Civil Code, the Bank of France, the prefectoral system and other institutional reforms as proof of the beneficial legacy of the Napoleonic era. However, Napoleon was incapable of establishing a stable and legitimate polity. His drive to conquer prolonged wars between France and the rest of Europe, leaving millions dead and wounded in their wake, and France materially and geographically worse off than it was before he started. Napoleon is also touted as the man who saved the Revolution, or at least as the man who consolidated the gains of the Revolution (not that they were in any danger of disappearing when he came to power in 1799). That too is part of the Bonapartist myth. Instead, he left France just as divided, if not more so, in 1815 as when he took power in 1799: the religious compromise that was the Concordat quickly turned sour; slavery was re-established; the opposition and parliamentary life were muzzled; and France was transformed into a virtual police state. One French scholar has gone so far as to suggest that Napoleon's two greatest legacies – the centralised state and the love of glory – delayed French modernity for a very long time.[21]

It is curious then that of all historical celebrities Napoleon is possibly the one with whom people most identify. He is a modern hero, the inspiration for businessmen and adolescents alike, all dreaming of achieving great things. Napoleon's story is also malleable. He can be modified and adapted so that he becomes the guru of business executives bent on eliminating competition or the darling of self-help manuals. He is the opposite of mediocrity. His venal image, in fact, is so strong, so deeply embedded in the western psyche, that advertisers can superimpose any face they like on Napoleon's body or uniform and he remains instantly recognisable. Not only does Napoleon appear on the labels of cognac bottles, but advertising agencies also use him to pitch anything from antacid to hi-fi systems. He attracts an inordinate number of fans. There are Napoleon magazines and associations throughout the western world. Military re-enactors gather periodically on former battlegrounds to commemorate if not celebrate past Napoleonic battles. As for the published lives of Napoleon, there are hundreds, alongside specialised monographs that examine every aspect of his life and reign.

The legend is what people yearn for. There is something deeply stirring in the story of a young, dynamic, victorious general who leads his ragtag army from victory to victory, sweeping aside all in his path through sheer willpower and against tremendous odds. Then there is the background love story with Josephine, even though it was a lopsided affair. That Napoleon went on to invade Egypt in the manner of a Caesar or an Alexander makes the story all the more fascinating. This is what Napoleon represents. It is a glorious adventure. It is the prospect of unlimited possibilities open to anyone with the will and imagination to accomplish great things. It is why Napoleon appeals to so many, why he ignites hearts and minds. That he conquered Europe and fell from power makes his story all the more fascinating and human.

Like the *Iliad*, Napoleon's story will be told and retold in a manner appropriate to each new generation. Biographers hold up their subjects like mirrors so the public can better see themselves and the world in which they live. What can Napoleon possibly teach us? That pride and arrogance inevitably lead to a fall, that a certain degree of humility is required in public and private lives, that military solutions to international problems create more difficulties than they resolve?

Perhaps all of these and more, but this is not how or why Napoleon will continue to be remembered. Napoleon fascinates us because he conquered, because he acquired absolute power, because he unashamedly pursued lasting fame. Isn't that what much of the modern western individual is all about?

Notes

CHAPTER I

1. On the history of the ship see David Cordingly, *The Billy Ruffian: The Bellerophon and the Downfall of Napoleon: The Biography of a Ship of the Line, 1782–1836* (London, 2003).
2. For the following account of the stay off Torbay see Norman MacKenzie, *Fallen Eagle: How the Royal Navy Captured Napoleon* (London, 2009), pp. 171–5.
3. Christopher Lloyd (ed.), *The Keith Papers: Selected from Letters and Papers of Admiral Viscount Keith*, 3 vols (London, 1927–55), iii. p. 332.
4. Keith to Anne Elphinstone (5 August 1815), in Henry Petty-Fitzmaurice, Marquess of Lansdowne (ed.), *The First Napoleon: Some Unpublished Documents from the Bowood Papers* (London, 1925), p. 169; Michael John Thornton, *Napoleon after Waterloo: England and the St. Helena Decision* (Stanford, Calif., 1968), p. 171.
5. John Smart, 'Napoleon on Board the Bellerophon at Torbay', in Clement Shorter (ed.), *Napoleon and his Fellow Travellers* (London, 1908), pp. 295–302; Paul F. Brunyee, *Napoleon's Britons and the St Helena Decision* (Stroud, 2009), pp. 50–3.
6. Smart, 'Napoleon on Board the Bellerophon at Torbay', p. 299.
7. Smart, 'Napoleon on Board the Bellerophon at Torbay', p. 300.
8. James Meek, 'Memorandum of Proceedings from June 24 to August 17, 1815', in Lloyd (ed.), *The Keith Papers*, iii. p. 339.
9. Louis-Joseph Marchand, *In Napoleon's Shadow* (San Francisco, 1998), pp. 314–15; Brian Unwin, *Terrible Exile: The Last Days of Napoleon on St Helena* (London, 2010), p. 37.
10. Frederick Maitland, *The Surrender of Napoleon: Being the Narrative of the Surrender of Buonaparte, and of His Residence on Board H.M.S.*

Bellerophon (Edinburgh and London, 1904), pp. 115–16, 135–6. Walter Scott wrote that this work was a 'as fine, manly, and explicit an account as ever was given', p. vii.

11. *The Naval Chronicle for 1815: Containing a General and Biographical History of the Royal Navy of the United Kingdom, with a Variety of Original Papers on Nautical Subjects*, 40 vols (Cambridge, 2010), xxxiv. p. 122.

12. Keith to Melville (1 August 1815) cited in Thornton, *Napoleon after Waterloo*, p. 146.

13. Keith to Anne Elphinstone (1 August 1815), in Lansdowne (ed.), *The First Napoleon*, p. 167; Gilbert Martineau, *Napoleon Surrenders*, trans. Frances Partridge (London, 1971), p. 176.

14. Lloyd (ed.), *The Keith Papers*, iii. p. 333.

15. Maitland, *The Surrender of Napoleon*, p. 136.

16. 'An Extract from a Journal Kept on Board H.M.S. Bellerophon, by Captain John Bowerbank, R.N.', in Shorter (ed.), *Napoleon and his Fellow Travellers*, pp. 315–16.

17. Stuart Semmel, *Napoleon and the British* (New Haven, 2004). On celebrity see Fred Inglis, *A Short History of Celebrity* (Princeton, 2010); and Clara Tuite, *Lord Byron and Scandalous Celebrity* (Cambridge, 2014), esp. pp. 73–7.

18. Benjamin Robert Haydon, *Correspondence and Table-Talk*, 2 vols (London, 1876), i. p. 288.

19. Crispin Gill, 'Some Diaries and Memoirs of Plymouth in the French Revolutionary and Napoleonic Wars', *Report and Transactions. The Devonshire Association for the Advancement of Science, Literature and Art*, 115 (1983), 1–17; Thornton, *Napoleon after Waterloo*, p. 99.

20. Lady Charlotte Fitzgerald, cited in James Davey, *In Nelson's Wake: The Navy and the Napoleonic Wars* (New Haven, 2016), p. 308. For Oskar Cox Jensen, *Napoleon and British Song, 1797–1822* (Basingstoke, 2015), p. 14, Napoleon was a hero to those disaffected by British politics and the state.

21. William Cobbett cited in Semmel, *Napoleon and the British*, p. 171; Thornton, *Napoleon after Waterloo*, p. 98.

22. *Cobbett's Weekly Political Register*, 28 (12 August 1815), p. 176; Semmel, *Napoleon and the British*, p. 226.

23. Keith to Melville (2 August 1815), in Lloyd (ed.), *The Keith Papers*, iii. p. 384; Thornton, *Napoleon after Waterloo*, p. 148.

24. William Lennox Bathurst to Henry Bathurst (31 July 1815), in *Report on the Manuscripts of Earl Bathurst*, pp. 364–5.

25. Haydon, *Correspondence and Table-Talk*, i. p. 288.
26. Stuart Semmel, 'Reading the Tangible Past: British Tourism, Collecting, and Memory after Waterloo', *Representations*, 69 (Winter, 2000), 9–37; A. V. Seaton, 'War and Thanatourism: Waterloo 1815–1914', *Annals of Tourism Research*, 26:1 (1999), 130–58.
27. On the panaroma see Stephan Oettermann, *The Panorama: History of a Mass Medium*, trans. Deborah Lucas Schneider (New York, 1997), esp. pp. 99–140; Denise Blake Oleksijczuk, *The First Panoramas: Visions of British Imperialism* (Minneapolis, 2011), p. 6.
28. Alan Forrest, *Waterloo* (Oxford, 2015), p. 114. See, for example, *Description of the Field of Battle, and Disposition of the Troops Engaged in the Action, Fought on the 18th of June, 1815, near Waterloo; Illustrative of the Representation of That Great Event, in the Panorama, Leicester-Square* (Quebec, 1817).
29. Richard D. Altick, *The Shows of London* (Cambridge, Mass., 1978), pp. 238–41; Semmel, 'Reading the Tangible Past', 12–13.
30. Judith Pascoe, *The Hummingbird Cabinet: A Rare and Curious History of Romantic Collectors* (Ithaca, NY, 2006), p. 91.
31. Pascoe, *The Hummingbird Cabinet*, pp. 85–109.
32. Georges-Adrien Crapelet, *Souvenirs de Londres en 1814 et 1816* (Paris, 1817), p. 128 (14 June 1816).
33. *A Description of the costly and curious military carriage of the late Emperor of France taken on the evening of the battle of Waterloo with its superb and curious contents* (London, 1818), p. 3. The carriage later toured some of the major British cities: Bristol, Dublin, Edinburgh. See James Grieg (ed.), *The Farrington Diary*, 8 vols (London, 1922–8), viii. p. 88 (24 August 1816).
34. *A Description of the costly and curious military carriage of the late Emperor of France*, p. 9.
35. Jean Hornn, *The Narrative of Jean Hornn, Military Coachman to Napoleon Bonaparte* (London, 1816).
36. Pascoe, *The Hummingbird Cabinet*, pp. 108–9. In a fabulous publicity stunt, Tussaud got permission to go on board the *Bellerophon* to model Napoleon's face. See Pamela Pilbeam, *Madame Tussaud and the History of Waxworks* (London, 2003), pp. 109–15, 118, 224–5.
37. Charles Doris, *Précis historique sur Napoléon Buonaparte* (Paris, 1815), pp. 17, 63, 81–2.
38. *Histoire amoureuse de Napoléon Bonaparte, extraite des mémoires particuliers composés par lui-même pendant son séjour à l'île d'Elbe, et continuée jusqu'au 14 juillet 1815. Par un ancien officier de sa maison, qui*

ne l'a quitté qu'au moment de monter sur le Northumberland, 2 vols
(Paris, 1815); [Charles Doris, de Bourges], *Amours secrètes de Napoléon
Bonaparte; par l'auteur du 'Précis historique' et des 'Mémoires secrets'*, 2
vols (Paris, 1815).

39. The insinuation that Hortense and Napoleon had sex can also be found
in the comic play by Alphonse Martainville, *Buonaparte, ou l'Abus de
l'abdication, pièce héroïco romantico-bouffonne* (Paris, 1815), p. 49.

40. Barry O' Meara, *Napoleon in Exile; or, A Voice from St. Helena*, 2 vols
(London, 1822), i. pp. 321–2. This was also the case for the fantastical
biography by Lewis Goldsmith, *Histoire secrète du cabinet de Napoléon
Buonaparté, et de la cour de Saint-Cloud* (London, 1814), read with
some amusement at Longwood. See Emmanuel, comte de Las Cases, *Le
Mémorial de Sainte-Hélène*, ed. and annotated by Marcel Dunan, 2 vols
(Paris, 1983), i. pp. 349–52 (15 January 1816).

41. Matthijs Lok, ' "Un oubli total du passé"? The Political and Social
Construction of Silence in Restoration Europe (1813–1830)', *History &
Memory*, 26:2 (2014), 53.

42. Jean Tulard, 'Le retour des cendres', in Pierre Nora (ed.), *Les lieux
de mémoire*, 3 vols (Paris, 1984–6), iii. p. 92; Sylvain Pagé, *Le mythe
napoléonien: de Las Cases à Victor Hugo* (Paris, 2013), p. 35. It was not
all that unusual for nineteenth-century writers to invent stories about
their biographical subjects. A number of other nineteenth-century political figures were also the subject of invented biographies. See, for example, Lucy Riall, *Garibaldi: Invention of a Hero* (New Haven, 2008), pp.
134–5, 194–203; John Plunkett, *Queen Victoria: First Media Monarch*
(Oxford, 2003); and Brian Hamnett, 'Fictitious Histories: The Dilemma
of Fact and Fiction in the Nineteenth Century Historical Novel',
European History Quarterly, 36:1 (2006), 31–60.

43. See, for example, [Charles Doris, de Bourges], *Mémoires secrets sur
Napoléon Buonaparte, écrits par un homme qui ne l'a pas quitté depuis
quinze ans* (Paris, 1815); *Histoire amoureuse de Napoléon Bonaparte*.

44. The most prominent of these essays is François-René, vicomte de
Chateaubriand's *De Buonaparte, des Bourbons, et de la nécessité de se
rallier à nos princes légitimes pour le bonheur de la France et celui de
l'Europe* (Paris, 1814).

45. See Germaine de Staël, *Portrait d'Attila* (Paris, 1814); Jean-Wendel
Wurtz, *L'Apollyon de l'Apocalypse, ou la révolution française prédite
par saint Jean l'évangéliste* (Lyons, 1816); Louis-André Pichon, *De
l'état de la France, sous la domination de Napoléon Bonaparte* (Paris,
1814), esp. pp. 13–30; Jacques-Barthélemy Salgues, *Mémoire pour servir
à l'histoire de France sous le gouvernement de Napoléon Buonaparte et*

pendant l'absence de la maison de Bourbon, 9 vols (Paris, 1814–26); A.-L.-J. Godin, *Histoire de Buonaparte, depuis sa naissance jusqu'à ce jour*, 2 vols (Paris, 1816), i. pp. 4–6; *Histoire de Napoléon Buonaparte, depuis sa naissance, en 1769, jusqu'à sa translation à l'île Sainte-Hélène, en 1815; par une société de gens de lettres*, 4 vols (Paris, 1817–18).

46. *Histoire secrète des amours de la famille N. Bonaparte* (Paris, 1815), pp. 60–1, 75–6, 98, 100, 106–10, 145.

47. *La Snapoleonazione. Opera buffa, ovvero il mago don Pilucca Dramma per musica* (Cagliari, 1814); Eileen Anne Millar, *Napoleon in Italian Literature, 1796–1821* (Rome, 1977), pp. 134–5.

48. Noël-Laurent Pissot, *Le mea culpa de Napoléon Bonaparte, l'aveu de ses perfidies et cruautés* (Paris, 1814); François Chéron, *Napoléon, ou le Corse dévoilé, ode aux Français* (Paris, 1814); *L'usurpateur remis à sa place dans les cieux, ou arrêt de la Cour céleste, extrait du Journal de l'Empirée* (Paris, 1814); *Apothéose de Napoleone Bonaparte, ou signalement de l'Ante-Christ, manifesté à tout l'univers, par l'esprit de vérité* (Paris, 1821); Georges Lote, 'La contre-légende napoléonienne et la mort de Napoléon', *Revue des études napoléoniennes*, 31 (1930), 331.

49. MacKenzie, *Fallen Eagle*, pp. 169, 175, 181, 183, 191–3.

50. Philip Dwyer, *Citizen Emperor: Napoleon in Power, 1799–1815* (London, 2013), pp. 561–2. On the Prince Regent, later George IV, see Saul David, *The Prince of Pleasure: The Prince of Wales and the Making of the Regency* (London, 1998).

51. Marcello Simonetta and Noga Arikha, *Napoleon and the Rebel: A Story of Brotherhood, Passion, and Power* (New York, 2011), pp. 221–6.

52. Gaspard Gourgaud, *Journal de Sainte-Hélène: 1815–1818*, introduction and notes by Octave Aubry, 2 vols (Paris, 1944), i. pp. 45, 46 (22 and 23 July 1815); Thornton, *Napoleon after Waterloo*, p. 71.

53. Thornton, *Napoleon after Waterloo*, pp. 94–5.

54. Gourgaud, *Journal de Sainte-Hélène*, i. p. 46 (24 July 1815); Las Cases, *Le Mémorial de Sainte-Hélène*, i. p. 38 (24 July 1815).

55. *The Times*, 22, 25 July 1815; Thornton, *Napoleon after Waterloo*, p. 153.

56. *The Times*, 6 July 1815.

57. *The Times*, 22 July, 3 August 1815; Jean-Paul Bertaud, Alan Forrest and Annie Jourdan, *Napoléon, le monde et les Anglais: guerre des mots et des images* (Paris, 2004), pp. 191–2.

58. Marcus Wood, *Radical Satire and Print Culture, 1790–1822* (Oxford, 1994), pp. 192–7.

59. Forrest, *Waterloo*, pp. 60–4. See, for example, Gilles Avril (ed.), *L'anti-Napoléon: écrits inédits et papiers de Noël-Antoine Apuril Du Pontreau, chanoine de la Congrégation de France* (Paris, 2006), pp. 180–1.

60. Thornton, *Napoleon after Waterloo*, pp. 60–1.

61. *The Times*, 22 and 27 July, 3 August 1815.

62. *The Times*, 31 July 1815.

63. Thornton, *Napoleon after Waterloo*, p. 151.

64. Las Cases, *Le Mémorial de Sainte-Hélène*, i. p. 42 (27 and 28 July 1815).

65. Paul Ganière, *Napoléon à Sainte-Hélène* (Paris, 1998), p. 43; Thornton, *Napoleon after Waterloo*, p. 73, says that Napoleon remained 'unruffled'.

66. Liverpool to Castlereagh, 20 July 1815, in Charles Duke Yonge (ed.), *The Life and Administration of Robert Banks, Second Earl of Liverpool*, 3 vols (London, 1868), ii. p. 199. See Norman Gash, *Lord Liverpool: The Life and Political Career of Robert Banks Jenkinson, Second Earl of Liverpool, 1770–1828* (London, 1984), pp. 120–1.

67. Castlereagh to Liverpool, 24 July 1815, in Charles William Vane (ed.), *Correspondence, Despatches, and Other Papers of Viscount Castlereagh*, 12 vols (London, 1848–53), x. p. 437.

68. Metternich to Marie Louise, 18 July 1815, in Klemens Wenzel von Metternich, *Mémoires: documents et écrits divers*, 8 vols (Paris, 1881–4), ii. pp. 525–6.

69. Richard Edgcumbe (ed.), *The Diary of Frances Lady Shelley*, 2 vols (London, 1913), i. p. 105; Thornton, *Napoleon after Waterloo*, p. 61.

70. Liverpool to Castlereagh, 21 July 1815, in *Supplementary Despatches, Correspondence, and Memoranda of Field Marshal Arthur, Duke of Wellington*, 15 vols (London, 1858–72), xi. p. 47; Thornton, *Napoleon after Waterloo*, p. 62; Neville Thompson, *Earl Bathurst and the British Empire, 1762–1834* (Barnsley, 1999), pp. 100–2.

71. Bathurst to Wellington, 24 July 1815, in *Supplementary Despatches*, xi. p. 55.

72. Ganière, *Napoléon à Sainte-Hélène*, p. 50; Dwyer, *Citizen Emperor*, p. 116.

73. Dwyer, *Citizen Emperor*, p. 513.

74. Lloyd (ed.), *The Keith Papers*, iii. p. 332.

75. Liverpool to Castlereagh, 15 and 20 July 1815, in Yonge (ed.), *The Life and Administration of Robert Banks*, ii. pp. 196, 199; Liverpool to Castlereagh, 21 July 1815, in *Supplementary Despatches*, xi. p. 47; Thornton, *Napoleon after Waterloo*, p. 62. On John Barrow see J. M. R. Cameron, 'John Barrow, the *Quarterly*'s Imperial Reviewer', in Jonathan Cutmore (ed.), *Conservatism and the Quarterly Review: A Critical Analysis* (London, 2007), pp. 133–49.

76. Melville to Keith (28 July 1815), in Lloyd (ed.), *The Keith Papers*, iii. p. 371.

77. Melville to Keith (25 July 1815), in Lloyd (ed.), *The Keith Papers*, iii. pp. 365–6.

78. Norwood Young, *Napoleon in Exile: St Helena*, 2 vols (London, 1915), i. p. 95; and Martin Howard, *Napoleon's Poisoned Chalice: The Emperor and his Doctors on St Helena* (Stroud, 2009), p. 13.

79. Melville to Keith (28 July 1815), in Lloyd (ed.), *The Keith Papers*, iii. pp. 371–2; and Torrens to Bathurst, 22 July 1815, in *Supplementary Despatches*, xi. p. 51.

80. For a range of descriptions of the island and its climate see Michel Dancoisne-Martineau, 'Sainte-Hélène, un aperçu historique', in Bernard Chevallier, Michel Dancoisne-Martineau and Thierry Lentz (eds), *Sainte-Hélène, île de mémoire* (Paris, 2005), pp. 13–45. For the island's environmental history see Richard H. Grove, *Green Imperialism: Colonial Expansion, Tropical Island Edens, and the Origins of Environmentalism, 1600–1860* (Cambridge, 1996), pp. 5–6, 42–4, 95–125.

81. *The Voyages and Travells of the Ambassadors Sent by Frederick Duke of Holstein, to the Great Duke of Muscovy, and the King of Persia: Begun in the Year 1633, and Finish'd in 1634: Containing a Compleat History of Muscovy, Tartary, Persia, and Other Adjacent Countries: with Several Publick Transactions Reaching Near the Present Times* (London, 1669), p. 210.

82. Thomas H. Brooke, *A History of the Island of St. Helena: From its Discovery by the Portuguese to the Year 1806* (London, 1808), p. 32.

83. 'Memorandum Concerning the Island of St Helena', in *Supplementary Despatches, Correspondence, and Memoranda of Field Marshal Arthur, Duke of Wellington*, xi. pp. 74–7.

84. Grove, *Green Imperialism*, pp. 343–64.

85. Thornton, *Napoleon after Waterloo*, p. 125.

86. Keith to Melville (1 August 1815) cited in Thornton, *Napoleon after Waterloo*, p. 146.

87. See Thornton, *Napoleon after Waterloo*, pp. 125–6.

88. Keith to Melville (31 July 1815), in Lansdowne (ed.), *The First Napoleon*, pp. 163–4; H. G. Bunbury, 'Memorandum of what passed at the Conference between Admiral Lord Keith and myself with Napoleon Bonaparte on 31st July, 1815', in Lloyd (ed.), *The Keith Papers*, iii. pp. 376–80.

89. Bunbury, 'Memorandum', in Lloyd (ed.), *The Keith Papers*, iii. p. 377.

90. Maitland, *The Surrender of Napoleon*, p. 142.

91. On Napoleon's previous attempt to commit suicide by poison see Dwyer, *Citizen Emperor*, pp. 152–4.

92. Marchand, *In Napoleon's Shadow*, p. 319; Paul Ganière, *Corvisart, médecin de l'Empereur* (Paris, 1985), pp. 367–8, 369–70.

93. Las Cases, *Le Mémorial de Sainte-Hélène*, i. p. 50 (2–3 August 1815); Thornton, *Napoleon after Waterloo*, pp. 158–9.

94. Bunbury to Bathurst (31 July 1815), in *Report on the Manuscripts of Earl Bathurst, Preserved at Cirencester* Park (London, 1923), p. 365.
95. Keith to his daughter (24 July 1815), in Lloyd (ed.), *The Keith Papers*, iii. p. 365.
96. Melville to Keith (28 July 1815), in Lloyd (ed.), *The Keith Papers*, iii. pp. 371–2; MacKenzie, *Fallen Eagle*, p. 184.
97. Thornton, *Napoleon after Waterloo*, p. 158.
98. Ganière, *Corvisart*, pp. 368–9.
99. Maitland, *The Surrender of Napoleon*, pp. 179–80, 194–5, 258; O'Meara, *Napoleon in Exile*, i. pp. 2–7. On O'Meara see Peter Hicks, 'Who was Barry O'Meara?', *Napoleonica. La Revue*, 17 (2013), 75–94; and Howard, *Napoleon's Poisoned Chalice*, pp. 35–61.
100. Maitland, *The Surrender of Napoleon*, p. 190.
101. John Cam Hobhouse, Lord Broughton, *Recollections of a Long Life (1786–1834)*, 4 vols (London, 1909–10), ii. p. 159.
102. See Dwyer, *Citizen Emperor*, p. 447.
103. 'Facts Illustrative of the Treatment of Napoleon Buonaparte in St Helena', *The Edinburgh Review, or Critical Journal*, 32 (July–October 1819), p. 154; and 'Reminiscences of Napoleon Bonaparte, on St Helena. By A Lady', *Edinburgh Magazine*, 35 (January–June 1834), p. 55; Henri-Gatien Bertrand, *Cahiers de Sainte-Hélène*, 3 vols (Paris, 1950), iii. p. 159 (14 April 1821).
104. Octave Aubry, *Sainte-Hélène* (Paris, 1973), p. 67.
105. On Gourgaud see the portrait in Archibald Philip Primrose, Earl of Rosebery, *Napoleon: The Last Phase* (London, 1904), pp. 35–57; and Jacques Macé, *Le général Gourgaud* (Paris, 2006).
106. On Las Cases see Jean-Pierre Gaubert, *Las Cases: l'abeille de Napoléon* (Portet-sur-Garonne, 2003); and Didier Le Gall, *Napoléon et Le mémorial de Sainte-Hélène* (Paris, 2003), pp. 31–51.
107. William Warden, *Letters Written on Board His Majesty's Ship the Northumberland and Saint Helena* (Brussels, 1817), p. 6.
108. On the atlas see Walter Goffart, *Historical Atlases: The First Three Hundred Years, 1570–1870* (Chicago, 2003), pp. 303–14.
109. Las Cases, *Le Mémorial de Sainte-Hélène*, i. p. 49 (1 August 1815).
110. Martineau, *Napoleon Surrenders*, p. 164; Maitland, *The Surrender of Napoleon*, pp. 154–8.
111. Las Cases, *Le Mémorial de Sainte-Hélène*, i. p. 49 (1 August 1815); Maitland, *The Surrender of Napoleon*, pp. 149–50; Thornton, *Napoleon after Waterloo*, pp. 137–40.
112. Mentioned in Gourgaud, *Journal de Sainte-Hélène*, i. p. 49 (31 July 1815); Louis Etienne Saint-Denis, *Souvenirs du Mameluck Ali sur l'empereur*

Napoléon (Paris, 2000), p. 135; Nicolas-Louis Planat de La Faye, *Vie de Planat de La Faye* (Paris, 1895), p. 240. Various accounts of this episode have been rendered by historians: Ganière, *Napoléon à Sainte-Hélène*, p. 53.

113. Lloyd (ed.), *The Keith Papers*, iii. pp. 397–8, 400–3; Thornton, *Napoleon after Waterloo*, pp. 220–1. For Gourgaud's letter see Macé, *Le général Gourgaud*, pp. 137–8.

114. Gourgaud to Keith, and O'Meara to Keith, in Lloyd (ed.), *The Keith Papers*, iii. pp. 397–8, 401–2.

115. Bertrand to Keith, in Lloyd (ed.), *The Keith Papers*, iii. p. 401.

116. Watson, *A Polish Exile with Napoleon*, pp. 51–2; Thornton, *Napoleon after Waterloo*, p. 221. Piontkowski's wishes were granted on 17 August 1815. He arrived at St Helena on 29 December 1815, but was sent home in October the following year.

117. Marchand, *In Napoleon's Shadow*, pp. 317, 318.

118. Marchand, *In Napoleon's Shadow*, p. 319.

119. Maitland, *The Surrender of Napoleon*, p. 206.

120. Maitland, *The Surrender of Napoleon*, p. 169.

121. Maitland, *The Surrender of Napoleon*, p. 160; Thornton, *Napoleon after Waterloo*, p. 167.

122. Napoléon Bonaparte, *Corr[espondance] de Napoléon I publiée par ordre de l'empereur Napoléon III*, 32 vols (Paris, 1858–70), xxviii. p. 348 (4 August 1815).

123. Richard Henry Horne, *The History of Napoleon*, 3 vols (London, 1841), ii. p. 437.

124. Keith to Anne Elphinstone (5 August 1815), in Lansdowne (ed.), *The First Napoleon*, p. 169.

125. Thornton, *Napoleon after Waterloo*, pp. 161–3, 189.

126. Meek, 'Memorandum', in Lloyd (ed.), *The Keith Papers*, iii. p. 342; John Holland Rose (ed.), *Napoleon's Last Voyages, Being the Diaries of Admiral Sir Thomas Ussher (on board the 'Undaunted'), and John R. Glover, Secretary to Rear Admiral Cockburn (on board the 'Northumberland')* (London, 1906), p. 118.

127. On 14 July, while still in Cambrai, Louis XVIII named fifty-seven individuals, generals and politicians, as leading or instigating what was termed 'the plot that had been hatched against royal authority' (Forrest, *Waterloo*, p. 76).

128. Keith to Melville (7 August 1815), in Lloyd (ed.), *The Keith Papers*, iii. pp. 395–6. On Cockburn see James Pack, *The Man Who Burned the White House: Admiral Sir George Cockburn, 1772–1853* (Emsworth, 1987); and Roger Morriss, *Cockburn and the British Navy in Transition: Admiral Sir George Cockburn, 1772–1853* (Exeter, 1997).

129. Lloyd (ed.), *The Keith Papers*, iii. p. 396; Keith to Anne Elphinstone (13 August 1815), in Lansdowne (ed.), *The First Napoleon*, pp. 176–7.

130. Lloyd (ed.), *The Keith Papers*, iii. pp. 379–80.

131. Savary, Lallemand and Planat de La Faye were transported to Malta. The Bourbons did indeed claim the extradition of Savary and Lallemand, at which point the British authorities allowed them to escape – Savary to England, Lallemand to America. Nineteen high-ranking generals were ordered to face court-martial in France after Waterloo, including Bertrand. Six were executed, of whom Marshal Ney, shot in December 1815, was the best known. The others either had their death sentences commuted or fled France. See Marcel Doher, *Proscrits et exilés après Waterloo* (Paris, 1965), pp. 37–42; Guillaume de Bertier de Sauvigny, *La Restauration* (Paris, 1963), pp. 178–81; Daniel Philip Resnick, *The White Terror and the Political Reaction after Waterloo* (Cambridge, Mass., 1966), pp. 67–70; Bertrand Goujon, *Monarchies postrévolutionnaires, 1814–1848* (Paris, 2012), pp. 74–6.

132. Las Cases, *Le Mémorial de Sainte-Hélène*, i. pp. 60–1 (7 August 1815).

133. According to Bowerbank, in Shorter (ed.), *Napoleon and his Fellow Travellers*, p. 322; and George Home, *Memoirs of an Aristocrat and Reminiscences of the Emperor Napoleon, by a midshipman of the 'Bellerophon'* (London, 1838), pp. 251–2.

134. Home, *Memoirs of an Aristocrat*, p. 253.

135. Maitland, *The Surrender of Napoleon*, p. ix.

136. Maitland, *The Surrender of Napoleon*, p. 220.

137. Home, *Memoirs of an Aristocrat*, pp. 253–4.

138. Keith to Anne Elphinstone (13 August 1815), in Lansdowne (ed.), *The First Napoleon*, p. 177.

139. *The Times*, 11 August 1815.

CHAPTER 2

1. Ross to Kingston, 26 July 1815, in Shorter (ed.), *Napoleon and his Fellow Travellers*, p. 60.

2. W. H. Lyttelton, 'Some Account of Bonaparte's coming on board H.M.S. The *Northumberland*', in Shorter (ed.), *Napoleon and his Fellow Travellers*, pp. 85–7.

3. 'Napoleon's Voyage to St. Helena by Sir George Bingham', in Shorter (ed.), *Napoleon and his Fellow Travellers*, p. 326 (7 August 1815).

4. Rose (ed.), *Napoleon's Last Voyages*, p. 231.

5. J. C. A. Stagg, *The War of 1812: Conflict for a Continent* (Cambridge, 2012), pp. 128–30.

6. O'Meara, *Napoleon in Exile*, i. p. 127. On the Rumbold affair see Dwyer, *Citizen Emperor*, p. 223.
7. Marchand, *In Napoleon's Shadow*, p. 332.
8. George Cockburn, *Extract from a Diary of Rear-Admiral Sir George Cockburn, with particular reference to General Napoleon Buonaparte, on the passage from England to Saint Helena in 1815* (London, 1888), pp. 10–11.
9. Cockburn, *Extract from a Diary*, p. 11; Marchand, *In Napoleon's Shadow*, p. 331; Rose (ed.), *Napoleon's Last Voyages*, p. 126.
10. Cockburn, *Extract from a Diary*, pp. 12–13.
11. Cited in Morriss, *Cockburn and the British Navy in Transition*, pp. 121–31, here p. 127.
12. Las Cases, *Le Mémorial de Sainte-Hélène*, i. p. 109 (1–6 September 1815); Elizabeth Balcombe Abell, *Recollections of the Emperor Napoleon during the First Three Years of his Captivity on the Island of St. Helena* (London, 1844), p. 254; Marchand, *In Napoleon's Shadow*, p. 401.
13. Cockburn, *Extract from a Diary*, p. 11; Marchand, *In Napoleon's Shadow*, p. 331; Rose (ed.), *Napoleon's Last Voyages*, p. 126.
14. Cockburn, *Extract from a Diary*, p. 14.
15. Pack, *The Man Who Burned the White House*, pp. 219–20.
16. Marchand, *In Napoleon's Shadow*, p. 336; Gourgaud, *Journal de Sainte-Hélène*, i. p. 53 (18 August 1815).
17. British Library (BL), Add Mss 20146, O'Meara to Finlaison (22 October 1815); Ross to Kingston, 26 July 1815, in Shorter (ed.), *Napoleon and his Fellow Travellers*, p. 61; Las Cases, *Le Mémorial de Sainte-Hélène*, i. pp. 72–4 (11–14 August 1815); Marchand, *In Napoleon's Shadow*, pp. 332–3; Saint-Denis, *Souvenirs*, pp. 138–40.
18. Rose (ed.), *Napoleon's Last Voyages*, pp. 115–220, which recounts in some detail Napoleon's conversations.
19. Las Cases, *Le Mémorial de Sainte-Hélène*, i. p. 134 (7–9 September 1815).
20. On the memoirs during this period see Philip Dwyer, 'Public Remembering, Private Reminiscing: French Military Memoirs and the Revolutionary and Napoleonic Wars', *French Historical Studies*, 33 (2010), 321–58; Natalie Petiteau, *Ecrire la mémoire: mémorialistes de la Révolution et de l'Empire* (Paris, 2012). For British war memoirs see Neil Ramsey, *The Military Memoir and Romantic Literary Culture, 1780–1835* (Farnham, 2011). On war memoirs in general see Philip Dwyer, ' "Making Sense of the Muddle": War and the Culture of Remembering', in Philip Dwyer (ed.), *War Stories: The War Memoir in History and Literature* (New York, 2016), pp. 1–26.

21. Alain Niderst, 'Les mémoires comme genre nostalgique?', in Madeleine Bertaud and François-Xavier Cuche (eds), *Le genre des mémoires, essai de définition* (Paris, 1995), pp. 111–18.

22. Cited in Geoffrey Ellis, *Napoleon* (London, 1997), p. 193.

23. Las Cases, *Le Mémorial de Sainte-Hélène*, ii. p. 70 (23 July 1816).

24. Las Cases, *Le Mémorial de Sainte-Hélène*, i. pp. 143, 174–5, 354–5 (19–22 September, 1–3 October 1815, 18–20 January 1816).

25. Gourgaud, *Journal de Sainte-Hélène*, i. p. 194 (18 November 1816); Bertrand, *Cahiers*, i. p. 130 (2 October 1816); Philippe Gonnard, *Les origines de la légende napoléonienne: l'oeuvre historique de Napoléon à Sainte-Hélène* (Paris, 1906), p. 86.

26. Las Cases, *Le Mémorial de Sainte-Hélène*, i. p. 179 (15 October 1815). Napoleon's exile on St Helena is one of the most written-about periods of his life. For a complete list of works see Chantal Lheureux-Prévot's bibliography in Chevallier, Dancoisne-Martineau and Lentz (eds), *Sainte-Hélène, île de mémoire*, pp. 361–94, which lists more than 1,700 items.

27. Keith Wren, 'Victor Hugo and the Napoleonic Myth', *European History Quarterly*, 10 (October 1980), 429–58, here 431.

28. On this see Stuart Semmel, *Napoleon and the British* (New Haven, 2004), pp. 222–5.

29. See, for example, the hand-coloured etching in the British Museum made by Jean Baptiste Gautier, *Le Promethée de l'Isle Ste Hélène*, September 1815 (Catherine Clerc, *La caricature contre Napoléon* (Paris, 1985), no. 173, p. 301).

30. François-René, vicomte de Chateaubriand, *Mémoires d'outre-tombe*, introduction and notes by Jean-Paul Clément, 2 vols (Paris, 1997), i. pp. 1529, 1531.

31. O'Meara, *Napoleon in Exile*, i. p. 8.

32. Warden, *Letters Written on Board His Majesty's Ship*, p. 101; Marchand, *In Napoleon's Shadow*, p. 339; Chateaubriand, *Mémoires d'outre-tombe*, i. pp. 1556–7; Johannes Willms, *Napoleon & St Helena: On the Island of Exile*, trans. John Brownjohn (London, 2008), p. 5. The only person who has Napoleon commenting on the appearance of the island is Gourgaud, *Journal de Sainte-Hélène*, i. p. 63 (15 October 1815): 'I would have done better to stay in Egypt: I would now be emperor of all the East.'

33. Heinrich Heine, *Reisebilder. Tableaux de voyage*, 2 vols (Paris, 1856), i. pp. 191–2.

34. Walter Henry, *Trifles from my Portfolio; or, Recollections of adventures during twenty-nine years' military service in the Peninsular war and invasion of France, the East Indies, etc.*, 2 vols (Quebec, 1839), i. p. 206. See also Georges Firmon-Didot, *La captivité de Sainte-Hélène, d'après*

les rapports inédits du marquis de Montchenu (Paris, 1894), pp. 14, 19 and 41.

35. Las Cases, *Le Mémorial de Sainte-Hélène*, i. p. 182 (16 October 1815); Marchand, *In Napoleon's Shadow*, p. 345; Henry, *Trifles from my Portfolio*, i. p. 206.

36. Hudson Ralph Janisch, *Extracts from the St. Helena Records* (St Helena, 1908), p. 219.

37. John Fryer, *A New Account of East India and Persia: Being Nine Years' Travels, 1672–1681*, ed. with notes and an introduction by William Crooke, 3 vols (London, 1915), iii. p. 184.

38. Although Gourgaud, *Journal de Sainte-Hélène*, i. p. 65; Marchand, *In Napoleon's Shadow*, p. 341; and O'Meara, *Napoleon in Exile*, i. p. 8, all state that it was the evening of 17 October, they are incorrect.

39. Abell, *Recollections of the Emperor Napoleon*, p. 15. Warden, *Letters Written on Board His Majesty's Ship*, p. 102, wrote that Napoleon came ashore in the evening, when everyone had tired of waiting for him and had gone home.

40. O'Meara, *Napoleon in Exile*, i. p. 8.

41. Pack, *The Man Who Burned the White House*, pp. 225–6.

42. Anne Whitehead, *Betsy and the Emperor* (Sydney, 2015), pp. 49–50.

43. Desmond Gregory, *Napoleon's Jailer: Lt. Gen. Sir Hudson Lowe: A Life* (Madison, 1996), pp. 133–4.

44. Las Cases, *Le Mémorial de Sainte-Hélène*, i. p. 184; O'Meara, *Napoleon in Exile*, i. pp. 11–13.

45. Robert Morrissey, 'The *Mémorial de Sainte-Hélène* and the Poetics of Fusion', *MLN*, 120:4 (2005), 726.

46. Gourgaud, *Journal de Sainte-Hélène*, i. pp. 79–80 (29, 30 November 1815); Marchand, *In Napoleon's Shadow*, p. 361.

47. Abell, *Recollections of the Emperor Napoleon*, pp. 72–5.

48. Las Cases, Gourgaud and Bertrand mention the Balcombe girls, but Betsy's cheeky behaviour is ever only alluded to. See Las Cases, *Le Mémorial de Sainte-Hélène*, i. p. 185; Gourgaud, *Journal de Sainte-Hélène*, i. pp. 70, 114, 325, 326; Bertrand, *Cahiers*, i. pp. 49, 197. Bertrand did not begin his diary until April 1816, four months after the Briars.

49. Willms, *Napoleon & St Helena*, p. 72.

50. Ganière, *Napoléon à Sainte-Hélène*, p. 99.

51. Annie Jourdan, 'Napoleon and History', *French History*, 10:3 (1996), 352–3.

52. Marchand, *In Napoleon's Shadow*, p. 363. Gourgaud accused Montholon of wanting to please the admiral by getting Napoleon out of the Briars (Gourgaud, *Journal de Sainte-Hélène*, i. p. 83 (7 December 1815)). Las

Cases, *Le Mémorial de Sainte-Hélène*, i. pp. 284, 285–6 (7, 8, 9 December 1815); Ganière, *Napoléon à Sainte-Hélène*, pp. 112–13.

53. Las Cases, *Le Mémorial de Sainte-Hélène*, i. p. 265 (26–28 November 1815); Marchand, *In Napoleon's Shadow*, p. 356.

54. Ganière, *Napoléon à Sainte-Hélène*, pp. 102, 110–11.

55. Ganière, *Napoléon à Sainte-Hélène*, p. 164.

56. O'Meara, *Napoleon in Exile*, i. pp. 48–9 (14 May 1816).

57. Bertrand, *Cahiers*, i. p. 148 (17 November 1816).

58. Gregory, *Napoleon's Jailer*, p. 128.

59. Martin Levy, 'Napoleon in Exile: The Houses and Furniture Supplied by the British Government for the Emperor and his Entourage on St Helena', *Furniture History*, 34 (1998), 1–211.

60. Willms, *Napoleon & St Helena*, pp. 112–13.

61. Las Cases, *Le Mémorial de Sainte-Hélène*, i. p. 478.

62. Philip Gosse, *St. Helena, 1502–1938* (London, 1938), pp. 54, 79.

63. Marchand, *In Napoleon's Shadow*, pp. 567–8.

64. Las Cases, *Le Mémorial de Sainte-Hélène*, i. p. 785 (27 June 1816); Gilbert Martineau, *La vie quotidienne à Sainte-Hélène au temps de Napoléon* (Paris, 2005), p. 103.

65. O'Meara, *Napoleon in Exile*, i. pp. 493–5; Stürmer to Metternich (10 January 1817), in Jacques St-Cère and H. Schlitter (eds), *Napoléon à Sainte-Hélène: rapports officiels du baron Stürmer, commissaire du gouvernement autrichien* (Paris, 1888), pp. 66–7.

66. Semmel, *Napoleon and the British*, p. 208.

67. *Morning Chronicle*, 18 October 1815, in *Napoleon: Extracts from the 'Times' and 'Morning Chronicle' 1815–1821 Relating to Napoleon's Life at St. Helena* (London, 1901), pp. 1–3.

68. *Morning Chronicle*, 28 December 1815, in *Napoleon: Extracts from the 'Times' and 'Morning Chronicle'*, p. 9.

69. *The Times*, 17 January 1816.

70. Las Cases, *Le Mémorial de Sainte-Hélène*, i. pp. 203, 304–5 (1–4 November, 18–19 December 1815); Gourgaud, *Journal de Sainte-Hélène*, ii. p. 93 (5 May 1817); Charles Tristan Montholon, *Récits de la captivité de l'empereur Napoléon*, 2 vols (Paris, 1847), ii. p. 267; O'Meara, *Napoleon in Exile*, i. pp. 25–6; Firmon-Didot, *La captivité de Sainte-Hélène*, p. 45 (28 June 1816).

71. See André Rossigneux, 'Ali le mameluk', *Bulletin de la Société des sciences historiques et naturelles de l'Yonne*, 65 (1911), 59–75; and G. Michaut, 'Saint-Denis dit Ali', in Saint-Denis, *Souvenirs*, pp. 17–31.

72. Montholon, *Récits*, ii. pp. 265–6.

73. Las Cases, *Le Mémorial de Sainte-Hélène*, i. pp. 373, 399 (28 January, 25–26 February 1816).
74. Despite assertions to the contrary from Las Cases, *Le Mémorial de Sainte-Hélène*, i. pp. 381–2 (3–6 February 1816).
75. Young, *Napoleon in Exile*, i. p. 165.
76. O'Meara, *Napoleon in Exile*, i. pp. 264–5, 365–6, 370; Martineau, *La vie quotidienne*, p. 74; Unwin, *Terrible Exile*, pp. 136–7.
77. Marchand, *In Napoleon's Shadow*, p. 609.
78. Clementine Malcolm to Margaret Elphinstone (28 June 1816), in Lansdowne (ed.), *The First Napoleon*, p. 187.
79. Gourgaud, *Journal de Sainte-Hélène*, i. p. 179 (14 May 1816).
80. Saint-Denis, *Souvenirs*, pp. 182–3, 239–40; Jacques Macé, 'Les soixante-huit mois de Napoléon à Sainte-Hélène', in Chevallier, Dancoisne-Martineau and Lentz (eds), *Sainte-Hélène, île de mémoire*, p. 60.
81. Marchand, *In Napoleon's Shadow*, p. 387; Ganière, *Napoléon à Sainte-Hélène*, pp. 150–3, 157–8,
82. Saint-Denis, *Souvenirs*, p. 179; Gourgaud, *Journal de Sainte-Hélène*, ii. p. 184 (12 July 1817); Arnold Chaplin, *A St. Helena Who's Who: Or a Directory of the Island during the Captivity of Napoleon* (London, 1919), pp. 132, 133.
83. Ganière, *Napoléon à Sainte-Hélène*, pp. 154–5.
84. Gourgaud, *Journal de Sainte-Hélène*, i. p. 71 (3 November 1815); J. David Markham, *Napoleon and Dr Verling on St Helena* (Barnsley, 2005), p. 47.
85. Rose (ed.), *Napoleon's Last Voyages*, p. 160; Basil Jackson, *Notes and Reminiscences of a Staff Officer, Chiefly Relating to the Waterloo Campaign and to St. Helena Matters during the Captivity of Napoleon* (London, 1903), p. 131.
86. On the struggle over Napoleon's title see Rosebery, *Napoleon: The Last Phase*, pp. 80–95.
87. See also Anna Keay, *The Magnificent Monarch: Charles II and the Ceremonies of Power* (London, 2008), about the importance of form and protocol in maintaining a sense of legitimacy for Charles as a monarch during the years of exile.
88. Las Cases, *Le Mémorial de Sainte-Hélène*, ii. pp. 45–6 (19 July 1816); Göran Blix, 'Heroic Genesis in the *Mémorial de Sainte-Hélène*', *Yale French Studies*, 111 (2007), 107.
89. Las Cases, *Le Mémorial de Sainte-Hélène*, ii. p. 217 (20 May 1816).
90. Las Cases, *Le Mémorial de Sainte-Hélène*, i. p. 628 (22 August 1816); Gourgaud, *Journal de Sainte-Hélène*, ii. pp. 76, 252 (23 April, 17 September 1817).

91. Ganière, *Napoléon à Sainte-Hélène*, p. 124.

92. Las Cases, *Le Mémorial de Sainte-Hélène*, i. pp. 347, 773–4 (12–14 January, 22 June 1816); Saint-Denis, *Souvenirs*, p. 176.

93. According to Albine de Montholon, *Journal secret d'Albine de Montholon, maîtresse de Napoléon à Sainte-Hélène* (Paris, 2002), pp. 135–6.

94. Gourgaud, *Journal de Sainte-Hélène*, i. pp. 102, 191, 194–6, 283–4 (13 December 1815, 14 and 18 November 1816, 14 January 1817).

95. Warden, *Letters Written on Board His Majesty's Ship*, p. 135.

96. Sir George Bingham to Lady Bingham, in Shorter (ed.), *Napoleon and his Fellow Travellers*, p. 333 (8 January 1816); and Thomas H. Brooke, in Clement Shorter (ed.), *Napoleon in his own Defence* (London, 1910), pp. 267–8 (7 February 1816).

97. Sir George Bingham to Lady Bingham, in Shorter (ed.), *Napoleon and his Fellow Travellers*, p. 333 (19 April 1816).

98. Las Cases, *Le Mémorial de Sainte-Hélène*, i. pp. 305, 346–7 (18–19 December 1815, 12–14 January 1816); Marchand, *In Napoleon's Shadow*, p. 385.

99. Charles-Tristan, Comte de Montholon, *History of the Captivity of Napoleon at St. Helena*, 2 vols (London, 1846–7), i. p. 176.

100. Las Cases, *Le Mémorial de Sainte-Hélène*, i. p. 305 (18, 19 December 1815).

101. Saint-Denis, *Souvenirs*, pp. 165–6.

102. Saint-Denis, *Souvenirs*, pp. 240–1.

CHAPTER 3

1. Las Cases, *Le Mémorial de Sainte-Hélène*, i. p. 807 (summary of April, May, June 1816).

2. Herbert Maxwell (ed.), *The Creevey Papers: A Selection from the Correspondence & Diaries of Thomas Creevey* (London, 1904), p. 288.

3. According to Ganière, *Napoléon à Sainte-Hélène*, p. 199; Jean-Pierre Fournier La Touraille, *Hudson Lowe, le geôlier de Napoléon* (Paris, 2006), p. 22.

4. Bathurst to Wellington (24 July 1815), in *Supplementary Despatches, Correspondence, and Memoranda of Field Marshal Arthur, Duke of Wellington*, xi. pp. 55–6.

5. Exmouth to Bathurst (1 August 1815), in *Report on the Manuscripts of Earl Bathurst*, p. 366.

6. Ganière, *Napoléon à Sainte-Hélène*, p. 170; Unwin, *Terrible Exile*, pp. 92–3.

7. Bathurst to Lowe (12 September 1815), in William Forsyth, *History of the Captivity of Napoleon at St. Helena*, 3 vols (London, 1853), i. pp. 437–8.

8. Forsyth, *History of the Captivity of Napoleon at St. Helena*, i. pp. 20–1, 199; Gregory, *Napoleon's Jailer*, p. 126.

9. MacKenzie, *Fallen Eagle*, p. 208.

10. For a description of Lowe see Montholon, *Récits*, i. pp. 244–6.

11. *Le Mémorial de Sainte-Hélène*, i. p. 515 (17 April 1816); Unwin, *Terrible Exile*, pp. 91–2.

12. Lowe gets off quite lightly at the hands of William Forsyth in his mid-nineteenth-century treatment of Napoleon's captivity, *History of the Captivity of Napoleon at St. Helena*, as well as those of Robert Cooper Seaton, *Sir Hudson Lowe and Napoleon* (London, 1898) fifty-odd years later, and T. Dundas Pillans, *The Real Martyr of St. Helena* (London, 1913); and more recently in Fournier La Touraille, *Hudson Lowe, le geôlier de Napoléon*. Lowe is, however, excoriated in Watson's revisionist work *A Polish Exile with Napoleon*.

13. James Kemble (ed.), *St. Helena during Napoleon's Exile: Gorrequer's Diary* (London, 1969), pp. 43, 44–5, 50 (23 and 26 February, 23 March 1818).

14. Philip Henry, Earl Stanhope, *Notes of Conversations with the Duke of Wellington, 1831–1851* (New York, 1888), pp. 104–5, 326–7 (19 October 1837 and 21 December 1848).

15. Kemble (ed.), *Gorrequer's Diary*, p. 34 (19 January 1818); O'Meara, *Napoleon in Exile*, i. p. 190.

16. Kemble (ed.), *Gorrequer's Diary*, pp. 39–40, 51–2, 122 (11 February, 2 April 1818 and March 1819); Gregory, *Napoleon's Jailer*, p. 165.

17. Kemble (ed.), *Gorrequer's Diary*, pp. 261 and 267 (end of 1821 and August 1823 or later).

18. David L. Smallman, *Quincentenary: A Story of St Helena, 1502–2002* (Penzance, 2003), p. 47.

19. Stürmer to Metternich, 13 December 1816, in St-Cère and Schlitter (eds), *Napoléon à Sainte-Hélène: rapports officiels du baron Stürmer*, p. 35.

20. Aleksandr Antonovich Graf Balmain, *Napoleon in Captivity: The Reports of Count Balmain, Russian Commissioner on the Island of St. Helena, 1816–1820*, trans. and ed. with introduction and notes by Julian Park (London, 1928), p. 85 (1 May 1817).

21. Alexandre Balmain, 'Comte de Balmain, Le prisonnier de Sainte-Hélène, d'après les rapports officiels du commissaire du gouvernement russe (1816–1820)', *La Revue politique et littéraire. Revue bleue*, 7 (8 May–12 June 1897), 578–84, 614–22, 647–55, 678–86, 716–22, 745–50.

22. Kemble (ed.), *Gorrequer's Diary*, p. 72 (24 July 1818).

23. Forsyth, *History of the Captivity of Napoleon at St. Helena*, i. p. 235.

24. Stürmer to Metternich (1 June 1818), in St-Cère and H. Schlitter (eds), *Napoléon à Sainte-Hélène: rapports officiels du baron Stürmer*, p. 189.

25. Kemble (ed.), *Gorrequer's Diary*, p. 65 (30 May 1818).

26. Stürmer to Metternich (1 June 1818), in St-Cère and H. Schlitter (eds), *Napoléon à Sainte-Hélène: rapports officiels du baron Stürmer*, p. 202.

27. Cited in Gregory, *Napoleon's Jailer*, pp. 153–4.

28. Warden's account was translated into French, published in Brussels and probably smuggled across the border. By all accounts, it received a 'passionate' reception in France (Jean Lucas-Dubreton, *Le culte de Napoléon, 1815–1848* (Paris, 1960), p. 125; Gonnard, *Les origines de la légende*, p. 28). The upshot of publishing a book favourable to Napoleon was that Warden was dismissed from the service (Howard, *Napoleon's Poisoned Chalice*, pp. 25–8).

29. See Linda Kelly, *Holland House: A History of London's Most Celebrated Salon* (London, 2013), esp. pp. 90–9.

30. BL Add Mss 20158, Montholon to Albine, 5 November 1819.

31. Gourgaud, *Journal de Sainte-Hélène*, ii. pp. 21–2, 23, 24–5, 26 (5, 6, 7, 9 March 1817); O'Meara, *Napoleon in Exile*, i. pp. 415–20; Bertrand, *Cahiers*, i. pp. 204, 205 (7, 8, 9 March 1817); Marchand, *In Napoleon's Shadow*, pp. 486–7; Ganière, *Napoléon à Sainte-Hélène*, p. 232.

32. It was translated into English with a preface by Barry O'Meara as *Letters from the Cape of Good Hope, in reply to Mr. Warden; with extracts from the great work now compiling for publication under the inspection of Napoleon* (London, 1817).

33. Gregory, *Napoleon's Jailer*, p. 147.

34. BL Add Mss 20124, 1 October 1818; Gregory, *Napoleon's Jailer*, pp. 172–3.

35. Henry, *Trifles from my Portfolio*, ii. p. 13; Forsyth, *History of the Captivity of Napoleon at St. Helena*, i. pp. 126–30.

36. Thomas Skinner, *Fifty Years in Ceylon: An Autobiography* (London, 1891), pp. 74–5; Lady Strachey (ed.), *Memoirs of a Highland Lady: The Autobiography of Elizabeth Grant of Rothiemurchus, 1797–1830* (London, 1898), pp. 459–60; Gregory, *Napoleon's Jailer*, p. 181. Jackson, *Notes and Reminiscences*, pp. 173–5, also came to his defence.

37. Bower J. Vernon, *Early Recollections of Jamaica* (London, 1848), pp. 179–81.

38. Willms, *Napoleon & St Helena*, p. 136.

39. For the meeting see BL Add Mss 20146, O'Meara to Finlaison, 22 April 1816; Marchand, *In Napoleon's Shadow*, pp. 401–3; Gourgaud,

Journal de Sainte-Hélène, i. pp. 122–3 (16 April 1816); Las Cases, *Le Mémorial de Sainte-Hélène*, i. pp. 507–8 (16 April 1816); O'Meara, *Napoleon in Exile*, i. pp. 27–8; Ganière, *Napoléon à Sainte-Hélène*, pp. 166–7, 172–3; James Kemble, *Napoleon Immortal: The Medical History and Private Life of Napoleon Bonaparte* (London, 1959), p. 239.

40. BL Add Mss 20122, Instructions for the Orderly Officer at Longwood, 1 May 1818. O'Meara writes that Napoleon sent word that he would receive Lowe between 1 and 5 p.m. (O'Meara to Finlaison, 22 April 1816, in Albert Benhamou, *Inside Longwood: Barry O'Meara's Clandestine Letters* (Hemel Hempstead, 2012), p. 43).

41. Las Cases, *Le Mémorial de Sainte-Hélène*, i. p. 512 (17 April 1816); Montholon, *Récits*, i. p. 244. See also Gourgaud, *Journal de Sainte-Hélène*, i. pp. 123–4 (17 April 1816); Marchand, *In Napoleon's Shadow*, pp. 402–3; Forsyth, *History of the Captivity of Napoleon*, i. pp. 181–2; and Sir George Bingham to Lady Bingham, in Shorter (ed.), *Napoleon and his Fellow Travellers*, p. 334 (19 April 1816).

42. Smallman, *Quincentenary: A Story of St Helena*, p. 50.

43. Las Cases, *Le Mémorial de Sainte-Hélène*, i. pp. 550–3 (30 April 1816); Bertrand, *Cahiers*, i. pp. 19–20 (30 April).

44. Gourgaud, *Journal de Sainte-Hélène*, i. p. 294 (6 December 1816); Las Cases, *Le Mémorial de Sainte-Hélène*, i. p. 673 (2 June 1816); and Marchand, *In Napoleon's Shadow*, pp. 506–7.

45. BL Add Mss 20146, O'Meara to Finlaison, 10 October 1816.

46. Montholon, *Récits*, i. p. 244; Gregory, *Napoleon's Jailer*, p. 129; Martineau, *Napoléon à Sainte-Hélène*, pp. 76, 140.

47. According to Clementine Malcolm to Mary Elphinstone (25 July 1816), in Lansdowne (ed.), *The First Napoleon*, p. 194.

48. Las Cases, *Le Mémorial de Sainte-Hélène*, i. pp. 515, 645–6 (17 April, 27 May 1816); Warden, *Letters Written on Board His Majesty's Ship*, pp. 176–7.

49. Napoleon was probably familiar with Johann Casper Laveter, a Swiss German *philosophe* best known for his work on physiognomy in the eighteenth century. See Lucy Hartley, *Physiognomy and the Meaning of Expression in Nineteenth-Century Culture* (Cambridge, 2001), esp. 15–43; and Richard T. Gray, *About Face: German Physiognomic Thought from Lavater to Auschwitz* (Detroit, 2004).

50. BL Add Mss 20146, O'Meara to Finlaison, 10 October 1816; O'Meara, *Napoleon in Exile*, i. pp. 129–30. Lowe adamantly denied putting his hand on his sword. See Lowe to O'Meara, 3 October 1816, in Forsyth, *History of the Captivity of Napoleon at St. Helena*, i. pp. 318–19.

51. Las Cases, *Le Mémorial de Sainte-Hélène*, i. pp. 571, 611–13; Marchand, *In Napoleon's Shadow*, pp. 411–12; Bertrand, *Cahiers*, i. pp. 30–1, 37–41, 145 (12 November 1816); O'Meara, *Napoleon in Exile*, i. pp. 50–1; Forsyth, *History of the Captivity of Napoleon at St. Helena*, i. pp. 171–6, 176–8.

52. See, for example, a letter from Bertrand to Lowe (30 September 1817) in Forsyth, *History of the Captivity of Napoleon at St. Helena*, ii. pp. 423–6.

53. Frank Giles, *Napoleon Bonaparte: England's Prisoner* (New York, 2001), p. 80.

54. Las Cases, *Le Mémorial de Sainte-Hélène*, i. p. 664 (31 May 1816); Forsyth, *History of the Captivity of Napoleon at St. Helena*, i. pp. 178–9.

55. Las Cases, *Le Mémorial de Sainte-Hélène*, i. p. 664 (31 May 1816).

56. See Gourgaud, *Journal de Sainte-Hélène*, i. pp. 162, 174 (16 July, 18 August 1816); Las Cases, *Le Mémorial de Sainte-Hélène*, ii. pp. 37–9, 205–8 (16 July, 18 August 1816); Bertrand, *Cahiers*, i. pp. 82–6, 106–8 (16 July, 18 August 1816); O'Meara, *Napoleon in Exile*, i. pp. 93–6 (19 August 1816); Marchand, *In Napoleon's Shadow*, pp. 432–3; Clementine Malcolm, *A Diary of St. Helena. The Journal of Lady Malcolm (1816, 1817)*, ed. Sir Arthur Wilson, with an introduction by Muriel Kent (London, 1929), pp. 54–5, 56–69 (16 and 18 August 1816); Forsyth, *History of the Captivity of Napoleon at St. Helena*, i. pp. 245–56. Malcolm was eventually replaced by Admiral Sir Robert Plampin from 1816 to 1820.

57. Forsyth, *History of the Captivity of Napoleon at St. Helena*, i. 246–51; Young, *Napoleon in Exile*, i. pp. 291–2; Ralph Korngold, *The Last Years of Napoleon: His Captivity on St. Helena* (London, 1960), p. 191; Gregory, *Napoleon's Jailer*, p. 205, n. 31.

58. Malcolm, *A Diary of St. Helena*, pp. 57–8.

59. Forsyth, *History of the Captivity of Napoleon at St. Helena*, i. pp. 245–56; Gregory, *Napoleon's Jailer*, p. 131.

60. Bertrand, *Cahiers*, i. p. 105 (16 August 1816); O'Meara, *Napoleon in Exile*, i. pp. 109–12; Forsyth, *History of the Captivity of Napoleon at St. Helena*, i. pp. 189–90.

61. Napoleon enjoyed a considerable personal fortune, some of which he had managed to smuggle on board the *Northumberland* – around 300,000 francs – with another seven million deposited with bankers in Europe or with his relatives. See Pierre Branda, *Le prix de la gloire: Napoléon et l'argent* (Paris, 2007), pp. 83–5. The silverware that he brought with him to the island was valued at over 128,000 francs (*Napoléon à Sainte-Hélène: la conquête de la mémoire* (Paris, 2016), pp. 284–5).

62. The 'Botany Bay' epithet was levelled at Lowe on a number of occasions. See BL Add Mss 20146, O'Meara to Finlaison, 29 June 1817.

63. Forsyth, *History of the Captivity of Napoleon at St. Helena*, iii. p. 336.

64. BL Add Mss 20146, O'Meara to Finlaison, 10 October 1816; Forsyth, *History of the Captivity of Napoleon at St. Helena*, i. pp. 288–90, 297, 360–2.

65. BL Add Mss 14059, 'Statement of the Allowance of Wine, Provisions and Supplies', October 1820. Napoleon's exile significantly stimulated the production of produce in the Cape during this period. See Susan Newton-King, 'The Labour Market of the Cape Colony, 1807–1828', in Shula Marks and Anthony Atmore (eds), *Economy and Society in Pre-Industrial South Africa* (London, 1980), p. 173.

66. BL Add Mss 20222, f. 136, 31 August 1820.

67. Young, *Napoleon in Exile*, i. pp. 157–8.

68. Rod Phillips, *Alcohol: A History* (Chapel Hill, NC, 2014), pp. 4, 92–6.

69. Maitland, *The Surrender of Napoleon*, p. 219; Saint-Denis, *Souvenirs*, p. 163. An indication of how much wine was imported into St Helena from the Cape is in Marcus Arkin, 'Supplies for Napoleon's Gaolers: John Company and the Cape-St. Helena Trade during the Captivity, 1815–21', *Archives Year Book for South African History*, 1 (1964), 200–6, in which we can see that 20,000 gallons (or over 90,000 litres) of wine was ordered for the civilian population for the year 1820–1 (I am assuming it is the white population), while another 120,000 gallons (or over 545,000 litres) was ordered for the garrison. The French servants, it has to be said, also played little games of non-cooperation and passive resistance. The bottles had to be filled from casks. Lowe tried to arrange for the collection of empty wine bottles, since there was a shortage on the island, but the servants used to smash them in a pile near the house just to exasperate the governor (Martineau, *La vie quotidienne*, p. 74).

70. Gourgaud, *Journal de Sainte-Hélène*, i. pp. 113, 158 (19 February, 2 July 1816); ii. p. 118 (28 May 1817). Ganière, *Napoléon à Sainte-Hélène*, p. 213, states that, for the month of October 1816, fifteen bottles of Bordeaux and one of champagne were delivered every day, along with seven chickens, 75 kilos of beef or mutton, thirty-four eggs, about 3.5 kilos of salted butter, 500 grams of cheese, 2 kilos of flour, 2 kilos of rice and so on. But then, the chef was feeding about fifty people.

71. Gourgaud, *Journal de Sainte-Hélène*, i. p. 158 (2 July 1816), accused Gentilini of making money by selling supplies to the English troops; Martineau, *La vie quotidienne*, pp. 95–6.

72. Marchand, *In Napoleon's Shadow*, pp. 434–40; Las Cases, *Le Mémorial de Sainte-Hélène*, ii. pp. 219–26 (23 August 1816).

73. Archives Nationales (AN) F7 6926, Police générale, dossier Santini, 22 April 1822; *Morning Chronicle*, 13 March 1817, in *Napoleon: Extracts from the 'Times' and 'Morning Chronicle'*, pp. 29–34; Marchand, *In Napoleon's Shadow*, p. 458; Charles Jean François Tristan de Montholon, *Bonaparte's Memorial in a letter addressed by General Count Montholon to Sir Hudson Lowe* (London, 1817); Forsyth, *History of the Captivity of Napoleon at St. Helena*, i. pp. 257–67; Giles, *Napoleon Bonaparte*, pp. 53–4. On Santini see Henri Rossi, *Les Corses des services secrets de Napoléon en exil* (Ajaccio, 2007), pp. 103–32.

74. *An appeal to the British nation on the treatment experienced by Napoleon Buonaparte in the Island of St. Helena, with an authentic copy of the official memoir dictated by Napoleon, and delivered to Sir Hudson Lowe* (London, 1817).

75. Henry Richard Vassall-Fox, Baron Holland, as well as the Duke of Sussex, the sixth son of George III, spoke out on at least two occasions against the restrictions that had been placed on Napoleon and his supposed persecution at the hands of Lowe. See *The Parliamentary Debates from the Year 1803 to the Present Time*, 41 vols (London, 1812–20), xxxiii. pp. 1011–20 (8 April 1816); xxxv. pp. 1137–66 (18 March 1817). See also D. C. Moylan (ed.), *The Opinions of Lord Holland, as Recorded in the Journals of the House of Lords, from 1797 to 1841* (London, 1841), pp. 84–7; Forsyth, *History of the Captivity of Napoleon at St. Helena*, i. p. 22).

76. See BL Add Mss 20146, O'Meara to Finlaison (10 October 1816), in which O'Meara states that it was an attempt on the part of Napoleon to undermine Lowe 'by saying that he has been obliged to sell his plate'. Also Add Mss 20146, O'Meara to Finlaison (13 and 17 September 1816).

77. Ganière, *Napoléon à Sainte-Hélène*, pp. 217–18. On 14 August according to Gourgaud, *Journal de Sainte-Hélène*, i. p. 173.

78. Las Cases, *Le Mémorial de Sainte-Hélène*, ii. pp. 362–3 (20 September 1816); Bertrand, *Cahiers*, i. pp. 124–5 (19 September 1816); Marchand, *In Napoleon's Shadow*, pp. 446, 448–51.

79. O'Meara, *Napoleon in Exile*, i. p. 122. On Cipriani see O'Meara, *Napoleon in Exile*, ii. p. 389.

80. Gourgaud, *Journal de Sainte-Hélène*, ii. p. 14 (28 February 1817); Unwin, *Terrible Exile*, pp. 119–20.

81. O'Meara, *Napoleon in Exile*, i. 299–300; Forsyth, *History of the Captivity of Napoleon at St. Helena*, ii. pp. 409–10; Ganière, *Napoléon à Sainte-Hélène*, pp. 217–19.

82. Gourgaud, *Journal de Sainte-Hélène*, ii. p. 244 (10 September 1817); O'Meara, *Napoleon in Exile*, ii. pp. 191–2; Lowe to Bathurst (17

September 1817), in Forsyth, *History of the Captivity of Napoleon at St. Helena*, ii. pp. 452–3.

83. Forsyth, *History of the Captivity of Napoleon at St. Helena*, ii. pp. 33, and Lowe to Bathurst (17 September 1817), pp. 452–3,

84. Ganière, *Napoléon à Sainte-Hélène*, p. 219, although this may be apocryphal.

85. Forsyth, *History of the Captivity of Napoleon at St. Helena*, i. pp. 58–62 (22 December 1815).

86. Marchand, *In Napoleon's Shadow*, pp. 445–6; Forsyth, *History of the Captivity of Napoleon at St. Helena*, i. pp. 41–3.

87. Rose (ed.), *Napoleon's Last Voyages*, pp. 41–2; Dwyer, *Citizen Emperor*, p. 498.

88. Las Cases, *Le Mémorial de Sainte-Hélène*, i. pp. 578–9 (11 May 1816).

89. Johann Willms, *Napoleon. Verbannung und Verklärung* (Munich, 2000), pp. 94–5.

90. BL Add Mss 20146, O'Meara to Finlaison, 22 October 1815; Add Mss 20216, O'Meara to Finlaison, 23 December 1816; Marchand, *In Napoleon's Shadow*, p. 445; O'Meara, *Napoleon in Exile*, i. pp. 156–9, 160–1; Forsyth, *History of the Captivity of Napoleon at St. Helena*, i. pp 346–53; Markham, *Napoleon and Dr Verling*, p. 39 (15 November 1818). On Muiron see Philip Dwyer, *Napoleon: The Path to Power* (London, 2007), pp. 2, 4.

91. Balmain, *Napoleon in Captivity*, p. 24 (6 September 1816).

92. Young, *Napoleon in Exile*, i. p. 324.

93. Young, *Napoleon in Exile*, ii. pp. 215–16; Ganière, *Napoléon à Sainte-Hélène*, p. 196; Forsyth, *History of the Captivity of Napoleon at St. Helena*, iii. pp. 155–6; Henry Edward Lord Holland (ed.), *Foreign Reminiscences* (Paris, 1854), pp. 42–3; Kelly, *Holland House*, p. 93. Napoleon was able by one means or another to put together a sizeable library at Longwood of 3,370 books. See Las Cases, *Le Mémorial de Sainte-Hélène*, i. pp. 773, 779, 780 (24, 25 June 1816); ii. p. 207 (18 August 1816); Gourgaud, *Journal de Sainte-Hélène*, i. pp. 154–5 (22 June 1816); Bertrand, *Cahiers*, i. p. 69 (22 June 1816); Albéric Cahuet, *Après la mort de l'Empereur* (Paris, 1913), pp. 201–48; Jacques Jourquin, 'La bibliothèque de Sainte-Hélène', in Chevallier, Dancoisne-Martineau and Lentz (eds), *Sainte-Hélène, île de mémoire*, pp. 121–5.

94. Bertrand, *Cahiers de Sainte-Hélène*, ii. p. 320 (26 March 1819).

95. Willms, *Verbannung und Verklärung*, p. 83.

96. AN F7 6668, Surveillance de la famille Bonaparte, Pius VII to Alexander, 17 November 1817; Aubry, *Sainte-Hélène*, p. 302. Cardinal Pacca, on the other hand, who had once been a prisoner of Napoleon, saw his

treatment on St Helena as divine retribution (Michael Sibalis, 'Political Prisoners and State Prisons in Napoleonic France', in Philip Dwyer and Alan Forrest (eds), *Napoleon and his Empire: Europe, 1804–1814* (New York, 2007), p. 109).

97. An imagery that was first employed by Heine, *Reisebilder*, i. p. 275. On the concept of martyrdom see Jolyon Mitchell, *Martyrdom: A Very Short Introduction* (Oxford, 2012).

98. Las Cases, *Le Mémorial de Sainte-Hélène*, i. p. 496 (9–10 April 1816). There are some studies on Napoleon as Messiah. See André Lebey, 'Le Messianisme napoléonien depuis 1815 jusqu'en 1848', *Le Censeur politique et littéraire*, 11 January 1908, pp. 33–40 – it is alluded to in a number of writings (like Jacques-Olivier Boudon, 'Grand homme ou demi-dieu? La mise en place d'une religion napoléonienne', *Romantisme*, 100 (1998), 131–41; Jean Tulard, *Le mythe de Napoléon* (Paris, 1971), pp. 85–92). Frank Paul Bowman, *Le Christ romantique* (Geneva, 1973), pp. 171–93 is the most complete to date. On the other hand, Jules Dechamps, *Sur la légende de Napoléon* (Paris, 1931) is convinced of the popular origins not only of the legend, but also of its Messianic aspects. See also Anne-Sophie Durozoy, 'Zu den französischen Quellen der Napoleon-Legende', in Marion George and Andrea Rudolph (eds), *Napoleons langer Schatten über Europa* (Dettelbach, 2008), pp. 157–69.

99. Gourgaud, *Sainte-Hélène, journal inédit*, ii. pp. 225–6 (23 July 1817). Montholon, *Récits*, ii. pp. 151–2, has Napoleon saying that 'if Christ had not been crucified, he would not be God' – that is, he was aware of the importance of martyrdom in the construction of Christianity.

100. For the 'saviour image', as well as the use of St Napoleon, see Dwyer, *Napoleon: The Path to Power*, pp. 452–62, 505–14; and *Citizen Emperor*, pp. 152–4, 212–15. See also Werner Telesko, *Erlösermythen in Kunst und Politik. Zwischen christlicher Tradition und Moderne* (Vienna, 2004), pp. 71–7.

101. At the time, the two terms Bonapartist and Napoleonist were used interchangeably. The distinction between Napoleonism and Bonapartism was first made by Frédéric Bluche, and later adopted by Bernard Ménager. Napoleonism, used by contemporaries to describe a sentiment of admiration for the person of Napoleon, had no political implications. An extreme form of Napoleonism was the cult, which verged on love for the man. Bonapartism was a political current, a (nostalgic) desire to see the return of the imperial regime in the person either of Napoleon or of his son. Of course the two sentiments were sometimes enmeshed or confused. Sudhir Hazareesingh has since rejected the

distinction between Napoleonist and Bonapartist, arguing that politics and sentiment are inextricably bound. This is true. Napoleonist sentiment could sometimes be transformed into Bonapartist will – that is, an emotional attachment to the man could sometimes find a political outlet. The memorial literature that appeared after Napoleon's death could transform a Napoleonist into a Bonapartist. However, sentiment does not always lead to political action. It was entirely possible, à la Victor Hugo, to be a Napoleonist but not a Bonapartist, to celebrate the man and his exploits without wanting to re-establish the Empire. Besides, as R. S. Alexander points out, Bonapartists could also be republicans. There were, of course, ways of recognizing a Bonapartist, if you knew what to look for. The most obvious sign was a violet in the lapel, but in certain cafés it was wearing a ring with the letter 'N', or a secret handshake which involved tracing an 'N' with the thumb (Lucas-Dubreton, *Le culte de Napoléon*, pp. 118, 158).

102. Charles Caillaux, *Arche de la Nouvelle-Alliance: prologue, par un apôtre évadien* (Paris, 1840), p. 115.

103. This kind of thinking was integral to a new Christian cult known as Evadism founded by Simon Vanneau in the 1830s. In it, the anniversary of Waterloo was to become the new Holy Friday. See Paul Bénichou, *Le temps des prophètes: doctrines de l'âge romantique* (Paris, 1977), pp. 429–35.

104. Sudhir Hazareesingh, 'Napoleonic Memory in Nineteenth-Century France: The Making of a Liberal Legend', *MLN*, 120:4 (2005), 757–9.

105. See Dwyer, *Citizen Emperor*, pp. 152–5; Pagé, *Le mythe napoléonien*, pp. 103–8.

106. Barbara Ann Day-Hickman, *Napoleonic Art: Nationalism and the Spirit of Rebellion in France (1815–1848)* (Newark, 1999), p. 104.

107. Bertrand, *Cahiers*, i. p. 113 (28 August 1816); ii. p. 159 (3 October 1818).

108. See, for example, BL Add Mss 20210, Journal of Captain Nicholls (6 July 1819); Giles, *England's Prisoner*, pp. 91–5.

109. BL Add Mss 20210, Journal of Captain Nicholls (18 September 1818).

110. Young, *Napoleon in Exile*, ii. pp. 161–5; Chaplin, *A St. Helena Who's Who*, p. 106.

111. BL Add Mss 20131, f. 297, Lutyens to Gorrequer (10 December 1820); Kemble (ed.), *Gorrequer's Diary*, p. 94 (3 October 1818); Watson, *A Polish Exile with Napoleon*, p. 15, n. 2.

112. According to O'Meara, *Napoleon in Exile*, ii. p. 516.

113. Bertrand to Lowe (24 July 1818), in Forsyth, *History of the Captivity of Napoleon at St. Helena*, ii. p. 545; and iii. p. 33; Marchand, *In Napoleon's Shadow*, p. 400, n. 285.

114. Kemble (ed.), *Gorrequer's Diary*, p. 27 (8 December 1817). On the challenge see Watson, *A Polish Exile with Napoleon*, pp. 18–20; Forsyth, *History of the Captivity of Napoleon at St. Helena*, iii. pp. 33–6.

115. Bathurst to Lowe, 26 June 1816, and Goulburn to Lowe, 20 July 1816, in Forsyth, *History of the Captivity of Napoleon at St. Helena*, ii. pp. 256–7 and 265–6.

116. Gregory, *Napoleon's Jailer*, p. 128.

117. Gregory, *Napoleon's Jailer*, p. 129.

118. Las Cases, *Le Mémorial de Sainte-Hélène*, ii. pp. 404 and 414–18 (9 October 1816), and Bertrand, *Cahiers*, i. pp. 130–1, place the interview on 4 October; Gourgaud, *Journal de Sainte-Hélène*, i. p. 178, on 3 October 1816. See also Montholon, *History of the Captivity of Napoleon*, i. pp. 273–8; Marchand, *In Napoleon's Shadow*, pp. 451–2, 456–7; and Forsyth, *History of the Captivity of Napoleon at St. Helena*, i. pp. 313–18, 319–21.

119. For what follows see BL Add Mss 20216, O'Meara to Finlaison (23 December 1816); O'Meara, *Napoleon in Exile*, i. pp. 154–5; Bertrand, *Cahiers de Sainte-Hélène*, i. pp. 136–8 (15–19 October 1816); Las Cases, *Le Mémorial de Sainte-Hélène*, ii. pp. 419–20, 430, 432–7, 448–9 (10, 14, 15, 18 October 1816); Montholon, *Récits*, i. pp. 405–20; Marchand, *In Napoleon's Shadow*, pp. 452–4; Forsyth, *History of the Captivity of Napoleon at St. Helena*, i. pp 152–7, 278–83; Ganière, *Napoléon à Sainte-Hélène*, p. 215.

120. Bertrand, *Cahiers de Sainte-Hélène*, i. p. 136.

121. Marchand, *In Napoleon's Shadow*, pp. 453–4; Ganière, *Napoléon à Sainte-Hélène*, p. 216.

122. Marchand, *In Napoleon's Shadow*, p. 452.

123. Marchand, *In Napoleon's Shadow*, p. 459.

CHAPTER 4

1. Rafe Blaufarb, *Bonapartists in the Borderlands: French Exiles and Refugees on the Gulf Coast, 1815–1835* (Tuscaloosa, 2006), pp. 77–8 and, for other escape plots, 79–81.

2. For escape plans see Ulane Bonnel, 'Espoirs de délivrance', in Ulane Bonnel (ed.), *Sainte-Hélène, terre d'exile* (Paris, 1971), pp. 229–57; Clarence Edward Macartney and Gordon Dorrance, *The Bonapartes in America* (Philadelphia, 1939), pp. 241–72; J. A. Da Costa, 'Napoléon Ier au Brésil', *Revue du monde latin*, 8 (January–April 1886), 205–16, 339–49. On French concerns about the exile community see Lucas-Dubreton, *Le culte de Napoléon*, pp. 96–108.

3. *Morning Chronicle*, 12 November 1818; Emilio Ocampo, *The Emperor's Last Campaign: A Napoleonic Empire in America* (Tuscaloosa, 2009), pp. 297–8.

4. Ocampo, *The Emperor's Last Campaign*, pp. 104–10.

5. Georges Ribe, *L'opinion publique et la vie politique à Lyon lors des premières années de la seconde Restauration, la réaction ultra et l'expérience constitutionnelle, 17 juillet 1815–9 janvier 1822* (Lyons, 1957), pp. 100–1.

6. Martyn Lyons, *Post-Revolutionary Europe, 1815–1856* (Basingstoke, 2006), p. 60; R. S. Alexander, 'Restoration Republicanism Reconsidered', *French History*, 8:4 (1994), 447. It is no longer considered accurate to describe the post-1815 era as the 'Restoration', largely because most governments of the time did not want to restore the old order. See Paul W. Schroeder, *The Transformation of European Politics, 1763–1848* (Oxford, 1994), p. 586. The period from 1814 to 1848 is often referred to as the *monarchie censitaire* in France, a reference to the level of property tax electors had to pay in order to vote.

7. See Natalie Petiteau, *Lendemains d'empire: les soldats de Napoléon dans la France du XIXe siècle* (Paris, 2003), pp. 83–8, 108–14, 141–58.

8. According to Frédéric Bluche, *Le bonapartisme: aux origines de la droite autoritaire, 1800–1850* (Paris, 1980), pp. 130–6, here p. 131. That number decreased over time as they were slowly reintegrated into society. On this group of veterans see Jean Vidalenc, *Les Demi-soldes, étude d'une catégorie sociale* (Paris, 1955).

9. The expression is from Sudhir Hazareesingh, *The Legend of Napoleon* (London, 2004), p. 37. See also Petiteau, *Lendemains d'empire*, pp. 131–4.

10. Vidalenc, *Les demi-soldes*, p. 183, argues that they 'slowly modified public opinion' in favour of Napoleon. On the other hand, Natalie Petiteau, *Napoléon, de la mythologie à l'histoire* (Paris, 2004), ch. 1; idem, *Lendemains d'empire*, pp. 269–81; idem, 'Les vétérans du Premier Empire: un groupe socioprofessionnel oublié', *Cahiers d'histoire*, 43:1 (1998), 25–45; Gilles Malandain, 'La haine des Bourbons sous la Restauration: quelques remarques sur un sentiment politique', in Frédéric Chauvaud and Ludovic Gaussot (eds), *La Haine: histoire et actualité* (Rennes, 2008), pp. 78–9, all question the traditional thesis of the legend propagated by veterans.

11. Bluche, *Le bonapartisme*, p. 135; Alexander, *Napoleon*, p. 152.

12. John A. Lynn, *The Bayonets of the Republic: Motivation and Tactics in the Army of Revolutionary France, 1791–94* (Urbana, 1984), pp. 61–3.

13. See Jean-François Bois, *Les anciens soldats dans la société française au XVIIIe siècle* (Paris, 1990); Isser Woloch, *The French Veteran from*

the Revolution to the Restoration (Chapel Hill, NC, 1979); Gérard de Puymège, Chauvin, le soldat-laboreur: contribution à l'étude des nationalisme (Paris, 1993); and Alexander, Napoleon, pp. 152–3, 156–7. This view, it should be noted, has been challenged by David M. Hopkin, 'La Ramée, the Archetypal Soldier, as an Indicator of Popular Attitudes to the Army in Nineteenth-Century France', French History, 14 (2000), 115–49; idem, Soldier and Peasant in French Popular Culture, 1766–1870 (Woodbridge, 2002), esp. pp. 282–352, who points to the disparity between peasant attitudes towards veterans on the one hand and cultural portrayals of them on the other. Hopkin concludes that peasant attitudes towards the veteran did not greatly evolve during the nineteenth century – that is, that soliders and veterans continued to be treated with a good deal of mistrust and as violent no-goods, a distinct class apart on the margins of society.

14. Lettres inédites du maréchal Bugeaud, duc d'Isly (1808–1809) (Paris, 1923), pp. 50–1; Bluche, Le bonapartisme, pp. 126–30.

15. Charles Clément, Géricault: étude biographique et critique (Paris, 1868), p. 211; Darcy Grimaldo Grigsby, Extremities: Painting Empire in Post-Revolutionary France (New Haven, 2002), pp. 178–80.

16. Jean-Noël Tardy, L'âge des ombres: complots, conspirations et sociétés secrètes au XIXe siècle (Paris, 2015), esp. pp. 47–75; Edouard Guillon, Les complots militaires sous la restauration (Paris, 1895); and Josiane Bourguet-Rouveyre, 'Les Bonapartistes dans les conspirations de 1815 à 1823', in Bernard Gainot et Pierre Serna (eds), Secret et République: 1795–1840 (Clermont-Ferrand, 2003), pp. 129–43.

17. Bluche, Le bonapartisme, pp. 140–3; Alan B. Spitzer, Old Hatreds and Young Hopes: The French Carbonari against the Bourbon Restoration (Cambridge, Mass., 1971), pp. 39–50.

18. Lucas-Dubreton, Le culte de Napoléon, pp. 146, 193.

19. On the relationship between liberals and Bonapartists see Hazareesingh, 'Napoleonic Memory in Nineteenth-Century France', 747–73.

20. In the words of George Beauchef, Mémoires pour servir à l'indépendance du Chili, trans. and ed. Patrick Puigmal (Paris, 2001), p. 7.

21. There is a considerable literature on the Bonapartist diaspora in the Americas, much of it dated. The most recent are Blaufarb, Bonapartists in the Borderlands; Ocampo, The Emperor's Last Campaign; and Eric Saugera, Reborn in America: French Exiles and Refugees in the United States and the Vine and Olive Adventure, 1815–1865, trans. Madeleine Velguth (Tuscaloosa, 2011), esp. pp. 165–70. See also Natasha S. Naujoks, 'Between Memory and History: Political Uses of the Napoleonic Past in

France, 1815–1840' (PhD dissertation, University of North Carolina at Chapel Hill, 2013), pp. 88–121.

22. Bluche, *Le bonapartisme*, pp. 138–9.

23. Jean-Guillaume Hyde de Neuville, *Mémoires et souvenirs du baron Hyde de Neuville*, 3 vols (Paris, 1888–92), ii. pp. 204–5; Ocampo, *The Emperor's Last Campaign*, pp. 81–4. On the duc de Richelieu's concerns about Napoleon see Sébastien Charléty (ed.), *Lettres du duc de Richelieu au marquis d'Osmond, 1816–1818* (Paris, 1939), pp. 46 (5 July 1816), 59 and 62 (2 and 12 September 1816) and 89–90 (6 January 1817); Michael Ross, *The Reluctant King: Joseph Bonaparte, King of the Two Sicilies and Spain* (London, 1976), pp. 252–3.

24. BL Add Mss 20119, 'Extrait d'une lettre Ecrite de Philadelphie' (24 July 1817); Hyde de Neuville, *Mémoires*, ii. pp. 317–18.

25. Charléty (ed.), *Lettres du duc de Richelieu*, pp. 133–61.

26. See, for example, Robert Harvey, *Cochrane: The Life and Exploits of a Fighting Captain* (London, 2000), pp. 226–8, 231, 249; Unwin, *Terrible Exile*, p. 188; William Edmundson, *A History of the British Presence in Chile: From Bloody Mary to Charles Darwin and the Decline of British Influence* (New York, 2009), p. 68.

27. BL Add Mss 20158, f. 6, 'Copy of a letter sent through the Post Office, explaining the means of effecting the escape of General Bonaparte from St Helena' (no date but probably around the end of 1816). See also Charléty (ed.), *Lettres du duc de Richelieu*, p. 190; Brian Vale, *Cochrane in the Pacific: Fortune and Freedom in Spanish America* (London, 2008), p. 203.

28. Walter Bruyère-Ostells, *La grande armée de la liberté* (Paris, 2009), pp. 35–6.

29. Montholon, *History of the Captivity of Napoleon*, ii. pp. 477–8; and Montholon, *Récits*, i. p. 348, ii. pp. 100–1, 427.

30. Montholon, *Récits*, ii. p. 435.

31. AN BB18 964, Correspondance générale de la division criminelle, Douai, 4 and 7 October 1816, mentions a proclamation posted in the commune of Sangatte supposedly by Marie-Louise announcing the arrival of Archduke Charles of Austria and Eugène at the head of two armies. The proclamation was full of spelling mistakes. See also Natalie Petiteau, 'La Monarchie de Juillet face aux héritages napoléoniens', in Patrick Harismendy (ed.), *La France des années 1830 et l'esprit de réforme* (Rennes, 2006), p. 57; François Ploux, *De bouche à l'oreille: naissance et propagation des rumeurs dans la France du XIXe siècle* (Paris, 2003), pp. 133, 134–8, 140–3; Gilles Malandain, 'Rumeurs et bavardages: indices

d'une appropriation ordinaire du politique dans la France censitaire', in Laurent Le Gall, Michel Offerlé and François Ploux (eds), *La politique sans en avoir l'air: aspects de la politique informelle, XIXe–XXIe siècle* (Rennes, 2012), pp. 149–62. On the role of rumour in history see Anjan Ghosh, 'The Role of Rumour in History Writing', *History Compass*, 6:5 (2008), 1235–43.

32. AN BB18 964, Correspondance générale de la division criminelle, in which a peasant from the Haute Loire in 1816 declared that 'The Emperor has come back once, he will come back again.' Also a judgement dated 1 August 1816 in BB18 964, in which the guilty party declared that Napoleon would be in Soisson in three weeks. Bernard Ménager, *Les Napoléon du peuple* (Paris, 1988), p. 16.

33. Ménager, *Les Napoléon*, pp. 21, 26; Lucas-Dubreton, *Le culte de Napoléon*, pp. 110–11.

34. Hazareesingh, *The Legend of Napoleon*, pp. 45–58.

35. Ploux, *De bouche à l'oreille*, pp. 140–3.

36. Ploux, *De bouche à l'oreille*, pp. 141–2; Ménager, *Les Napoléon*, p. 21.

37. AN F7 3792, Bulletin de police, 8–11 March 1820.

38. Hazareesingh, *The Legend of Napoleon*, p. 51.

39. Ploux, *De bouche à l'oreille*, p. 144.

40. Other examples in Ploux, *De bouche à l'oreille*, pp. 144–5.

41. Ploux, *De bouche à l'oreille*, pp. 137, 143.

42. Sudhir Hazareesingh, 'Memory and Political Imagination: The Legend of Napoleon Revisited', *French History*, 18 (2004), 465–8.

43. According to Bertier de Sauvigny, *La Restauration*, p. 136, some 50,000–80,000 bureaucrats, or around one-quarter of the total number, were purged. See also Jean Tulard, 'Les épurations administratives en France de 1800 à 1830', in *Les épurations administratives: XIXe et XXe siècles* (Geneva, 1977), pp. 49–63.

44. Bertier de Sauvigny, *La Restauration*, pp. 3–157; Ménager, *Les Napoléon*, pp. 16, 19.

45. Malandain, 'La haine des Bourbons sous la Restauration', pp. 73–83.

46. AN F7 3792, Bulletin de police, October 1819; Claude Guillet, *La rumeur de Dieu: apparitions, prophéties et miracles sous la Restauration* (Paris, 1994), pp. 69–76.

47. Lucas-Dubreton, *Le culte de Napoléon*, pp. 67–8.

48. Jean Tulard, 'Sainte-Hélène et l'opinion française', in Bonnel (ed.), *Sainte-Hélène, terre d'exil*, p. 189; E.D., 'Un faux empereur', *Visages de l'Ain*, 101 (1969), 78–80.

49. Ménager, *Les Napoléon*, p. 26.

50. Both instances cited in Hazareesingh, *The Legend of Napoleon*, p. 55.

51. AN F7 3736, Bulletin de police, 7 February 1816.

52. See the mention in BL Add Mss 20146, O'Meara to Finlaison (10 October 1816), in which O'Meara writes, 'you [Finlaison] have said that Mr Croker wishes to hear everything that I can pick up concerning him [Napoleon]'. Also, Add Mss 38263, O'Meara to Finlaison (6 October 1816).

53. Benhamou, *Inside Longwood*, p. 13.

54. At least according to Dr Verling, in Markham, *Napoleon and Dr Verling*, p. 144; Unwin, *Terrible Exile*, p. 159.

55. O'Meara, *Napoleon in Exile*, i. pp. 46–7; Howard, *Napoleon's Poisoned Chalice*, p. 47.

56. Gourgaud, *Journal de Sainte-Hélène*, ii. p. 244 (10 September 1817); Forsyth, *History of the Captivity of Napoleon at St. Helena*, i. pp. 76–8; Frédéric Masson, *Autour de Sainte-Hélène*, 3 vols (Paris, 1909–12), iii. p. 178.

57. BL Add Mss 20146, O'Meara to Finlaison (10 October 1816).

58. O'Meara, *Napoleon in Exile*, ii. p. 347.

59. See, for example, O'Meara, *Napoleon in Exile*, ii. p. 375.

60. Marchand, *In Napoleon's Shadow*, pp. 481–2; O'Meara, *Napoleon in Exile*, i. pp. vii–viii, 392; ii. pp. 136, 163–4, 385–6; Forsyth, *History of the Captivity of Napoleon at St. Helena*, ii. pp. 582–6; Young, *Napoleon in Exile*, i. p. 78.

61. Forsyth, *History of the Captivity of Napoleon at St. Helena*, i. pp. 302–3; Gregory, *Napoleon's Jailer*, pp. 142–6; Howard, *Napoleon's Poisoned Chalice*, pp. 48–53.

62. See, for example, BL Add Mss 20119, 'Notes of a Conversation between the Governor and Surgeon O'Meara' (18, 21, 24 July, and 23 August 1817); Kemble (ed.), *Gorrequer's Diary*, p. 29 (18 December 1817).

63. Gourgaud, *Journal de Sainte-Hélène*, i. pp. 193, 194 (16 and 18 November 1816); Forsyth, *History of the Captivity of Napoleon at St. Helena*, ii. p. 93.

64. Forsyth, *History of the Captivity of Napoleon at St. Helena*, ii. pp. 74–5.

65. Bertrand, *Cahiers*, ii. p. 327 (5 April 1819).

66. Willms, *Napoleon & St Helena*, pp. 119–23; Gregory, *Napoleon's Jailer*, pp. 134–5.

67. BL Add Mss 20216, O'Meara to Finlaison (23 December 1816); Marchand, *In Napoleon's Shadow*, pp. 462–8.

68. The letters are published in Forsyth, *History of the Captivity of Napoleon at St. Helena*, ii. pp. 298–311.

69. O'Meara, *Napoleon in Exile*, i. pp. 222–5; Gourgaud, *Journal de Sainte-Hélène*, i. pp. 199–201 (25, 26 November 1816); Bertrand, *Cahiers*, i. pp. 152–3 (26 November 1816).

70. BL Add Mss 20216, O'Meara to Finlaison (23 December 1816).

71. BL Add Mss 20216, O'Meara to Finlaison (29 December 1816); Forsyth, *History of the Captivity of Napoleon at St. Helena*, i. pp. 367–93.

72. O'Meara, *Napoleon in Exile*, i. p. 298.

73. BL Add Mss 20216, O'Meara to Finlaison (23 December 1816); Bertrand, *Cahiers*, i. pp. 165, 167 (23, 28 December 1816); Marchand, *In Napoleon's Shadow*, pp. 471, 472.

74. Montholon, *History of the Captivity of Napoleon*, i. p. 286.

75. BL Add Mss 20216, O'Meara to Finlaison (23 December 1816); Gourgaud, *Journal de Sainte-Hélène*, i. p. 247 (28 December 1816).

76. O'Meara, *Napoleon in Exile*, i. p. 225; Gourgaud, *Journal de Sainte-Hélène*, i. p. 207 (4 December 1816).

77. Gourgaud, *Journal de Sainte-Hélène*, i. p. 250 (30 December 1816); Bertrand, *Cahiers*, i. pp. 156, 171 (3, 30 December 1816); Marchand, *In Napoleon's Shadow*, p. 472.

78. Bathurst to Lowe, 7 February 1817, in Forsyth, *History of the Captivity of Napoleon at St. Helena*, ii. pp. 323–4.

79. See the debate about Las Cases in *The Parliamentary Debates*, xxxviii. pp. 704–8 (14 May 1818).

80. One often forgets Las Cases' son, also called Emmanuel, in this story. He shared his father's hardships and returned to Europe with him. The years in exile must have left their mark and certainly he developed a hatred for the man he saw as his father's tormentor, Hudson Lowe. Some years later, on 22 October 1822, Las Cases' son, aged twenty-two, was in London when, riding in a carriage with a friend along the road near Paddington Green, he recognised Lowe standing in front of his house. Las Cases leapt from the carriage and proceeded to hit him twice in the face with his riding crop. Las Cases then dropped his calling card – it was a way of saying that if Lowe wanted 'satisfaction' he knew where to find him. Lowe didn't as it turned out, instead filing a complaint for assault with the police. By the time the police found Las Cases' hotel, he had already left for Paris (Emmanuel Las Cases, *Journal écrit à bord de la frégate la Belle-Poule* (Paris, 1841), pp. vii–viii; Albéric Cahuet, *Retours de Sainte-Hélène (1821–1840)* (Paris, 1932), pp. 61–4, has a slightly different version of events). Three years later, Las Cases was set upon as he was coming out of his father's house in Passy and lightly stabbed twice. Lowe happened to be in Paris at the time. Despite the rumours circulating at the time, there is nothing to connect the two events.

81. Lowe to Bathurst, 3 December 1816, in Forsyth, *History of the Captivity of Napoleon at St. Helena*, i. pp. 382–5.

82. Laurence Montroussier, *L'éthique du chef militaire dans le 'Mémorial de Sainte-Hélène'* (Montpellier, 1998), p. 21,

83. See, for example, Gourgaud, *Journal de Sainte-Hélène*, i. pp. 156, 159, 160, 171 (25–30 June, 5, 10, 11 July, 4–8 August 1816); and ii. p. 165 (29 June 1817).

84. Gourgaud, *Journal de Sainte-Hélène*, i. pp. 75–6, 86 (20 November, 17 December 1815); ii. pp. 55, 57 (1, 2 April 1817).

85. Marchand, *In Napoleon's Shadow*, p. 418; Gourgaud, *Journal de Sainte-Hélène*, i. pp. 241–3 (25 December 1816).

86. Rosebery, *Napoleon: The Last Phase*, pp. 36–7.

87. See, for example, Gourgaud, *Journal de Sainte-Hélène*, i. p. 167 (22 July 1816); ii. pp. 53, 54, 74, 280 (30, 31 March, 19 April, 10 October 1817).

88. See, for example, Gourgaud, *Journal de Sainte-Hélène*, ii. pp. 41–2, 316 (20 March, 18 December 1817).

89. Gourgaud, *Journal de Sainte-Hélène*, i. pp. 242–3 (25 December 1816).

90. Gourgaud, *Journal de Sainte-Hélène*, ii. pp. 188–9, 204–5 (15, 29 July 1817).

91. See Stürmer to Metternich (31 March 1818), in St-Cère and H. Schlitter (eds), *Napoléon à Sainte-Hélène: rapports officiels du baron Stürmer*, p. 174.

92. Gourgaud, *Journal de Sainte-Hélène*, ii. p. 30 (10 March 1817).

93. See, for example, Gourgaud, *Journal de Sainte-Hélène*, ii. pp. 138, 141 (11, 13 June 1817).

94. Gourgaud, *Journal de Sainte-Hélène*, ii. p. 301 (18 November 1817); Bertrand, *Cahiers*, i. p. 365; Ganière, *Napoléon à Sainte-Hélène*, p. 293; Martineau, *Napoléon à Sainte-Hélène*, p. 329.

95. Bertrand, *Cahiers*, ii. p. 233 (5 January 1819). See also Macé, *Le général Gourgaud*, p. 167.

96. See, for example, Gourgaud, *Journal de Sainte-Hélène*, i. pp. 294–7 (20, 21 January 1817).

97. Gourgaud, *Journal de Sainte-Hélène*, ii. pp. 349–51 (2 February 1818).

98. Jackson, *Notes and Reminiscences*, p. 153.

99. Willms, *Verbannung und Verklärung*, p. 33. On the implications of Gourgaud's venting see Masson, *Autour de Sainte-Hélène*, ii. pp. 43–126, who argues that as a result the allied powers meeting at Aix decided to tighten the noose around Napoleon's neck and never to let him off the island. Aubry, 'Introduction', in Gourgaud, *Journal de Sainte-Hélène*, i. pp. 17–19, has countered this argument.

100. Gourgaud, *Journal de Sainte-Hélène*, ii. pp. 357, 360 (23 February, 11 March 1818); Bertrand, *Cahiers*, ii. p. 93 (13 March 1818).

101. Willms, *Verbannung und Verklärung*, p. 33.

102. Forsyth, *History of the Captivity of Napoleon at St. Helena*, iii. pp. 37–41; Young, *Napoleon in Exile*, ii. pp. 90–3; Ganière, *Napoléon à Sainte-Hélène*, p. 303.

103. On New Longwood House see Levy, 'Napoleon in Exile', p. 46; Ganière, *Napoléon à Sainte-Hélène*, pp. 302–4; Macé, *Le général Gourgaud*, pp. 171–4, 313–22. It was initially meant to be built on St Francis Plain, at some distance from Longwood. It was the site of Rosemary Hall, occupied by the Russian and Austrian commissioners, Balmain and Stürmer. Napoleon was in two minds about whether he would move into it once it was built. On the one hand, to do so was almost an admission that he would never get off the island; on the other, they were badly housed at Longwood. See Gourgaud, *Journal de Sainte-Hélène*, i. p. 99 (11 January 1816).

104. J. R. Dinwiddy, *Radicalism and Reform in Britain, 1780–1850* (London, 1992), pp. 164–6.

105. And this includes the servants, such as Noverraz, who obviously asked to leave but then changed his mind (BL Add Mss 20158, Noverraz to Lowe (3 February 1820)). By the end of 1819, the Bertrands were talking about returning to Europe, although Montholon's belief that nothing would come of it was borne out, and they were still talking about leaving in January 1821 (BL Add Mss 20158, Montholon to Albine, 26 September 1919 and 19 January 1821).

106. AN F7 6668, baron de Marandret to the comte de Richelieu, Hamburg, 26 August 1818; Masson, *Autour de Sainte-Hélène*, ii. pp. 253–73; Ganière, *Napoléon à Sainte-Hélène*, pp. 290–1; Hazareesingh, *The Legend of Napoleon*, p. 116.

107. O'Meara, *Napoleon in Exile*, ii. pp. 386–9; Marchand, *In Napoleon's Shadow*, pp. 517–18; Kemble, *Napoleon Immortal*, p. 251; Howard, *Napoleon's Poisoned Chalice*, pp. 55–60, 75. On Cipriani see Rossi, *Les Corses des services secrets de Napoléon*, pp. 77–101.

108. AN F7 6668, baron de Marandret to the comte de Richelieu, Hamburg, 26 August 1818.

109. See Dwyer, *Citizen Emperor*, pp. 301–3.

110. Las Cases, *Le Mémorial de Sainte-Hélène*, i. p. 479; Marchand, *In Napoleon's Shadow*, p. 588; Montholon, *Journal secret*, p. 149.

111. Saint-Denis, *Souvenirs*, pp. 157, 158, 170, 231, 232, 236–7, 266.

112. According to Gourgaud, *Journal de Sainte-Hélène*, i. p. 74 (10 November 1815), she was 'in love' with Cockburn.

113. Gourgaud, *Journal de Sainte-Hélène*, ii. p. 352 (5 February 1818).

114. O'Meara to Reade, 24 July 1816, in Forsyth, *History of the Captivity of Napoleon at St. Helena*, i. pp. 239–40.

115. Gourgaud, *Journal de Sainte-Hélène*, i. p. 228 (15 December 1816).

116. Gourgaud, *Journal de Sainte-Hélène*, ii. p. 295 (5 November 1817).

117. Martineau, *Napoléon à Sainte-Hélène*, p. 223. See also Aubry, *Sainte-Hélène*, pp. 234–7.

118. Ganière, *Napoléon à Sainte-Hélène*, p. 341.

119. Bertrand, *Cahiers*, ii. p. 391 (9 September 1819); Ganière, *Napoléon à Sainte-Hélène*, pp. 341–4.

120. Jackson, *Notes and Reminiscences*, p. 129.

121. Bertrand, *Cahiers*, ii. pp. 295–6, 317–18 (9 February, 18 March 1819); iii. p. 200 (8 May 1821).

122. Macé, 'Les soixante-huit mois de Napoléon à Sainte-Hélène', pp. 64, 66 and 71, nn. 12 and 13.

123. Bertrand, *Cahiers*, iii. p. 200 (8 May 1821).

124. Montholon to Albine, 2 July 1819, in Philippe Gonnard (ed.), *Lettres du comte et de la comtesse de Montholon, 1819–1821* (Paris, 1906), p. 17.

125. At least according to Montholon in BL Add Mss 20158, Montholon to Albine (5 December 1820).

126. BL Add Mss 20158, Montholon to Albine, 26 September 1919.

127. BL Add Mss 20158, Albine to Montholon, 12 June 1820. According to Albine (Add Mss 20158, 4 July 1820, Pauline replied that she would not undertake any action to send someone to St Helena because, after consulting with her mother and uncle, she and they were concerned it might counter Napoleon's own wishes on the matter (Add Mss 20158, the countess to Montholon (31 August 1820)).

128. BL Add Mss 20158, Albine to Montholon (24 October, 13 December 1820).

129. BL Add Mss 20158, Montholon to Albine (20 December 1820).

130. BL Add Mss 20158, Montholon to Albine (6 November 1820).

131. Martineau, *La vie quotidienne*, p. 105.

132. See, for example, Las Cases, *Le Mémorial de Sainte-Hélène*, i. pp. 381, 392, 396, 404, 430, 461, 475, 476, where in the space of two months, February and March 1816, he frequently references the rain and the bad weather; Martineau, *La vie quotidienne*, p. 106.

133. Philippe de Ségur, *Histoire et mémoires, par le général comte de Ségur*, 7 vols (Paris, 1873), vi. p. 138.

134. Marchand, *In Napoleon's Shadow*, pp. 484, 490.

135. BL Add Mss 20216, O'Meara to Finlaison (1 November 1817).

136. O'Meara, *Napoleon in Exile*, ii. p. 285.

137. O'Meara, *Napoleon in Exile*, ii. p. 257.

138. O'Meara, *Napoleon in Exile*, i. p. 188 (5 November 1817); Unwin, *Terrible Exile*, p. 171. Napoleon came to the same conclusion as early as May 1818 in O'Meara, *Napoleon in Exile*, ii. p. 60.

139. Cited in Kemble, *Napoleon Immortal*, p. 250.

140. Kemble, *Napoleon Immortal*, p. 251.

141. Gourgaud, *Journal de Sainte-Hélène*, i. pp. 115–16 (27 February–3 April 1816).

142. Kemble, *Napoleon Immortal*, pp. 251–2; Jacalyn Duffin, *Lovers and Livers: Disease Concepts in History* (Toronto, 2005), pp. 82–8.

143. For the state of early nineteenth-century medicine see W. F. Bynum, *Science and the Practice of Medicine in the Nineteenth Century* (Cambridge, 1994), pp. 1–24; and Jean-François Lemaire, Paul Fornès, Pascal Kintz and Thierry Lentz, *Autour de 'l'empoisonnement' de Napoléon* (Paris, 2001), pp. 16–19.

144. Marchand, *In Napoleon's Shadow*, p. 491; Young, *Napoleon in Exile*, ii. p. 102; Howard, *Napoleon's Poisoned Chalice*, p. 52.

145. Kemble (ed.), *Gorrequer's Diary*, pp. 33, 43 (first days of January, 23 February 1818); Forsyth, *History of the Captivity of Napoleon at St. Helena*, i. 549–50.

146. BL Add Mss 20122, Bathurst to Lowe (29 April 1818); and Benhamou, *Inside Longwood*, p. 145.

147. BL Add Mss 20122, Henry Goulbourn to Bathurst (10 May 1818), and Bathurst to Lowe (16 May 1818); and Forsyth, *History of the Captivity of Napoleon at St. Helena*, iii. pp. 399–400.

148. Kemble (ed.), *Gorrequer's Diary*, pp. 70–1 (24 July 1818).

149. BL Add Mss 20216, O'Meara to Finlaison (10 May, 30 June 1818).

150. Reade to O'Meara, in Marchand, *In Napoleon's Shadow*, pp. 522–9.

151. Bertrand, *Cahiers*, ii. p. 151.

152. BL Add Mss 20146, O'Meara to the Admiralty, 20 October 1818; and in Benhamou, *Inside Longwood*, pp. 175–200.

153. Henry, *Trifles from my Portfolio*, i. p. 235.

154. See also Walter Henry, *Events of a Military Life*, 2 vols (London, 1843), ii. pp. 42–4; Howard, *Napoleon's Poisoned Chalice*, pp. 66–8.

155. See Croker to O'Meara, 2 November 1818, in Benhamou, *Inside Longwood*, pp. 201–2.

156. According to Lemaire et al., *Autour de 'l'empoisonnement' de Napoléon*, p. 27.

157. Markham, *Napoleon and Dr Verling*, p. 39 (19 November 1818).

158. The journal was recently re-edited by David Markham. On Verling see Howard, *Napoleon's Poisoned Chalice*, pp. 139–64.

159. Markham, *Napoleon and Dr Verling*, pp. 131–2.
160. Kemble (ed.), *Gorrequer's Diary*, pp. 124–5, 126, 140–1 (4, 6 April and 8 September 1819).
161. Markham, *Napoleon and Dr Verling*, p. 46 (18 January 1819).
162. Bertrand, *Cahiers*, ii. pp. 245–6 (17 January 1819); Balmain, *Napoleon in Captivity*, pp. 186–7; John Stokoe, *With Napoleon at St Helena* (London, 1902), pp. 83–6, 217–19; Marchand, *In Napoleon's Shadow*, pp. 555–8. On Stokoe see Howard, *Napoleon's Poisoned Chalice*, pp. 87–113.
163. Bertrand, *Cahiers*, ii. pp. 246–8 (18, 19, 20, 21 January 1819); Kemble (ed.), *Gorrequer's Diary*, pp. 125, 127, 140–1 (4, 6 April, 8 September 1819).
164. Stokoe, *With Napoleon at St Helena*, pp. 92–3, 100. Gregory, *Napoleon's Jailer*, p. 148, considers Napoleon's ill-health during this period to be born of his refusal to take any exercise, which was nothing less than a political move to get off the island, but that view does not withstand scrutiny.
165. BL Add Mss 20125, f. 281, Lowe to Bathurst (6 February 1819); Bertrand, *Cahiers*, ii. p. 295; Gregory, *Napoleon's Jailer*, p. 149.
166. BL Add Mss 20126, ff. 61–4; Howard, *Napoleon's Poisoned Chalice*, pp. 115–38; and Charles Harrison to Colonel Bingham, in Gareth Glover (ed.), *Wellington's Lieutenant, Napoleon's Gaoler: The Peninsula and St Helena Diaries and Letters of Sir George Ridout Bingham, 1809–21* (Barnsley, 2005), pp. 281–2 (9 September 1819).

CHAPTER 5

1. Schroeder, *The Transformation of European Politics*, pp. 592–3; Mark Jarrett, *The Congress of Vienna and its Legacy: War and Great Power Diplomacy after Napoleon* (London, 2013), pp. 180–205.
2. Young, *Napoleon in Exile*, ii. pp. 119–20; Ganière, *Napoléon à Sainte-Hélène*, pp. 315–19.
3. Aubry, *Sainte-Hélène*, pp. 303–4.
4. According to Lemaire et al., *Autour de 'l'empoisonnement' de Napoléon*, pp. 26–7, he knew as early as 19 January.
5. See, for example Las Cases, *Le Mémorial de Sainte-Hélène*, i. pp. 517, 687, 765–6 (2 April, 7–8, 21 June 1816).
6. Gourgaud, *Journal de Sainte-Hélène*, i. p. 124 (18 April 1816).
7. Gourgaud, *Journal de Sainte-Hélène*, ii. pp. 207, 209, 211, 250 (6, 15, 17 August, 14 September 1817).
8. Major Charles Harrison to George and Lady Bingham, in Sir Herbert Maxwell, 'More Light on St. Helena', *Cornhill Magazine* (February 1901), 158–60.

9. Las Cases, *Le Mémorial de Sainte-Hélène*, i. pp. 544–5, 554, 555, 556 (29 April, 1, 2, 3, 4 May 1816); Balmain, *Napoleon in Captivity*, p. 142 (2 November 1817).

10. O'Meara, *Napoleon in Exile*, ii. p. 407.

11. According to Balmain, *Napoleon in Captivity*, pp. 208–9 (1 March 1819).

12. According to Martineau, *La vie quotidienne*, p. 73.

13. Las Cases, *Le Mémorial de Sainte-Hélène*, i. p. 478.

14. Las Cases, *Le Mémorial de Sainte-Hélène*, ii. p. 15 (9–11 July 1816); O'Meara, *Napoleon in Exile*, i. pp. 37–8, 69, 149–50; Watson, *A Polish Exile with Napoleon*, pp. 22–3.

15. BL Add Mss 20204, f. 127.

16. Young, *Napoleon in Exile*, ii. pp. 152–4; Korngold, *The Last Years of Napoleon*, pp. 333–5.

17. BL Add Mss 20158, Montholon to Albine (26 September 1919).

18. Marchand, *In Napoleon's Shadow*, pp. 583–4; Saint-Denis, *Souvenirs*, pp. 208–9; and Bertrand, *Cahiers*, ii. p. 397 (21 September 1819).

19. Kemble, *Napoleon Immortal*, p. 248. On Antommarchi see Howard, *Napoleon's Poisoned Chalice*, pp. 165–88.

20. Pauline's letters are cited in Len Ortzen, *Imperial Venus: The Story of Pauline Bonaparte-Borghese* (London, 1974), pp. 188–9. See also Gilbert Martineau, *Madame Mère: Napoleon's Mother*, trans. Frances Partridge (London, 1978), pp. 159–63.

21. On this episode see Frédéric Masson, 'L'énigme de Sainte-Hélène', *Revue des deux mondes*, 38 (1917), 756–88.

22. François Antommarchi, *Mémoires du docteur F. Antommarchi, ou Les derniers momens de Napoléon*, 2 vols (Paris, 1825), i. pp. 144–5 (9 October 1819).

23. Antommarchi, *Mémoires*, i. pp. 109–10 (23 September 1819).

24. Antommarchi, *Mémoires*, ii. p. 40 (17 March 1821).

25. BL Add Mss 20210, Journal of Captain Nicholls (29 November 1819); Bertrand, *Cahiers*, ii. pp. 407, 412, 413, 414 (1, 14, 22 November, December 1819); Marchand, *In Napoleon's Shadow*, pp. 591–2, 609–10; Saint-Denis, *Souvenirs*, pp. 186–204.

26. Antommarchi, *Mémoires*, i. p. 401 (19 November 1820).

27. Bertrand, *Cahiers*, iii. p. 120 (15 April 1821).

28. BL Add Mss 20131, f. 88; Charles Harrison to Colonel Bingham, in Glover (ed.), *Wellington's Lieutenant*, pp. 287–8 (9 October 1820).

29. Forsyth, *History of the Captivity of Napoleon at St. Helena*, iii. pp. 242–5.

30. Bertrand, *Cahiers*, iii. pp. 40–1, 218 (21, 22 January 1821); Saint-Denis, *Souvenirs*, p. 244.

31. BL Add Mss 20158, Montholon to Albine (5 December 1820).
32. Bertrand, *Cahiers*, iii. p. 89 (2 March 1821); Las Cases, *Le Mémorial de Sainte-Hélène*, i. pp. 481–2 (1–2 April 1816). By 1819, he was shaving every second day, but only gave it up entirely about a month before his death. Marchand, *In Napoleon's Shadow*, pp. 596, 646; Saint-Denis, *Souvenirs*, pp. 243, 259.
33. Saint-Denis, *Souvenirs*, pp. 242–3.
34. BL Add Mss 20158, Montholon to Albine (30 March 1821), in which he writes that he had not left Napoleon's side for the last thirteen days.
35. Marchand, *In Napoleon's Shadow*, pp. 633–5, 646; Bertrand, *Cahiers*, iii. p. 89 (2 March 1821).
36. Alessandro Lugli, A. K. Lugli and M. N. Horcic, 'Napoleon's Autopsy: New Perspectives', *Human Pathology*, 36:4 (2005), 320–4.
37. BL Add Mss 20207, f. 341, Reade to Lowe (27 March 1821); Watson, *A Polish Exile with Napoleon*, p. 17, n. 2. The reference to the declaration concerns the Congress of Troppau, held in that city in October 1820, where Austria, Prussia and Russia signed a treaty agreeing to quash any revolution and to bring that state into the conservative fold. The declaration in effect blamed Napoleon as 'representative of the Revolution' for unrest in Italy and Spain.
38. BL Add Mss 20158, Montholon to Albine (1 September 1920). See also Gourgaud, *Journal de Sainte-Hélène*, i. p. 126 (20 April 1816).
39. Gourgaud, *Journal de Sainte-Hélène*, i. p. 71 (5 November 1815); ii. pp. 318–19, 348 (21 December 1817, 31 January 1818); Bertrand, *Cahiers*, iii. pp. 110, 111 (9 April 1821); Montholon, *Journal secret*, 151.
40. Gourgaud, *Journal de Sainte-Hélène*, ii. pp. 353, 354 (6, 11 February 1818).
41. Gonnard (ed.), *Lettres du comte et de la comtesse de Montholon*, pp. 18, 40, 71–2 (3 July, 31 October 1819, 11 February 1821).
42. Ganière, *Napoléon à Sainte-Hélène*, pp. 380–1.
43. BL Add Mss 20158, Montholon to Albine (6 November 1820).
44. Montholon, *History of the Captivity of Napoleon*, ii. p. 353; O'Meara, *Napoleon in Exile*, ii. pp. 255–6, 499, 502, 509; Bertrand, *Cahiers*, ii. pp. 176–7 (October 1818); iii. pp. 77, 91, 104, 113, 115, 120, 123, 125, 135, 166, 167 (24 February, 6, 19 March, 10, 13, 15, 17, 18, 21, 26 April 1821); Marchand, *In Napoleon's Shadow*, pp. 484, 530, 635, 648, 649, 664, 678; Saint-Denis, *Souvenirs*, pp. 169, 181–2, 240–1, 249, 252–3; Stokoe, *With Napoleon at St Helena*, p. 164.
45. BL Add Mss 20158, Montholon to Albine (19 January 1821); Add Mss 20133, Arnott to Gorrequer (1 April 1821).
46. Gonnard (ed.), *Lettres du comte et de la comtesse de Montholon*, pp. 68, 71 (19 January, 11 February 1821).

47. Gonnard (ed.), *Lettres du comte et de la comtesse de Montholon*, pp. 72–3, 75 (5 and 17 March 1821).

48. See BL Add Mss 20157 (1 and 2 April 1821); Archibald Arnott, *An Account of the Last Illness, Decease, and Post Mortem Appearances of Napoleon Bonaparte* (London, 1822), pp. 2–5; Marchand, *In Napoleon's Shadow*, pp. 642–3; Bertrand, *Cahiers*, iii. pp. 107–9 (31 March, 1, 2 April 1821); Major Harrison to George Bingham, in Maxwell, 'More Light on St. Helena', 165 (3 April 1821). On Arnott see Howard, *Napoleon's Poisoned Chalice*, pp. 190–214.

49. See, for example, BL Add Mss 20157, Arnott's reports dated 23, 25, 27 April and 4 May 1821. They are substantially different to the views later expressed in his *An Account of the Last Illness*, largely a whitewash of his role.

50. BL Add Mss 20133, Reade to Lowe (6 April 1821); Arnott, *An Account of the Last Illness*, p. 7; Howard, *Napoleon's Poisoned Chalice*, p. 204. On 9 April, Arnott went to Plantation House to apply for permission to return to Europe (Forsyth, *History of the Captivity of Napoleon at St. Helena*, iii. pp. 275–6).

51. Kemble (ed.), *Gorrequer's Diary*, pp. 220–1 (7 April 1821); Major Harrison to George Bingham, in Maxwell, 'More Light on St. Helena', 166 (22 April 1821).

52. Lowe collated them in one volume, BL Add Mss 20157; and Kemble (ed.), *Gorrequer's Diary*, p. 220 (6 April 1821); Howard, *Napoleon's Poisoned Chalice*, pp. 209–12.

53. BL Add Mss 20133, Lowe to Bathurst (13 April 1821).

54. See BL Add Mss 20133, Lowe to Bathurst (18 April 1821); Add Mss 20157 (23 April 1821); Kemble (ed.), *Gorrequer's Diary*, p. 222 (17 April 1821).

55. BL Add Mss 20133, Reade to Lowe (22 October 1822).

56. Bertrand, *Cahiers*, iii. p. 61 (11 February 1821).

57. Bertrand, *Cahiers*, iii. pp. 105–6 (27 March 1821).

58. Ganière, *Napoléon à Sainte-Hélène*, pp. 404–5.

59. Marchand, *In Napoleon's Shadow*, pp. 647–8; Bertrand, *Cahiers*, iii. pp. 116, 117; Saint-Denis, *Souvenirs*, pp. 260–1. A translation of the will can be found in Marchand, *In Napoleon's Shadow*, pp. 718–36; Young, *Napoleon in Exile*, pp. 278–9.

60. Montholon, *Récits*, ii. pp. 504–9, 529, 530–7.

61. Bertrand, *Cahiers*, iii. pp. 136–46, 148 (22, 23 April 1821). See also Emmanuel Fureix, *La France des larmes: deuils politiques à l'âge*

romantique, 1814–1840 (Seyssel, 2009), pp. 424–5; and Jean Lemaire, *Le testament de Napoleon: un étonnant destin* (Paris, 1957), esp. pp. 17–41.

62. For details see Branda, *Le prix de la gloire*, pp. 82–99.

63. Hélie Guillaume Hubert de Noailles, *Le Comte Molé, 1781–1855: sa vie, ses mémoires*, 6 vols (Paris, 1924), iii. p. 241; J. B. Rye, 'The Lost and the New Letters of Napoleon', *English Historical Review*, 13:51 (1898), 484–5. On the bequest to Cantillon see William Stirling Maxwell, *Napoleon's Bequest to Cantillon: A Fragment of International History* (London, 1858).

64. Bertrand, *Cahiers*, iii. p. 110 (9 April 1821).

65. Gonnard, *Les origines de la légende*, pp. 277–86; André-Jean Tudesq, 'La légende napoléonienne en France en 1848', *Revue historique*, 218 (1957), 72–3.

66. Montholon, *Récits*, ii. pp. 516–28.

67. Montholon, *Récits*, ii. p. 538.

68. See Add Mss 20133, Lowe to Montholon (28 April 1821); Arnold Chaplin, *The Illness and Death of Napoleon Bonaparte* (London, 1913), pp. 61–2; Howard, *Napoleon's Poisoned Chalice*, p. 196.

69. Forsyth, *History of the Captivity of Napoleon at St. Helena*, iii. p. 280.

70. On Shortt see Arnold Chaplin, *Thomas Shortt, Principal Medical Officer in St. Helena* (London, 1914), pp. 7–26; and Howard, *Napoleon's Poisoned Chalice*, pp. 215–24.

71. Add Mss 20133, Lowe to Bathurst (1 May 1821).

72. Blistering consisted of placing irritating substances on the patient's body, such as plasters made of mustard flour and sulphuric acid, which were kept in place until a blister formed. The reasoning was that the blisters would draw out the toxins and infection (Heather Beatty, *Nervous Disease in Late Eighteenth-Century Britain: The Reality of a Fashionable Disorder* (London, 2015), pp. 133–4).

73. *Corr.* xxxii. p. 387 (19 April 1821); Saint-Denis, *Souvenirs*, p. 262; Etienne-Denis Pasquier, *Mémoires du Chancelier Pasquier: histoire de mon temps*, 6 vols (Paris, 1895), v. pp. 206–7; Ganière, *Napoléon à Sainte-Hélène*, p. 417.

74. Ganière, *Napoléon à Sainte-Hélène*, pp. 427–8.

75. Bertrand, *Cahiers*, iii. pp. 167, 171–8 (26, 29 April 1821); Saint-Denis, *Souvenirs*, pp. 263–71.

76. Cited in Georges Mauguin, *Napoléon et la superstition: anecdotes et curiosités* (Rodez, 1946), p. 91.

77. Add Mss 20133, Reade to Lowe (1 May 1821).

78. What we know of Napoleon's final hours during the night of 4–5 May comes from the detailed account left by Bertrand, *Cahiers*, iii. pp. 192–6; Marchand, *In Napoleon's Shadow*, pp. 678, 680; Saint-Denis, *Souvenirs*, pp. 262–70; and less reliable Antommarchi, *Mémoires*, ii. pp. 147–54.
79. Bertrand, *Cahiers*, iii. p. 137, 184 (22 April, 1 May 1821); Jacques-Olivier Boudon, *Napoléon et les cultes: les religions en Europe à l'aube du XIXe siècle, 1800–1815* (Paris, 2002), pp. 43–4.
80. On Napoleon and religion see Gonnard, *Les origines de la légende*, pp. 250–69.
81. Saint-Denis, *Souvenirs*, pp. 263–4.
82. Bertrand, *Cahiers*, iii. pp. 194, 195. It is less likely that, according to Marchand, *In Napoleon's Shadow*, p. 678, he said something like 'France ... my son ... The army ...'. That sounds apocryphal. Montholon, *Récits*, ii. p. 548, has him saying, 'France, armée, tête d'armé, Joséphine', but Saint-Denis, *Souvenirs*, p. 267 asserts that Montholon was the only person to have heard this.
83. Fureix, *La France des larmes*, p. 423.
84. See, for example, *Le Constitutionnel: journal du commerce, politique et littéraire*, 13 July 1821; *Le coucher du soleil du 5 mai 1821, par M. P**A* (Paris, 1821), p. 12.
85. A number of early St Helena historians state that a storm began to rage, as though nature were reacting to Napoleon's passing. It was initially reported by Antommarchi, *Mémoires*, ii. pp. 147–8 (4 May 1821). However, we know from ships' logs that 'on the days in question, 3rd, 4th and 5th of May, the weather was very generally fine, with a few cloudy spells'. See George L. de St Macaire Watson, *The Story of Napoleon's Death-Mask* (London, 1915), pp. 3–6. My thanks to Michael Sibalis for pointing this out.
86. Thomas A. Kselman, *Death and Afterlife in Modern France* (Princeton, 1993), pp. 50–1.
87. 'Discours de Lyon', in Frédéric Masson and Guido Biagi, *Napoléon inconnu, papiers inédits (1786–1793)*, 2 vols (Paris, 1895), ii. p. 327.
88. BL Add Mss 20133, Reade to Lowe (22 October 1822).
89. Saint-Denis, *Souvenirs*, pp. 271–2.
90. Marchand, *In Napoleon's Shadow*, pp. 690–1; Bertrand, *Cahiers*, iii. pp. 196–7 (6 May 1821); Saint-Denis, *Souvenirs*, pp. 272–6; Montholon, *Récits*, ii. p. 555; Duncan Darroch to his mother, 6 May 1821, in Sir Lees Knowles (ed.), *Letters of Captain Engelbert Lutyens, orderly officer at Longwood, Saint Helena: Feb. 1820 to Nov. 1823* (London, 1915), pp. 189–92; Thomas H. Brooke, 12 May 1821, in Shorter (ed.), *Napoleon in his own Defence*, pp. 269–70.

91. See, for example, Major Harrison to George Bingham, in Maxwell, 'More Light on St. Helena', 167 (7 May 1821).

92. Marchand, *In Napoleon's Shadow*, p. 695; Aubry, *Sainte-Hélène*, p. 414.

93. Young, *Napoleon in Exile*, ii. p. 245.

94. Claudia Hattendorff, *Napoleon I. und die Bilder. System und Umriss bildgewordener Politik und politischen Bildgebrauchs* (Petersberg, 2012), pp. 34 and n. 97, 244–5 for a discussion on the various deathbed sketches in circulation.

95. Antommarchi, *Mémoires*, ii. pp. 160–6; Young, *Napoleon in Exile*, ii. pp. 226–42; Lemaire et al., *Autour de 'l'empoisonnement' de Napoléon*, pp. 107–15.

96. Bertrand, *Cahiers*, iii. pp. 196–7 (6 May 1821); Ganière, *Napoléon à Sainte-Hélène*, p. 445; Martineau, *Napoléon à Sainte-Hélène*, pp. 496–9.

97. See Emmanuel Fureix, 'Sensibilité et politique: l'exemple du culte des mort à l'âge romantique', in Anne-Emmanuelle Demartini and Dominique Kalifa (eds), *Imaginaire et sensibilités au XIXe siècle: études pour Alain Corbin* (Paris, 2005), pp. 141–2.

98. Montholon to Albine, 6 May 1821, cited in J. Holland Rose, 'The Funeral of Napoleon and his Last Supper', *English Historical Review*, 17 (1902), 311–12.

99. Kemble, *Napoleon Immortal*, pp. 272–8. David P. Jordan, *Napoleon and the Revolution* (Basingstoke, 2012), p. 296, points out that the words 'tumour' and 'ulcer' were used interchangeably when speaking of cancer. Montholon reported that the cause of Napoleon's death was the same as his father's, namely, 'un squirre ulcereux a l'estomac' (BL Add Mss 20158, Montholon to Albine (6 May 1821)). For analyses see Thierry Lentz and Jacques Macé, *La mort de Napoléon: mythes, légendes et mystères* (Paris, 2009), pp. 61–9.

100. Alessandro Lugli et al., 'Napoleon Bonaparte's Gastric Cancer: A Clinicopathologic Approach to Staging, Pathogenesis, and Etiology', *Nature Clinical Practice Gastroenterology & Hepatology*, 4:1 (2007), 52–7; Alain Goldcher, *Napoléon Ier: l'ultime autopsie* (Paris, 2012); and idem, 'Napoléon Ier: l'ultime autopsie', *Revue de l'Institut Napoléon*, 202–3 (2011), 115–36.

101. Antommarchi, *Mémoires*, ii. pp. 169–70; Marchand, *In Napoleon's Shadow*, pp. 695–7.

102. Kemble (ed.), *Gorrequer's Diary*, p. 234 (7 May 1821); Kemble, *Napoleon Immortal*, pp. 272–81; Howard, *Napoleon's Poisoned Chalice*, pp. 218–23.

103. Much of what follows surrounding the autopsy is based on Thomas W. Laqueur, 'Bodies, Details, and the Humanitarian Narrative', in Lynn

Hunt (ed.), *The New Cultural History* (Berkeley, 1989), pp. 176–204, here pp. 181–4. See also Fureix, 'Sensibilité et politique: l'exemple du culte des mort à l'âge romantique', 141–2.

104. BL Add Mss 20133, Reade to Lowe (6 May 1821). See also *The Times*, 11 July 1821. Similar remarks about Napoleon's fat can be found in the *Evening Mail*, 11 July 1821; and the *Annual Register*, 1821, pp. 105–6.

105. *La Quotidienne*, 11 July 1821; Major Harrison to George Bingham, in Maxwell, 'More Light on St. Helena', 167–8 (7 May 1821).

106. *Le Drapeau blanc: journal de la politique, de la littérature et des théâtres*, 8 July 1821; and *Gazette de France*, 8 and 13 July 1821. The royalist newspapers were no doubt echoing the British newspaper reports, probably based on a report from Reade to Lowe (6 May 1821), BL Add Mss 20133, in which he underlines the 'extraordinary quantity of fat which covered almost every part of the interior, under the chest, but particularly about the heart, which was literally enveloped in fat'.

107. *Relation de la maladie et de la mort de Napoléon Bonaparte, extraite de plusieurs lettres venues de Sainte-Hélène* (Paris, 1821).

108. See, for example, the detailed report in *Bonaparte n'est pas mort d'un cancer; dédié aux mânes de Napoléon* (Paris, 1821), pp. 12–13, which went through twelve editions in 1821.

109. See *Napoléon: le retour des cendres: 1840–1990* (Courbevoie, 1990), pp. 62–8.

110. BL Add Mss 20133, Reade to Lowe (6 May 1821).

111. Christine Quigley, *The Corpse: A History* (Jefferson, NC, 1996), pp. 82, 251. Napoleon's intestines, or at least pieces of them, were acquired by the Museum of the Royal College of Surgeons of England in 1841. In 1883, Sir James Paget called into question the authenticity of the specimens (L. W. Proger, 'A Napoleonic Relic', *Annals of the Royal College of Surgeons of England*, 26:1 (1960), 57–62). The specimens were destroyed in an air raid during the Second World War.

112. Napoleon's son would also have his heart and his entrails buried separately when he died in 1832 (Jean Tulard, *Napoléon II* (Paris, 1992), p. 197).

113. *Gazette de France*, 13 July 1821.

114. The Vignali family sold their Napoleonic collection to a London bookseller, Maggs Brothers, in 1916. It was purchased by the A. S. W. Rosenbach Company of Philadelphia in 1924. In 1927, the collection was exhibited in New York at the Museum of French Arts. It was auctioned at Christie's in 1971, only to be passed in, and finally sold to an American urologist, John K. Lattimer, in 1977 for 13,000 francs.

Lattimer died in 2007. As far as I am aware, the relic in question that belonged to this collection is still in the possession of Lattimer's daughter, Evan. See Harvey Rachlin, *Lucy's Bones, Sacred Stones, & Einstein's Brain: The Remarkable Stories behind the Great Objects and Artifacts of History, from Antiquity to the Modern Era* (New York, 1996), pp. 190–6; and Tony Perrottet, *Napoleon's Privates: 2500 Years of History Unzipped* (New York, 2008), pp. 20–4.

115. Saint-Denis, *Souvenirs*, p. 274.

116. Fureix, *La France des larmes*, p. 56.

117. Emmanuel Fureix, 'L'iconoclasme: une pratique politique? (1814–1848)', in Le Gall, Offerlé and Ploux (eds), *La politique sans en avoir l'air*, pp. 121–2.

118. See Richard Wrigley, *The Politics of Appearance: Representations of Dress in Revolutionary France* (Oxford, 2002), pp. 1–57; and Eva Giloi, *Monarchy, Myth, and Material Culture in Germany, 1750–1950* (Cambridge, 2011), p. 33. French Romantics in particular were not always politically liberal, as they were in Germany, Italy and England. They could be apologists for the monarchy. See F. W. J. Hemmings, *Culture and Society in France, 1789–1848* (Leicester, 1987), pp. 166–72.

119. Quigley, *The Corpse*, p. 42; Philippe Ariès, *The Hour of our Death*, trans. Helen Weaver (New York, 1981), p. 262.

120. Antommarchi, *Mémoires*, ii. pp. 156–7. On the death masks see Watson, *The Story of Napoleon's Death-Mask*; Eugène de Veauce, *Les masques mortuaires de Napoléon* (Paris, 1971); Alain Pougetoux, 'Le masque de Napoléon: de la relique au bibelot' (Paris, 2002), pp. 146–57; Howard, *Napoleon's Poisoned Chalice*, pp. 224–33. For a complete bibliography see Chantal Lheureux-Prévot, 'L'affaire des masques mortuaires de Napoléon: éléments bibliographiques commentés', *Napoleonica. La Revue*, 3:3 (2008), 60–75.

121. David d'Angers, *Les carnets de David d'Angers*, 2 vols (Paris, 1958), i. p. 23.

122. Other examples are in Mauguin, *Napoléon et la superstition*, p. 223; Ernest Legouvé, *Dernier travail, derniers souvenirs: école normale de Sèvres* (Paris, 1898), p. 188. Cuttings from the tree ended up as far afield as Christchurch in New Zealand.

123. Cited in Fureix, *La France des larmes*, p. 57; Agricol Perdiguier, *Mémoires d'un compagnon*, presentation by Maurice Agulhon (Paris, 1992), pp. 234–5.

124. See Susan M. Pearce, *On Collecting: An Investigation into Collecting in the European Tradition* (London, 1995), esp. pp. 122–39; and Russell

Belk, *Collecting in a Consumer Society* (Hoboken, 2013), pp. 31–42. For a related discussion on royal memorabilia see Giloi, *Monarchy, Myth, and Material Culture in Germany*, pp. 1–45; Pascoe, *The Hummingbird Cabinet*. A good introduction on the material culture surrounding relics is Alexandra Walsham, 'Introduction: Relics and Remains', *Past & Present*, Supplement 5 (2010), 9–36.

125. Roustam Raza, *Souvenirs de Roustam, mamelouck de Napoléon Ier* (Paris, 1911), p. 220.

126. Todd Porterfield and Susan L. Siegfried, *Staging Empire: Napoleon, Ingres, and David* (University Park, Pa., 2006), p. 36; Marie-Anne Dupuy (ed.), *Dominique-Vivant Denon: l'oeil de Napoleon* (Paris, 1999), pp. 420–1, 480–1.

127. See, for example, BL Add Mss 20133, Montholon to Lowe (5 May 1821).

128. This from a letter from Hudson Lowe, 12 May 1821, cited in Holland Rose, 'The Funeral of Napoleon', 312–13.

129. J. Marquerie, *Le Deuil: histoire, règlements, usages, modes d'autrefois et d'aujourd'hui* (Paris, 1877), p. 66.

130. Marchand, *In Napoleon's Shadow*, pp. 708–10.

131. Kemble (ed.), *Gorrequer's Diary*, p. 242 (May 1821).

132. As many of his biographers: Aubry, *Sainte-Hélène*, pp. 418–19; Martineau, *Napoléon à Sainte-Hélène*, pp. 503–4.

133. Knowles (ed.), *Letters of Captain Engelbert Lutyens*, pp. viii–x, and the interminable correspondence that resulted from a seemingly innocent gesture, pp. 135–87; Korngold, *The Last Years of Napoleon*, pp. 377–8; Forsyth, *History of the Captivity of Napoleon at St. Helena*, iii. pp. 277–9; Young, *Napoleon in Exile*, ii. pp. 215–16.

134. Las Cases, *Le Mémorial de Sainte-Hélène*, ii. pp. 202–3, 232–3, 543–4 (17, 24 August and 11 November 1816).

135. Las Cases, *Le Mémorial de Sainte-Hélène*, i. pp. 329, 749 (30 December 1815, 17 June 1816); ii. p. 242 (25 August 1816); Nina Athanassoglou-Kallmyer, 'Sad Cincinnatus: Le Soldat-Laboureur as an Image of the Napoleonic Veteran after the Empire', *Arts Magazine*, 60 (May 1986), 72–3. One of the most important of Charlet's illustrations, which evidently struck a chord with the readers of the *Mémorial*, was that recounting the story of Napoleon taking a tiller from a peasant on the island, and then proceeding to plough a straight furrow. The illustration described him as the 'soldier-laboureur'.

136. Marchand, *In Napoleon's Shadow*, pp. 711–12; Saint-Denis, *Souvenirs*, pp. 284–6.

137. Levy, 'Napoleon in Exile', 57–67.

138. Fournier La Touraille, *Hudson Lowe*, p. 191.

139. Marchand, *In Napoleon's Shadow*, pp. 714–15.
140. According to Marchand, *In Napoleon's Shadow*, p. 738.
141. See Holland (ed.), *Foreign Reminiscences*, pp. 40–1.
142. AN F7 6668–9, Surveillance de la famille Bonaparte.

CHAPTER 6

1. Duncan Wu, *William Hazlitt: The First Modern Man* (Oxford, 2008), p. 299.
2. Cited in Wu, *William Hazlitt*, p. 299.
3. *The Examiner*, 8 July 1821, p. 417.
4. See Stuart Semmel, *Napoleon and the British* (New Haven, 2004), pp. 218–20.
5. *Annual Register*, 1821, pp. 142, 144.
6. *Morning Post*, 10 July 1821.
7. *The Times*, 5 July 1821.
8. *Blackwood's Edinburgh Magazine*, July 1821, p. 464.
9. *Journal des débats politiques et littéraires*, 7 July 1821.
10. AN F7 6668, Surveillance de la famille Bonaparte, 15 July 1821; F7 3875, Bulletin de police, 20 July 1821. Engravings appeared without permission, which indicated a slight disregard for the police and the law concerning their publication (Maurice d'Irisson, comte d'Hérisson, *Les girouettes politiques: un pair de France policier: 1815–1822* (Paris, 1894), p. 428).
11. Emmanuel Fureix, 'La mort de Napoléon: images et cristallisations de l'événement (1821–1831)', in Christian Delporte and Annie Duprat (eds), *L'événement: images, représentation, mémoire* (Paris, 2003), pp. 159–77, here p. 166.
12. According to a police report, AN F7 6668, Surveillance de la famille Bonaparte, 19 July 1821; and F7 3875, Bulletin de police, 12 and 15 August 1821; Fureix, *La France des larmes*, pp. 410–11.
13. For one fight on the Boulevard des Capucines, AN F7 6668, Surveillance de la famille Bonaparte, 15 July 1821.
14. Alphonse Aulard, 'La mort de Napoléon et les journaux parisiens en 1821', in *Etudes et leçons sur la Révolution française*, 9e série (Paris, 1924), pp. 92–103, here p. 94.
15. According to Aulard, 'La mort de Napoléon', p. 95.
16. Pasquier, *Mémoires*, v. p. 357.
17. Eléonore-Adèle d'Osmond, comtesse de Boigne, *Récits d'une tante: mémoires de la comtesse de Boigne*, 5 vols (Paris, 1921–3), iii. pp. 59–60.

18. Astolphe de Custine, *Lettres inédites au marquis de La Grange* (Paris, 1925), pp. 132–3; Jean-Pons-Guillaume Viennet, *Mémoires et journal: 1777–1867* (Paris, 2006), p. 449; Prosper Brugière, baron de Barante, *Souvenirs du Bon de Barante: 1782–1866*, 8 vols (Paris, 1890–1901), ii p. 501; Pasquier, *Mémoires*, v. pp. 207, 357; M. Thomassy, *De la sensation qu'a faite en France la mort de Buonaparte, et des écrits publiés à ce sujet* (Paris, 1821), pp. 14–15; Maurice d'Irisson, comte d'Hérisson, *Le cabinet noir: Louis XVII–Napoléon–Marie-Louise* (Paris, 1887), pp. 255–6 (12 July 1821); Lord Granville Leveson Gower, *Private Correspondence, 1781 to 1821*, 2 vols (London, 1916), ii. p. 548 (9 July 1821).

19. Maximilien-Sébastien Foy, *Notes journalières du général Foy: 1820–1825*, 3 vols (Compiègne, 1925), i. p. 209.

20. Georges Lacour-Gayet, *Talleyrand: 1754–1838*, 5 vols (Paris, 1928–34), iii. p. 117 or v. p. 136.

21. AN F7 3875, Préfet de Police, 7 and 8 July 1821. At Rennes, Marseilles and in the Jura, same general indifference (F7 3794, 20–25 July 1821).

22. AN F7 3794, Bulletin de police, 18–19 July 1821; Ernest Dupuy, *Alfred de Vigny: ses amitiés, son rôle littéraire. Les amitiés*, 2 vols (Paris, 1910), i. p. 135; Ernest Daudet, *La police politique: chronique des temps de la Restauration, 1815–1820* (Paris, 1912), p. 202; Ménager, *Les Napoléon*, p. 28.

23. AN F7 6916, prefect of Rhône to the general director of the Department of Police, Lyons, 21 July 1821.

24. AN F7 6916, prefect of the Eure-et-Loir to the general director of the Department of Police, Marseilles, 14 July 1821.

25. AN F7 6916, prefect of Bouches-du-Rhône to the general director of the Department of Police, Marseilles, 20 July 1821.

26. Letter from General of the 13th Division to the minister of war, 14 July 1821, cited in Fureix, *La France des larmes*, p. 406.

27. See David Skuy, *Assassination, Politics, and Miracles: France and the Royalist Reaction of 1820* (Montreal, 2003); Gilles Malandain, *L'introuvable complot: attentat, enquête et rumeur dans la France de la Restauration* (Paris, 2011); and Philip Mansel, *Paris between Empires: Monarchy and Revolution, 1814–1852* (London, 2003), pp. 167–70. Louvel was guillotined on 7 June 1820 in front of the Hôtel de Ville. Unbeknown to Louvel, Berry's wife was pregnant and would give birth to a son, Henri, duc de Bordeaux, seven months later. After the abdication of Charles X, Legitimists recognised him as Henri V.

28. Irene Collins, *The Government and the Newspaper Press in France, 1814–1881* (London, 1959), pp. 31–5; Claude Bellanger, Jacques Godechot,

Pierre Guiral and Fernand Terrou Lien (eds), *Histoire générale de la presse française*, 5 vols (Paris, 1969–76), ii. pp. 67–70, 72–7.

29. AN F7 3798, Bulletin de police, 21 July 1829; BB30 215, Versements divers, dossier 1, n. 7, 23 April 1822.

30. Malandain, 'La haine des Bourbons sous la Restauration', pp. 74–5.

31. Lucas-Dubreton, *Le culte de Napoléon*, pp. 110–16; Nicolas Boisson, 'Une approche socio-historique de la violence au XIXème siècle: le cas d'une conspiration à Lyon en 1817' (MA dissertation, Université Pierre Mendès France, Grenoble, 2008); Pamela M. Pilbeam, *Republicanism in Nineteenth-Century France, 1814–1871* (Basingstoke, 1995), pp. 76–7.

32. On political prisoners during this period see Emile Louret, *Le pavillon des princes: histoire complète de la prison politique de Sainte-Pélagie depuis sa fondation jusqu'à nos jours* (Paris, 1895), pp. 64–82; Jean-Claude Vimont, 'Enfermer les politiques: la mise en place progressive des "régimes politiques" d'incarcération', in Philippe Vigier and Alain Faure (eds), *Répression et prison politique en France et en Europe au XIXe siècle* (Paris, 1990), pp. 189–203.

33. The argument adopted by Fureix, 'La mort de Napoléon', pp. 159–77; and Lote, 'La contre-légende napoléonienne et la mort de Napoléon', 324–49.

34. Ménager, *Les Napoléon*, pp. 29–33.

35. AN F7 6916, General Secretary of the Doubs Prefecture to the General Director of the Department of Police, Besançon, 23 July 1821.

36. Foy, *Notes journalières*, p. 209.

37. Kirstin Buchinger, '"La pierre et l'empereur": Remembering the Revolutionary and Napoleonic Wars in French Lithography', in Alan Forrest, Etienne François and Karen Hagemann (eds), *War Memories: The Revolutionary and Napoleonic Wars in Modern European Culture* (Basingstoke, 2012), pp. 322–3.

38. Ménager, *Les Napoléon*, pp. 31–2.

39. AN F7 3794, Bulletin de police, 20–25 July 1821.

40. Ménager, *Les Napoléon*, p. 33; Victor Hugo, *Les Misérables*, 2 vols (Paris, 1951), i. p. 390; Honoré de Balzac, *Le médecin de campagne*, in *La comédie humaine*, 10 vols (Paris, 1949–59), viii. p. 469.

41. AN BB30 230, Versements divers, 16 August 1822.

42. AN BB30 230, Versements divers, Fontenoy-le-Comte, 28 April 1822.

43. Paul-Louis Courier, *Oeuvres complètes*, 4 vols (Brussels, 1828), i. p. 290.

44. Pascal Greppe, 'L'empereur est mort: propos du colonel Perraton', *Revue des études napoléoniennes*, 34 (1932), 277–97.

45. AN F7 6668, Surveillance de la famille Bonaparte, 17–18 July 1821.

46. Barante, *Souvenirs*, ii. p. 508; Victor de Broglie, *Souvenirs, 1785–1870, du feu duc de Broglie*, 4 vols (Paris, 1886), ii. pp. 209–10; Fureix, *La France des larmes*, p. 405.

47. Lucas-Dubreton, *Le culte de Napoléon*, p. 243; Fureix, 'La mort de Napoléon', p. 159.

48. *Morning Chronicle*, 21 July 1821.

49. AN F7 3794, Bulletin de police, 13–14 July 1821; *Morning Chronicle*, 21 July 1821.

50. *Morning Chronicle*, 21 July 1821.

51. AN F7 3794, Bulletin de police, 18–19 July 1821; and F7 6758, Police générale, 16 July 1821, in this case a Polish officer by the name of Debinski who had been in the Grande Armée; and AN F7 6668, Surveillance de la famille Bonaparte, 28 July 1821.

52. AN F7 6668, Surveillance de la famille Bonaparte, 11 July 1821.

53. Robert Gildea, *Children of the Revolution: The French, 1799–1914* (London, 2008), pp. 6–9.

54. Alfred de Musset, *La confession d'un enfant du siècle*, 2 vols (Paris, 1836), i. pp. 7–12.

55. Louis-Florimond Fantin des Odoards, *Journal du général Fantin des Odoards, étapes d'un officier de la Grande Armée, 1800–1830* (Paris, 1895), pp. 472–3.

56. Planat de La Faye, *Vie de Planat de La Faye*, p. vi; idem, *Correspondance intime de Planat de La Faye* (Paris, 1895), p. vi.

57. Louis Bro, *Mémoires du général Bro (1796–1844)* (Paris, 1914), pp. 177–8.

58. Maurice Persat, *Mémoires du commandant Persat, 1806 à 1844* (Paris, 1910), pp. 75–6.

59. Charlotte von Schönberg, comtesse von Kielmannsegge, *Mémoires de la comtesse de Kielmannsegge sur Napoléon Ier*, trans. Joseph Delage, 2 vols (Paris, 1928), ii. pp. 157, 163, 207.

60. Kielmannsegge, *Mémoires*, ii. p. 207.

61. Legouvé, *Dernier travail, derniers souvenirs*, p. 188; Chateaubriand, *Mémoires d'outre-tombe*, i. pp. 1568–9.

62. Greppe, 'L'empereur est mort', 278–9.

63. Jean Boisson, *Le retour des cendres* (Paris, 1973), p. 34.

64. Jacques-Olivier Boudon, *Le roi Jérôme, frère prodigue de Napoléon (1784–1860)* (Paris, 2008), p. 468.

65. Bernard Nabonne, *Joseph Bonaparte: le roi philosophe* (Paris, 1949), p. 222; Ross, *The Reluctant King*, p. 257; Patricia Tyson Stroud, *The Man Who Had Been King: The American Exile of Napoleon's Brother Joseph* (Philadelphia, 2005), pp. 84, 87.

66. Ross, *The Reluctant King*, p. 257.

67. Henri Welschinger, *Le roi de Rome (1811–1832)* (Paris, 1897) p. 266; Boisson, *Le retour des cendres*, p. 36.

68. Cited in Welschinger, *Le roi de Rome*, p. 266.

69. See Dwyer, *Citizen Emperor*, pp. 501, 508–9.

70. *Correspondance de Marie Louise, 1799–1847; lettres intimes et inédites à la comtesse de Colloredo et à Mlle de Poutet, depuis 1810 comtesse de Crenneville* (Vienna, 1887), pp. 225–9.

71. Hanns Schlitter, *Die Stellung der österreichischen Regierung zum Testamente Napoleon Bonaparte's* (Vienna, 1893), pp. 15–16.

72. Interestingly, any hawker mentioning the word 'Napoleon' was likely to be quickly arrested (AN F7 3875, Préfet de Police, 17 July 1821). Planat de La Faye to Eugène Lebon (11 July 1821), in Planat de La Faye, *Vie de Planat de La Faye*, p. 394; *Accusation contre les meurtriers de Napoléon* (Paris, 1821), p. 4.

73. Lote, 'La mort de Napoléon', 44–6; Fureix, *La France des larmes*, pp. 407–8; Fiona Parr, 'The Death of Napoleon Bonaparte and the Retour des Cendres: French and British Perspectives', http://www.napoleon.org/en/reading_room/articles/files/479507.asp.

74. Frédéric Degeorge, *Sentiment d'un citoyen sur les cancers héréditaires* (Paris, 1821), p. 6; and *Bonaparte n'est pas mort d'un cancer*, (Paris, 1821) p. 3.

75. *Accusation contre les meurtriers de Napoléon*, p. 3.

76. *Bonaparte n'est pas mort d'un cancer*, p. 12.

77. Jean-Claude Bésuchet de Saunois, *Réflexions sur la mort de Napoléon, suivies de quelques considérations sur l'empoisonnement par les substances introduites dans l'estomac, par un chirurgien-major de la vieille armée* (Paris, 1821), pp. 5 and 6; Alexandre Barginet, *De la reine d'Angleterre et de Napoléon Bonaparte, tous deux morts d'un cancer* (Paris, 1821), p. 20; *Napoléon et la reine d'Angleterre aux bords du Styx, dialogue* (Paris, 1821).

78. J. Héreau, *Napoléon à Sainte-Hélène: opinion d'un médecin sur la maladie de l'Empereur Napoléon et sur la cause de sa mort; offerte à son fils au jour de sa majorité* (Paris, 1829).

79. On works that debunk the poisoning thesis see Volker Sellin, 'Der Tod Napoleons', *Francia*, 35 (2008), 273–94; Lentz and Macé, *La mort de Napoléon*.

80. The most notorious of the modern poison proponents is: Sten Forshufvud, *Who Killed Napoleon?*, trans. A. H. Broderick (London, 1962); idem, *Napoléon a-t-il été empoisonné?* (Paris, 1961). The story of Forshufvud

and his research is told in Ben Weider and David Hapgood, *The Murder of Napoleon* (Toronto, 1982). Also Sten Forshufvud and Ben Weider, *Assassination at St. Helena: The Poisoning of Napoleon Bonaparte* (Vancouver, 1978) and *Assassination at St. Helena Revisited* (New York, 1995). An overview of the conspiracy theories is in Michael Sibalis, 'Conspiracy on St. Helena? (Mis)remembering Napoleon's Exile', *French History and Civilization*, 4 (2011), 94–105. There is an extensive literature on the 'causes' of Napoleon's death. A bibliography, which is now out of date, can be found in Lemaire et al., *Autour de 'l'empoisonnement' de Napoléon*, pp. 119–28.

81. René Maury, *L'assassin de Napoléon, ou Le mystère de Sainte-Hélène* (Paris, 1994).

82. Alessandro Lugli et al., 'The Medical Mystery of Napoleon Bonaparte: An Interdisciplinary Exposé', *Advances in Anatomic Pathology*, 18:2 (March 2011), 152–8; and P. F. Corso and T. Hindmarsh, 'Further Scientific Evidence of the Non-Poisonous Death of Napoleon', *Science Progress*, 79:2 (1996), 89–96.

83. Quigley, *The Corpse*, pp. 238–9.

84. Bertrand, *Cahiers*, iii. p. 267; Marchand, *In Napoleon's Shadow*, pp. 709–10.

85. For these and the following figures see Fureix, *La France des larmes*, pp. 410–11; idem, 'La mort de Napoléon', p. 162. For the French pamphlet literature produced by Napoleon's death see Paul Holzhausen, *Napoleons Tod im Spiegel der zeitgenössischen Presse und Dichtung* (Frankfurt am Main, 1902), pp. 95–111.

86. On the 'monster' in nineteenth-century France see Anne-Emmanuelle Demartini, *L'affaire Lacenaire* (Paris, 2001).

87. *L'Ami de la religion et du Roi: journal ecclésiastique, politique et littéraire*, 722 (11 July 1821), pp. 283–4; *La Quotidienne*, 29 July 1821. On the assassination of Enghien see Dwyer, *Citizen Emperor*, pp. 119–24.

88. Pagé, *Le mythe napoléonien*, pp. 62–6. See, for example, J.-J. de Cousso, *Observations relatives au despotisme militaire exercé en France pendant la trop longue domination de Napoléon Buonaparte* (Paris, 1821); *Apothéose de Napoleone Bonaparte, ou signalement de l'Ante-Christ*.

89. Louis de Bonald, *Considérations politiques sur le projet de loi relatif aux donataires* (Paris, n.d.).

90. Antoine-Jean Cassé de Saint-Prosper, *Oraison funèbre de N. Buonaparte, où l'on trouve établi, d'après 'Le Moniteur', ce que les vertus du ci-devant empereur ont coûté d'hommes et d'argent à la France; suivi du testament dudit N. Buonaparte. Le tout recueilli par un conscrit jambe de bois* (Paris, 1821), p. 3.

91. Jean-Baptiste Pérès, *Comme quoi Napoléon n'a jamais existé, ou Grand erratum, source d'un grand nombre infini d'errata à noter dans l'histoire du XIXe siècle* (Paris, 1827). This was, however, very much the exception to the rule, a satire directed not against Napoleon but against rationalist arguments against religion, and that somehow has become incorporated into the anti-Napoleonic literature. See Albert Sonnenfeld, 'Napoleon as Sun Myth', *Yale French Studies*, 26 (1960), 32, 36.

92. André-François-Victoire-Henri, marquis de Carrion-Nisas, *Bonaparte et Napoléon, parallèle* (Paris, 1821).

93. Carrion-Nisas, *Bonaparte et Napoléon, parallèle*, pp. 3–7.

94. Albin Thourel, *Les accens de la liberté au tombeau de Napoléon* (Paris, 1821), pp. 4, 7.

95. *L'éloge des éloges, ou encore du Bonaparte* (Paris, 1821).

96. *Le Drapeau blanc: journal de la politique, de la littérature et des théâtres*, 8 July 1821; *La Quotidienne* (9 July 1821). A similar sentiment expressed in the *Nouveaux détails sur la mort de Bonaparte* (Paris, n.d.), pp. 1–2.

97. See *La Quotidienne*, 7 July 1821; *Le Drapeau blanc: journal de la politique, de la littérature et des théâtres*, 7, 8 and 9 July 1821; *Gazette de France*, 7 and 8 July 1821.

98. For a selection of extracts from the press see Boisson, *Le retour des cendres*, pp. 20–1.

99. Georges Lote, 'La mort de Napoléon et l'opinion bonapartiste en 1821', *Revue des études napoléoniennes*, 31 (1930), 19–58; Tudesq, 'La légende napoléonienne', pp. 418–19.

100. Léonard-Charles-André-Gustave Gallois, *Eloge funèbre de Napoléon, prononcé sur sa tombe, le 9 mai 1821, par le grand maréchal Bertrand* (Paris, n.d.), p. 1. On the cult of the genius see Maurice Z. Shroder, *Icarus: The Image of the Artist in French Romanticism* (Cambridge, Mass., 1961), pp. 26–40.

101. *L'homme au petit chapeau* (Paris, 1821), 6; *Le coucher du soleil de 5 mai 1821*, 8; Gallois, *Eloge funèbre de Napoléon*, pp. 8–10; *Panégyrique d'un mort, par un homme sans titre* (Paris, 1821), pp. 5–6; *Le Constitutionnel*, 11 July 1821.

102. Fureix, *La France des larmes*, p. 428; *De profundis, par un invalide* (Paris, 1821), pp. 14–17.

103. P. J. F. D. S. M., *Bonaparte jugé par lui-même dialogue* (Paris, 1823), p. 52.

104. Barbara Beßlich, *Der deutsche Napoleon-Mythos. Literatur und Erinnerung, 1800–1945* (Darmstadt, 2007), pp. 137–68.

105. Alain Pougetoux, 'La mort de Napoléon', in Jérémie Benoît, Agnès Delannoy and Alain Pougetoux, *Napoléon: le retour des cendres (1840–1990)* (Paris, 1990), pp. 41–55.

106. Maria dell'Isola, 'La mort de Napoléon', *Revue des études napoléoniennes*, 36 (1933), 280–4; idem, *Napoléon dans la poésie italienne à partir de 1821* (Paris, 1927), pp. 15–36; Millar, *Napoleon in Italian Literature*, pp. 154–7; and Pagé, *Le mythe napoléonien*, pp. 80–4.

107. See Kenneth Cornell, 'May 5, 1821 and the Poets', *Yale French Studies*, 26 (1960), 50–4; Guglielmo Alberti, 'Alessandro Manzoni', in Emilio Cecchi and Natalino Sapegno (eds), *Storia della letteratura italiana* (Milan, 1969), pp. 663–809.

108. On Grillparzer and Napoleon see Claudio Magris, *Danube*, trans. Patrick Creagh (London, 1989), pp. 78–82. On Lamey see Fritz L. Cohn, 'The Worship of Napoleon in German Poetry', *Modern Language Quarterly*, 1 (1940), 539–49. On the mourning poetry in Germany see Walther Klein, *Der Napoleonkult in der Pfalz* (Munich, 1934), pp. 7–9; and Holzhausen, *Napoleons Tod im Spiegel*, pp. 68–91.

109. See Jean-Marcel Humbert (ed.), *Napoléon aux Invalides: 1840, le retour des cendres* (Paris, 1991), pp. 110–15, 258–67; Benoît, Delannoy and Pougetoux, *Napoléon: le retour des cendres, fig. 14–44*; Suzanne Glover Lindsay, 'Mummies and Tombs: Turenne, Napoleon, and Death Ritual', *Art Bulletin*, 82 (2000), 492–7; and Claudia Hattendorff, *Napoleon I. und die Bilder* (Petersberg, 2012), pp. 19–33.

110. *Morning Chronicle*, 21 July 1821.

111. For a somewhat later date see the poem by Auguste-Marseille Barthélemy and Joseph Méry, *Le fils de l'homme, ou souvenirs de Vienne* (Paris, 1829), which gave rise to a famous political trial known as the Trial of the Son of Man. See Jules Garsou, *Les créateurs de la légende napoléonienne: Barthélemy et Méry* (Paris, 1899), pp. 48–50, 156–7.

112. Buchinger, 'La pierre et l'empereur', pp. 320–1. Napoleon's son received the title Duc de Reichstadt in 1818 after the estates he had been granted by his grandfather, Francis I.

113. According to Heinrich Heine, *De la France* (Paris, 1857), pp. 46–7, 117–18.

114. There is, surprisingly, no scholarly study of Vernet. See, however, *Horace Vernet: 1789–1863* (Paris, 1980); Armand Dayot, *Les Vernet: Joseph, Carle, Horace* (Paris, 1898); Katie Hornstein, 'Episodes in Political Illusion: The Proliferation of War Imagery in France (1804–1856)', (PhD dissertation, University of Michigan, 2010), esp. chs 3 and 4; and Daniel Harkett and Katie Hornstein (eds), *Horace Vernet and the Thresholds of Nineteenth-Century Visual Culture* (Hanover, NH, 2017).

115. Jean-Paul Kauffmann, *The Black Room at Longwood: Napoleon's Exile on Saint Helena* (New York, 1999), p. 276; Nina Maria

Athanassoglou-Kallmyer, '*Imago Belli*: Horace Vernet's *L'Atelier* as an Image of Radical Militarism under the Restoration', *Art Bulletin*, 68:2 (1986), 268–80, here 278; Hornstein, 'Episodes in Political Illusion', pp. 115–17.

116. Bro, *Mémoires du général Bro*, pp. 163–5; Fureix, 'La mort de Napoléon', p. 166.

117. Fureix, *La France des larmes*, p. 406.

118. For the following see Ploux, *De bouche à l'oreille*, pp. 179–81; and Day-Hickman, *Napoleonic Art*, pp. 32–3. The rumours coincided with the French expedition sent to help put down the liberal revolt in Spain.

119. See, for example, Gavriel D. Rosenfeld, *The World Hitler Never Made: Alternate History and the Memory of Nazism* (Cambridge, 2005), pp. 199–270.

120. See, for example, Laure Junot, duchesse d'Abrantès, *Mémoires sur la Restauration, ou Souvenirs historiques sur cette époque, la Révolution de 1830, et les premières années du règne de Louis-Philippe*, 7 vols (Brussels, 1837), vii. p. 4.

121. Ménager, *Les Napoléon*, pp. 27–33.

122. See AN F7 6913, Bulletin de police, fol. 8195, for his dossier.

123. AN F7 6913, fol. 8195, Requisitoire du substitut du procureur du roi, 26 May 1821; Copy of interrogation, 30 June 1821; prefect of police to Baron Mounier (6 July 1821).

124. Hazareesingh, *Legend of Napoleon*, pp. 70–1.

125. AN BB30 215, Versements divers, dossier 1, n. 7, 20 April 1822; d. 2, n. 9, 9 April 1823 and n. 17, 17 March 1823; Ploux, *De bouche à l'oreille*, pp. 180–1.

126. Day-Hickman, *Napoleonic Art*, p. 104.

127. G. Lenôtre, *Napoléon: croquis de l'épopée* (Paris, 1932), p. 279; Boisson, *Le retour des cendres*, p. 28; Lucas-Dubreton, *Le culte de Napoléon*, pp. 191–2.

128. AN BB18 1145, Correspondance générale de la division criminelle, 31 October 1826; Day-Hickman, *Napoleonic Art*, p. 34.

129. Balzac, *Le médecin de campagne*, in *La comédie humaine*, viii. p. 469. English quotation from *The Country Doctor*, trans. Ellen Marriage (London, 1961), p. 201. On Napoleon in Balzac see Saint-Paulien [M. I. Sicard], *Napoléon, Balzac et l'empire de la Comédie humaine* (Paris, 1979), esp. pp. 145–75; Pagé, *Le mythe napoléonien*, pp. 124–31.

130. AN F7 6772 (28 May 1828).

131. Ploux, *De bouche à l'oreille*, p. 274, n. 243 (F7 6672)

132. Frances Trollope, *Paris and the Parisians in 1835*, 2 vols (London, 1836), i. pp. 259–62.

133. Ploux, *De bouche à l'oreille*, p. 182.

CHAPTER 7

1. Thierry Lentz, 'A Brief History of an Oft-Forgotten Secondary Source for the Revolution and Empire Period: The Memoirs of Napoleon', *Napoleonica. La Revue*, 13:1 (2012), 52–64.

2. Las Cases, *Le Mémorial de Sainte-Hélène*, ii. pp. 405–6, 407–8 (5, 6–7 October 1816).

3. On Montholon's memoirs see Hélène Michaud, 'Que vaut le témoignage de Montholon à la lumière du fonds Masson', *Revue de l'Institut Napoléon*, 120 (1971), 113–20, here 117.

4. See Pierre Nora, 'Les mémoires d'état: de Commynes à de Gaulle', in Pierre Nora (ed.), *Les lieux de mémoire*, 3 vols (Paris, 1984–6), ii.2, p. 385; Morrissey, 'The *Mémorial de Sainte-Hélène*', 716–32; Antoine Casanova, *Napoléon et la pensée de son temps: une histoire intellectuelle singulière* (Paris, 2001).

5. Las Cases, *Le Mémorial de Sainte-Hélène*, i. p. 247 (16 November 1815).

6. Las Cases, *Le Mémorial de Sainte-Hélène*, i. p. 657 (30 May 1816).

7. A point made by Blix, 'Heroic Genesis', 107–28.

8. Las Cases, *Le Mémorial de Sainte-Hélène*, ii. p. 460 (25 October 1816).

9. Jay Winter, 'Thinking about Silence', in Efrat Ben-Ze'ev, Ruth Ginio and Jay Winter (eds), *Shadows of War: A Social History of Silence in the Twentieth Century* (Cambridge, 2010), pp. 3–31; Luisa Passerini, 'Memories between Silence and Oblivion', in Katherine Hodgkin and Susannah Radstone (eds), *Contested Pasts: The Politics of Memory* (London, 2003), pp. 238–54. On the relation between narratives, memory and forgetting see Geoffrey Cubitt, *History and Memory* (Manchester, 2007), pp. 90–111.

10. R. S. Alexander, *Bonapartism and the Revolutionary Tradition in France: The Fédérés of 1815* (Cambridge, 1991), pp. 5–7.

11. Philippe Gonnard, 'La légende napoléonienne dans la press libérale', *Revue des études napoléoniennes*, 1 (1912), 235–58; idem, 'La légende napoléonienne dans la press libérale: *La Minerve*', *Revue des études napoléoniennes*, 3 (1914), 28–49.

12. Albert Léon Guérard, *Reflections on the Napoleonic Legend* (London, 1924), pp. 134–9.

13. François Antommarchi's *Mémoires* found little echo among the public (Gonnard, *Les origines de la légende*, pp. 172–81).

14. Gérard Gengembre, *Napoléon: l'empereur immortel* (Paris, 2002), p. 98; Otto W. Johnston, *The Myth of a Nation: Literature and Politics in Prussia under Napoleon* (Columbia, SC, 1989), p. 187.

15. They included Napoleon's account of the siege of Toulon, the first Italian campaign, the coup of Brumaire, the early years of the Consulate and the

campaign of 1815. Gaspard Gourgaud, *Mémoires pour servir à l'histoire de France, sous Napoléon, écrits à Sainte-Hélène par les généraux qui ont partagé sa captivité, et publiés sur les manuscrits entièrement corrigés de Napoléon*, 2 vols (Paris, 1823); Charles Tristan Montholon, *Mémoires pour servir à l'histoire de France, sous Napoléon, écrits à Sainte-Hélène par les généraux qui ont partagé sa captivité, et publiés sur les manuscrits entièrement corrigés de Napoléon*, 6 vols (Paris, 1823).

16. Thomas Hook, *Facts Illustrative of the Treatment of Napoleon Bonaparte* (London, 1819). It was translated into French as Carnet d'un voyageur ou recueil de notes curieuses sur la vie, les occupations, les habitudes de Buonaparte à Longwood (Paris, 1819).

17. Barry O'Meara, *An Exposition of Some of the Transactions that Have Taken Place at St Helena* (London, 1819), p. 3.

18. Cited in Hicks, 'Who was Barry O'Meara?', 85–6.

19. According to Joseph Shaylor, *The Fascination of Books: With Other Papers on Books & Bookselling* (London, 1912), p. 207.

20. Maxwell (ed.), *The Creevey Papers*, p. 39. For a discussion of the book see Gonnard, *Les origines de la légende*, pp. 115–43.

21. O'Meara, *Napoleon in Exile*, i. pp. 165–7.

22. O'Meara, *Napoleon in Exile*, i. pp. 174–6, 385.

23. O'Meara, *Napoleon in Exile*, i. pp. 463–6, 479–80; and Bertrand, *Cahiers*, i. p. 102 (14 August 1816). Waterloo is often mentioned in Gourgaud's *Journal de Sainte-Hélène*, but then Gourgaud was writing on the history of the battle.

24. O'Meara, *Napoleon in Exile*, i. pp. 191–6.

25. O'Meara, *Napoleon in Exile*, ii. p. 56.

26. O'Meara, *Napoleon in Exile*, ii. p. 157; Las Cases, *Le Mémorial de Sainte-Hélène*, i. p. 473 (27 March 1816).

27. Las Cases, *Le Mémorial de Sainte-Hélène*, ii. p. 579 (14 November 1816).

28. O'Meara, *Napoleon in Exile*, i. pp. 207, 250, 329–30, 333–4, 349–50, 381; ii. pp. 341, 393.

29. Jean Tulard, *Napoléon ou le mythe du sauveur* (Paris, 1977), p. 448; Le Gall, *Napoléon*, p. 13; Robert Morrissey, *Napoléon et l'héritage de la gloire* (Paris, 2010), p. 173; Hazareesingh, 'Napoleonic Memory in Nineteenth-Century France', 757. On the other hand, a study carried out by Martyn Lyons, *Le triomphe du livre: une histoire sociologique de la lecture dans la France du XIXe siècle* (Paris, 1987), pp. 91, 93, shows that a number of novels by far outsold Las Cases.

30. Louis A. Rozelaar, 'Le Mémorial de Sainte-Helene et Victor Hugo en 1827', *French Quarterly*, 9 (1927), 53–68; idem, 'Mémorial de Sainte-Hélène et le Romantisme', *Revue des études napoléoniennes*, 29 (1929),

203–26; Nada Tomiche, *Napoléon écrivain* (Paris, 1952), pp. 237–88; and Morrissey, *Napoléon et l'héritage de la gloire*, pp. 176–209.

31. Stendhal, *Le rouge et le noir* (Paris, 2000), p. 66; Pagé, *Le mythe napoléonien*, pp. 84–102.

32. Maxwell (ed.), *The Creevey Papers*, p. 403.

33. André-Jean Tudesq, *L'élection présidentielle de Louis-Napoléon Bonaparte, 10 decembre 1848* (Paris, 1965), p. 14. On the various editions see Morrissey, *Napoléon et l'héritage de la gloire*, pp. 174–5; and Montroussier, *L'éthique du chef militaire*, pp. 26–9. The best critical edition is that by Marcel Dunan, first published in 1951, from which the following references are taken. The 1830 edition is considered to be the most complete because it contains passages about the Bourbons that were not included in the earlier editions.

34. Philippe Burty, 'Les desseins de Charlet pour le mémorial de Sainte-Hélène', *Gazette des Beaux-Arts*, 1 (1 March 1860), 275–82.

35. André Fugier, 'Introduction', in *Mémorial de Sainte-Hélène*, ed. and annotated by André Fugier, 2 vols (Paris, 1961), i. p. xxiv; Montroussier, *L'éthique du chef militaire*, pp. 24–5.

36. Annie Jourdan, *L'empire de Napoléon* (Paris, 2000) p. 159.

37. Hazareesingh, *The Legend of Napoleon*, pp. 164–71.

38. Morrissey, *Napoléon et l'héritage de la gloire*, pp. 188–9.

39. Las Cases, *Le Mémorial de Sainte-Hélène*, i. pp. 126–30 (1–6 September 1815).

40. Las Cases, *Le Mémorial de Sainte-Hélène*, i. p. 147 (26–30 September 1815).

41. Las Cases, *Le Mémorial de Sainte-Hélène*, i. pp. 298–9 (15–16 December 1815).

42. Las Cases, *Le Mémorial de Sainte-Hélène*, i. p. 480 (1–2 April 1816), points to two paintings and a bust of the King of Rome in Napoleon's bedroom; and ii. pp. 371–2 (23 September 1816). On Napoleon's feelings towards his son see Charles Doris, *Chagrins domestiques de Napoléon Bonaparte à l'île Sainte-Hélène* (Paris, 1821), pp. 218–21; Antoine Jean-Baptiste Simonnin, *Histoire des trois derniers mois de la vie de Napoléon Bonaparte* (Paris, 1821), pp. 27, 29.

43. Las Cases, *Le Mémorial de Sainte-Hélène*, i. pp. 243–4 (16 November 1815).

44. Such as Las Cases, *Le Mémorial de Sainte-Hélène*, ii. p. 77 (29 July 1816).

45. Las Cases, *Le Mémorial de Sainte-Hélène*, i. p. 399 (25–28 February 1816).

46. See also Morrissey, 'The *Mémorial de Sainte-Hélène*', 729.

47. See Dwyer, *Citizen Emperor*, pp. 341–3.

48. For the following see Day-Hickman, *Napoleonic Art*, pp. 24–6.

49. Las Cases, *Le Mémorial de Sainte-Hélène*, i. p. 452 (17 March 1816).

50. Las Cases, *Le Mémorial de Sainte-Hélène*, i. p. 311 (18, 19 December 1815); Bluche, *Le bonapartisme*, pp. 172–92.

51. Las Cases, *Le Mémorial de Sainte-Hélène*, i. pp. 109–33, 469 (1–6 September 1815, 27 March 1816).

52. Las Cases, *Le Mémorial de Sainte-Hélène*, i. pp. 495–6 (9–10 April 1816).

53. Las Cases, *Le Mémorial de Sainte-Hélène*, i. p. 271 (29–30 November 1815).

54. Las Cases, *Le Mémorial de Sainte-Hélène*, i. p. 472 (27 March 1816).

55. Las Cases, *Le Mémorial de Sainte-Hélène*, i. p. 471 (27 March 1816).

56. Las Cases, *Le Mémorial de Sainte-Hélène*, i. p. 543 (28 April 1816); Bertrand, *Cahiers*, i. p. 230 (2 June 1817); Gourgaud, *Journal de Sainte-Hélène*, ii. p. 129 (2 June 1817).

57. Las Cases, *Le Mémorial de Sainte-Hélène*, ii. p. 544 (11 November 1816).

58. Las Cases, *Le Mémorial de Sainte-Hélène*, ii. p. 233 (24 August 1816).

59. Las Cases, *Le Mémorial de Sainte-Hélène*, i. pp. 277–8, 760–2 (4–5 December 1815, 18 June 1816; ii. pp. 244–58 (26 August 1816); Gourgaud, *Journal de Sainte-Hélène*, ii. p. 111 (20 May 1817).

60. Montholon, *History of the Captivity of Napoleon*, i. p. 130; and Montholon, *Récits*, i. p. 254.

61. Las Cases, *Le Mémorial de Sainte-Hélène*, ii. pp. 542–3 (11 November 1816).

62. Dwyer, *Citizen Emperor*, pp. 345–9; and idem, 'Napoleon and the Universal Monarchy', *History*, 95:319 (2010), 293–307.

63. Las Cases, *Le Mémorial de Sainte-Hélène*, i. pp. 439, 704–9 (10–12 March, 14 June 1816); O'Meara, *Napoleon in Exile*, i. pp. 354, 461.

64. Las Cases, *Le Mémorial de Sainte-Hélène*, i. pp. 492–3 (3 April 1816); Hazareesingh, 'Napoleonic Memory in Nineteenth-Century France', 759.

65. Gourgaud, *Journal de Sainte-Hélène*, ii. p. 444 (20 January 1818).

66. Las Cases, *Le Mémorial de Sainte-Hélène*, i. p. 274 (29–30 November 1815).

67. O'Meara, *Napoleon in Exile*, ii. p. 60.

68. O'Meara, *Napoleon in Exile*, ii. p. 156.

69. O'Meara, *Napoleon in Exile*, ii. p. 340.

70. Las Cases, *Le Mémorial de Sainte-Hélène*, i. pp. 243, 730 (16 November 1815, 14 June 1816).

71. Las Cases, *Le Mémorial de Sainte-Hélène*, i. pp. 412, 476 (3, 30–31 March 1816); ii. pp. 231–2 (24 August 1816).

72. Las Cases, *Le Mémorial de Sainte-Hélène*, i. pp. 714–16 (12 June 1816); O'Meara, *Napoleon in Exile*, ii. pp. 198–200.

73. Las Cases, *Le Mémorial de Sainte-Hélène*, i. pp. 661–2 (30 May 1816); ii. pp. 622–8 (20 November 1816).

74. Las Cases, *Le Mémorial de Sainte-Hélène*, i. pp. 569–70 (6 May 1816).

75. In Paris between 1816 and 1820, literacy rates may have been as high as 84 per cent for men and 60 per cent for women. They would have increased into the 1830s. See James Smith Allen, *Popular French Romanticism: Authors, Readers, and Books in the 19th Century* (Syracuse, NY, 1981), pp. 154–5; idem, *In the Public Eye: A History of Reading in Modern France, 1800–1940* (Princeton, 2014), p. 64; William H. Sewell, Jr, 'Social Mobility in a Nineteenth-Century European City: Some Findings and Implications', *Journal of Interdisciplinary History*, 7:2 (Autumn, 1976), 217–33.

76. Sydney Morgan, *France in 1829–30*, 2 vols (London, 1831), i. pp. 383–4.

77. Antoine Vincent Arnault, *Vie politique et militaire de Napoléon*, 2 vols (Paris, 1822–6).

78. Petiteau, *Napoléon*, pp. 68–9; James Clifton and Leslie M. Scattone, *The Plains of Mars: European War Prints, 1500–1825* (New Haven, 2008), pp. 87–9; Hornstein, 'Episodes in Political Illusion', pp. 142–3, 146.

79. Some of the more important monumental histories of Napoleon (in French) for this period are: Jacques Marquet de Montbreton de Norvins, *Histoire de Napoléon*, 4 vols (Paris, 1827–8), with illustrations by the artist Denis-Auguste-Marie Raffet; Louis-Pierre-Edouard Bignon, *Histoire de France, depuis le 18 brumaire, novembre 1799, jusqu'à la paix de Tilsitt, juillet 1807*, 6 vols (Paris, 1829–30); Antoine-Clair Thibaudeau, *Histoire générale de Napoléon Bonaparte, de sa vie privée et publique, de sa carrière politique et militaire, de son administration et de son gouvernement*, 6 vols (Paris, 1827–8); followed by a more detailed history by the same author entitled *Le Consulat et l'Empire, ou Histoire de la France et de Napoléon Bonaparte, de 1799 à 1815*, 10 vols (Paris, 1834–5); and Paul-Mathieu Laurent de L'Ardèche, *Histoire de l'empereur Napoléon* (Paris, 1839), illustrated by Horace Vernet. For a discussion of the works by Norvins and Laurent see Maurice Samuels, *The Spectacular Past: Popular History and the Novel in Nineteenth-Century France* (Ithaca, NY, 2004), pp. 69–79.

80. Léonard-Charles-André-Gustave Gallois, *Histoire de Napoléon d'après lui-même* (Paris, 1825). Also Jean-Joseph Regnault-Warin, *Introduction à l'histoire de l'empire français, ou essai sur la monarchie de Napoléon*, 2 vols (Paris, 1821); *Vie civile et militaire de Napoléon Bonaparte, depuis*

sa naissance jusqu'à sa mort, par L***** R******, officier de l'ancienne armée, 2 vols (Paris, 1821).

81. Gallois, *Histoire de Napoléon*, p. 79; Petiteau, *Napoléon*, pp. 41, 71.

82. Auguste de Chambure, *Napoléon et ses contemporains* (Paris, 1828); Michael Paul Driskel, 'The Proletarian's Body: Charlet's Representations of Social Class during the July Monarchy', in Petra ten-Doesschate Chu and Gabriel P. Weisberg (eds), *The Popularization of Images: Visual Culture under the July Monarchy* (Princeton, 1994), pp. 76–7.

83. Alain Ruiz, 'Bemerkungen zur Entstehung der Napoleon-Legende', in George and Rudolph (eds), *Napoleons langer Schatten über Europa*, p. 419.

84. The theme of exile and return is also very much a Judaic and Christian conception. See, for example, Martien A. Halvorson-Taylor, *Enduring Exile: The Metaphorization of Exile in the Hebrew Bible* (Leiden, 2011); and James M. Scott (ed.), *Exile: Old Testament, Jewish, and Christian Conceptions* (Leiden, 1997). My thanks to Peter James for pointing this out.

85. Frank Paul Bowman, 'Illuminism, Utopia, Mythology', in D. G. Charlton (ed.), *The French Romantics*, 2 vols (Cambridge, 1984), i. p. 102.

86. For this, my thanks to Francis O'Gormen for a copy of his unpublished paper, 'Waterloo and the History of Loneliness', delivered at the conference 'Waterloo: Representation and Memory, 1815–2015', University of York, 27 June 2015.

87. Georges Minois, *Histoire de la solitude et des solitaires* (Paris, 2013), pp. 10–11, 359–61, 387–93.

88. Alain Laurent, *Histoire de l'individualisme* (Paris, 1993), pp. 39–44.

89. See, for example, Françoise Guizot, *Histoire de la civilisation en Europe* (Paris, 1868), p. 26; Laurent, *Histoire de l'individualisme*, p. 47.

90. Peter Fritzsche, *Stranded in the Present: Modern Time and the Melancholy of History* (Cambridge, Mass., 2004), p. 57.

91. Alison Hafera, 'Visual Mediations of Mourning and Melancholia in France, 1790–1830' (PhD dissertation, University of North Carolina at Chapel Hill, 2015), p. 125.

CHAPTER 8

1. See, for example, Annie Duprat, 'Le roi a été chassé à Rambouillet', *Sociétés & Représentations*, 12:2 (2001), 30–43. Robert Gildea, *The Past in French History* (New Haven, 1994), pp. 89–111, adopts a different approach and points to three types of cult: the official cult promoted by Napoleon and his heirs; the popular cult, which remembered Napoleon

as a revolutionary emperor; and what might be termed the 'anti-cult' or the 'black legend'.

2. See, for example, Skuy, *Assassination, Politics, and Miracles*, pp. 14–16; Goujon, *Monarchies postrévolutionnaires*, esp. chs 3 and 4.

3. Alphonse Karr, *Le livre de bord, souvenirs, portraits, notes au crayon*, 4 vols (Paris, 1879–1880), i. p. 117; Louis de Carné, *Vues sur l'histoire contemporaine, ou Essai sur l'histoire de la Restauration*, 2 vols (Paris, 1835), i. p. 257; Lucas-Dubreton, *Le culte de Napoléon*, pp. 133–5; R. S. Alexander, *Re-Writing the French Revolutionary Tradition: Liberal Opposition and the Fall of the Bourbon Monarchy* (Cambridge, 2003), pp. 140–1.

4. F. W. J. Hemmings, *The Theatre Industry in Nineteenth-Century France* (Cambridge, 1993), p. 83.

5. On the politics of forgetting (oubli) see Natalie Scholz, *Die imaginierte Restauration: Repräsentationen der Monarchie im Frankreich Ludwigs XVIII* (Darmstadt, 2006), pp. 58–9, and T. Lawrence Larkin, 'Louis XVIII's Cult[ural] Politics, 1815–1820', *Aurora*, 5 (2004), 28–55; Pierre Rosanvallon, *La monarchie impossible: les Chartes de 1814 et de 1830* (Paris, 1994), pp. 15–89; and for the politics of forgetting in post-1815 Europe see Lok, 'Un oubli total du passé?', esp. 44–8. On iconoclasm see Fureix, 'L'iconoclasme: une pratique politique?', pp. 117–32; and Anne M. Wagner, 'Outrages: Sculpture and Kingship in France after 1789', in Ann Bermingham and John Brewer (eds), *The Consumption of Culture, 1600–1800: Image, Object, Text* (New York, 1995), pp. 294–318. On the destruction of the symbols of Empire see Pierre Boyries, *De plâtre, de marbre, ou de bronze, Napoléon: essai d'iconographie sculptée* (Tauriac, 1998), pp. 119–21.

6. Achille de Vaulabelle, *Histoire des deux Restaurations: jusqu'à l'avènement de Louis-Philippe, de janvier 1813 à octobre 1830*, 8 vols (Paris, 1860), iv. pp. 230–2; Jean Baptiste Auguste Barrès, *Souvenirs d'un officier de la Grande Armée* (Paris, 1923), pp. 222–3; Lucas-Dubreton, *Le culte de Napoléon*, p. 501. On this phenomenon see Martyn Lyons, *Reading Culture and Writing Practices in Nineteenth-Century France* (Toronto, 2008), ch. 4.

7. On the fate of these paintings see Sébastien Allard and Marie-Claude Chaudonneret, *Le suicide de Gros: les peintres de l'Empire et la génération romantique* (Paris, 2010), pp. 54–5, 102–3.

8. Fureix, *La France des larmes*, pp. 172–7. On the contradictory nature of monarchy and the image of Louis XVIII see Martin Wrede, 'Le portrait du roi restauré, ou la fabrication de Louis XVIII', *Revue d'histoire*

moderne et contemporaine, 53:2 (2006), 112–38. On the Bourbon regime's attempts to reconcile competing political interests see Bettina Frederking, '"Il ne faut pas être le roi de deux peuples": Strategies of National Reconciliation in Restoration France', *French History*, 22:4 (2008), 446–68; Natalie Scholz, 'Past and Pathos: Symbolic Practices of Reconciliation during the French Restoration', *History & Memory*, 22:1 (2010), 48–80; and Maximilian Paul Owre, 'United in Division: The Polarized French Nation, 1814–1830' (PhD dissertation, University of North Carolina at Chapel Hill, 2008), pp. 34–101.

9. The AN F7 6678–4, Police générale, contain thousands of reports on opponents of the Bourbons that include details of confiscated material.

10. Bluche, *Le bonapartisme*, p. 125.

11. Such as Antoine-Marie Chamans La Valette, *Mémoires et souvenirs du comte Lavallette, aide-de-camp du général Bonaparte* (Paris, 1831), pp. 340–1. Lavallette housed Bertrand when he returned from St Helena.

12. Sheryl Kroen, *Politics and Theatre* (Berkeley, 2000), p. 164.

13. Lucas-Dubreton, *Le culte de Napoléon*, p. 71; Vincent Robert, *Le temps des banquets: politique et symbolique d'une génération, 1818–1848* (Paris, 2010), pp. 50–1.

14. Edgar L. Newman, 'What the Crowd Wanted in the French Revolution of 1830', in John M. Merriman (ed.), *1830 in France* (New York, 1975), p. 29; Goujon, *Monarchies postrévolutionnaires*, p. 116.

15. The expression is from Susanna Barrows, cited in Kroen, *Politics and Theatre*, p. 165. On the use of festivals by the Bourbons see Rémi Dalisson, *Les trois couleurs, Marianne et l'empereur: fêtes libérales et politiques symboliques en France, 1815–1870* (Paris, 2004), pp. 17–62; Françoise Waquet, *Les fêtes royales sous la Restauration ou l'Ancien Régime retrouvé* (Geneva, 1981).

16. AN F7 9890 (23 February 1816), the prefect of Lot-et-Garonne to the minister of police. Cited in Kroen, *Politics and Theatre*, p. 165.

17. See for example the market at Digne, the préfecture of the Alpes-de-Haute-Provence, in AN F7 3797, Bulletin de police, nos 80, 85, 96 (2, 7, 15 September, 28 October 1826).

18. Kroen, *Politics and Theatre*, pp. 180–1; Eugène Ténot, *Paris en décembre 1851: étude historique sur le coup d'état* (Paris, 1868), p. 33; Ménager, *Les Napoléon*, p. 16.

19. AN BB18 964–1179, Correspondance générale de la division criminelle. See Ménager, *Les Napoléon*, pp. 15–83; Day-Hickman, *Napoleonic Art*, pp. 32–3; Alexander, *Napoleon*, pp. 154–5. Bertier de Sauvigny, *La Restauration*, pp. 132–3, asserted that some prison terms went up to five

years and that some fines were as much as 20,000 francs. On popular Bonapartism in Alsace, see Paul Leuilliot, *L'Alsace au début du XIXe siècle: essais d'histoire politique, économique et religieuse (1815–1830)*, 3 vols (Paris, 1959–60), i. pp. 148–52, 181–9, 255–6, 451–4.

20. More than 5,700 convictions in the early years of the Restoration according to Bluche, *Le bonapartisme*, p. 128. Emile Couret, *Le pavillon des princes: histoire complète de la prison politique de Sainte-Pélagie depuis sa fondation jusqu'à nos jours* (Paris, 1895), p. 66, asserts that 2,484 people were brought before the courts in the 1820s. Resnick, *The White Terror*, p. 111, states that 1,885 convictions in political cases were obtained in the last three months of 1815.

21. Newman, 'What the Crowd Wanted in the French Revolution of 1830', pp. 39–40, n. 93.

22. AN F7 6772 (28 May 1818), cited in Petiteau, 'La Monarchie de Juillet face aux héritages napoléoniens', p. 56.

23. AN F7 6678–84 (1815–38), Objets généraux des affaires politiques, also contains descriptions of objets d'art seized by the police. Hazareesingh, *The Legend of Napoleon*, pp. 74–80.

24. Henri d'Alméras, *La vie parisienne sous la Restauration* (Paris, n.d.), p. 371; Lucas-Dubreton, *Le culte de Napoléon*, p. 184.

25. Anatoliï Nicolaïevich Demidov, *Voyage dans la Russie méridionale et la Crimée, par la Hongrie, la Valachie et la Moldavie, exécuté en 1837* (Paris, 1840), p. 11.

26. Henry Houssaye, *1815: la première Restauration, le retour de l'île d'Elbe, les Cent Jours* (Paris, 1896), p. 57; Day-Hickman, *Napoleonic Art*, pp. 100–2; Durozoy, 'Zu den französischen Quellen der Napoleon-Legende', p. 164.

27. Alméras, *La vie parisienne sous la Restauration*, pp. 369–71; Lucas-Dubreton, *Le culte de Napoléon*, p. 129.

28. See Gaillard, commissaire de police de la librairie, *Catalogue des écrits, gravures et dessins condamnés depuis 1814 jusqu'au 1er janvier 1850: suivi de la liste des individus condamnés pour délits de presse* (Paris, 1850), pp. 5, 7, 11, 19, 20, 27, 30, 88, for Bonapartiana destroyed by the Bourbon government. The accumulated list of destroyed objects seems quite small given the number produced.

29. On the busts see Simon Bainbridge, 'Battling Bonaparte after Waterloo: Re-enactment, Representation and "The Napoleon Bust Business"', in Neil Ramsey and Gillian Russell (eds), *Tracing War in British Enlightenment and Romantic Culture* (Basingstoke, 2015), pp. 141–6.

30. Anthony Oliver, *Staffordshire Pottery: The Tribal Art of England* (London, 1981), p. 136; P. D. Gordon Pugh, *Staffordshire Portrait Figures and Allied Subjects of the Victorian Era* (Woodbridge, 1987), pp. 49–51, 91, 94–5, 226–35.

31. Théo Fleischman, 'Popularité de Napoléon en Angleterre', *Bulletin de la Société belge d'études napoléoniennes*, 54 (March 1966), 5–11.

32. On Canova's statue see Christopher M. S. Johns, *Antonio Canova and the Politics of Patronage in Revolutionary and Napoleonic Europe* (Berkeley, 1998), esp. pp. 98–104.

33. Lucas-Dubreton, *Le culte de Napoléon*, p. 115.

34. Robert Goldstein, *Censorship of Political Caricature in Nineteenth-Century France* (Kent, Oh., 1989), pp. 49–50.

35. On the growth of French consumerism see, for example, Michael B. Miller, *The Bon Marché: Bourgeois Culture and the Department Store, 1869–1920* (Princeton, 1981). The Bon Marché became the world's first department store in the 1850s.

36. Stephen C. Behrendt, *Royal Mourning and Regency Culture: Elegies and Memorials of Princess Charlotte* (London, 1997), pp. 177–8.

37. Boigne, *Récits d'une tante*, iii. pp. 184–5.

38. Maxime du Camp, *Souvenirs littéraires*, 2 vols (Paris, 1906), i. p. 25. The strangest thing in all of that, commented the author, was that his mother, grandmother and uncles were convinced legitimists.

39. Kroen, *Politics and Theatre*, pp. 181–4; and Owre, 'United in Division', pp. 305–20, 332–45. Similarly, in Britain after 1815, there was not a single song that spoke ill of Napoleon. See Cox Jensen, *Napoleon and British Song*, pp. 127–33.

40. Nicolas Brazier, *Chansons nouvelles* (Paris, 1836), pp. 23–30. For Germany see Ute Planert, 'Bonapartismus und Nationalismus in der Berliner Klassik. Goethe, Zelter und der deutsche Männergesang', in Axel Fischer and Matthias Kornemann (eds), *Integer vitae. Die Zeltersche Liedertafel als kulturgeschichtliches Phänomen* (Hanover, 2014), pp. 169–92.

41. Day-Hickman, *Napoleonic Art*, pp. 103–4.

42. Lucas-Dubreton, *Le culte de Napoléon*, pp. 238–9; David H. Pinkney, *The French Revolution of 1830* (Princeton, 1972), p. 50.

43. Anik Devriès, 'La "musique à bon marché" dans les années 1830', in Peter Bloom (ed.), *Music in Paris in the Eighteen-Thirties* (Stuyvesant, NY, 1987), pp. 229–50, here p. 232; and Ralph P. Locke, 'The Music of the French Chanson, 1810–1850', in Bloom (ed.), *Music in Paris in the Eighteen-Thirties*, pp. 431–47. See Lyons, *Le triomphe du livre*, pp. 91,

93, 94–5. For Béranger in Germany see Valentin Pollak, *Béranger in Deutschland* (Vienna, 1908); and Waltraud Linder-Beroud, ' "Schier dreißig Jahre bist du alt …". Zur populären Wirkung des Chansonniers Pierre-Jean de Béranger (1780–1857) in Deutschland', *Lied und populäre Kultur/Song and Popular Culture*, 57 (2012), 57–79. For the popularity of Béranger's songs in Russia see Fortuné Du Boisgobey, *Du Rhin au Nil, carnet de voyage d'un Parisien* (Paris, 1880), pp. 20–1.

44. Examples in Sophie-Anne Leterrier, *Béranger, des chansons pour un peuple citoyen* (Rennes, 2013), pp. 127–9, 130–3, 136, 140.

45. Sophie-Anne Leterrier, 'Béranger en prison: "Mes fers sont prêts; la liberté m'inspire; Je vais chanter son hymne glorieux"', *Criminocorpus* (2013), http://criminocorpus.revues.org/2594; Allen, *In the Public Eye*, p. 97, n. 60; Pierre-Jean de Béranger, *Procès fait aux chansons de P.-J. de Béranger* (Paris, 1821). Studies on Béranger include Jules Garsou, *Béranger et la légende napoléonienne* (Brussels, 1897); Jean Touchard, *La gloire de Béranger*, 2 vols (Paris, 1968); and Leterrier, *Béranger*.

46. Suzanne d'Huart, 'Le dernier préfet de police de Charles X, Claude Mangin', in *Actes du quatre-vingt quatrieme Congrès national des Sociétés savantes, Dijon, 1959* (Paris, 1960), pp. 603–16.

47. AN F7 6926, Police générale, 20 July 1822; Leuilliot, *L'Alsace au début du XIXe siècle*, p. 149.

48. AN F7 3798, Bulletin de police, 18 July and 1 August 1829.

49. Walter Markov, *Napoleon und seine Zeit. Geschichte und Kultur des Grand Empire* (Leipzig, 1996), p. 196.

50. Charles François, *Journal du capitaine François: dit le Dromadaire d'Egypte, 1792–1830* (Paris, 2003), p. 821; Lucas-Dubreton, *Le culte de Napoléon*, p. 253. See also Boigne, *Récits d'une tante*, iii. pp. 135–6.

51. François Guizot, *Mémoires pour servir à l'histoire de mon temps*, 8 vols (Paris, 1858–67), i. pp. 276–7; Vincent W. Beach, *Charles X of France: His Life and Times* (Boulder, Colo., 1971), pp. 216–18.

52. Beach, *Charles X of France*, p. 339.

53. Sandy Petrey, *In the Court of the Pear King: French Culture and the Rise of Realism* (Ithaca, NY, 2005), p. 23. The best biography of the July Monarch is Guy Antonetti, *Louis-Philippe* (Paris, 1994), pp. 545–634, for the manoeuvrings that brought him to power.

54. Pamela M. Pilbeam, *The 1830 Revolution in France* (London, 1991). For a detailed history of the July Revolution see Jean-Louis Bory, *La Révolution de Juillet: 29 juillet 1830* (Paris, 1972).

55. For a good summary see Tulard, *Napoléon II*, pp. 169–74; and Walter R. Herscher, 'Evoking the Eagle: The July Monarchy's Use of Napoleonic

Imagery' (PhD dissertation, Marquette University, 1992), pp. 54–100, although I think Herscher underestimates the part played by liberals and Bonapartists.

56. Hippolyte Bonnellier, *Mémorial de l'Hôtel-de-Ville de Paris, 1830* (Paris, 1835), pp. 75–7; Etienne Cabet, *Révolution de 1830* (Paris, 1833), p. 143; Marie de Flavigny, comtesse d'Agoult, *Mes souvenirs, 1806–1833* (Paris, 1880), p. 329; Comte Edmond d'Alton-Shée, *Mes mémoires (1826–1848)*, 2 vols (Paris, 1869), i. p. 53; Martial Côme Annibal Perpétue Magloire de Guernon-Ranville, *Journal d'un ministre* (Caen, 1874), p. 177; Odilon Barrot, *Mémoires posthumes de Odilon Barrot*, 4 vols (Paris, 1875–6), i. p. 114; Newman, 'What the Crowd Wanted in the French Revolution of 1830', pp. 28–30.

57. Pinkney, *The French Revolution of 1830*, pp. 257, 271; Newman, 'What the Crowd Wanted in the French Revolution of 1830', p. 30. On the street fighting and the lack of military response to it see Jonathan M. House, *Controlling Paris: Armed Forces and Counter-Revolution, 1789–1848* (New York, 2014), pp. 28–37.

58. Pinkney, *The French Revolution of 1830*, p. 293. Of the 561 deputies elected in 1831, around sixty were veterans of the Revolution and the Empire. Patrick-Bernard Higonnet, 'La Composition de la Chambre des Députés de 1827 à 1831', *Revue historique*, 239 (1968), 363–4.

59. Adolphe Thiers, *La monarchie de 1830* (Paris, 1831), pp. 27–8, 148–9; Charles Bocher, *Mémoires de Charles Bocher (1816–1907), précédés des souvenirs de famille (1760–1816)*, 2 vols (Paris, 1907–9), i. pp. 144–5.

60. Camp, *Souvenirs littéraires*, i. p. 36.

61. Lucas-Dubreton, *Le culte de Napoléon*, pp. 271–97; Pilbeam, *Republicanism in Nineteenth-Century France*, pp. 95–128; Alexander, *Napoleon*, p. 45.

62. See Bertier de Sauvigny, *La Restauration*, pp. 7–41; Emmanuel de Waresquiel and Benoît Yvert, *Histoire de la Restauration, 1814–1830: naissance de la France moderne* (Paris, 1996), pp. 126–7.

63. Paul Thureau-Dangin, *Histoire de la monarchie de juillet*, 7 vols (Paris, 1888–92), i. pp. 594–601; Sylvie Vielledent, *1830 aux théâtres* (Paris, 2009), pp. 395–552.

64. Robert Justin Goldstein, 'France', in idem (ed.), *The Frightful Stage: Political Censorship of the Theater in Nineteenth-Century Europe* (New York, 2009), pp. 73–4; Odile Krakovitch, 'Le théâtre sous la Restauration et la monarchie de Juillet: lecture et spectacle', in Alain Vaillant (ed.), *Mesure(s) du livre: colloque organisé par la Bibliothèque nationale et la Société des études romantiques* (Paris, 1992), pp. 147–64.

65. See Kroen, *Politics and Theatre*, pp. 172–4. See also Ernest Daudet, *Conspirateurs et comédiennes, épisodes d'histoire d'après des documents inédits, 1796–1825* (Paris, 1902), pp. 224–31; Alain Corbin, 'L'agitation dans les théâtres de province sous la Restauration', in Marc Bertrand (ed.), *Popular Traditions and Learned Culture in France: From the Sixteenth to the Twentieth Century* (Saratoga, Calif., 1985), pp. 93–114; Hemmings, *The Theatre Industry in Nineteenth-Century France*, pp. 83–6; and Romuald Féret, 'Le théâtre de province au XIXe siècle: entre révolutions et conservatisme', *Annales historiques de la Révolution française*, 367 (2012), 119–43.

66. Barante, *Souvenirs*, ii. pp. 271–2; F. W. J. Hemmings, *Theatre and State in France, 1760–1905* (Cambridge, 1994), pp. 210–11; Louis Péricaud, *Le Théâtre des Funambules, ses mimes, ses acteurs et ses pantomimes, depuis sa fondation jusqu'à sa démolition* (Paris, 1897), pp. 88–9.

67. Madeleine and Francis Ambrière, *Talma ou L'histoire au théâtre* (Paris, 2007), p. 557.

68. Lucas-Dubreton, *Le culte de Napoléon*, pp. 120–2; Hemmings, *Culture and Society in France*, p. 164.

69. Théodore de Banville, *Mes souvenirs* (Paris, 1883), pp. 248–9; Hemmings, *The Theatre Industry in Nineteenth-Century France*, pp. 126–7.

70. Sylvie Vielledent, 'Le retour du "petit chapeau" en 1830', in *Napoléon, de l'histoire à la légende* (Paris, 2000), pp. 351–72; and idem, *1830 aux théâtres*, esp. pp. 391–552.

71. Lucas-Dubreton, *Le culte de Napoléon*, pp. 286–92; Samuels, *The Spectacular Past*, pp. 119–20.

72. Those plays included Charles Nombret Saint-Laurent and Félix-Auguste Duvert, *Bonaparte, lieutenant d'artillerie, ou 1789 et 1800, comédie historique en 2 actes, mêlée de couplets*, presented at the Vaudeville on 9 October 1830 (Paris, 1830); Clairville (pseudonym), *Quatorze ans de la vie de Napoléon, ou Berlin, Potsdam, Paris, Waterloo et Sainte-Hélène, pièce historique en 4 actes et en 7 tableaux*, presented at the Théâtre du Luxembourg on 23 November 1830.

73. Alexander, *Napoleon*, p. 157; Jennifer E. Sessions, *By Sword and Plow: France and the Conquest of Algeria* (Ithaca, NY, 2011), pp. 125–9.

74. Samuels, *The Spectacular Past*, pp. 106–50.

75. Heine, *De la France*, pp. 278–9; Adolphe Laferrière, *Mémoires de Laferrière* (Paris, 1876), pp. 82–3; Esprit Victor Elisabeth Boniface, comte de Castellane, *Journal du maréchal de Castellane, 1804–1862*, 5 vols (Paris, 1895–7), ii. p. 393; Jules Claretie, *Brichanteau comédien* (Paris, 1896), pp. 236–7.

76. Hugues Marie Désiré Bouffé, *Mes souvenirs, 1800–1880* (Paris, 1880), pp. 179–80; Jules Levallois, *Milieu du siècle: mémoires d'un critique* (Paris, 1896), p. 7.

77. Hemmings, *Theatre and State in France*, pp. 211–12; Anne Vincent-Buffault, *The History of Tears: Sensibility and Sentimentality in France*, trans. Teresa Bridgeman (New York, 1991), pp. 54–5, 236–7.

78. Naujoks, 'Between Memory and History', pp. 131–2.

79. *Napoléon, son élévation, sa chute et son parti par un prolétaire* (Lyons, 1833), p. 32; Sébastien Charléty, *La Monarchie de Juillet (1830–1848)* (Paris, 1920), p. 41.

80. Lazare A. (Augé), *Quelques pensées apologétiques sur Bonaparte* (Paris, 1821), p. 3.

81. Vielledent, 'Le retour du "petit chapeau" en 1830', pp. 352, 354.

82. Kirstin Buchinger, *Napoléomanie* (Berlin, 2013), pp. 159–60.

83. Cited in Vielledent, *1830 aux théâtres*, p. 431.

84. Day-Hickman, *Napoleonic Art*, p. 22.

85. For the literature on Epinal see Day-Hickman, *Napoleonic Art*; John Grand-Carteret, 'La légende napoléonienne par l'image, vue sous un jour nouveau', *Revue des études napoléoniennes*, 20 (1923), 28–46.

86. See Day-Hickman, *Napoleonic Art*, pp. 84–110.

87. Fureix, *La France des larmes*, p. 419.

88. Victoria E. Thompson, 'The Creation, Destruction and Recreation of Henri IV: Seeing Popular Sovereignty in the Statue of a King', *History and Memory*, 24:2 (2012), 5–40.

89. Kroen, *Politics and Theatre*, p. 201.

90. Jean-Claude Caron, 'Louis-Philippe face à l'opinion publique, ou l'impossible réconciliation des Français, 1830–1835', *French Historical Studies*, 30:4 (Fall 2007), 597–621, here 606–7.

91. Taxile Delord, *Histoire du second empire (1848–1869)* (Paris, 1869), i. pp. 37–8; Bluche, *Le bonapartisme*, p. 219.

92. Banville, *Mes souvenirs*, pp. 203–4; John McCormick, *Popular Theatres of Nineteenth-Century France* (London, 1993), pp. 103, 168–9. The July Monarch was, however, just as censorious as the Bourbons; the number of engravings and writings condemned was about the same under both regimes (Gaillard, *Catalogue des écrits*, p. ii).

93. For example, *Napoléon: journal anecdotique et biographique de l'Empire et de la Grande armée* (Paris, 1833–5), from May 1833 to April 1835; and *Rationalisme napoléonien, ou Napoléonisme* (Paris, 1834). See Eugène Hatin, *Bibliographie historique et critique de la presse périodique française* (Paris, 1866), pp. 389, 392.

94. Christian Delacroix, François Dosse and Patrick Garcia, *Les courants historiques en France: XIXe–XXe siècle* (Paris, 2007), pp. 34–5; Petiteau, 'La Monarchie de Juillet face aux héritages napoléoniens', pp. 55, 56; Henri-François Imbert, 'Evolutîon et fonctîon du mythe napoléonien sous la Restauration', *Rivista italiana di studi napoleonici*, 18:1 (1981), 9–22.

95. Theodore Zeldin, *The Political System of Napoleon III* (London, 1958), p. 4.

96. Heinrich Heine, *The Works of Heinrich Heine*, trans. Charles Godfrey Leland, 12 vols (London, 1891–1905), vii. p. 358.

97. Avner Ben-Amos, *Funerals, Politics, and Memory in Modern France, 1789–1996* (Oxford, 2000), p. 70.

98. Gérard Hubert and Guy Ledoux-Lebard, *Napoléon: portraits contemporains, bustes et statues* (Paris, 1999), p. 154.

99. At least according to Armand Augustin Louis, marquis de Caulaincourt, *Memoirs of General de Caulaincourt, Duke of Vicenza*, ed. Jean Hanoteau, 3 vols (London, 1950), ii. p. 245.

100. Albert Boime, *Art and the French Commune* (Princeton, 1995), pp. 22–3; Jules Dementhe, 'Histoire de la Colonne', *L'Illustration. Journal universel*, nos 1590, 1591, 1592, 1593, 1594 (16, 23, 30 August, 6, 13 September 1873), pp. 115, 118, 134–5, 150–1, 163, 166–7, 178–9.

101. June Hargrove, *The Statues of Paris: An Open Air Pantheon* (New York, 1989), p. 44.

102. Wagner, 'Outrages', p. 307; Edgar Schmitz, 'Das trojanische Pferd und die Restauration. Die Auseinandersetzung um die *Colonne de la Place Vendôme* als Paradigma der gescheiterten Restauration', in Gudrun Gersmann and Hubertus Kohle (eds), *Frankreich 1815–1830. Trauma oder Utopie? Die Gesellschaft der Restauration und das Erbe der Revolution* (Stuttgart, 1993), pp. 187–96.

103. Auguste Hus, *Paris, le 1er septembre 1822: la Colonne de la place Vendôme bourbonisée, suivie de quelques pensées sur l'éloquent ouvrage de M. de Châteaubriant* (Paris, n.d. [1822]).

104. David O'Brien, 'Censorship of Visual Culture in France, 1815–1852', *Yale French Studies*, 122 (2012), 37–52, here 50.

105. Benjamin Appert, *Dix ans à la cour du roi Louis-Philippe, et souvenirs du temps de l'empire et de la Restauration*, 3 vols (Paris, 1846), iii. p. 241; Alain Pougetoux, 'La Colonne Vendôme', in Benoît, Delannoy and Pougetoux, *Napoléon: le retour des cendres*, p. 75.

106. Fureix, 'La mort de Napoléon', p. 174.

107. Achille Murat, *La Colonne Vendôme* (Paris, 1970), p. 124; Herscher, 'Evoking the Eagle', p. 220.

108. AN F7 12329, Bulletin de police, 5, 10, 11 and 12 May 1831; Petiteau, 'La Monarchie de Juillet face aux héritages napoléoniens', p. 61.

109. Henri Gisquet, *Mémoires de M. Gisquet, ancien préfet de police*, 4 vols (Paris, 1840), ii. pp. 117–19.

110. Philippe Vigier, *Nouvelle histoire de Paris: Paris pendant la Monarchie de Juillet (1830–1848)* (Paris, 1991), p. 89.

111. Gildea, *The Past in French History*, p. 89; Hazareesingh, *The Legend of Napoleon*, pp. 200, 202.

112. Maurice Agulhon, 'Paris: A Traversal from East to West', in Pierre Nora (ed.), *Realms of Memory: The Construction of the French Past*, trans. Arthur Goldhammer, 3 vols (New York, 1992), iii. p. 538; Gildea, *The Past in French History*, p. 103.

113. Castellane, *Journal du maréchal de Castellane*, iii. pp. 84–5 (28 July 1833).

114. One of the first uses of the term 'little corporal' was by Las Cases, *Le Mémorial de Sainte-Hélène*, i. p. 132 (1–6 September 1815), repeated by a number of contemporary Napoleon biographers, as well as by Hugo, Stendhal and Thiers.

115. Henry Jouin, *David d'Angers, sa vie, son oeuvre, ses écrits et ses contemporains*, 2 vols (Paris, 1878), ii. pp. 308–9.

116. Albert Boime, *Art in an Age of Counterrevolution, 1815–1848* (Chicago, 2004), pp. 308–9; Michael Marrinan, *Painting Politics for Louis-Philippe: Art and Ideology in Orléanist France, 1830–1848* (New Haven, 1988), p. 160; André-Jean Tudesq, *Les grands notables en France (1840–1849): étude historique d'une psychologie sociale* (Paris, 1964), p. 534. A new plinth, made of Corsican granite, was installed in 1835 (Albert Mousset, *Petite histoire des grands monuments, rues et statues de Paris* (Paris, 1950), p. 152).

117. Gisquet, *Mémoires*, iii. p. 97; Henry Jouin, *Histoire et description de la Colonne de Juillet* (Paris, 1879). One view of the distaste of Bonapartists for the frock coat and hat can be seen in the preface to Auguste-Louis Pétiet, *Souvenirs militaires de l'histoire contemporaine, par le général, baron, Auguste Pétiet* (Paris, 1844), xxi–xxiii.

118. Hazareesingh, *The Legend of Napoleon*, pp. 240–1; Maurice Bottet, *Vétérans frères d'armes de l'Empire français* (Paris, 1906), pp. 36–7.

119. On the Vendôme Column as contested site see Matt K. Matsuda, 'Idols of the Emperor', in Jeffrey K. Olick (ed.), *States of Memory: Continuities,*

Conflicts, and Transformations in National Retrospection (Durham, NC, 2003), pp. 72–100.

120. On the arch see Isabelle Rouge-Ducos, *L'Arc de Triomphe de l'Etoile: panthéon de la France guerrière: art et histoire* (Dijon, 2008), pp. 119–20; Maxime Weygand, *L'Arc de Triomphe de l'Etoile* (Paris, 1960), p. 39; Edouard Driault, *Napoléon architecte* (Paris, 1942), pp. 119–30.

121. On the political debate surrounding the war see Owre, 'United in Division', pp. 155–236; and for a different take, Kôbô Seigan, 'L'influence de la mémoire de la Révolution française et de l'empire napoléonien dans l'opinion publique française face à la guerre d'Espagne de 1823', *Annales historiques de la Révolution française*, 335 (2004), 159–81.

122. Weygand, *L'Arc de Triomphe*, p. 45.

123. Albert Boime, *Hollow Icons: The Politics of Sculpture in Nineteenth-Century France* (Kent, Ohio, 1987), p. 38; and Boime, *Art in an Age of Counterrevolution*, pp. 311–16.

124. Antoine Etex, *Les souvenirs d'un artiste* (Paris, 1877), pp. 192–5.

125. Antonetti, *Louis-Philippe*, pp. 758–9.

126. *Journal des artistes*, 31 July 1836; Weygand, *L'Arc de Triomphe*, pp. 49–50.

127. Charles Simond (ed.), *La vie parisienne à travers le XIXe siècle: Paris de 1800 à 1900 d'après les estampes et les mémoires du temps*, 3 vols (Paris, 1900–1), ii. p. 115.

128. On Louis-Philippe and the museum at Versailles see Marrinan, *Painting Politics*, pp. 150–5, 164–72; idem, 'Historical Vision and the Writing of History at Louis-Philippe's Versailles', in Chu and Weisberg (eds), *The Popularization of Images*, pp. 113–43; Thomas W. Gaehtgens, *Versailles als Nationaldenkmal. Die Gallerie des Batailles im Musée Historique von Louis-Philippe* (Berlin, 1985), also as *Versailles: de la résidence royale au musée historique: la galerie des batailles dans le musée histo-rique de Louis-Philippe*, trans. Patrick Poirot (Paris, 1984), pp. 59–256; Maureen Meister, 'To All the Glories of France: The Versailles of Louis-Philippe', in *All the Banners Wave: Art and War in the Romantic Era, 1792–1851* (Providence, 1982), pp. 20–6; Marie-Claude Chaudonneret, 'Peinture et histoire dans les années, 1820–1830', in *L'histoire au musée: actes du colloque* (Versailles, 2004), pp. 127–37; and Hornstein, 'Episodes in Political Illusion', pp. 180–5.

129. Marthe-Camille Bachasson Montalivet, *Le Roi Louis-Philippe et sa liste civile* (Paris, 1850), p. 41.

130. Axelle de Gaigneron, 'La stratégie de Louis-Philippe à Versailles', *Connaissance des arts*, 272 (October 1974), 74–81; Albert Boime, *The*

Academy and French Painting in the Nineteenth Century (New Haven, 1986), p. 14; and Buchinger, *Napoléomanie*, pp. 158–9.

131. Gustave Planche in *Chronique de Paris*, 7 April 1836, pp. 21–4.

132. *Gazette de France*, 2 August 1837; and Dominique Pety, 'Le Versailles des Goncourt: patrimoine public ou collection privée?', in Véronique Léonard-Roques (ed.), *Versailles dans la littérature: mémoire et imaginaire aux XIXe et XXe siècles* (Clermont-Ferrand, 2005), pp. 139–54.

133. Charles de Rémusat, *Mémoires de ma vie*, 5 vols (Paris, 1960), iii. pp. 395–401; Agulhon, *Marianne into Battle*, pp. 45–6.

134. For example, Bonapartists largely appropriated the conquest of Algeria, which took place during this period and which the monarchy attempted to present to the French public as a shining example of its ability to take control of an overseas possession (Sessions, *By Sword and Plow*, pp. 125–73).

CHAPTER 9

1. Alain Corbin, 'L'impossible présence du roi', in Alain Corbin, Noëlle Gérôme and Danielle Tartakowsky (eds), *Les usages politiques des fêtes aux XIXe–XXe siècles* (Paris, 1994), pp. 77–116; Goujon, *Monarchies postrévolutionnaires*, p. 331.

2. Thiers had been called to form a government in March 1840 after the dismissal of the government of Marshal Soult, the consequence of a crisis over monies requested for the king's son, the duc de Nemours. Janet Ladner, 'Napoleon's Repatriation – Why 1840?', in *Selected Papers: The Consortium on Revolutionary Europe, 1750–1850* (Tallahassee, Fla., 1995), pp. 489–501.

3. Ernest Daudet (ed.), *Journal de Victor de Balabine, secrétaire de l'ambassade de Russie* (Paris, 1914), p. 107.

4. Pierre Guiral, *Adolphe Thiers ou De la nécessité en politique* (Paris, 1986), pp. 286–92; J. P. T. Bury and Robert Tombs, *Thiers: 1797–1877: A Political Life* (London, 1986), pp. 146–53; Hazareesingh, 'Napoleonic Memory in Nineteenth-Century France', 264–70.

5. Tudesq, *Les grands notables en France*, pp. 537–8.

6. See Tudesq, *Les grands notables en France*, p. 535; Marrinan, *Painting Politics*, pp. 184–5; Thureau-Dangin, *Histoire de la monarchie de juillet*, iv. pp. 146–53.

7. See, for example, the letter from Dorothée de Lieven to François Guizot, *Lettres de François Guizot et de la princesse de Lieven* (Paris, 1963–4), ii. p. 122 (14 May 1840); Hazareesingh, *The Legend of Napoleon*, p. 155; Fureix, *La France des larmes*, p. 282.

8. Tudesq, *Les grands notables en France*, pp. 490–511; Guiral, *Adolphe Thiers*, p. 163; Marrinan, *Painting Politics*, pp. 189–92.

9. Dorothée de Lieven to François Guizot, *Lettres de François Guizot et de la princesse de Lieven*, ii. pp. 137–8, 140–2, 144–5 (19, 20, 21 May 1840). Herscher, 'Evoking the Eagle', pp. 308–14, believes that Louis-Philippe came to the decision independently of Thiers, but Herscher's conclusion is based on the diary of Gourgaud, who cannot be entirely relied upon.

10. According to Marrinan, *Painting Politics*, pp. 186, 199–200.

11. François Ferdinand Philippe d'Orléans, prince de Joinville, *Vieux souvenirs: 1818–1848* (Paris, 1894), p. 207.

12. d'Hérisson, *Le cabinet noir*, p. 260 (6 July 1821); Jean Lucas-Dubreton, 'Le monde apprend sa mort', *Miroir de l'histoire*, 109 (1959), 82; Sylvia Neely, *Lafayette and the Liberal Ideal, 1814–1824: Politics and Conspiracy in an Age of Reaction* (Carbondale, Ill., 1991), pp. 193–4.

13. AN 314 AP 10, fonds Gourgaud, letters to Mme Mère and Stéphanie de Beauharnais, 7 July 1821; Herscher, 'Evoking the Eagle', p. 257; and Lentz and Macé, *La mort de Napoléon*, pp. 72–3.

14. *Lettre du prince Eugène de Beauharnais aux souverains alliés, ou Protestation contre le pouvoir arbitraire que s'est arrogé l'Angleterre de retenir à Sainte-Hélène le corps de Napoléon Bonaparte* (Paris, 1821).

15. Pierre Barthélemy, *Demande de la translation des dépouilles mortelles de l'empereur Napoléon* (Paris, 1821), for which he was put on trial in November 1821; *Panégyrique d'un mort*; Alexandre Goujon, *Pensée d'un soldat sur la sépulture de Napoléon* (Paris, 1821); L. Picquot, *Encore un mot sur Napoléon-le-Grand* (Paris, 1821). See also Naujoks, 'Between Memory and History', pp. 157–67; and idem, '*Reconnaissance* and the Politics of Memory in Demands to Repatriate Napoleon's Remains in 1821', *Proceedings of the Western Society for French History*, 37 (2009), 163–73.

16. Herscher, 'Evoking the Eagle', pp. 257–76, here p. 261.

17. On the attempts to bring back Napoleon's remains see Boisson, *Le retour des cendres*, pp. 77–105.

18. *Napoléon à Paris, ou translation de ses cendres sous le dôme des Invalides* (Paris, 1841), p. 233.

19. Boisson, *Le retour des cendres*, pp. 77–149; Bernard Ménager, 'Contexte politique et sociale', in Humbert (ed.), *Napoléon aux Invalides*, p. 22.

20. Ménager, 'Contexte politique et sociale', pp. 22–3.

21. Tulard, *Napoléon II*, pp. 198–9.

22. A brief summary of the diplomatic negotiations can be found in Boisson, *Le retour des cendres*, pp. 108–15. Marrinan disagrees with

Michael Driskel, 'Eclecticism and Ideology in the July Monarchy', *Arts Magazine*, 56:9 (1982), 121, about the complexity of the negotiations. But as Marrinan points out, and as Guizot's letters show (*Lettres de François Guizot et de la princesse de Lieven*, ii. pp. 117, 127 (10 and 14 May 1840)), the negotiations went surprisingly quickly and smoothly. On the other hand, it is possible that Palmerston may have been playing the devil's advocate and may have agreed to the request in the hope of undermining the French regime's stability. See also Herscher, 'Evoking the Eagle', pp. 315–18, 321–3.

23. *Journal des débats politiques et littéraires*, 13 May 1840; *Moniteur universel*, 13 May 1840, pp. 1034–5. See also *Archives parlementaires; procès-verbaux des séances de la Chambre des Députés*, 143 vols (Paris, 1840), v. pp. 336–9; Tulard, 'Le retour des cendres', p. 81; Hazareesingh, *Legend of Napoleon*, p. 155.

24. Thiers to Guizot, 13 May 1840, cited in Marrinan, *Painting Politics*, p. 186.

25. *Le Siècle*, 28 May 1840.

26. Alphonse de Lamartine, *Discours de M. de Lamartine, sur la loi relative aux restes mortels de Napoléon* (Paris, n.d.). An account of the debate is in the *Moniteur universel*, 27 May 1840, pp. 1188–90. Also *Archives parlementaires*, vii. pp. 10–20; and Michael Driskel, *As Befits a Legend* (Kent, Ohio, 1993), pp. 18–19; Ménager, 'Contexte politique et sociale', p. 24.

27. Ménager, 'Contexte politique et sociale', p. 24.

28. Valentine de Lamartine (ed.), *Correspondance de Lamartine*, 5 vols (Paris, 1873–4), v. pp. 438–9.

29. AN F7 3890, Police générale, 14 May 1840.

30. Driskel, *As Befits a Legend*, pp. 33–4; Chantal Georgel, 'Panorama de l'événement', in Humbert (ed.), *Napoléon aux Invalides*, p. 109. An example of a play is Auguste Jouhaud, *Les cendres de Napoléon, ou le retour en France* (Paris, 1841), first performed in January of that year.

31. Theodore Ziolkowski, 'Napoleon's Impact on Germany: A Rapid Survey', *Yale French Studies*, 26 (1960), 97.

32. Marrinan, *Painting Politics*, pp. 186–7.

33. *Le Courrier Français*, 13 and 14 May 1840; and *Le National*, 14 May 1840.

34. Rémusat, *Mémoires*, iii. pp. 314–16.

35. *Le Siècle*, 14 and 27 May 1840; Albéric Cahuet, *Napoléon délivré* (Paris, 1914), p. 64. *Le Siècle* also compared Napoleon's suffering on St Helena to Christ's agony on Calvary, except that Napoleon's lasted much longer.

36. *Le National*, 13 May 1840; André-Jean Tudesq, 'Le reflet donné par la presse', in Humbert (ed.), *Napoléon aux Invalides*, pp. 85–91, here p. 86.

37. *Journal des débats politiques et littéraires*, 14 May 1840. As did *La Quotidienne*, 14 May 1840, a newspaper close to the Legitimists. Legitimists were outraged by the term.

38. *Gazette de France*, 15, 16 May 1840.

39. *L'Orléanais: journal politique, littéraire et commercial*, 17 May 1840.

40. Ben-Amos, *Funerals, Politics, and Memory*, pp. 71–2.

41. Petrey, *In the Court of the Pear King*, pp. 1–19.

42. See Philippe de Rohan-Chabot, *Les 5 cercueils de l'Empereur: souvenirs inédits* (Paris, 1985), pp. 125–6; Jean Vidalenc, 'L'opinion publique en Normandie et le retour des restes de Napoléon en décembre 1840', in *La France au XIXe siècle: études historiques. Mélanges offerts à Charles Hippolyte Pouthas* (Paris, 1973), pp. 212–24.

43. AN F21 742, Beaux-Arts, Mairie of Toulouse to the Minister of the Interior, 20 May 1840, as well as another letter in the same vein from the municipal council of the commune of Donzy in the Nièvre (18 November 1840). See also AN C 2180, Assemblées nationales, Choisy-le-Roi, 29 May 1840, petitioning that one mayor (the eldest) from each department be allowed to participate in the procession; or again AN C 2180, Assemblées nationales, Marseilles, 24 May 1840, asking that representatives of the former Grande Armée be allowed to participate.

44. AN CC 461, Sénat, chambre et cour des pairs, Marseilles, 28 May 1840.

45. AN C 2180, Assemblées nationales, Saint-Denis, 17 May 1840.

46. AN CC 461, Sénat, chambre et cour des pairs, Paris, 26 May 1840.

47. AN C 2180, Assemblées nationales, Paris, 16 May 1840, accompanying a demand to change the name of the Place Vendôme to Place de la Colonne Napoleon. See also Frédéric Soulié, *Le tombeau de Napoléon* (Paris, 1840), pp. 15–19.

48. AN C 2180, Assemblées nationales, Paris, 15 May 1840.

49. *Le National*, 16 May 1840.

50. AN C 2180, Assemblées nationales, Montmartre, 16 May 1840.

51. AN C 2180, Assemblées nationales, Paris, 18 May 1840.

52. AN CC 461, Sénat, chambre et cour des pairs, Champlemy, 29 May 1840; AN C 2180, Assemblées nationales, Camille Reveillé, Blois, 25 May 1840, Bordeaux, 15 May 1840; AN C 2180, Assemblées nationales, Lyons, 26 May 1840.

53. AN C 2180, Assemblées nationales, Paris, 19 May 1840.

54. On this question see Marrinan, *Painting Politics*, pp. 187–8; Driskel, *As Befits a Legend*, pp. 35–58; Corinna Engel, *Napoleons Grab Im Invalidendom* (Frankfurt am Main, 2007), pp. 55–147; Jean-Marcel Humbert, 'Avant-propos', in Humbert (ed.), *Napoléon aux Invalides*,

pp. 11–12; Edouard Péclet, *Napoléon, où sera le tombeau?* (Paris, 1840); Rouge-Ducos, *L'Arc de Triomphe de l'Etoile*, pp. 251–5.

55. Benoît Agnès, 'La pétition, reine de l'opinion? Les autorités françaises et britanniques entre réfutations et légitimations (1814–1848)', in Laurent Bourquin, Philippe Hamon, Pierre Karila-Cohen et Cédric Michon (eds), *S'exprimer en temps de troubles: conflits, opinion(s) et politisation de la fin du Moyen Âge au début du XXe siècle* (Rennes, 2011), p. 307.

56. See Iouda Tchernoff, *Le parti républicain sous la monarchie de juillet: formation et évolution de la doctrine républicaine* (Paris, 1901), p. 48; Emmanuelle Fureix, 'République et républicains sous les monarchies censitaires (1814–1848)', in Vincent Duclert and Christophe Prochasson (eds), *Dictionnaire critique de la République* (Paris, 2007), pp. 1306–13; Sudhir Hazareesingh and Karma Nablusi, 'Entre Robespierre et Napoléon: les paradoxes de la mémoire républicaine sous la monarchie de juillet', *Annales*, 65 (2010), 1238–44. See Hazareesingh, *The Legend of Napoleon*, pp. 157–83, on how leading liberals came to terms with the legacy of Napoleon. Pilbeam, *Republicanism in Nineteenth-Century France*, pp. 64–5, 93–4, 109–10.

57. My thanks to Peter McPhee for pointing this out.

58. The expression is from Sudhir Hazareesingh and Karma Nablusi, 'Entre Robespierre et Napoléon: les paradoxes de la mémoire républicaine sous la monarchie de Juillet', *Annales. Histoire, Sciences Sociales*, 65:5 (2010), 1225–47. See also Alexander, *Bonapartism and the Revolutionary Tradition*, pp. 5–7.

59. See Tulard, 'Le retour des cendres', pp. 84–92, even if the notions of popular, collective or national memory pose some problems. See Maurice Halbwachs, *On Collective Memory*, trans. Lewis A. Coser (Chicago, 1992); Patrick Hutton, *History as an Art of Memory* (Hanover, 1993), pp. 73–90; Natahn Wachtel, 'Memory and History: Introduction', *History and Anthropology*, 2 (1986), 207–24; Iwona Irwin-Zarecka, *Frames of Remembrance: The Dynamics of Collective Memory* (New Brunswick, 1994); Noa Gedi and Yigal Elam, 'Collective Memory: What is it?', *History and Memory*, 8 (1996), 3–50; Alon Confino, 'Collective Memory and Cultural History: Problems of Method', *American Historical Review*, 102 (1997), 1386–1403.

60. There are a number of memoirs decribing the voyage to St Helena, the exhumation of the body and the return trip. See Louis Etienne Saint-Denis (Mameluck Ali), *Journal inédit du retour des cendres, 1840* (Paris, 2003), pp. 105–49; Rohan-Chabot, *Les 5 cercueils de l'Empereur*; Joinville, *Vieux souvenirs*, pp. 208–19; Gourgaud, *Le retour des cendres*

de l'empereur Napoléon (Paris, 2003); Félix Coquereau, *Souvenirs du voyage à Sainte-Hélène* (Paris, 1841).

61. Coquereau, *Souvenirs du voyage*, p. 55.

62. Coquereau, *Souvenirs du voyage*, pp. 55–6.

63. Joinville, *Vieux souvenirs*, p. 217.

64. Coquereau, *Souvenirs du voyage*, p. 68.

65. Coquereau, *Souvenirs du voyage*, p. 72. See also Albéric Cahuet, *Après la mort de l'Empereur* (Paris, 1913), pp. 285–315; Gilles Malandain, 'Jalons pour une histoire du pèlerinage au(x) tombeau(x) de Napoléon', in Luc Chantre, Paul D'Hollander and Jérôme Grévy (eds), *Politiques du pèlerinage, du XVIIe siècle à nos jours* (Rennes, 2014), pp. 297–313.

66. Coquereau, *Souvenirs du voyage*, p. 70.

67. Edouard Pujol, *Napoléon, de la vallée du tombeau au dôme des Invalides* (Paris, 1841), pp. 41, 43; and Cahuet, *Après la mort de l'Empereur*, p. 302. Cuttings from the willows on St Helena were planted around the world in places as far away as Akaroa in New Zealand, the Invalides in Paris and a churchyard in Dyrham near Bath.

68. Legouvé, *Dernier travail, derniers souvenirs*, p. 190; Alfred-Auguste Cuvillier-Fleury, *Journal intime de Cuvillier-Fleury*, 2 vols (Paris, 1900–3), i. p. 150.

69. Other examples can be had in Joseph Lockwood, *A Guide to St. Helena, Descriptive and Historical, with a Visit to Longwood, and Napoleon's Tomb* (St Helena, 1851), pp. 82–93. Christopher Woodward, 'Napoleon's Last Journey', *History Today*, 55:7 (2005), 55, writes that more than 4,000 people had signed their names in the visitors' book for the year 1836.

70. A number of memoirs were written and later published around these pilgrimages. See, for example, Marius Villers, *Pèlerinage à Sainte-Hélène, ou Souvenirs d'un voyage autour du monde* (Paris, 1829); and Volcy Boze, *Pèlerinage à Ste Hélène en 1826* (Marseilles, 1879).

71. Lockwood, *A Guide to St. Helena*, p. 101.

72. Gilbert Martineau, *Le retour des cendres* (Paris, 1990), p. 110.

73. Coquereau, *Souvenirs du voyage*, pp. 72–4.

74. Coquereau, *Souvenirs du voyage*, pp. 91–3.

75. Coquereau, *Souvenirs du voyage*, p. 107.

76. Saint-Denis, *Journal inédit*, pp. 177–9.

77. Saint-Denis, *Journal inédit*, p. 179.

78. Gourgaud, AN 314 AP 15, fonds Gourgaud, 30 November 1840.

79. *Retour des cendres de Napoléon: procès-verbal d'exhumation des restes de l'empereur Napoléon* (Orthez, n.d.), p. 2.

80. Gaspard Gourgaud, 'Expédition de Sainte-Hélène en 1840', *Nouvelle revue rétrospective*, 43 (1898), 1–48.

81. Coquereau, *Souvenirs du voyage*, pp. 109–10; Chateaubriand, *Mémoires d'outre-tombe*, i. p. 1585.

82. *Moniteur universel*, 3 December 1840, p. 338. Las Cases, *Journal écrit à bord de la frégate 'la Belle-Poule'*, p. 292; Rohan-Chabot, *Les 5 cercueils de l'Empereur*, p. 80; *Translation des cendres de Napoléon, de Sainte-Hélène en France* (Cherbourg, n.d.), p. 18.

83. Gourgaud, 'Expédition de Sainte-Hélène en 1840', p. 32.

84. Gourgaud, 'Expédition de Sainte-Hélène en 1840', p. 34.

85. On the 'incorruptible' bodies of saints see Quigley, *The Corpse*, pp. 254–7.

86. Isabelle Julia in *Les années romantiques: la peinture française de 1815 à 1850* (Paris, 1995), pp. 405–6.

87. Chateaubriand, *Mémoires d'outre-tombe*, i. pp. 1585–7.

88. See Suzanne Glover Lindsay, *Funerary Arts and Tomb Cult: Living with the Dead in France, 1750–1870* (Farnham, 2012), pp. 37–40.

89. *Moniteur universel*, 2, 3, 4 December 1840, pp. 354, 363, 373–4.

90. Jérémie Benoît, 'La Résurrection', in Benoît, Delannoy and Pougetoux, *Napoléon, le retour des cendres*, p. 144.

91. Which, in turn, may have had its roots in the Messianism of the Revolution. See Noel Parker, *Portrayals of Revolution: Images, Debates and Patterns of Thought on the French Revolution* (London, 1990), pp. 199–200. On Napoleon as Saviour see Dwyer, *Napoleon: The Path to Power*, pp. 513–16.

92. Lindsay, 'Mummies and Tombs: Turenne, Napoleon, and Death Ritual', 476, 478.

93. Cited in Mauguin, *Napoléon et la superstition*, p. 213.

94. Boudon, 'Grand homme ou demi-dieu?', 135.

95. Ploux, *De bouche à l'oreille*, p. 274, n. 240. See, for example, Jean-Marie Déguignet, *Mémoires d'un paysan bas-breton* (Le Relecq-Kerhuon, 1998), pp. 65–6.

96. Driskel, *As Befits a Legend*, pp. 22–3, briefly touches on the theme.

CHAPTER 10

1. Bowman, *Le Christ romantique*, p. 171; Laure Murat, *L'homme qui se prenait pour Napoléon: pour une histoire politique de la folie* (Paris, 2011), pp. 163–219, here p. 163. The figure is based on a report written in 1847 by the writer and historian Henri-François-Alphonse Esquiros, *Paris, ou Les sciences, les institutions et les moeurs au XIXe siècle*, 2 vols (Paris, 1847), ii. p. 118. See also the wonderful novel by Simon Leys, *La mort de Napoléon* (Paris, 1986).

2. Murat, *L'homme qui se prenait pour Napoléon*, pp. 183–6.

3. Murat, *L'homme qui se prenait pour Napoléon*, pp. 186–7.

4. Marrinan, *Painting Politics*, p. 192.

5. On the Eastern crisis see Schroeder, *The Transformation of European Politics*, pp. 736–56; James L. Richardson, *Crisis Diplomacy: The Great Powers since the Mid-Nineteenth Century* (Cambridge, 1994), pp. 37–68; Munro Price, *The Perilous Crown: France between Revolutions, 1814–1848* (London, 2007), pp. 297–305; Bury and Tombs, *Thiers*, pp. 63–79, for the 'Syrian Gamble'.

6. David H. Pinkney, *Decisive Years in France, 1840–1847* (Princeton, 1986), pp. 131–2.

7. Lucas-Dubreton, *Le culte de Napoléon*, pp. 364–74; William Smith, *Napoléon III* (Paris, 1983), pp. 75–86; Louis Girard, *Napoleon III* (Paris, 1986), pp. 55–60; Fenton Bresler, *Napoleon III: A Life* (London, 1999), pp. 153–65; Eric Anceau, *Napoléon III* (Paris, 2008), pp. 79–84; Juliette Glikman, *Louis-Napoléon prisonnier: du fort de Ham aux ors des Tuileries* (Paris, 2011), pp. 15–42.

8. Marrinan, *Painting Politics*, p. 192.

9. A point picked up by Victor Hugo, *Oeuvres inédites de Victor Hugo*, 10 vols (Paris, 1886–93), iii. p. 36; and Jean-Marie Roulin, 'Le retour des cendres de Napoléon: une cérémonie palimseste', in Corinne and Eric Perrin-Saminadayar (eds), *Imaginaire et représentations des entrées royales au XIXe siècle: une sémiologie du pouvoir politique* (Saint-Etienne, 2006), p. 89; Marrinan, *Painting Politics*, pp. 199–200.

10. Jérémie Benoît, 'Le retour des cendres', in Benoît, Dellanoy and Pougetoux, *Napoléon: le retour des cendres*, p. 108.

11. AN C 2180, Assemblées nationales, 19 May 1840.

12. Boisson, *Le retour des cendres*, p. 308; Marrinan, *Painting Politics*, p. 186.

13. AN F21 742, Beaux-Arts, minister of the interior to the prefect of the Eure, 4 and 8 December 1840.

14. Cited in Marie-Françoise Huyghues des Etages, 'L'expédition maritime et fluviale', in Humbert (ed.), *Napoléon aux Invalides*, p. 43; Boisson, *Le retour des cendres*, pp. 332–3.

15. *Le Siècle*, 15 December 1840.

16. Boisson, *Le retour des cendres*, p. 360; E. M. Laumann, *L'épopée napoléonienne. Le retour des cendres* (Paris, 1904), p. 104. See also Nicolas Jacques Noël-Agnès, *Relation de ce qui s'est passé à Cherbourg à l'occasion du transbordement des restes mortels de l'empereur Napoléon* (Cherbourg, 1841), p. 8.

17. Coquereau, *Souvenirs*, p. 145, estimated about 100,000 visitors in all. See also Vidalenc, 'L'opinion publique en Normandie', pp. 213–14;

Boisson, *Le retour des cendres*, p. 360; Rohan-Chabot, *Les 5 cercueils de l'Empereur*, pp. 114–15; Jean Bourguignon, *Le retour des cendres, 1840* (Paris, 1941), p. 129.

18. Vidalenc, 'L'opinion publique en Normandie', p. 217.

19. Balzac to Mme Hanksa, in Roger Pierrot (ed.), *Lettres à Madame Hanska*, 2 vols (Paris, 1990), i. pp. 521–2; Coquereau, *Souvenirs*, pp. 152–3; Boisson, *Le retour des cendres*, p. 373.

20. *Journal de Rouen*, 19 December 1840.

21. *Journal de Rouen*, 31 December 1840.

22. AN F7 3890, Police générale, 9 and 10 December 1840; *Le Siècle*, 11 December 1840; *La Presse*, 11 December 1840; Théodore Villenave, *Relation des funérailles de Napoléon, exhumation, translation, pièces officielles, etc.* (Paris, 1840), pp. 60–1.

23. *Journal de Rouen*, 3 and 7 December 1840.

24. Herscher, 'Evoking the Eagle', p. 386.

25. Eugène Noel, *Rouen, rouennais, rouenneries* (Rouen, 1894), pp. 114–16; Boisson, *Le retour des cendres*, p. 327.

26. Vidalenc, 'L'opinion publique en Normandie', p. 215.

27. *Passage des cendres de l'empereur Napoléon à Rouen: procès-verbal* (Rouen, 1842), p. 24.

28. Vidalenc, 'L'opinion publique en Normandie', p. 217. At least, this is to be found in the letters from sub-prefects to the prefect of the Eure (AN Pontaudemer, 9 December 1840), but this may very well have been a case of one bureaucrat telling another what he wanted to hear. They conveniently forgot to report the 'Vives l'Empereur' that were heard. Cited in Boisson, *Le retour des cendres*, p. 374.

29. Cited in Boisson, *Le retour des cendres*, p. 386.

30. *Moniteur universel*, 2, 3, 4 December 1840, pp. 337, 338 and 339.

31. *Journal des débats politiques et littéraires*, 13 December 1840.

32. There is an extensive literature on the 'return of the ashes', the phrase often mistakenly used for the return of Napoleon's body. The French word *cendres* does not mean in this context 'ashes', but rather 'remains', and is a Christian reference to the decomposition of the body in liturgical texts. It was a word that confused some contemporaries, as it did Lamartine when he said, 'Napoleon's ashes are not extinguished, and they are blowing on the sparks.' They believed that the British had burned Napoleon's body (see *Le National*, 15 May 1840; Cahuet, *Napoléon délivré*, p. 83). The literature on the return is mostly descriptive. Some of the more notable works include Boisson, *Le retour des cendres* (Paris, 1973); Tulard, 'Le retour des cendres'; Martineau, *Le retour des cendres* (Paris, 1990); and Georges Poisson, *L'aventure du retour des cendres* (Paris, 2004). See

NOTES

also Uwe Fleckner, 'Le retour des cendres de Napoléon. Vergängliche Denkmäler zur Domestizierung einer Legende', in Michael Diers (ed.), *Mo(nu)mente. Formen und Funktionen ephemerer Denkmäler* (Berlin, 1993), pp. 61–76. Fureix, *La France des larmes*, pp. 314–17, examines the 'multiple voices' surrounding the ceremony, and postulates that the July Monarchy invented national mourning, of which the return of Napoleon's remains was a fundamental part. For a similar approach to Nelson's funeral see Timothy Jenks, 'Contesting the Hero: The Funeral of Admiral Lord Nelson', *Journal of British Studies*, 39:4 (2000), 422–53.

33. Alfred Villeroy, *Histoire de 1840, annuaire historique et politique*, 2 vols (Paris, 1841–2), i. p. 429, Boisson, *Le retour des cendres*, p. 406.
34. Marie Célestine Amélie de Ségur, comtesse d'Armaillé, *Quand on savait vivre heureux: 1830–1860* (Paris, 2012), p. 65; Boisson, *Le retour des cendres*, p. 405.
35. Bocher, *Mémoires de Charles Bocher*, i. pp. 355–8.
36. Hugo, *Oeuvres inédites de Victor Hugo*, iii. p. 20.
37. *Journal des débats politiques et littéraires*, 16 December 1840; Hugo, *Oeuvres inédites de Victor Hugo*, iii. pp. 25–6. Marengo died at the age of thirty-eight. His skeleton, minus two hoofs, was preserved and is now on display at the National Army Museum in Chelsea.
38. Hazareesingh, *The Legend of Napoleon*, p. 238; Laumann, *L'épopée napoléonienne*, pp. 153–4.
39. Cited in Laumann, *L'épopée napoléonienne*, pp. 153–4.
40. Hugo, *Oeuvres inédites de Victor Hugo*, iii. pp. 35–6; Comte Rodolphe Apponyi, *Vingt-cinq ans à Paris (1826–1850): journal du comte Rodolphe Apponyi*, 4 vols (Paris, 1913), iii. pp. 448–9; Viennet, *Mémoires et journal*, p. 1286.
41. Dorothée, princesse de Courlande, duchesse de Dino, *Mémoires*, 4 vols (Clermont-Ferrand, 2004), iv. p. 190.
42. *Le Siècle*, 17 December 1840; *Le Commerce*, 17 December 1840.
43. Cited in Laumann, *L'épopée napoléonienne*, p. 133; Roger Dupuy, *La Garde nationale, 1789–1872* (Paris, 2010), pp. 437–8; Georges Carrot, *La Garde nationale, 1789–1871: une force politique ambiguë* (Paris, 2001), p. 266. A police report considered the National Guard 'very numerous, but ill disposed and not very obedient' (Tudesq, *Les grands notables en France*, p. 542).
44. *La Quotidienne*, 16 December 1840, estimates the crowd at between 500,000 and 600,000; *Le Siècle*, 16 and 17 December 1840, at between 700,000 and 800,000; *Moniteur universel*, 18 December 1840, p. 353, at 600,000; Dino, *Mémoires*, iv. p. 184, at 800,000; Tudesq, *Les grands*

notables, p. 542, at 750,000; Boisson, *Le retour des cendres*, p. 408, at one million.

45. This is especially the case for the series F7. It is also possible that it was because, up till 1818, the prefecture of police depended on the ministry of general police. After 1818, it became increasingly independent, hence the lack of documentation. Jean Tulard, *La Préfecture de Police sous la monarchie de juillet* (Paris, 1964), pp. 21–2.

46. See Michael Driskel, 'Singing "The Marseillaise" in 1840: The Case of Charlet's Censored Prints', *Art Bulletin*, 69 (1987), 611–12.

47. *La Quotidienne*, 17 December 1840.

48. AN F7 3890, Police générale, 15 December 1840. For other examples of public exclamations see *Journal des débats politiques et littéraires*, 16 December 1840; *Le National*, 16 December; *Le Charivari* (18 December); Laumann, *L'épopée napoléonienne*, p. 143; Boisson, *Le retour des cendres*, p. 416.

49. *Le Constitutionnel*, 16 December 1840; Boisson, *Le retour des cendres*, p. 417.

50. AN F7 3890, Police générale, 15 December 1840; Dino, *Mémoires*, iv. p. 188; Boisson, *Le retour des cendres*, p. 424.

51. Hugo, *Oeuvres inédites de Victor Hugo*, iii. p. 35.

52. Hugo, *Oeuvres inédites de Victor Hugo*, iii. pp. 33-4.

53. Alfred Hachette, 'Le dossier de la journée du retour des cendres', *Revue des études napoléoniennes*, 24 (1925), 239–80.

54. Rohan-Chabot, *Les 5 cercueils de l'Empereur*, pp. 142–5.

55. Ben-Amos, *Funerals, Politics, and Memory*, p. 75. For a discussion on the visual representations of the procession and the temporariness of the decorations made of wood, plaster and canvas see Marrinan, *Painting Politics*, pp. 192–5.

56. Driskel, *As Befits a Legend*, p. 32.

57. Marrinan, *Painting Politics*, p. 194; Driskel, 'Eclecticism and Ideology in the July Monarchy', 119–29.

58. For a similar context see Peter W. Sinnema, *The Wake of Wellington: Englishness in 1852* (Athens, Ohio, 2006), p. 75.

59. Nigel Llewellyn, *The Art of Death: Visual Culture in the English Death Ritual, c.1500–c.1800* (London, 1991), p. 54.

60. For a similar interpretation of the crowd see Thompson, 'The Creation, Destruction and Recreation of Henri IV', 25–6.

61. *Le Siècle*, 17 December 1840; *Le Constitutionnel*, 16 December 1840; as did Guizot, *Mémoires pour servir à l'histoire de mon temps*, xi. pp. 21–2.

62. *Gazette de France*, 15, 16 December 1840.

63. *Le Constitutionnel*, 16 December 1840; *Le Siècle*, 17 December 1840. This sentiment was not universal, however. At least one member of the National Guard considered the whole thing to be a political farce (Apponyi, *Vingt-cinq ans à Paris*, iii. p. 447).

64. *Journal des débats politiques et littéraires*, 16 December 1840.

65. *La Presse*, 16 December 1840.

66. *La Quotidienne*, 17 December 1840.

67. *L'Atelier: organe des intérêts moraux et matériels des ouvriers*, December 1840, 27–8.

68. *Journal de Rouen*, 12 December 1840.

69. Cf. N. Jorga, 'Un témoin roumain de la translation des Cendres de Napoléon', *Revue des études napoléoniennes*, 2 (1912), 130.

70. Philippe de Massa, *Souvenirs et impressions, 1840–1871* (Paris, 1897), p. 18; d'Armaillé, *Quand on savait vivre heureux*, p. 65.

71. Heinrich Heine, *Deutschland: A Winter's Tale*, trans. T. J. Reed (London, 1986), p. 50.

72. A similar sentiment is expressed in *Relation exacte de la translation des restes mortels de l'empereur Napoléon* (Paris, 1840), p. 5.

73. Dino, *Mémoires*, iv. p. 187.

74. Charles Robert, Vasilievitch de Nesselrode, *Lettres et papiers, 1760–1850, extraits de ses archives*, 11 vols (Paris, 1908–12), viii. pp. 88–90.

75. Apponyi, *Vingt-cinq ans à Paris*, iii. pp. 446–7; Tudesq, 'Le reflet donné par la presse', 92.

76. William Makepeace Thackeray, *The Second Funeral of Napoleon* (New York, 1883).

77. Mme Mollien to the duchesse de Dino, in Dorothée, princesse de Courlande, duchesse de Dino, *Chronique de 1831 à 1862*, 4 vols (Paris, 1909–10), ii. p. 436.

78. Saint-Denis, *Journal inédit*, p. 214.

79. *Journal de Rouen*, 20 December 1840; Boisson, *Le retour des cendres*, p. 432.

80. The *Moniteur* regularly published the number of entries; *La Presse*, 19, 20, 23 December 1840; Laumann, *L'épopée napoléonienne*, p. 157. There are slight variations in the figures in Boisson, *Le retour des cendres*, p. 446; Louis-Eustache Audot, *Funérailles de l'empereur Napoléon, exhumation, retour en France, cérémonies, faits et anecdotes* (Paris, 1841), p. 60.

81. Hugo, *Oeuvres inédites de Victor Hugo*, iii. p. 44.

82. Jorga, 'Un témoin roumain', 130–1.

83. *Le Commerce*, 23, 25 December 1840, which also tells the tale of a woman who gave birth to a child in the gardens of the Invalides and named him Napoléon-Sauveur-Bienvenu.

84. Guizot, *Mémoires pour servir à l'histoire de mon temps*, xi. p. 21.

85. Jean-Claude Caron, *Générations romantiques: les étudiants de Paris et le Quartier latin, 1814–1851* (Paris, 1991), pp. 249–50, 279–81; Emmanuel Fureix, 'La violence et la mort: funérailles opposantes sous les monarchies censitaires (Paris, 1820–1830)', in Philippe Bourdin, Jean-Claude Caron and Mathias Bernard (eds), *La voix et le geste: une approche culturelle de la violence socio-politique* (Paris, 2005), pp. 115–32; and on the political funeral, idem, 'De l'hommage funèbre à la prise de parole: l'enterrement du général Foy (novembre 1825)', *Sociétés & Représentations*, 12:2 (2001), 176–203.

86. Spitzer, *Old Hatreds and Young Hopes*, pp. 37–8.

87. On the cholera epidemic and on Lamarque's funeral see Catherine J. Kudlick, *Cholera in Post-Revolutionary Paris: A Cultural History* (Berkeley, 1996), esp. pp. 192–8; Apponyi, *Vingt-cinq ans à Paris*, ii. pp. 204–9 (5 June 1832). On contestatory funeral processions see Emmanuel Fureix, 'La construction rituelle de la souveraineté populaire: deuils protestataires (Paris, 1815–1840)', *Revue d'histoire du XIXe siècle*, 42 (2011), 21–39.

88. Thureau-Dangin, *Histoire de la monarchie de juillet*, ii. pp. 130–1; Lucas-Dubreton, *Le culte de Napoléon*, p. 309.

89. AN F7 3890, Police générale, 14, 15 and 28 December 1840; *La Quotidienne*, 17 December 1840.

90. AN F7 3890, Police générale, 16 and 18 December 1840.

91. For example, Théodore Fadeville, *Aperçu critique sur Napoléon et sur les hommes de son époque* (Paris, 1840), p. 2.

92. Thiers had yet to publish his monumental history of the Consulate and the Empire, but Baptiste Capefigue, *L'Europe pendant le Consulat et l'Empire de Napoléon*, 10 vols (Paris, 1840), had already done so. Other histories include François-Gilbert de Coston, *Biographie des premières années de Napoléon Bonaparte, c'est-à-dire depuis sa naissance jusqu'à l'époque de son commandement en chef de l'armée d'Italie*, 2 vols (Paris and Valence, 1840); Etienne Laborde, *Napoléon et sa garde, ou Relation du voyage de Fontainebleau à l'île d'Elbe en 1814, du séjour de l'Empereur dans cette île et de son retour en France* (Paris, 1840).

93. Anonymous, *Couronne poétique de Napoléon* (Paris, 1840), pp. 3–4.

94. *Relation exacte de la translation des restes mortels de l'empereur Napoléon*, p. 11; *Translation des cendres de Napoléon, de Sainte-Hélène en France* (Cherbourg, n.d.), p. 4; Jacques Marquet de Montbreton, baron de Norvins, *Translation des cendres de Napoléon* (Paris, 1840), pp. 7–8; Justin Bonnaire, *Les cendres de Napoléon* (Paris, 1840), pp. 27–8; Anonymous, *Napoléon aux Invalides: dédié à tous les Français* (Paris, 1840), pp. 28–31.

95. One author refers to Napoleon's remains as a 'holy relic'. Anonymous, *Renseignements historiques sur l'Empereur Napoléon et sa famille* (Paris, 1840), p. 7.

96. Such as the account by the surgeon major of the *Belle-Poule*, Remi-Julien Guillard, in Ferdinand Langlé, *Funérailles de l'empereur Napoléon, relation officielle de la translation de ses restes* (Paris, 1840), pp. 15–17, which also contains an illustration of Napoleon in the open coffin; and Villenave, *Relation des funérailles de Napoléon*, pp. 18, 24–9, which also published the surgeon major's written report.

97. Las Cases, *Journal écrit à bord de la frégate 'la Belle-Poule'*, p. 237.

98. Cited in Fureix, 'L'iconoclasme: une pratique politique?', p. 121.

99. Anonymous, *Description de l'intérieur et de l'extérieur de l'hôtel royal des Invalides: contenant un précis historique sur la translation des cendres de Napoléon* (Paris, 1840), pp. 22–3.

100. Bonnaire, *Les cendres de Napoléon*, pp. 5–12; Anonymous, *La voix du peuple aux funérailles de Napoléon* (Paris, 1840); Anonymous, *Napoléon aux Invalides*, p. 8; J.-L.-M. Lecomte, *Napoléon!! De l'oeuvre sainte qui va mettre à sa place si grande chose!* (Paris, 1840), pp. 7, 9, 10.

101. Fadeville, *Aperçu critique sur Napoléon*, p. 119.

102. Joseph Cresp, *Eloge funèbre de Napoléon* (Paris, 1840), pp. 8–9.

103. Cresp, *Eloge funèbre de Napoléon*, pp. 10, 12, 13.

104. Coston, *Biographie des premières années de Napoléon Bonaparte*, i. p. 151.

105. Anonymous, *Napoléon et les prophéties* (Paris, 1840).

106. Joseph Ottavi, *Napoléon* (Paris, 1840), p. 29.

107. Heinrich Heine, *Lutèce: lettres sur la vie politique* (Paris, 1855), pp. 53–5; Lloyd S. Kramer, *Threshold of a New World: Intellectuals and the Exile Experience in Paris, 1830–1848* (Ithaca, NY, 1988), p. 78.

108. Viennet, *Mémoires et journal*, p. 1287.

109. Specifically, the funerals of Louis XVI and Marie-Antoinette, the prince of Condé, the duc de Berry and Louis XVIII. See Fureix, *La France des larmes*, pp. 245–65; Bettina Frederking, '"Les funérailles de la monarchie" ou "l'impossible oubli"', in Natalie Scholz and Christina Schröe (eds), *Représentation et pouvoir: la politique symbolique en France, 1789–1830* (Rennes, 2007), pp. 213–33.

110. See Jo Burr Margadant, 'Gender, Vice, and the Political Imaginary in Nineteenth-Century France: Reinterpreting the Failure of the July Monarchy, 1830–1848', *American Historical Review*, 104 (1999), 1461–96.

111. Girard, *Napoleon III*, p. 95. See also Robert Pimienta, *La propagande bonapartiste en 1848* (Paris, 1911), esp. pp. 49–52, 113–15; and Tudesq, 'La légende napoléonienne', 65–72.

112. D. B. Wehs, *Some Account of the Political Life of Louis Napoleon* (London, 1859), p. 3; Alphonse d'Hautpoul, *Mémoires du général marquis Alphonse d'Hautpoul, pair de France, 1789–1865* (Paris, 1906), p. 319; Tudesq, 'La légende napoléonienne', 80–4; Peter McPhee, *The Politics of Rural Life: Political Mobilization in the French Countryside, 1846–1852* (Oxford, 1992), pp. 114–20; William Fortescue, *France and 1848: The End of Monarchy* (London, 2005), p. 153.

EPILOGUE

1. Sudhir Hazareesingh, *The Saint-Napoleon: Celebrations of Sovereignty in Nineteenth-Century France* (Cambridge, Mass., 2004), pp. 66–7.

2. Stéphane Rials, *Nouvelle histoire de Paris: de Trochu à Thiers, 1870–1873* (Paris, 1985), p. 476.

3. *L'Illustration*, 12 December 1863; Matthew Truesdell, *Spectacular Politics: Louis-Napoleon Bonaparte and the Fête Impériale, 1849–1870* (New York, 1997), p. 157.

4. Francis Magnard, 'La Résurrection d'une légende', *La Revue de Paris*, 1 (1 February 1894), 92.

5. Cited in Gildea, *The Past in French History*, p. 99; *Le Père Duchesne*, 25 germinal An 79.

6. Antoine Chollier, *La vraie Route Napoléon* (Paris, 1950), p. 25; Hazareesingh, *The Saint-Napoleon*, pp. 232–3.

7. See Richard D. E. Burton, *Blood in the City: Violence and Revelation in Paris, 1789–1945* (Ithaca, NY, 2001), pp. 77–8, 84–8; Matt K. Matsuda, *The Memory of the Modern* (Oxford, 1996), pp. 21–2, 25–8, 31–2, 34–5, 37–8; idem, 'Idols of the Emperor', pp. 72–100; and Seth Whidden, *Authority in Crisis in French Literature, 1850–1880* (Farnham, 2014), pp. 68–76.

8. Zeldin, *The Political System of Napoleon III*, p. 3.

9. See, for example, John Rothney, *Bonapartism after Sedan* (Ithaca, NY, 1969). For its literary implications see Venita Datta, *Heroes and Legends of Fin-de-Siècle France: Gender, Politics, and National Identity* (Cambridge, 2011), ch. 3. And for the continuation of the legend into the nineteenth and twentieth centuries see Gengembre, *Napoléon: l'empereur immortel*, pp. 152–244; and Buchinger, *Napoléomanie*, pp. 200–67.

10. David Chanteranne and Isabelle Veyrat-Masson, *Napoléon à l'écran: cinéma et télévision* (Paris, 2003).

11. On the (spurious) public contest to design the tomb see Michael Paul Driskel, 'By Competition or Administrative Decree? The Contest for the Tomb of Napoleon in 1841', *Art Journal*, 48 (Spring 1989), 46–52;

and Thierry Issartel, 'Les projets pour le tombeau de Napoléon', in Humbert (ed.), *Napoléon aux Invalides*, pp. 121–45.

12. Driskel, *As Befits a Legend*, pp. 126–7.

13. Georges Poisson, *Le retour des cendres de l'Aiglon* (Paris, 2006).

14. Chateaubriand, *Mémoires d'outre-tombe*, xxiv. ch. 8.

15. R. Ben Jones, *Napoleon: Man and Myth* (London, 1977), pp. 35–6.

16. Aleksandr Pushkin, *The Queen of Spades and Other Stories*, trans. Sutherland Edwards (London, 1892), p. 53.

17. Alexander, *Napoleon*, pp. 106–14; Steven Englund, 'Napoleon and Hitler', *Journal of the Historical Society*, 6 (2006), 151–69; and Michael Rowe, 'Napoleon's France: A Forerunner of Europe's Twentieth-Century Dictators', in Claus-Christian Szejnmann (ed.), *Rethinking History, Dictatorship and War: New Approaches and Interpretations* (London, 2009), pp. 87–106.

18. Peter Burke, *The Fabrication of Louis XIV* (New Haven, 1992).

19. Charles A. Porter, *Chateaubriand: Composition, Imagination, and Poetry* (Saratoga, Calif., 1978), p. 71; Jeffrey L. Sammons, *Heinrich Heine: A Modern Biography* (Princeton, 1979), pp. 67–8.

20. Elie Faure, *Napoléon* (Paris, 1983), esp. pp. 31–4; and Henri Peyre, 'Napoleon: Devil, Poet, Saint', *Yale French Studies*, 26 (1960), 28–9.

21. Gérard Grunberg, *Napoléon Bonaparte: le noir génie* (Paris, 2015).

NOTES TO PLATE CAPTIONS

1. Charles Lock Eastlake, *Contributions to the Literature of the Fine Arts. 2. Series* (London, 1870), pp. 54–6.

2. He was later allowed to sail with Hudson Lowe and to join Napoleon as his equerry. See George L. de St Macaire Watson, *A Polish Exile with Napoleon* (London, 1912).

3. Miles Chappell, *Form, Function, and Finesse: Drawings from the Frederick and Lucy S. Herman Foundation* (Williamsburg, 1983), p. 143.

4. Alain Pougetoux, 'Le masque de Napoléon: de la relique au bibelot', in Emmanuelle Héran (ed.), *Le dernier portrait* (Paris, 2002), pp. 150, 151.

5. Maurice Agulhon, *Marianne into Battle: Republican Imagery and Symbolism in France, 1789–1880*, trans. Janet Lloyd (Cambridge, 1981), p. 37.

6. Simonnin, *Histoire des trois derniers mois de la vie de Napoléon Bonaparte*, p. 8.

7. François-René, vicomte de Chateaubriand, *Vie de Napoléon* (Paris, 1999), p. 434.

8. See, for example, Charles-Joseph Bail, *Napoléon aux Champs-Elysées, nouveau dialogue des morts, par un vieux soldat* (Paris, 1821).

9. Hafera, 'Visual Mediations of Mourning and Melancholia', p. 143.

Picture Credits

Select Bibliography

A. (Augé), Lazare. *Quelques pensées apologétiques sur Bonaparte*. Paris: Ravelle, 1821.

Abell, Elizabeth Balcombe. *Recollections of the Emperor Napoleon during the First Three Years of his Captivity on the Island of St. Helena*. London: John Murray, 1844.

Abrantès, Laure Junot, duchesse de. *Mémoires sur la Restauration, ou Souvenirs historiques sur cette époque, la Révolution de 1830, et les premières années du règne de Louis-Philippe*. 7 vols. Brussels: L. Hauman, 1835–7.

Accusation contre les meurtriers de Napoléon. Paris: L'Huillier, 1821.

Agnès, Benoît. 'La pétition, reine de l'opinion? Les autorités françaises et britanniques entre réfutations et légitimations. 1814–1848', in Laurent Bourquin, Philippe Hamon, Pierre Karila-Cohen et Cédric Michon (eds), *S'exprimer en temps de troubles: conflits, opinion(s) et politisation de la fin du Moyen Âge au début du XXe siècle*. Rennes: Presses universitaires de Rennes, 2011, pp. 307–20.

Agoult, Marie de Flavigny, comtesse d'. *Mes souvenirs, 1806–1833*. Paris, 1880.

Agulhon, Maurice. *Marianne into Battle: Republican Imagery and Symbolism in France, 1789–1880*. Trans. Janet Lloyd. Cambridge: Cambridge University Press, 1981.

Agulhon, Maurice. 'Paris: A Traversal from East to West', in Pierre Nora (ed.), *Realms of Memory: The Construction of the French Past*. Trans. Arthur Goldhammer. 3 vols. New York: Columbia University Press, 1992, pp. 523–52.

Alberti, Guglielmo. 'Alessandro Manzoni', in Emilio Cecchi and Natalino Sapegno (eds), *Storia della letteratura italiana*. Milan: Garzanti, 1969, pp. 663–809.

Alexander, R. S. *Bonapartism and the Revolutionary Tradition in France: The Fédérés of 1815*. Cambridge: Cambridge University Press, 1991.

Alexander, R. S., 'Restoration Republicanism Reconsidered', *French History*, 8:4 (1994): 442–69.

Alexander, R. S. *Re-Writing the French Revolutionary Tradition: Liberal Opposition and the Fall of the Bourbon Monarchy*. Cambridge: Cambridge University Press, 2003.

Allard, Sébastien and Chaudonneret, Marie-Claude. *Le suicide de Gros: les peintres de l'Empire et la génération romantique*. Paris: Gourcuff Gradenigo, 2010.

Allen, James Smith. *In the Public Eye: A History of Reading in Modern France, 1800–1940*. Princeton: Princeton University Press, 2014.

Allen, James Smith. *Popular French Romanticism: Authors, Readers, and Books in the 19th Century*. Syracuse, NY: Syracuse University Press, 1981.

Alméras, Henri de. *La vie parisienne sous la Restauration*. Paris: Albin Michel, n.d.

Altick, Richard D. *The Shows of London*. Cambridge, Mass.: Belknap Press of Harvard University Press, 1978.

Alton-Shée, Comte Edmond de. *Mes mémoires. 1826–1848*. 2 vols. Paris: A. Lacroix, 1869.

Ambrière, Madeleine and Francis. *Talma ou L'histoire au theatre*. Paris: Fallois, 2007.

Anceau, Eric. *Napoléon III*. Paris: Tallandier, 2008.

Angers, David de. *Les carnets de David d'Angers*. 2 vols. Paris: Plon, 1958.

Les années romantiques: la peinture française de 1815 à 1850. Paris: Société française de promotion artistique, 1995.

Anonymous. *Couronne poétique de Napoléon*. Paris: Amyot, 1840.

Anonymous. *Description de l'intérieur et de l'extérieur de l'hôtel royal des Invalides: contenant un précis historique sur la translation des cendres de Napoléon*. Paris: Gauthier, 1840.

Anonymous. *Napoléon aux Invalides: dédié à tous les Français*. Paris: F. Knab, 1840.

Anonymous. *Napoléon et les prophéties*. Paris: chez tous les marchands de nouveautés, 1840.

Anonymous. *Renseignements historiques sur l'Empereur Napoléon et sa famille*. Paris: H.-L. Delloye, 1840.

Anonymous. *La voix du peuple aux funérailles de Napoléon*. Paris: E. Brière, 1840.

Antommarchi, François. *Mémoires du docteur F. Antommarchi, ou Les derniers moments de Napoléon*. 2 vols. Paris: Barrois l'aîné, 1825.

Antonetti, Guy. *Louis-Philippe*. Paris: Fayard, 1994.

Apothéose de Napoleone Bonaparte, ou signalement de l'Ante-Christ, manifesté à tout l'univers, par l'esprit de vérité. Paris: chez l'auteur, 1821.

An appeal to the British nation on the treatment experienced by Napoleon Buonaparte in the Island of St. Helena, with an authentic copy of the official memoir dictated by Napoleon, and delivered to Sir Hudson Lowe. London: Ridgway, 1817.

Appert, Benjamin. *Dix ans à la cour du roi Louis-Philippe, et souvenirs du temps de l'empire et de la Restauration*. 3 vols. Paris: J. Renouard, 1846.

Apponyi, Comte Rodolphe. *Vingt-cinq ans à Paris. 1826–1850: journal du comte Rodolphe Apponyi*. 4 vols. Paris: Plon-Nourrit, 1913.

Archives parlementaires; procès-verbaux des séances de la Chambre des Députés. 143 vols. Paris: A. Henry, 1837–47.

Ariès, Philippe. *The Hour of our Death*. Trans. Helen Weaver. New York: Knopf, 1981.

Arkin, Marcus. 'Supplies for Napoleon's Gaolers: John Company and the Cape-St. Helena Trade during the Captivity, 1815–21', *Archives Year Book for South African History*, 1 (1964): 169–230.

Armaillé, Marie Célestine Amélie de Ségur, comtesse de. *Quand on savait vivre heureux: 1830–1860*. Paris: Lacurne, 2012.

Arnault, Antoine Vincent. *Vie politique et militaire de Napoléon*. 2 vols. Paris: E. Babeuf, 1822–6.

Arnott, Archibald. *An Account of the Last Illness, Decease, and Post Mortem Appearances of Napoleon Bonaparte*. London: John Murray, 1822.

Athanassoglou-Kallmyer, Nina Maria. '*Imago Belli*: Horace Vernet's *L'Atelier* as an Image of Radical Militarism under the Restoration', *Art Bulletin*, 68:2 (1986): 268–80.

Athanassoglou-Kallmyer, Nina. 'Sad Cincinnatus: Le Soldat-Laboureur as an Image of the Napoleonic Veteran after the Empire', *Arts Magazine*, 60 (May 1986): 65–75.

Aubry, Octave. *Sainte-Hélène*. Paris: Flammarion, 1973.

Audot, Louis-Eustache. *Funérailles de l'empereur Napoléon, exhumation, retour en France, cérémonies, faits et anecdotes*. Paris: Fain et Thunot, 1841.

Aulard, Alphonse. 'La mort de Napoléon et les journaux parisiens en 1821', in *Etudes et leçons sur la Révolution française*, 9e série. Paris: F. Alcan, 1924, pp. 92–103

Avril, Gilles (ed). *L'anti-Napoléon: écrits inédits et papiers de Noël-Antoine Apuril Du Pontreau, chanoine de la Congrégation de France*. Paris: Nouveau monde éd., 2006.

Bail, Charles-Joseph. *Napoléon aux Champs-Elysées, nouveau dialogue des morts, par un vieux soldat.* Paris: L'Huillier, 1821.

Bainbridge, Simon. 'Battling Bonaparte after Waterloo: Re-enactment, Representation and "The Napoleon Bust Business"', in Neil Ramsey and Gillian Russell (eds), *Tracing War in British Enlightenment and Romantic Culture.* Basingstoke: Palgrave Macmillan, 2015, pp. 132–50

Balmain, Alexandre. 'Comte de Balmain, Le prisonnier de Sainte-Hélène, d'après les rapports officiels du commissaire du gouvernement russe (1816–1820)', *La Revue politique et littéraire. Revue bleue,* 7 (8 May–12 June 1897): 578–84, 614–22, 647–55, 678–86, 716–22, 745–50.

Balmain, Aleksandr Antonovich Graf. *Napoleon in Captivity: The Reports of Count Balmain, Russian Commissioner on the Island of St. Helena, 1816–1820.* Trans. and ed. with introduction and notes by Julian Park. London: Allen & Unwin, 1928.

Balzac, Honoré de. *Le médecin de campagne,* in *La comédie humaine.* 10 vols. Paris: Gallimard, 1949–59.

Balzac, Honoré de. *The Country Doctor.* Trans. Ellen Marriage. London: J. M. Dent, 1961.

Banville, Théodore de. *Mes souvenirs.* Paris: G. Charpentier, 1883.

Barante, Prosper Brugière, baron de. *Souvenirs du Bon de Barante: 1782–1866.* 8 vols. Paris: Calmain Lévy, 1890–1901, ii.

Barginet, Alexandre. *De la reine d'Angleterre et de Napoléon Bonaparte, tous deux morts d'un cancer.* Paris: chez tous les marchands de nouveautés, 1821.

Barrès, Jean Baptiste Auguste. *Souvenirs d'un officier de la Grande Armée.* Paris: Plon-Nourrit, 1923.

Barrot, Odilon. *Mémoires posthumes de Odilon Barrot.* 4 vols. Paris: Charpentier, 1875–6.

Barthélemy, Auguste-Marseille and Méry, Joseph. *Le fils de l'homme, ou souvenirs de Vienne.* Paris: les marchands de nouveautés, 1829.

Barthélemy, Pierre. *Demande de la translation des dépouilles mortelles de l'empereur Napoléon.* Paris: Galliot, 1821.

Beach, Vincent W. *Charles X of France: His Life and Times.* Boulder, Colo.: Pruett, 1971.

Beatty, Heather. *Nervous Disease in Late Eighteenth-Century Britain: The Reality of a Fashionable Disorder.* London: Routledge, 2015.

Beauchef, George. *Mémoires pour servir à l'indépendance du Chili.* Trans. and ed. Patrick Puigmal. Paris: La Vouivre, 2001.

Behrendt, Stephen C. *Royal Mourning and Regency Culture: Elegies and Memorials of Princess Charlotte.* London: Macmillan Press, 1997.

Bellanger, Claude, Godechot, Jacques, Guiral, Pierre and Terrou Lien, Fernand (eds). *Histoire générale de la presse française*. 5 vols. Paris: Presses universitaires de France, 1969–76.

Ben-Amos, Avner. *Funerals, Politics, and Memory in Modern France, 1789–1996*. Oxford: Oxford University Press, 2000.

Benhamou, Albert. *Inside Longwood: Barry O'Meara's Clandestine Letters*. Hemel Hempstead: Albert Benhamou Pub., 2012.

Bénichou, Paul. *Le temps des prophètes: doctrines de l'âge romantique*. Paris: Gallimard, 1977.

Benoît, Jérémie. 'La Résurrection', in Jérémie Benoît, Agnès Dellanoy and Alain Pougetoux, *Napoléon: le retour des cendres (1840–1990)*. Courbevoie: Musée Roybet-Fould, 1990, pp. 144–54.

Benoît, Jérémie. 'Le retour des cendres', in Jérémie Benoît, Agnès Dellanoy and Alain Pougetoux, *Napoléon: le retour des cendres (1840–1990)*. Courbevoie: Musée Roybet-Fould, 1990, pp. 97–134.

Benoît, Jérémie, Delannoy, Agnès and Pougetoux, Alain. *Napoléon: le retour des cendres (1840–1990)*. Courbevoie: Musée Roybet-Fould, 1990.

Béranger, Pierre-Jean de. *Procès fait aux chansons de P.-J. de Béranger*. Paris: les marchands de nouveautés, 1821.

Bertaud, Jean-Paul, Forrest, Alan and Jourdan, Annie. *Napoléon, le monde et les Anglais: guerre des mots et des images*. Paris: Ed. Autrement, 2004.

Bertier de Sauvigny, Guillaume de. *La Restauration*. Paris: Flammarion, 1963.

Bertrand, Henri-Gatien. *Cahiers de Sainte-Hélène*. 3 vols. Paris: Albin Michel, 1950.

Beßlich, Barbara. *Der deutsche Napoleon-Mythos. Literatur und Erinnerung, 1800–1945*. Darmstadt: Wissenschaftliche Buchgesellschaft, 2007.

Bésuchet de Saunois, Jean-Claude. *Réflexions sur la mort de Napoléon, suivies de quelques considérations sur l'empoisonnement par les substances introduites dans l'estomac, par un chirurgien-major de la vieille armée*. Paris: chez tous les marchands de nouveautés, 1821.

Bignon, Louis-Pierre-Edouard. *Histoire de France, depuis le 18 brumaire, novembre 1799, jusqu'à la paix de Tilsitt, juillet 1807*. 6 vols. Paris: F. Didot Frères, 1829–30.

Blaufarb, Rafe. *Bonapartists in the Borderlands: French Exiles and Refugees on the Gulf Coast, 1815–1835*. Tuscaloosa: University of Alabama Press, 2006.

Blix, Göran. 'Heroic Genesis in the *Mémorial de Sainte-Hélène*', *Yale French Studies*, 111 (2007): 107–28.

Bluche, Frédéric. *Le bonapartisme: aux origines de la droite autoritaire, 1800–1850*. Paris: Nouvelles éditions latines, 1980.

Bocher, Charles. *Mémoires de Charles Bocher (1816–1907), précédés des souvenirs de famille (1760–1816)*. 2 vols. Paris: Flammarion, 1907–9.

Boigne, Eléonore-Adèle d'Osmond, comtesse de. *Récits d'une tante: mémoires de la comtesse de Boigne*. 5 vols. Paris: Emile-Paul, 1921–3.

Boime, Albert. *The Academy and French Painting in the Nineteenth Century*. New Haven: Yale University Press, 1986.

Boime, Albert. *Art and the French Commune*. Princeton: Princeton University Press, 1995.

Boime, Albert. *Art in an Age of Counterrevolution, 1815–1848*. Chicago: University of Chicago Press, 2004.

Boime, Albert. *Hollow Icons: The Politics of Sculpture in Nineteenth-Century France*. Kent, Ohio: Kent State University Press, 1987.

Bois, Jean-François. *Les anciens soldats dans la société française au XVIIIe siècle*. Paris: Economica, 1990.

Boisson, Jean. *Le retour des cendres*. Paris: Etudes et recherches historiques, 1973.

Boisson, Nicolas. 'Une approche socio-historique de la violence au XIXème siècle: le cas d'une conspiration à Lyon en 1817'. MA dissertation, Université Pierre Mendès France, Grenoble, 2008.

Bonald, Louis de. *Considérations politiques sur le projet de loi relatif aux donataires*. Paris: A. Egron, n.d.

Bonaparte, Napoléon. *Correspondance de Napoléon I publiée par ordre de l'empereur Napoléon III*. 32 vols. Paris: Henri Plon, 1858–70.

Bonaparte n'est pas mort d'un cancer; dédié aux mânes de Napoléon. Paris: Bataille et Bousquet, 1821.

Bonnaire, Justin. *Les cendres de Napoléon*. Paris: A. André, 1840.

Bonnel, Ulane, 'Espoirs de délivrance', in Ulane Bonnel (ed.), *Sainte-Hélène, terre d'exile*. Paris: Hachette, 1971, pp. 229–57.

Bonnellier, Hippolyte. *Mémorial de l'Hôtel-de-Ville de Paris: 1830*. Paris: 1835.

Bory, Jean-Louis. *La Révolution de Juillet: 29 juillet 1830*. Paris: Gallimard, 1972.

Bottet, Maurice. *Vétérans frères d'armes de l'Empire français*. Paris: J. Leroy fils, 1906.

Boudon, Jacques-Olivier. 'Grand homme ou demi-dieu? La mise en place d'une religion napoléonienne', *Romantisme*, 100 (1998): 131–41.

Boudon, Jacques-Olivier. *Napoléon et les cultes: les religions en Europe à l'aube du XIXe siècle, 1800–1815*. Paris: Fayard, 2002.

Boudon, Jacques-Olivier. *Le roi Jérôme, frère prodigue de Napoléon, 1784–1860*. Paris: Fayard, 2008.

Bouffé, Hugues Marie Désiré. *Mes souvenirs, 1800–1880*. Paris: E. Dentu, 1880.

Bourguet-Rouveyre, Josiane. 'Les Bonapartistes dans les conspirations de 1815 à 1823', in Bernard Gainot et Pierre Serna (eds), *Secret et République: 1795–1840*. Clermont-Ferrand: Presses Universitaire Blaise Pascal, 2003, pp. 129–43.

Bourguignon, Jean. *Le retour des cendres, 1840*. Paris: Plon, 1941.

Bowman, Frank Paul. *Le Christ romantique*. Geneva: Droz, 1973.

Bowman, Frank Paul. 'Illuminism, Utopia, Mythology', in D. G. Charlton (ed.), *The French Romantics*. 2 vols. Cambridge: Cambridge University Press, 1984, i. pp. 76–112.

Boyries, Pierre. *De plâtre, de marbre, ou de bronze, Napoléon: essai d'iconographie sculptée*. Tauriac: Burgus, 1998.

Boze, Volcy. *Pèlerinage à Ste Hélène en 1826*. Marseilles: Doucet, 1879.

Branda, Pierre. *Le prix de la gloire: Napoléon et l'argent*. Paris: Fayard, 2007.

Brazier, Nicolas. *Chansons nouvelles*. Paris: Rossignol, 1836.

Bresler, Fenton. *Napoleon III: A Life*. London: HarperCollins, 1999.

Bro, Louis. *Mémoires du général Bro (1796–1844)*. Paris: Plon-Nourrit, 1914.

Broglie, Victor de. *Souvenirs, 1785–1870, du feu duc de Broglie*. 4 vols. Paris: C. Lévy, 1886.

Brooke, Thomas H. *A History of the Island of St. Helena: From its Discovery by the Portuguese to the Year 1806*. London: Black, Parry and Kingsbury, 1808.

Broughton, John Cam Hobhouse, Lord. *Recollections of a Long Life. 1786–1834*. 4 vols. London: John Murray, 1909–10.

Brunyee, Paul F. *Napoleon's Britons and the St Helena Decision*. Stroud: The History Press, 2009.

Bruyère-Ostells, Walter. *La grande armée de la liberté*. Paris: Tallandier, 2009.

Buchinger, Kirstin. *Napoléomanie*. Berlin: Goldencalb Verlag, 2013.

Buchinger, Kirstin. '"La pierre et l'empereur": Remembering the Revolutionary and Napoleonic Wars in French Lithography', in Alan Forrest, Etienne François and Karen Hagemann (eds), *War Memories: The Revolutionary and Napoleonic Wars in Modern European Culture*. Basingstoke: Palgrave Macmillan, 2012, pp. 317–39.

Burke, Peter. *The Fabrication of Louis XIV*. New Haven: Yale University Press, 1992.

Burton, Richard D. E. *Blood in the City: Violence and Revelation in Paris: 1789–1945.* Ithaca, NY: Cornell University Press, 2001.

Burty, Philippe. 'Les desseins de Charlet pour le mémorial de Sainte-Hélène', *Gazette des Beaux-Arts*, 1 (1 March 1860): 275–82.

Bury, J. P. T. and Tombs, Robert. *Thiers: 1797–1877: A Political Life.* London: Allen & Unwin, 1986.

Bynum, W. F. *Science and the Practice of Medicine in the Nineteenth Century.* Cambridge: Cambridge University Press, 1994.

Cabet, Etienne. *Révolution de 1830.* Paris: Deville-Cavellin et Pagnerre, 1833.

Cahuet, Albéric. *Après la mort de l'Empereur.* Paris: Emile-Paul, 1913.

Cahuet, Albéric. *Napoléon délivré.* Paris: Emile-Paul, 1914.

Cahuet, Albéric. *Retours de Sainte-Hélène. 1821–1840.* Paris: Fasquelle, 1932.

Caillaux, Charles. *Arche de la Nouvelle-Alliance: prologue, par un apôtre évadien.* Paris: Desessarts, 1840.

Cameron, J. M. R. 'John Barrow, the *Quarterly*'s Imperial Reviewer', in Jonathan Cutmore (ed.), *Conservatism and the Quarterly Review: A Critical Analysis.* London: Pickering & Chatto, 2007, pp. 133–49.

Camp, Maxime du. *Souvenirs littéraires.* 2 vols. Paris: Hachette, 1906.

Capefigue, Baptiste. *L'Europe pendant le Consulat et l'Empire de Napoléon.* 10 vols. Paris: Pitois-Levrault, 1840.

Carné, Louis de. *Vues sur l'histoire contemporaine, ou Essai sur l'histoire de la Restauration.* 2 vols. Paris: Paulin, 1835.

Caron, Jean-Claude. *Générations romantiques: les étudiants de Paris et le Quartier latin, 1814–1851.* Paris: Armand Colin, 1991.

Caron, Jean-Claude. 'Louis-Philippe face à l'opinion publique, ou l'impossible réconciliation des Français, 1830–1835', *French Historical Studies*, 30:4 (Fall 2007): 597–621.

Carrion-Nisas, André-François-Victoire-Henri, marquis de. *Bonaparte et Napoléon, parallèle.* Paris: Bousquet, 1821.

Carrot, Georges. *La Garde nationale, 1789–1871: une force politique ambiguë.* Paris: l'Harmattan, 2001.

Casanova, Antoine. *Napoléon et la pensée de son temps: une histoire intellectuelle singulière.* Paris: Boutique de l'histoire, 2001.

Cassé de Saint-Prosper, Antoine-Jean. *Oraison funèbre de N. Buonaparte, où l'on trouve établi, d'après 'Le Moniteur', ce que les vertus du ci-devant empereur ont coûté d'hommes et d'argent à la France; suivi du testament dudit N. Buonaparte. Le tout recueilli par un conscrit jambe de bois.* Paris: N. Pichard, 1821.

Castellane, Esprit Victor Elisabeth Boniface, comte de. *Journal du maréchal de Castellane. 1804–1862.* 4 vols. Paris: E. Plon, Nourrit, 1895.

Caulaincourt, Armand Augustin Louis, marquis de, duc de Vicence. *Memoirs of General de Caulaincourt, Duke of Vicenza.* Ed. Jean Hanoteau. 3 vols. London: Cassell, 1950.

Chambure, Auguste de. *Napoléon et ses contemporains.* Paris: J. Renouard, 1828.

Chanteranne, David and Veyrat-Masson, Isabelle. *Napoléon à l'écran: cinéma et télévision.* Paris: Nouveau monde éd., 2003.

Chaplin, Arnold. *The Illness and Death of Napoleon Bonaparte.* London: Hirschfeld, 1913.

Chaplin, Arnold. *A St. Helena Who's Who: Or a Directory of the Island during the Captivity of Napoleon.* London: Published by the author, 1919.

Chaplin, Arnold. *Thomas Shortt, Principal Medical Officer in St. Helena.* London: Stanley Paul, 1914.

Chappell, Miles. *Form, Function, and Finesse: Drawings from the Frederick and Lucy S. Herman Foundation.* Williamsburg: Joseph and Margaret Muscarelle Museum of Art, 1983.

Charléty, Sébastien (ed.). *Lettres du duc de Richelieu au marquis d'Osmond, 1816–1818.* Paris: Gallimard, 1939.

Charléty, Sébastien. *La Monarchie de Juillet. 1830–1848.* Paris: Hachette, 1920.

Chateaubriand, François-René, vicomte de. *De Buonaparte, des Bourbons, et de la nécessité de se rallier à nos princes légitimes pour le bonheur de la France et celui de l'Europe.* Paris: n.p., 1814.

Chateaubriand, François-René, vicomte de. *Mémoires d'outre-tombe*, introduction and notes by Jean-Paul Clément. 2 vols. Paris: Flammarion, 1997.

Chateaubriand, François-René, vicomte de. *Vie de Napoléon.* Paris: Fallois, 1999.

Chaudonneret, Marie-Claude. 'Peinture et histoire dans les années, 1820–1830', in *L'histoire au musée: actes du colloque.* Arles: Actes Sud; Versailles: Château de Versailles, 2004, pp. 127–37.

Chéron, François. *Napoléon, ou le Corse dévoilé, ode aux Français.* Paris: Le Normant, 1814.

Chevallier, Bernard, Dancoisne-Martineau, Michel and Lentz, Thierry (eds). *Sainte-Hélène, île de mémoire.* Paris: Fayard, 2005.

Chollier, Antoine. *La vraie Route Napoléon.* Paris: Editions Alpina, 1950.

Clairville (pseudonym). *Quatorze ans de la vie de Napoléon, ou Berlin, Potsdam, Paris, Waterloo et Sainte-Hélène, pièce historique en 4 actes et en 7 tableaux*, presented at the Théâtre du Luxembourg on 23 November 1830. Paris: A. Barbier, 1830.

Claretie, Jules. *Brichanteau comédien*. Paris: E. Fasquelle, 1896.

Clément, Charles. *Géricault: étude biographique et critique*. Paris: Didier, 1868.

Clerc, Catherine. *La caricature contre Napoléon*. Paris: Promodis, 1985.

Clifton, James and Scattone, Leslie M. *The Plains of Mars: European War Prints, 1500–1825*. New Haven: Yale University Press, 2008.

Cockburn, George. *Extract from a Diary of Rear-Admiral Sir George Cockburn, with particular reference to General Napoleon Buonaparte, on the passage from England to Saint Helena in 1815*. London: Simpkin, Marshall, 1888.

Cohn, Fritz L. 'The Worship of Napoleon in German Poetry', *Modern Language Quarterly*, 1 (1940): 539–49.

Collins, Irene. *The Government and the Newspaper Press in France, 1814–1881*. London: Oxford University Press, 1959.

Confino, Alon. 'Collective Memory and Cultural History: Problems of Method', *American Historical Review*, 102 (1997): 1386–1403

Coquereau, Félix. *Souvenirs du voyage à Sainte-Hélène*. Paris: H.-L. Delloye, 1841.

Corbin, Alain. 'L'agitation dans les théâtres de province sous la Restauration', in Marc Bertrand (ed.), *Popular Traditions and Learned Culture in France: From the Sixteenth to the Twentieth Century*. Saratoga, Calif.: Anma libri, 1985, pp. 93–114.

Corbin, Alain. 'L'impossible présence du roi', in Alain Corbin, Noëlle Gérôme and Danielle Tartakowsky (eds), *Les usages politiques des fêtes aux XIXe–XXe siècles*. Paris: Publications de la Sorbonne, 1994, pp. 77–116.

Cordingly, David. *The Billy Ruffian: The Bellerophon and the Downfall of Napoleon: The Biography of a Ship of the Line, 1782–1836*. London: Bloomsbury, 2003.

Cornell, Kenneth, 'May 5, 1821 and the Poets', *Yale French Studies*, 26 (1960): 50–4.

Correspondance de Marie Louise, 1799–1847; lettres intimes et inédites à la comtesse de Colloredo et à Mlle de Poutet, depuis 1810 comtesse de Crenneville. Vienna: C. Gerold, 1887.

Corso, P. F. and Hindmarsh, T. 'Further Scientific Evidence of the Non-Poisonous Death of Napoleon', *Science Progress*, 79:2 (1996): 89–96.

Coston, François-Gilbert de. *Biographie des premières années de Napoléon Bonaparte, c'est-à-dire depuis sa naissance jusqu'à l'époque de son commandement en chef de l'armée d'Italie.* 2 vols. Paris and Valence: Marc Aurel frères, 1840.

Le coucher du soleil du 5 mai 1821, par M. P**A. Paris: passage Feydeau, 1821.

Couret, Emile. *Le pavillon des princes: histoire complète de la prison politique de Sainte-Pélagie depuis sa fondation jusqu'à nos jours.* Paris: Flammarion, 1895.

Courier, Paul-Louis. *Oeuvres completes.* 4 vols. Brussels: Librairie parisienne, 1828.

Cousso, J.-J. de. *Observations relatives au despotisme militaire exercé en France pendant la trop longue domination de Napoléon Buonaparte.* Paris: Ponthieu, 1821.

Cox Jensen, Oskar. *Napoleon and British Song, 1797–1822.* Basingstoke: Palgrave Macmillan, 2015.

Crapelet, Georges-Adrien. *Souvenirs de Londres en 1814 et 1816.* Paris: Crapelet, 1817.

Cresp, Joseph. *Eloge funèbre de Napoléon.* Paris: Lépagnez, 1840.

Cubitt, Geoffrey. *History and Memory.* Manchester: Manchester University Press, 2007.

Custine, Astolphe de. *Lettres inédites au marquis de La Grange.* Paris: les Presses françaises, 1925.

Cuvillier-Fleury, Alfred-Auguste. *Journal intime de Cuvillier-Fleury.* 2 vols. Paris: Plon-Nourrit, 1900–3.

Da Costa, J. A. 'Napoléon Ier au Brésil', *Revue du monde latin*, 8 (January–April 1886): 205–16, 339–49.

Dalisson, Rémi. *Les trois couleurs, Marianne et l'empereur: fêtes libérales et politiques symboliques en France, 1815–1870.* Paris: Boutique de l'histoire, 2004.

Datta, Venita. *Heroes and Legends of Fin-de-Siècle France: Gender, Politics, and National Identity.* Cambridge: Cambridge University Press, 2011.

Daudet, Ernest. *Conspirateurs et comédiennes, épisodes d'histoire d'après des documents inédits, 1796–1825.* Paris: F. Juven, 1902.

Daudet, Ernest (ed.). *Journal de Victor de Balabine, secrétaire de l'ambassade de Russie.* Paris: Emile-Paul, 1914.

Daudet, Ernest. *La police politique: chronique des temps de la Restauration, 1815–1820.* Paris: Plon-Nourrit, 1912.

Davey, James. *In Nelson's Wake: The Navy and the Napoleonic Wars.* New Haven: Yale University Press, 2016.

David, Saul. *The Prince of Pleasure: The Prince of Wales and the Making of the Regency.* London: Little, Brown, 1998.

Day-Hickman, Barbara Ann. *Napoleonic Art: Nationalism and the Spirit of Rebellion in France (1815–1848)*. Newark: University of Delaware Press, 1999.

Dayot, Armand. *Les Vernet: Joseph, Carle, Horace*. Paris: H. Laurens, 1898.

Dechamps, Jules. *Sur la légende de Napoléon*. Paris: Champion, 1931.

Degeorge, Frédéric. *Sentiment d'un citoyen sur les cancers héréditaires*. Paris: chez les marchands de nouveautés, 1821.

Déguignet, Jean-Marie. *Mémoires d'un paysan bas-breton*. Le Relecq-Kerhuon: Association de recherches historiques Arkae, 1998.

Delacroix, Christian, Dosse, François and Garcia, Patrick. *Les courants historiques en France: XIXe–XXe siècle*. Paris: Gallimard, 2007.

Delord, Taxile. *Histoire du second empire. 1848–1869*. Paris: G. Baillière, 1869.

Demartini, Anne-Emmanuelle. *L'affaire Lacenaire*. Paris: Aubier, 2001.

Demidov, Anatoliĭ Nicolaïevich. *Voyage dans la Russie méridionale et la Crimée, par la Hongrie, la Valachie et la Moldavie, exécuté en 1837*. Paris: Bourdin, 1840.

De profundis, par un invalide. Paris: chez les marchands de nouveautés, 1821.

A Description of the costly and curious military carriage of the late Emperor of France taken on the evening of the battle of Waterloo with its superb and curious contents. London: London Museum, 1818.

Description of the Field of Battle, and Disposition of the Troops Engaged in the Action, Fought on the 18th of June, 1815, near Waterloo; Illustrative of the Representation of That Great Event, in the Panorama, Leicester-Square. Quebec: L. Bedard, 1817.

Devriès, Anik. 'La "musique à bon marché" dans les années 1830', in Peter Bloom (ed.), *Music in Paris in the Eighteen-Thirties*. Stuyvesant, NY: Pendragon Press, 1987, pp. 229–50.

Dino, Dorothée, princesse de Courlande, duchesse de. *Chronique de 1831 à 1862*. 4 vols. Paris: Plon, 1909–10.

Dino, Dorothée, princesse de Courlande, duchesse de. *Mémoires* , 4 vols. Clermont-Ferrand: Paleo, 2004.

Dinwiddy, J. R. *Radicalism and Reform in Britain, 1780–1850*. London: Hambledon, 1992.

Doher, Marcel. *Proscrits et exilés après Waterloo*. Paris: Peyronnet, 1965.

Doris, Charles. *Chagrins domestiques de Napoléon Bonaparte à l'île Sainte-Hélène*. Paris: Mathiot, 1821.

Doris, Charles. *Précis historique sur Napoléon Buonaparte*. Paris: Mathiot, 1815.

Doris, Charles, de Bourges. *Amours secrètes de Napoléon Bonaparte; par l'auteur du 'Précis historique' et des 'Mémoires secrets'*. 2 vols. Paris: Mathiot, 1815.

Doris, Charles, de Bourges. *Mémoires secrets sur Napoléon Buonaparte, écrits par un homme qui ne l'a pas quitté depuis quinze ans*. Paris: Mathiot, 1815.

Driault, Edouard. *Napoléon architecte*. Paris: Presses universitaires de France, 1942.

Driskel, Michael. *As Befits a Legend: Building a Tomb for Napoleon, 1840–1861*. Kent, Ohio: Kent State University Press, 1993.

Driskel, Michael Paul. 'By Competition or Administrative Decree? The Contest for the Tomb of Napoleon in 1841', *Art Journal*, 48 (Spring 1989): 46–52.

Driskel, Michael. 'Eclecticism and Ideology in the July Monarchy', *Arts Magazine*, 56:9 (1982): 119–29.

Driskel, Michael Paul. 'The Proletarian's Body: Charlet's Representations of Social Class during the July Monarchy', in Petra ten-Doesschate Chu and Gabriel P. Weisberg. (eds), *The Popularization of Images: Visual Culture under the July Monarchy*. Princeton: Princeton University Press, 1994, pp. 58–89

Driskel, Michael. 'Singing "The Marseillaise" in 1840: The Case of Charlet's Censored Prints', *Art Bulletin*, 69 (1987): 603–24.

Du Boisgobey, Fortuné. *Du Rhin au Nil, carnet de voyage d'un Parisien*. Paris: E. Plon, 1880.

Duffin, Jacalyn. *Lovers and Livers: Disease Concepts in History*. Toronto: University of Toronto Press, 2005.

Duprat, Annie. 'Le roi a été chassé à Rambouillet', *Sociétés & Représentations*, 12:2 (2001): 30–43.

Dupuy, Ernest. *Alfred de Vigny: ses amitiés, son rôle littéraire. Les amities*. 2 vols. Paris: Société française d'imprimerie et de librairie, 1910.

Dupuy, Marie-Anne (ed.). *Dominique-Vivant Denon: l'oeil de Napoleon*. Paris: Réunion des musées nationaux, 1999.

Dupuy, Roger. *La Garde nationale, 1789–1872*. Paris: Gallimard, 2010.

Durozoy, Anne-Sophie. 'Zu den französischen Quellen der Napoleon-Legende', in Marion George and Andrea Rudolph (eds), *Napoleons langer Schatten über Europa*. Dettelbach: Röll, 2008.

Dwyer, Philip. *Citizen Emperor: Napoleon in Power, 1799–1815*. London: Bloomsbury, 2013.

Dwyer, Philip. ' "Making Sense of the Muddle": War and the Culture of Remembering', in Philip Dwyer (ed.), *War Stories: The War Memoir in History and Literature*. New York: Berghahn, 2016, pp. 1–26.

Dwyer, Philip. 'Napoleon and the Universal Monarchy', *History*, 95:319 (2010): 293–307.

Dwyer, Philip. *Napoleon: The Path to Power*. London: Bloomsbury, 2007.

Dwyer, Philip. 'Public Remembering, Private Reminiscing: French Military Memoirs and the Revolutionary and Napoleonic Wars', *French Historical Studies*, 33 (2010): 321–58.

Eastlake, Charles Lock. *Contributions to the Literature of the Fine Arts. Second Series*. London: John Murray, 1870.

Edgcumbe, Richard (ed.). *The Diary of Frances Lady Shelley*. 2 vols. London: John Murray, 1913.

Edmundson, William. *A History of the British Presence in Chile: From Bloody Mary to Charles Darwin and the Decline of British Influence*. New York: Palgrave Macmillan, 2009.

Ellis, Geoffrey. *Napoleon*. London: Longman, 1997.

L'éloge des éloges, ou encore du Bonaparte. Paris: librairie grecque-latine-française, 1821.

Engel, Corinna. *Napoleons Grab Im Invalidendom*. Frankfurt am Main: Engel, 2007.

Englund, Steven. 'Napoleon and Hitler', *Journal of the Historical Society*, 6 (2006): 151–69.

Esquiros, Henri-François-Alphonse. *Paris, ou Les sciences, les institutions et les moeurs au XIXe siècle*. 2 vols. Paris: au Comptoir des imprimeurs-unis, 1847.

Etex, Antoine. *Les souvenirs d'un artiste*. Paris: E. Dentu, 1877.

'An Extract from a Journal Kept on Board H.M.S. Bellerophon, by Captain John Bowerbank, R.N.', in Clement Shorter (ed.), *Napoleon and his Fellow Travellers*. London: Cassell, 1908, pp. 303–23.

'Facts Illustrative of the Treatment of Napoleon Buonaparte in St Helena', *The Edinburgh Review, or Critical Journal*, 32 (July–October 1819): 148–70.

Fadeville, Théodore. *Aperçu critique sur Napoléon et sur les hommes de son époque*. Paris: l'auteur, 1840.

Fantin des Odoards, Louis-Florimond. *Journal du général Fantin des Odoards, étapes d'un officier de la Grande Armée, 1800–1830*. Paris: E. Plon, Nourrit, 1895.

Faure, Elie. *Napoléon*. Paris: Denoël-Gonthier, 1983.

Féret, Romuald. 'Le théâtre de province au XIXe siècle: entre révolutions et conservatisme', *Annales historiques de la Révolution française*, 367 (2012): 119–43.

Firmon-Didot, Georges. *La captivité de Sainte-Hélène, d'après les rapports inédits du marquis de Montchenu*. Paris: Firmin-Didot, 1894.

Fleckner, Uwe. 'Le retour des cendres de Napoléon. Vergängliche Denkmäler zur Domestizierung einer Legende', in Michael Diers (ed.), *Mo(nu)mente. Formen und Funktionen ephemerer Denkmäler.* Berlin: Akademieverlag, 1993, pp. 61–76.

Fleischman, Théo. 'Popularité de Napoléon en Angleterre', *Bulletin de la Société belge d'études napoléoniennes*, 54 (March 1966): 5–11.

Forrest, Alan. *Waterloo*. Oxford: Oxford University Press, 2015.

Forshufvud, Sten. *Napoléon a-t-il été empoisonné?* Paris: Plon, 1961.

Forshufvud, Sten. *Who Killed Napoleon?* Trans. A. H. Broderick. London: Hutchinson, 1962.

Forshufvud, Sten and Weider, Ben. *Assassination at St. Helena: The Poisoning of Napoleon Bonaparte*. Vancouver: Mitchell Press, 1978.

Forshufvud, Sten and Weider, Ben. *Assassination at St. Helena Revisited*. New York: Wiley, 1995.

Forsyth, William. *History of the Captivity of Napoleon at St. Helena*. 3 vols. London: John Murray, 1853.

Fortescue, William. *France and 1848: The End of Monarchy*. London: Routledge, 2005.

Fournier La Touraille, Jean-Pierre. *Hudson Lowe, le geôlier de Napoléon*. Paris: Perrin, 2006.

Foy, Maximilien-Sébastien. *Notes journalières du général Foy: 1820–1825*. 3 vols. Compiègne: Impr. de Compiègne, 1925.

François, Charles. *Journal du capitaine François: dit le Dromadaire d'Egypte, 1792–1830*. Paris: Tallandier, 2003.

Frederking, Bettina. ' "Les funérailles de la monarchie" ou "l'impossible oubli"', in Natalie Scholz and Christina Schröe (eds), *Représentation et pouvoir: la politique symbolique en France, 1789–1830*. Rennes: Presses universitaires de Rennes, 2007, pp. 213–33.

Frederking, Bettina, ' "Il ne faut pas être le roi de deux peuples": Strategies of National Reconciliation in Restoration France', *French History*, 22:4 (2008): 446–68.

Fritzsche, Peter. *Stranded in the Present: Modern Time and the Melancholy of History*. Cambridge, Mass.: Harvard University Press, 2004.

Fryer, John. *A New Account of East India and Persia: Being Nine Years' Travels, 1672–1681*. Ed. with notes and an introduction by William Crooke. 3 vols. London: Chiswell, 1915.

Fureix, Emmanuel. 'La construction rituelle de la souveraineté populaire: deuils protestataires (Paris, 1815–1840)', *Revue d'histoire du XIXe siècle*, 42 (2011): 21–39.

Fureix, Emmanuel. 'De l'hommage funèbre à la prise de parole: l'enterrement du général Foy (novembre 1825)', *Sociétés & Représentations*, 12:2 (2001): 176–203.

Fureix, Emmanuel. *La France des larmes: deuils politiques à l'âge romantique, 1814–1840*. Seyssel: Champ Vallon, 2009.

Fureix, Emmanuel. 'L'iconoclasme: une pratique politique? (1814–1848)', in Laurent Le Gall, Michel Offerlé and François Ploux (eds), *La politique sans en avoir l'air: aspects de la politique informelle, XIXe–XXIe siècle*. Rennes: Presses universitaires de Rennes, 2012, pp. 117–32.

Fureix, Emmanuel. 'La mort de Napoléon: images et cristallisations de l'événement (1821–1831)', in Christian Delporte and Annie Duprat (eds), *L'événement: images, représentation, mémoire*. Paris: Créaphis, 2003, pp. 159–77.

Fureix, Emmanuelle. 'République et républicains sous les monarchies censitaires (1814–1848)', in Vincent Duclert and Christophe Prochasson (eds), *Dictionnaire critique de la République*. Paris: Flammarion, 2007, pp. 1306–13.

Fureix, Emmanuel. 'Sensibilité et politique: l'exemple du culte des mort à l'âge romantique', in Anne-Emmanuelle Demartini and Dominique Kalifa (eds), *Imaginaire et sensibilités au XIXe siècle: études pour Alain Corbin*. Paris: Créaphis, 2005, pp. 137–46.

Fureix, Emmanuel. 'La violence et la mort: funérailles opposantes sous les monarchies censitaires (Paris, 1820–1830)', in Philippe Bourdin, Jean-Claude Caron and Mathias Bernard (eds), *La voix et le geste: une approche culturelle de la violence socio-politique*. Paris: Presses universitaires Blaise Pascal, 2005, pp. 115–32.

Gaehtgens, Thomas W. *Versailles als Nationaldenkmal. Die Gallerie des Batailles im Musée Historique von Louis-Philippe*. Berlin: Fonds Mercator, 1985; also as *Versailles: de la résidence royale au musée historique: la galerie des batailles dans le musée historique de Louis-Philippe*. Trans. Patrick Poirot. Paris: A. Michel, 1984.

Gaigneron, Axelle de. 'La stratégie de Louis-Philippe à Versailles', *Connaissance des arts*, 272 (October 1974): 74–81.

Gaillard, commissaire de police de la librairie. *Catalogue des écrits, gravures et dessins condamnés depuis 1814 jusqu'au 1er janvier 1850: suivi de la liste des individus condamnés pour délits de presse*. Paris: Pillet fils aîné, 1850.

Gallois, Léonard-Charles-André-Gustave. *Eloge funèbre de Napoléon, prononcé sur sa tombe, le 9 mai 1821, par le grand maréchal Bertrand*. Paris: les marchands de nouveautés, n.d.

Gallois, Léonard-Charles-André-Gustave. *Histoire de Napoléon d'après lui-même*. Paris: J.-M. Boursy, 1825.

Ganière, Paul. *Corvisart, médecin de l'Empereur*. Paris: Perrin, 1985.

Ganière, Paul. *Napoléon à Sainte-Hélène*. Paris: Perrin, 1998.

Garsou, Jules. *Béranger et la légende napoléonienne.* Brussels: P. Weissenbruch, 1897.

Garsou, Jules. *Les créateurs de la légende napoléonienne: Barthélemy et Méry.* Paris, 1899.

Gash, Norman. *Lord Liverpool: The Life and Political Career of Robert Banks Jenkinson, Second Earl of Liverpool, 1770–1828.* London: Weidenfeld & Nicolson, 1984.

Gaubert, Jean-Pierre. *Las Cases: l'abeille de Napoléon.* Portet-sur-Garonne: Loubatières, 2003.

Gedi, Noa and Elam, Yigal. 'Collective Memory: What is it?', *History and Memory*, 8 (1996): 3–50.

Gengembre, Gérard. *Napoléon: l'empereur immortel.* Paris: Ed. du Chêne, 2002.

George, Marion and Rudolph, Andrea (eds). *Napoleons langer Schatten über Europa.* Dettelbach: Röll, 2008.

Georgel, Chantal. 'Panorama de l'événement', in Jean-Marcel Humbert (ed.), *Napoléon aux Invalides: 1840, le retour des cendres.* Paris: Musée de l'armée, Fondation Napoléon, 1991, pp. 109–19.

Ghosh, Anjan. 'The Role of Rumour in History Writing', *History Compass*, 6:5 (2008): 1235–43.

Gildea, Robert. *Children of the Revolution: The French, 1799–1914.* London: Allen Lane, 2008.

Gildea, Robert. *The Past in French History.* New Haven: Yale University Press, 1994.

Giles, Frank. *Napoleon Bonaparte: England's Prisoner.* New York: Carroll & Graf, 2001.

Gill, Crispin. 'Some Diaries and Memoirs of Plymouth in the French Revolutionary and Napoleonic Wars', *Report and Transactions. The Devonshire Association for the Advancement of Science, Literature and Art*, 115 (1983): 1–17.

Giloi, Eva. *Monarchy, Myth, and Material Culture in Germany, 1750–1950.* Cambridge: Cambridge University Press, 2011.

Girard, Louis. *Napoleon III.* Paris: Fayard, 1986.

Gisquet, Henri. *Mémoires de M. Gisquet, ancien préfet de police.* 4 vols. Paris: Marchant, 1840.

Glikman, Juliette. *Louis-Napoléon prisonnier: du fort de Ham aux ors des Tuileries.* Paris: Aubier, 2011.

Glover, Gareth (ed.). *Wellington's Lieutenant, Napoleon's Gaoler: The Peninsula and St Helena Diaries and Letters of Sir George Ridout Bingham, 1809–21.* Barnsley: Pen & Sword, 2005.

Godin, A.-L.-J. *Histoire de Buonaparte, depuis sa naissance jusqu'à ce jour.* 2 vols. Paris: Ménard et Desenne, 1816.

Goffart, Walter. *Historical Atlases: The First Three Hundred Years, 1570–1870.* Chicago: University of Chicago Press, 2003.

Goldcher, Alain. *Napoléon Ier: l'ultime autopsie.* Paris: SPM, 2012.

Goldcher, Alain. 'Napoléon Ier: l'ultime autopsie', *Revue de l'Institut Napoléon*, 202–3 (2011): 115–36.

Goldsmith, Lewis. *Histoire secrète du cabinet de Napoléon Buonaparté, et de la cour de Saint-Cloud.* London: T. Harper, 1814.

Goldstein, Robert. *Censorship of Political Caricature in Nineteenth-Century France.* Kent, Ohio: Kent State University Press, 1989.

Goldstein, Robert Justin. 'France', in Robert Justin Goldstein (ed.), *The Frightful Stage: Political Censorship of the Theater in Nineteenth-Century Europe.* New York: Berghahn, 2009, pp. 70–129.

Gonnard, Philippe. 'La légende napoléonienne dans la press libérale', *Revue des études napoléoniennes*, 1 (March 1912): 235–58.

Gonnard, Philippe. 'La légende napoléonienne dans la press libérale: *La Minerve*', *Revue des études napoléoniennes*, 3 (1914): 28–49.

Gonnard, Philippe (ed.). *Lettres du comte et de la comtesse de Montholon, 1819–1821.* Paris: A. Picard, 1906).

Gonnard, Philippe. *Les origines de la légende napoléonienne: l'oeuvre historique de Napoléon à Sainte-Hélène.* Paris: C. Lévy, 1906.

Gosse, Philip. *St. Helena, 1502–1938.* London: Cassell, 1938.

Goujon, Alexandre. *Pensée d'un soldat sur la sépulture de Napoléon.* Paris: les marchands de nouveautés, 1821.

Goujon, Bertrand. *Monarchies postrévolutionnaires, 1814–1848.* Paris: Seuil, 2012.

Gourgaud, Gaspard. *Journal de Sainte-Hélène: 1815–1818.* Introduction and notes by Octave Aubry. 2 vols. Paris: Flammarion, 1944.

Gourgaud, Gaspard. *Mémoires pour servir à l'histoire de France, sous Napoléon, écrits à Sainte-Hélène par les généraux qui ont partagé sa captivité, et publiés sur les manuscrits entièrement corrigés de Napoléon.* 2 vols. Paris: Firmin-Didot, 1823.

Gourgaud, General. *Le retour des cendres de l'empereur Napoléon.* Paris: Arléa, 2003.

Grand-Carteret, John. 'La légende napoléonienne par l'image, vue sous un jour nouveau', *Revue des études napoléoniennes*, 20 (1923): 28–46.

Gray, Richard T. *About Face: German Physiognomic Thought from Lavater to Auschwitz.* Detroit: Wayne State University Press, 2004.

Gregory, Desmond. *Napoleon's Jailer: Lt. Gen. Sir Hudson Lowe: A Life.* Madison: Fairleigh Dickinson University Press, 1996.

Greppe, Pascal. 'L'empereur est mort: propos du colonel Perraton', *Revue des études napoléoniennes*, 32 (1932): 277–97.

Grigsby, Darcy Grimaldo. *Extremities: Painting Empire in Post-Revolutionary France*. New Haven: Yale University Press, 2002.

Grove, Richard H. *Green Imperialism: Colonial Expansion, Tropical Island Edens, and the Origins of Environmentalism, 1600–1860*. Cambridge: Cambridge University Press, 1996.

Grunberg, Gérard. *Napoléon Bonaparte: le noir génie*. Paris: CNRS Editions, 2015.

Guérard, Albert Léon. *Reflections on the Napoleonic Legend*. London: T. F. Unwin, 1924.

Guernon-Ranville, Martial Côme Annibal Perpétue Magloire de. *Journal d'un ministre*. Caen: F. Le Blanc-Hardel, 1874.

Guillet, Claude. *La rumeur de Dieu: apparitions, prophéties et miracles sous la Restauration*. Paris: Ed. Imago, 1994.

Guillon, Edouard. *Les complots militaires sous la restauration*. Paris: E. Plon, Nourrit, 1895.

Guiral, Pierre. *Thiers*. Paris: Fayard, 1986.

Guizot, François. *Mémoires pour servir à l'histoire de mon temps*. 8 vols. Paris: Michel-Lévy, 1858–67.

Hachette, Alfred. 'Le dossier de la journée du retour des cendres', *Revue des études napoléoniennes*, 24 (1925): 239–80.

Hafera, Alison. 'Visual Mediations of Mourning and Melancholia in France, 1790–1830'. PhD dissertation, University of North Carolina at Chapel Hill, 2015.

Halbwachs, Maurice. *On Collective Memory*. Trans. Lewis A. Coser. Chicago: University of Chicago Press, 1992.

Hamnett, Brian. 'Fictitious Histories: The Dilemma of Fact and Fiction in the Nineteenth Century Historical Novel', *European History Quarterly*, 36:1 (2006): 31–60.

Hargrove, June. *The Statues of Paris: An Open Air Pantheon*. New York: Vendome Press, 1989.

Harkett, Daniel and Hornstein, Katie (eds). *Horace Vernet and the Thresholds of Nineteenth-Century Visual Culture*. Hanover, NH: Dartmouth College Press, 2017.

Hartley, Lucy. *Physiognomy and the Meaning of Expression in Nineteenth-Century Culture*. Cambridge: Cambridge University Press, 2001.

Harvey, Robert. *Cochrane: The Life and Exploits of a Fighting Captain*. London: Constable, 2000.

Hatin, Eugène. *Bibliographie historique et critique de la presse périodique française*. Paris: Firmin-Didot, 1866.

Hattendorff, Claudia. *Napoleon I. und die Bilder. System und Umriss bildgewordener Politik und politischen Bildgebrauchs.* Petersberg: Michael Imhof, 2012.

Hautpoul, Alphonse de. *Mémoires du général marquis Alphonse d'Hautpoul, pair de France, 1789–1865.* Paris: Perrin, 1906.

Haydon, Benjamin Robert. *Correspondence and Table-Talk.* 2 vols. London: Chatto & Windus, 1876.

Hazareesingh, Sudhir. *The Legend of Napoleon.* London: Granta, 2004.

Hazareesingh, Sudhir. 'Memory and Political Imagination: The Legend of Napoleon Revisited', *French History*, 18 (2004): 463–83.

Hazareesingh, Sudhir, 'Napoleonic Memory in Nineteenth-Century France: The Making of a Liberal Legend', *MLN*, 120:4 (2005): 747–73.

Hazareesingh, Sudhir. *The Saint-Napoleon: Celebrations of Sovereignty in Nineteenth-Century France.* Cambridge, Mass.: Harvard University Press, 2004.

Hazareesingh, Sudhir and Nablusi, Karma. 'Entre Robespierre et Napoléon: les paradoxes de la mémoire républicaine sous la monarchie de juillet', *Annales. Histoire, Sciences Sociales,* 65:5 (2010): 1225–47.

Heine, Heinrich. *De la France.* Paris: Michel Lévy, 1857.

Heine, Heinrich, *Lutèce: Lettres sur la vie politique, artistique et sociale de la France.* Paris: M. Lévy, 1855.

Heine, Heinrich. *Reisebilder. Tableaux de voyage.* 2 vols. Paris: M. Lévy frères, 1856.

Heine, Heinrich. *The Works of Heinrich Heine.* Trans. Charles Godfrey Leland. 12 vols. London: Heinemann, 1891–1905.

Heine, Heinrich. *Deutschland. A Winter's Tale.* Trans. T. J. Reed. London: Angel Books, 1986.

Hemmings, F. W. J. *Culture and Society in France, 1789–1848.* Leicester: Leicester University Press, 1987.

Hemmings, F. W. J. *Theatre and State in France, 1760–1905.* Cambridge: Cambridge University Press, 1994.

Hemmings, F. W. J. *The Theatre Industry in Nineteenth-Century France.* Cambridge: Cambridge University Press, 1993.

Henry, Walter. *Events of a Military Life.* 2 vols. London: Chatto & Windus, 1843.

Henry, Walter. *Trifles from my Portfolio; or, Recollections of adventures during twenty-nine years' military service in the Peninsular war and invasion of France, the East Indies, etc.* 2 vols. Quebec: W. Neilson, 1839.

Héreau, J. *Napoléon à Sainte-Hélène: opinion d'un médecin sur la maladie de l'Empereur Napoléon et sur la cause de sa mort; offerte à son fils au jour de sa majorité.* Paris: F. Louis, 1829.

Hérisson, Maurice d'Irisson, comte de. *Le cabinet noir: Louis XVII–Napoléon–Marie-Louise*. Paris: P. Ollendorff, 1887.

Hérisson, Maurice d'Irisson, comte de. *Les girouettes politiques: un pair de France policier: 1815–1822*. Paris: P. Ollendorff, 1894.

Herscher, Walter R. 'Evoking the Eagle: The July Monarchy's Use of Napoleonic Imagery'. PhD dissertation, Marquette University, 1992.

Hicks, Peter. 'Who was Barry O'Meara?', *Napoleonica. La Revue*, 17 (2013): 75–94.

Higonnet, Patrick-Bernard. 'La Composition de la Chambre des Députés de 1827 à 1831', *Revue historique*, 239 (1968): 351–78.

Histoire amoureuse de Napoléon Bonaparte, extraite des mémoires particuliers composés par lui-même pendant son séjour à l'île d'Elbe, et continuée jusqu'au 14 juillet 1815. Par un ancien officier de sa maison, qui ne l'a quitté qu'au moment de monter sur le Northumberland. 2 vols. Paris: Le Dentu, 1815.

Histoire de Napoléon Buonaparte, depuis sa naissance, en 1769, jusqu'à sa translation à l'île Sainte-Hélène, en 1815; par une société de gens de lettres. 4 vols. Paris: L.-G. Michaud, 1817–18.

Histoire secrète des amours de la famille N. Bonaparte. Paris: Davi et Locard, 1815.

Holland, Henry Edward Lord (ed.). *Foreign Reminiscences*. Paris: Longman, Brown, Green & Longmans, 1854.

Holzhausen, Paul. *Napoleons Tod im Spiegel der zeitgenössischen Presse und Dichtung*. Frankfurt am Main: M. Diesterweg, 1902.

Home, George. *Memoirs of an Aristocrat and Reminiscences of the Emperor Napoleon, by a midshipman of the 'Bellerophon'*. London: Whittaker, 1838.

L'homme au petit chapeau. Paris: chez tous les marchands de nouveautés, 1821.

Hook, Thomas. *Facts Illustrative of the Treatment of Napoleon Bonaparte*. London: n.p., 1819; translated into French as *Carnet d'un voyageur ou recueil de notes curieuses sur la vie, les occupations, les habitudes de Buonaparte à Longwood*. Paris: Pillet aîné, 1819.

Hopkin, David M. '*La Ramée*, the Archetypal Soldier, as an Indicator of Popular Attitudes to the Army in Nineteenth-Century France', *French History*, 14 (2000): 115–49.

Hopkin, David M. *Soldier and Peasant in French Popular Culture, 1766–1870*. Woodbridge: Boydell Press, 2002.

Horace Vernet: 1789–1863. Paris: Ecole des beaux-arts, 1980.

Horne, Richard Henry. *The History of Napoleon*. 3 vols. London: R. Tyas, 1841.

Hornn, Jean. *The Narrative of Jean Hornn, Military Coachman to Napoleon Bonaparte*. London: Ken Trotman, 1816.

Hornstein, Katie. 'Episodes in Political Illusion: The Proliferation of War Imagery in France. 1804–1856'. PhD dissertation, University of Michigan, 2010.

House, Jonathan M. *Controlling Paris: Armed Forces and Counter-Revolution, 1789–1848*. New York: New York University Press, 2014.

Houssaye, Henry. *1815: la première Restauration, le retour de l'île d'Elbe, les Cent Jours*. Paris: Perrin, 1896.

Howard, Martin. *Napoleon's Poisoned Chalice: The Emperor and his Doctors on St Helena*. Stroud: History, 2009.

Huart, Suzanne d'. 'Le dernier préfet de police de Charles X, Claude Mangin', in *Actes du quatre-vingt quatrieme Congrès national des Sociétés savantes, Dijon, 1959*. Paris: Impr. nationale, 1960, pp. 603–16

Hugo, Victor. *Les Misérables*, 2 vols. Paris: Gallimard, 1951.

Hugo, Victor. *Oeuvres inédites de Victor Hugo*, 10 vols. Paris: J. Hetzel, 1886–93.

Humbert, Jean-Marcel. 'Avant-propos', in Jean-Marcel Humbert (ed.), *Napoléon aux Invalides: 1840, le retour des cendres*. Paris: Musée de l'armée, Fondation Napoléon, 1991, pp. 11–17.

Humbert, Jean-Marcel (ed.). *Napoléon aux Invalides: 1840, le retour des cendres*. Paris: Musée de l'armée, Fondation Napoléon, 1991.

Hus, Auguste. *Paris: le 1er septembre 1822: la Colonne de la place Vendôme bourbonisée, suivie de quelques pensées sur l'éloquent ouvrage de M. de Châteaubriant*. Paris, n.d. 1822.

Hutton, Patrick. *History as an Art of Memory*. Hanover: University of Vermont, 1993.

Huyghues des Etages, Marie-Françoise. 'L'expédition maritime et fluviale', in Jean-Marcel Humbert (ed.), *Napoléon aux Invalides: 1840, le retour des cendres*. Paris: Musée de l'armée, Fondation Napoléon, 1991, pp. 19–45.

Hyde de Neuville, Jean-Guillaume. *Mémoires et souvenirs du baron Hyde de Neuville*. 3 vols. Paris: E. Plon, Nourrit, 1888–92.

Imbert, Henri-François, 'Evolution et fonction du mythe napoléonien sous la Restauration', *Rivista italiana di studi napoleonici*, 18:1 (1981): 9–22.

Inglis, Fred. *A Short History of Celebrity*. Princeton: Princeton University Press, 2010.

Irwin-Zarecka, Iwona. *Frames of Remembrance: The Dynamics of Collective Memory*. New Brunswick: Transaction, 1994.

Isola, Maria dell'. 'La mort de Napoléon', *Revue des études napoléoniennes*, 36 (1933): 280–4.

Isola, Maria dell'. *Napoléon dans la poésie italienne à partir de 1821*. Paris: J. Camber, 1927.

Issartel, Thierry. 'Les projets pour le tombeau de Napoléon', in Jean-Marcel Humbert (ed.), *Napoléon aux Invalides: 1840, le retour des cendres*. Paris: Musée de l'armée, Fondation Napoléon, 1991, pp. 121–45.

Jackson, Basil. *Notes and Reminiscences of a Staff Officer, Chiefly Relating to the Waterloo Campaign and to St. Helena Matters during the Captivity of Napoleon*. London: John Murray, 1903.

Janisch, Hudson Ralph. *Extracts from the St. Helena Records*. St Helena: Benjamin Grant, 1908.

Jarrett, Mark. *The Congress of Vienna and its Legacy: War and Great Power Diplomacy after Napoleon*. London: I. B. Tauris, 2013.

Jenks, Timothy. 'Contesting the Hero: The Funeral of Admiral Lord Nelson', *Journal of British Studies*, 39:4 (2000): 422–53.

Johns, Christopher M. S. *Antonio Canova and the Politics of Patronage in Revolutionary and Napoleonic Europe*. Berkeley: University of California Press, 1998.

Johnston, Otto W. *The Myth of a Nation: Literature and Politics in Prussia under Napoleon*. Columbia, SC: Camden House, 1989.

Joinville, François Ferdinand Philippe d'Orléans, prince de. *Vieux souvenirs: 1818–1848*. Paris: C. Lévy, 1894.

Jones, R. Ben. *Napoleon: Man and Myth*. London: Hodder & Stoughton, 1977.

Jordan, David P. *Napoleon and the Revolution*. Basingstoke: Palgrave Macmillan, 2012.

Jorga, N. 'Un témoin roumain de la translation des Cendres de Napoléon', *Revue des études napoléoniennes*, 2 (1912): 129–31.

Jouhaud, Auguste. *Les cendres de Napoléon, ou le retour en France*. Paris: L.-A. Gallet, 1841.

Jouin, Henry. *David d'Angers, sa vie, son oeuvre, ses écrits et ses contemporains*. 2 vols. Paris: 1878.

Jouin, Henry. *Histoire et description de la Colonne de Juillet*. Paris: E. Plon, Nourrit, 1879.

Jourdan, Annie. *L'empire de Napoléon*. Paris: Flammarion, 2000.

Jourdan, Annie. 'Napoleon and History', *French History*, 10:3 (1996): 334–54.

Jourquin, Jacques. 'La bibliothèque de Sainte-Hélène', in Bernard Chevallier, Michel Dancoisne-Martineau and Thierry Lentz (eds), *Sainte-Hélène, île de mémoire*. Paris: Fayard, 2005, pp. 121–5.

Karr, Alphonse. *Le livre de bord, souvenirs, portraits, notes au crayon*, 4 vols. Paris: C. Lévy, 1879–1880.

Kauffmann, Jean-Paul. *The Black Room at Longwood: Napoleon's Exile on Saint Helena*. New York, NY: Four Walls Eight Windows, 1999.

Keay, Anna. *The Magnificent Monarch: Charles II and the Ceremonies of Power*. London: Continuum, 2008.

Kelly, Linda. *Holland House: A History of London's Most Celebrated Salon*. London: I. B. Tauris, 2013.

Kemble, James. *Napoleon Immortal: The Medical History and Private Life of Napoleon Bonaparte*. London: John Murray, 1959.

Kemble, James (ed.). *St. Helena during Napoleon's Exile: Gorrequer's Diary*. London: Heinemann, 1969.

Kielmannsegge, Charlotte von Schönberg, comtesse von. *Mémoires de la comtesse de Kielmannsegge sur Napoléon Ier*. Trans. Joseph Delage. 2 vols. Paris and Neuchâtel: Victor Attinger, 1928.

Klein, Walther. *Der Napoleonkult in der Pfalz*. Munich: C. H. Beck, 1934.

Knowles, Sir Lees (ed.). *Letters of Captain Engelbert Lutyens, Orderly Officer at Longwood, Saint Helena: Feb. 1820 to Nov. 1823*. London: John Lane, 1915.

Korngold, Ralph. *The Last Years of Napoleon: His Captivity on St. Helena*. London: Victor Gollancz, 1960.

Krakovitch, Odile. 'Le théâtre sous la Restauration et la monarchie de Juillet: lecture et spectacle', in Alain Vaillant (ed.), *Mesure(s) du livre: colloque organisé par la Bibliothèque nationale et la Société des études romantiques*. Paris: Bibliothèque nationale, 1992, pp. 147–64.

Kramer, Lloyd S. *Threshold of a New World: Intellectuals and the Exile Experience in Paris: 1830–1848*. Ithaca, NY: Cornell University Press, 1988.

Kroen, Sheryl. *Politics and Theatre: The Crisis of Legitimacy in Restoration France, 1815–1830*. Berkeley: University of California Press, 2000.

Kselman, Thomas A. *Death and Afterlife in Modern France*. Princeton: Princeton University Press, 1993.

Kudlick, Catherine J. *Cholera in Post-Revolutionary Paris: A Cultural History*. Berkeley: University of California Press, 1996.

Laborde, Etienne. *Napoléon et sa garde, ou Relation du voyage de Fontainebleau à l'île d'Elbe en 1814, du séjour de l'Empereur dans cette île et de son retour en France*. Paris: A. Desrez, 1840.

Lacour-Gayet, Georges. *Talleyrand: 1754–1838*. 5 vols. Paris: Payot, 1928–34.

Ladner, Janet. 'Napoleon's Repatriation – Why 1840?', in *Selected Papers: The Consortium on Revolutionary Europe, 1750–1850*. Tallahassee, Fla.: Institute on Napoleon and the French Revolution, 1995, pp. 489–50.

Laferrière, Adolphe. *Mémoires de Laferrière*. Paris: E. Dentu, 1876.

Lamartine, Alphonse de. *Discours de M. de Lamartine, sur la loi relative aux restes mortels de Napoléon.* Paris: Béthune et Plon, n.d.

Lamartine, Valentine de (ed.). *Correspondance de Lamartine.* 5 vols. Paris: Hachette, Furne, Jouvet, 1873–4.

Langlé, Ferdinand. *Funérailles de l'empereur Napoléon, relation officielle de la translation de ses restes.* Paris: L. Curmer, 1840.

Lansdowne, Henry Petty-Fitzmaurice, Marquess of (ed.). *The First Napoleon: Some Unpublished Documents from the Bowood Papers.* London: Constable, 1925.

Laqueur, Thomas W. 'Bodies, Details, and the Humanitarian Narrative', in Lynn Hunt (ed.). *The New Cultural History.* Berkeley: University of California Press, 1989, pp. 176–204.

Larkin, T. Lawrence. 'Louis XVIII's Cult[ural] Politics, 1815–1820', *Aurora*, 5 (2004): 28–55.

Las Cases, Emmanuel. *Journal écrit à bord de la frégate la Belle-Poule.* Paris: H.-L. Delloye, 1841.

Las Cases, Emmanuel, comte de. *Le Mémorial de Sainte-Hélène.* Ed. and annotated by André Fugier. 2 vols. Paris: Flammarion, 1961.

Las Cases, Emmanuel, comte de. *Le Mémorial de Sainte-Hélène.* Ed. and annotated by Marcel Dunan. 2 vols. Paris: Flammarion, 1983.

Laumann, E. M. *L'épopée napoléonienne. Le retour des cendres.* Paris: H. Daragon, 1904.

Laurent, Alain. *Histoire de l'individualisme.* Paris: Presses universitaires de France, 1993.

Laurent de L'Ardèche, Paul-Mathieu. *Histoire de l'empereur Napoléon.* Illustrated by Horace Vernet. Paris: Dubochet, 1839.

La Valette, Antoine-Marie Chamans. *Mémoires et souvenirs du comte Lavallette, aide-de-camp du général Bonaparte.* Paris: H. Fournier, 1831.

Lebey, André. 'Le Messianisme napoléonien depuis 1815 jusqu'en 1848', *Le Censeur politique et littéraire*, 11 January 1908, pp. 33–40.

Lecomte, J.-L.-M. *Napoléon!! De l'oeuvre sainte qui va mettre à sa place si grande chose!* Paris: l'auteur, 1840.

Le Gall, Didier. *Napoléon et Le mémorial de Sainte-Hélène.* Paris: Ed. Kimé, 2003.

Le Gall, Laurent, Offerlé, Michel and Ploux, François (eds). *La politique sans en avoir l'air: aspects de la politique informelle, XIXe–XXIe siècle.* Rennes: Presses universitaires de Rennes, 2012.

Legouvé, Ernest. *Dernier travail, derniers souvenirs: école normale de Sèvres.* Paris: J. Hetzel, 1898.

Lemaire, Jean. *Le testament de Napoleon: un étonnant destin.* Paris: Plon, 1957.

Lemaire, Jean-François, Fornès, Paul, Kintz, Pascal and Lentz, Thierry. *Autour de 'l'empoisonnement' de Napoléon*. Paris: Nouveau monde éd., 2001.

Lenôtre, G. *Napoléon: croquis de l'épopée*. Paris: B. Grasset, 1932.

Lentz, Thierry. 'A Brief History of an Oft-Forgotten Secondary Source for the Revolution and Empire Period: The Memoirs of Napoleon', *Napoleonica. La Revue*, 13:1 (2012): 52–64.

Lentz, Thierry and Macé, Jacques. *La mort de Napoléon: mythes, légendes et mystères*. Paris: Perrin, 2009.

Leterrier, Sophie-Anne. *Béranger, des chansons pour un peuple citoyen*. Rennes: Presses universitaires de Rennes, 2013.

Leterrier, Sophie-Anne. 'Béranger en prison: "Mes fers sont prêts; la liberté m'inspire; Je vais chanter son hymne glorieux"', *Criminocorpus* (2013): http://criminocorpus.revues.org/2594

Letters from the Cape of Good Hope, in reply to Mr. Warden; with extracts from the great work now compiling for publication under the inspection of Napoleon. London: Ridgway, 1817.

Lettre du prince Eugène de Beauharnais aux souverains alliés, ou Protestation contre le pouvoir arbitraire que s'est arrogé l'Angleterre de retenir à Sainte-Hélène le corps de Napoléon Bonaparte. Paris: chez les marchands de nouveautés, 1821.

Lettres de François Guizot et de la princesse de Lieven. 3 vols. Paris: Mercure de France, 1963–4.

Lettres inédites du maréchal Bugeaud, duc d'Isly. 1808–1809. Paris: Emile-Paul, 1923.

Leuilliot, Paul. *L'Alsace au début du XIXe siècle: essais d'histoire politique, économique et religieuse. 1815–1830*. 3 vols. Paris: SEVPEN, 1959–60.

Levallois, Jules. *Milieu du siècle: mémoires d'un critique*. Paris: Librairie illustrée, 1896.

Leveson Gower, Lord Granville. *Private Correspondence, 1781 to 1821*. 2 vols. London: John Murray, 1916.

Levy, Martin. 'Napoleon in Exile: The Houses and Furniture Supplied by the British Government for the Emperor and his Entourage on St Helena', *Furniture History*, 34 (1998): 1–211.

Leys, Simon. *La mort de Napoléon*. Paris: Hermann, 1986.

Lheureux-Prévot, Chantal. 'L'affaire des masques mortuaires de Napoléon: éléments bibliographiques commentés', *Napoleonica. La Revue*, 3:3 (2008): 60–75.

Linder-Beroud, Waltraud. ' "Schier dreißig Jahre bist du alt ...". Zur populären Wirkung des Chansonniers Pierre-Jean de Béranger (1780–1857) in Deutschland', *Lied und populäre Kultur/Song and Popular Culture*, 57 (2012): 57–79.

Lindsay, Suzanne Glover. *Funerary Arts and Tomb Cult: Living with the Dead in France, 1750–1870*. Farnham: Ashgate, 2012.

Lindsay, Suzanne Glover. 'Mummies and Tombs: Turenne, Napoleon, and Death Ritual', *Art Bulletin*, 82 (2000): 492–7.

Llewellyn, Nigel. *The Art of Death: Visual Culture in the English Death Ritual, c.1500–c.1800*. London: Reaktion, 1991.

Lloyd, Christopher (ed.). *The Keith Papers: Selected from Letters and Papers of Admiral Viscount Keith*. 3 vols. London: Navy Records Society, 1927–55.

Locke, Ralph P. 'The Music of the French Chanson, 1810–1850', in Peter Bloom (ed.), *Music in Paris in the Eighteen-Thirties*. Stuyvesant, NY: Pendragon Press, 1987, pp. 431–47.

Lockwood, Joseph. *A Guide to St. Helena, Descriptive and Historical, with a Visit to Longwood, and Napoleon's Tomb*. St Helena: Geo. Gibb, 1851.

Lok, Matthijs. '"Un oubli total du passé"? The Political and Social Construction of Silence in Restoration Europe (1813–1830)', *History & Memory*, 26:2 (2014): 40–75.

Lote, Georges. 'La contre-légende napoléonienne et la mort de Napoléon', *Revue des études napoléoniennes*, 31 (1930): 324–49.

Lote, Georges. 'La mort de Napoléon et l'opinion bonapartiste en 1821', *Revue des études napoléoniennes*, 31 (1930): 19–58.

Louret, Emile. *Le pavillon des princes: histoire complète de la prison politique de Sainte-Pélagie depuis sa fondation jusqu'à nos jours*. Paris: Flammarion, 1895.

Lucas-Dubreton, Jean. *Le culte de Napoléon, 1815–1848*. Paris: A. Michel, 1960.

Lucas-Dubreton, Jean. 'Le monde apprend sa mort', *Miroir de l'histoire*, 109 (1959): 76–83.

Lugli, Alessandro, Lugli, A. K. and Horcic, M. N. 'Napoleon's Autopsy: New Perspectives', *Human Pathology*, 36:4 (2005): 320–4.

Lugli, Alessandro et al. 'The Medical Mystery of Napoleon Bonaparte: An Interdisciplinary Exposé', *Advances in Anatomic Pathology*, 18:2 (March 2011): 152–8.

Lugli, Alessandro et al. 'Napoleon Bonaparte's Gastric Cancer: A Clinicopathologic Approach to Staging, Pathogenesis, and Etiology', *Nature Clinical Practice Gastroenterology & Hepatology*, 4:1 (2007): 52–7.

Lynn, John A. *The Bayonets of the Republic: Motivation and Tactics in the Army of Revolutionary France, 1791–94*. Urbana: University of Illinois Press, 1984.

Lyons, Martyn. *Post-Revolutionary Europe, 1815–1856*. Basingstoke: Palgrave Macmillan, 2006.

Lyons, Martyn. *Reading Culture and Writing Practices in Nineteenth-Century France*. Toronto: University of Toronto Press, 2008.

Lyons, Martyn. *Le triomphe du livre: une histoire sociologique de la lecture dans la France du XIXe siècle*. Paris: Promodis, 1987.

Lyttelton, W. H. 'Some Account of Bonaparte's coming on board H.M.S. The *Northumberland*', in Clement Shorter (ed.), *Napoleon and his Fellow Travellers*. London: Cassell, 1908, pp. 71–108.

Macartney, Clarence Edward and Dorrance, Gordon. *The Bonapartes in America*. Philadelphia: Dorrance, 1939.

McCormick, John. *Popular Theatres of Nineteenth-Century France*. London: Routledge, 1993.

Macé, Jacques. *Le général Gourgaud*. Paris: Nouveau monde éd., 2006.

Macé, Jacques. 'Les soixante-huit mois de Napoléon à Sainte-Hélène', in Bernard Chevallier, Michel Dancoisne-Martineau and Thierry Lentz (eds), *Sainte-Hélène, île de mémoire*, Paris: Fayard, 2005, pp. 55–71.

MacKenzie, Norman. *Fallen Eagle: How the Royal Navy Captured Napoleon*. London: Bellerophon Books, 2009.

McPhee, Peter. *The Politics of Rural Life: Political Mobilization in the French Countryside, 1846–1852*. Oxford: Oxford University Press, 1992.

Magnard, Francis. 'La Résurrection d'une légende', *La Revue de Paris*, 1 (1 February 1894): 89–111.

Magris, Claudio. *Danube*. Trans. Patrick Creagh. London: Harvill Press, 1989.

Maitland, Frederick. *The Surrender of Napoleon: Being the Narrative of the Surrender of Buonaparte, and of His Residence on Board H.M.S. Bellerophon*. Edinburgh and London: William Blackwood, 1904.

Malandain, Gilles. 'La haine des Bourbons sous la Restauration: quelques remarques sur un sentiment politique', in Frédéric Chauvaud and Ludovic Gaussot (eds), *La Haine: histoire et actualité*. Rennes: Presses universitaires de Renne, 2008, pp. 73–83.

Malandain, Gille. *L'introuvable complot: attentat, enquête et rumeur dans la France de la Restauration*. Paris: Ecole des hautes études en sciences sociales, 2011.

Malandain, Gilles. 'Jalons pour une histoire du pèlerinage au(x) tombeau(x) de Napoléon', in Luc Chantre, Paul D'Hollander and Jérôme Grévy (eds), *Politiques du pèlerinage, du XVIIe siècle à nos jours*. Rennes: Presses universitaires de Renne, 2014, pp. 297–313.

Malandain, Gilles. 'Rumeurs et bavardages: indices d'une appropriation ordinaire du politique dans la France censitaire', in Laurent Le Gall, Michel Offerlé and François Ploux (eds), *La politique sans en avoir l'air:*

aspects de la politique informelle, XIXe–XXIe siècle. Rennes: Presses universitaires de Renne, 2012, pp. 149–62.

Malcolm, Clementine. *A Diary of St. Helena: The Journal of Lady Malcolm. 1816, 1817.* Ed. Sir Arthur Wilson, with an introduction by Muriel Kent. London: Allen & Unwin, 1929.

Mansel, Philip. *Paris between Empires: Monarchy and Revolution, 1814–1852.* London: Phoenix, 2003.

Marchand, Louis-Joseph. *In Napoleon's Shadow.* San Francisco: Proctor Jones, 1998.

Margadant, Jo Burr. 'Gender, Vice, and the Political Imaginary in Nineteenth-Century France: Reinterpreting the Failure of the July Monarchy, 1830–1848', *American Historical Review*, 104 (1999): 1461–96.

Markham, J. David. *Napoleon and Dr Verling on St Helena.* Barnsley: Pen & Sword Military, 2005.

Markov, Walter. *Napoleon und seine Zeit: Geschichte und Kultur des Grand Empire.* Leipzig: Ed. Leipzig, 1996.

Marquerie, J. *Le Deuil: histoire, règlements, usages, modes d'autrefois et d'aujourd'hui.* Paris: rue de la Paix, 1877.

Marrinan, Michael. 'Historical Vision and the Writing of History at Louis-Philippe's Versailles', in Petra ten-Doesschate Chu and Gabriel P. Weisberg (eds), *The Popularization of Images: Visual Culture under the July Monarchy.* Princeton: Princeton University Press, 1994, pp. 113–43.

Marrinan, Michael. *Painting Politics for Louis-Philippe: Art and Ideology in Orléanist France, 1830–1848.* New Haven: Yale University Press, 1988.

Martainville, Alphonse. *Buonaparte, ou l'Abus de l'abdication, pièce héroïco-romantico-bouffonne.* Paris: J. G. Dentu, 1815.

Martineau, Gilbert. *Madame Mère: Napoleon's Mother.* Trans. Frances Partridge. London: John Murray, 1978.

Martineau, Gilbert. *Le retour des cendres.* Paris: Tallandier, 1990.

Martineau, Gilbert. *La vie quotidienne à Sainte-Hélène au temps de Napoléon.* Paris: Tallandier, 2005.

Massa, Philippe de. *Souvenirs et impressions, 1840–1871.* Paris: Calmann-Lévy, 1897.

Masson, Frédéric. *Autour de Sainte-Hélène.* 3 vols. Paris: P. Ollendorff, 1909–12.

Masson, Frédéric. 'L'énigme de Sainte-Hélène', *Revue des deux mondes*, 38 (1917): 756–88.

Masson, Frédéric and Biagi, Guido. *Napoléon inconnu, papiers inédits. 1786–1793.* 2 vols. Paris: P. Ollendorff, 1895.

Matsuda, Matt K. 'Idols of the Emperor', in Jeffrey K. Olick (ed.), *States of Memory: Continuities, Conflicts, and Transformations in National Retrospection*. Durham, NC: Duke University Press, 2003, pp. 72–100.

Matsuda, Matt K. *The Memory of the Modern*. Oxford: Oxford University Press, 1996.

Mauguin, Georges. *Napoléon et la superstition: anecdotes et curiosités*. Rodez: Carrère, 1946.

Maury, René. *L'assassin de Napoléon, ou Le mystère de Sainte-Hélène*. Paris: A. Michel, 1994.

Maxwell, Herbert (ed.). *The Creevey Papers: A Selection from the Correspondence & Diaries of Thomas Creevey*. London: John Murray, 1904.

Maxwell, Sir Herbert. 'More Light on St. Helena', *Cornhill Magazine* (February 1901): 155–74.

Maxwell, William Stirling. *Napoleon's Bequest to Cantillon: A Fragment of International History*. London: John W. Parker, 1858.

Meister, Maureen. 'To All the Glories of France: The Versailles of Louis-Philippe', in *All the Banners Wave: Art and War in the Romantic Era, 1792–1851*. Providence, RI: The Department (Brown University), 1982, pp. 20–6.

Ménager, Bernard. 'Contexte politique et sociale', in Jean-Marcel Humbert (ed.), *Napoléon aux Invalides: 1840, le retour des cendres*. Paris: Musée de l'armée, Fondation Napoléon, 1991, pp. 21–7.

Ménager, Bernard. *Les Napoléon du peuple*. Paris: Aubier, 1988.

Metternich, Klemens Wenzel von. *Mémoires: documents et écrits divers*. 8 vols. Paris: E. Plon, Nourrit, 1881–4.

Michaud, Hélène. 'Que vaut le témoignage de Montholon à la lumière du fonds Masson', *Revue de l'Institut Napoléon*, 120 (1971): 113–20.

Millar, Eileen Anne. *Napoleon in Italian Literature, 1796–1821*. Rome: Edizioni di Storia e letteratura, 1977.

Miller, Michael B. *The Bon Marché: Bourgeois Culture and the Department Store, 1869–1920*. Princeton: Princeton University Press, 1981.

Minois, Georges. *Histoire de la solitude et des solitaires*. Paris: Fayard, 2013.

Mitchell, Jolyon. *Martyrdom: A Very Short Introduction*. Oxford: Oxford University Press, 2012.

Montalivet, Marthe-Camille Bachasson. *Le Roi Louis-Philippe et sa liste civile*. Paris: Michel-Lévy, 1850.

Montholon, Albine de. *Journal secret d'Albine de Montholon, maîtresse de Napoléon à Sainte-Hélène*. Paris: A. Michel, 2002.

Montholon, Charles-Tristan de. *Bonaparte's Memorial in a letter addressed by General Count Montholon to Sir Hudson Lowe.* London: Hebert & Mann, 1817.

Montholon, Charles-Tristan de. *History of the Captivity of Napoleon at St. Helena.* 2 vols. London: Colburn, 1846–7.

Montholon, Charles-Tristan de. *Mémoires pour servir à l'histoire de France, sous Napoléon, écrits à Sainte-Hélène par les généraux qui ont partagé sa captivité, et publiés sur les manuscrits entièrement corrigés de Napoléon.* 6 vols. Paris: Firmin Didot, 1823.

Montholon, Charles-Tristan de. *Récits de la captivité de l'empereur Napoléon.* 2 vols. Paris: Paulin, 1847.

Montroussier, Laurence. *L'éthique du chef militaire dans le 'Mémorial de Sainte-Hélène'.* Montpellier: Centre d'histoire militaire et d'études de défense nationale, 1998.

Morgan, Sydney. *France in 1829–30.* 2 vols. London: Saunders & Otley, 1831.

Morriss, Roger. *Cockburn and the British Navy in Transition: Admiral Sir George Cockburn, 1772–1853.* Exeter: University of Exeter Press, 1997.

Morrissey, Robert. 'The *Mémorial de Sainte-Hélène* and the Poetics of Fusion', *MLN*, 120:4 (2005): 716–32.

Morrissey, Robert. *Napoléon et l'héritage de la gloire.* Paris: Presses universitaires de France, 2010.

Mousset, Albert. *Petite histoire des grands monuments, rues et statues de Paris.* Paris: Amiot-Dumont, 1950.

Moylan, D. C. (ed.). *The Opinions of Lord Holland, as Recorded in the Journals of the House of Lords, from 1797 to 1841.* London: James Ridgway, 1841.

Murat, Achille. *La Colonne Vendôme.* Paris: Edition du Palais Royal, 1970.

Murat, Laure. *L'homme qui se prenait pour Napoléon: pour une histoire politique de la folie.* Paris: Gallimard, 2011.

Musset, Alfred de. *La confession d'un enfant du siècle.* 2 vols. Paris: F. Bonnaire, 1836.

Nabonne, Bernard. *Joseph Bonaparte: le roi philosophe.* Paris: Hachette, 1949.

Napoléon à Paris: ou translation de ses cendres sous le dôme des Invalides. Paris: P.-H. Krabbe, 1841.

Napoléon à Sainte-Hélène: la conquête de la mémoire. Paris: Gallimard; Musée de l'armée, 2016.

Napoléon et la reine d'Angleterre aux bords du Styx, dialogue. Paris: chez tous les marchands de nouveautés, 1821.

Napoleon: Extracts from the 'Times' and 'Morning Chronicle' 1815–1821 Relating to Napoleon's Life at St. Helena. London: A. L. Humphreys, 1901.

Napoléon: journal anecdotique et biographique de l'Empire et de la Grande armée. Paris: n.p., 1833–5.

Napoléon: le retour des cendres: 1840–1990. Courbevoie: Musée de l'armée, Fondation Napoléon, 1990.

Napoléon, son élévation, sa chute et son parti par un prolétaire. Lyons: chez tous les marchands de nouveautés, 1833.

'Napoleon's Voyage to St. Helena by Sir George Bingham', in Clement Shorter (ed.), *Napoleon and his Fellow Travellers.* London: Cassell, 1908, pp. 325–36

Naujoks, Natasha S. 'Between Memory and History: Political Uses of the Napoleonic Past in France, 1815–1840'. PhD dissertation, University of North Carolina at Chapel Hill, 2013.

Naujoks, Natasha S. '*Reconnaissance* and the Politics of Memory in Demands to Repatriate Napoleon's Remains in 1821', *Proceedings of the Western Society for French History*, 37 (2009): 163–73.

The Naval Chronicle for 1815: Containing a General and Biographical History of the Royal Navy of the United Kingdom, with a Variety of Original Papers on Nautical Subjects. Cambridge: Cambridge University Press, 2010.

Neely, Sylvia. *Lafayette and the Liberal Ideal, 1814–1824: Politics and Conspiracy in an Age of Reaction.* Carbondale, Ill.: Southern Illinois University Press, 1991.

Nesselrode, Charles Robert, Vasilievitch de. *Lettres et papiers, 1760–1850, extraits de ses archives.* 11 vols. Paris: A. Lahure, 1908–12.

Newman, Edgar L. 'What the Crowd Wanted in the French Revolution of 1830', in John M. Merriman (ed.), *1830 in France.* New York: New Viewpoints, 1975, pp. 17–40.

Newton-King, Susan. 'The Labour Market of the Cape Colony, 1807–1828', in Shula Marks and Anthony Atmore (eds), *Economy and Society in Pre-Industrial South Africa.* London: Longman, 1980, pp. 171–207.

Niderst, Alain. 'Les mémoires comme genre nostalgique?', in Madeleine Bertaud and François-Xavier Cuche (eds), *Le genre des mémoires, essai de définition.* Paris: Klincksieck, 1995, pp. 111–18.

Noailles, Hélie Guillaume Hubert de. *Le Comte Molé, 1781–1855: sa vie, ses mémoires.* 6 vols. Paris: Champion, 1922–1930.

Noel, Eugène. *Rouen, rouennais, rouenneries.* Rouen: Schneider frères, 1894.

Noël-Agnès, Nicolas Jacques. *Relation de ce qui s'est passé à Cherbourg à l'occasion du transbordement des restes mortels de l'empereur Napoléon.* Cherbourg: Noblet, 1841.

Nombret Saint-Laurent, Charles and Duvert, Félix-Auguste. *Bonaparte, lieutenant d'artillerie, ou 1789 et 1800, comédie historique en 2 actes, mêlée de couplets.* Paris: Bezou, 1830.

Nora, Pierre. 'Les mémoires d'état: de Commynes à de Gaulle', in Pierre Nora (ed.), *Les lieux de mémoire.* 3 vols. Paris: Gallimard, 1984–6, ii. pp. 354–400.

Norvins, Jacques Marquet de Montbreton de. *Histoire de Napoléon.* 4 vols. With illustrations by the artist Denis-Auguste-Marie Raffet. Paris: Dupont, 1827–8.

Norvins, Jacques Marquet de Montbreton, baron de. *Translation des cendres de Napoléon.* Paris: Furne, 1840.

Nouveaux détails sur la mort de Bonaparte. Paris: Jeunehomme-Crémière, n.d.

O'Brien, David. 'Censorship of Visual Culture in France, 1815–1852', *Yale French Studies*, 122 (2012): 37–52.

Ocampo, Emilio. *The Emperor's Last Campaign: A Napoleonic Empire in America.* Tuscaloosa: University of Alabama Press, 2009.

Oettermann, Stephan. *The Panorama: History of a Mass Medium.* Trans. Deborah Lucas Schneider. New York: MIT Press, 1997.

O'Gormen, Francis. 'Waterloo and the History of Loneliness', unpublished paper delivered at the conference 'Waterloo: Representation and Memory, 1815–2015', University of York, 27 June 2015.

Oleksijczuk, Denise Blake. *The First Panoramas: Visions of British Imperialism.* Minneapolis: University of Minnesota Press, 2011.

Oliver, Anthony. *Staffordshire Pottery: The Tribal Art of England.* London: Heinemann, 1981.

O'Meara, Barry. *An Exposition of Some of the Transactions that Have Taken Place at St Helena.* London: J. Ridgway, 1819.

O'Meara, Barry. *Napoleon in Exile; or, A Voice from St. Helena.* 2 vols. London: Simpkin, Marshall, 1822.

Ortzen, Len. *Imperial Venus: The Story of Pauline Bonaparte-Borghese.* London: Constable, 1974.

Ottavi, Joseph. *Napoléon.* Paris: bureau de la 'Revue de France', 1840.

Owre, Maximilian Paul. 'United in Division: The Polarized French Nation, 1814–1830'. PhD dissertation, University of North Carolina at Chapel Hill, 2008.

Pack, James. *The Man Who Burned the White House: Admiral Sir George Cockburn, 1772–1853.* Emsworth: Mason, 1987.

Pagé, Sylvain. *Le mythe napoléonien: de Las Cases à Victor Hugo*. Paris: CNRS, 2013.

Panégyrique d'un mort, par un homme sans titre. Paris: chez tous les marchands de nouveautés, 1821.

Parker, Noel. *Portrayals of Revolution: Images, Debates and Patterns of Thought on the French Revolution*. London: Harvester Wheatsheaf, 1990.

The Parliamentary Debates from the Year 1803 to the Present Time. 41 vols. London: Longman, 1812–20.

Parr, Fiona. 'The Death of Napoleon Bonaparte and the Retour des Cendres: French and British Perspectives', http://www.napoleon.org/en/reading_room/articles/files/479507.asp.

Pascoe, Judith. *The Hummingbird Cabinet: A Rare and Curious History of Romantic Collectors*. Ithaca, NY: Cornell University Press, 2006.

Pasquier, Etienne-Denis. *Mémoires du Chancelier Pasquier: histoire de mon temps*. 6 vols. Paris: E. Plon, Nourrit, 1895.

Passage des cendres de l'empereur Napoléon à Rouen: procès-verbal. Rouen: Périaux, 1842.

Passerini, Luisa. 'Memories between Silence and Oblivion', in Katherine Hodgkin and Susannah Radstone (eds), *Contested Pasts: The Politics of Memory*. London: Routledge, 2003, pp. 238–54.

Pearce, Susan M. *On Collecting: An Investigation into Collecting in the European Tradition*. London: Routledge, 1995.

Péclet, Edouard. *Napoléon, où sera le tombeau?* Paris: Delaunay, 1840.

Perdiguier, Agricol. *Mémoires d'un compagnon, presentation by Maurice Agulhon*. Paris: Imprimerie nationale, 1992.

Pérès, Jean-Baptiste. *Comme quoi Napoléon n'a jamais existé, ou Grand erratum, source d'un grand nombre infini d'errata à noter dans l'histoire du XIXe siècle*. Paris: Pérès, 1827.

Péricaud, Louis. *Le Théâtre des Funambules, ses mimes, ses acteurs et ses pantomimes, depuis sa fondation jusqu'à sa démolition*. Paris: L. Sapin, 1897.

Perrottet, Tony. *Napoleon's Privates: 2500 Years of History Unzipped*. New York: HarperCollins, 2008.

Persat, Maurice. *Mémoires du commandant Persat, 1806 à 1844*. Paris: Plon-Nourrit, 1910.

Pétiet, Auguste-Louis. *Souvenirs militaires de l'histoire contemporaine, par le général, baron, Auguste Pétiet*. Paris: Dentu, 1844.

Petiteau, Natalie. *Ecrire la mémoire: mémorialistes de la Révolution et de l'Empire*. Paris: les Indes savantes, 2012.

Petiteau, Natalie. *Lendemains d'empire: les soldats de Napoléon dans la France du XIXe siècle.* Paris: Boutique de l'histoire, 2003.

Petiteau, Natalie. 'La Monarchie de Juillet face aux héritages napoléoniens', in Patrick Harismendy (ed.), *La France des années 1830 et l'esprit de réforme.* Rennes: Presses universitaires de Rennes, 2006, pp. 55–62.

Petiteau, Natalie. *Napoléon, de la mythologie à l'histoire.* Paris: Seuil, 2004.

Petiteau, Natalie. 'Les vétérans du Premier Empire: un groupe socioprofessionnel oublié', *Cahiers d'histoire*, 43:1 (1998): 25–45.

Petrey, Sandy. *In the Court of the Pear King: French Culture and the Rise of Realism.* Ithaca, NY: Cornell University Press, 2005.

Pety, Dominique. 'Le Versailles des Goncourt: patrimoine public ou collection privée?', in Véronique Léonard-Roques (ed.), *Versailles dans la littérature: mémoire et imaginaire aux XIXe et XXe siècles.* Clermont-Ferrand: Presses universitaires Blaise Pascal, 2005, pp. 139–54

Peyre, Henri. 'Napoleon: Devil, Poet, Saint', *Yale French Studies*, 26 (1960): 21–31.

Phillips, Roderick. *Alcohol: A History.* Chapel Hill: University of North Carolina Press, 2014.

Pichon, Louis-André. *De l'état de la France, sous la domination de Napoléon Bonaparte.* Paris: J. G. Dentu, 1814.

Picquot, L. *Encore un mot sur Napoléon-le-Grand.* Paris: les marchands de nouveautés, 1821.

Pierrot, Roger (ed.). *Lettres à Madame Hanska.* 2 vols. Paris: Laffont, 1990.

Pilbeam, Pamela M. *The 1830 Revolution in France.* London: Macmillan, 1991.

Pilbeam, Pamela, M. *Madame Tussaud and the History of Waxworks.* London: Hambledon and London, 2003.

Pilbeam, Pamela M. *Republicanism in Nineteenth-Century France, 1814–1871.* Basingstoke: Palgrave Macmillan, 1995.

Pillans, T. Dundas. *The Real Martyr of St. Helena.* London: Andrew Melrose, 1913.

Pimienta, Robert. *La propagande bonapartiste en 1848.* Paris: E. Cornély, 1911.

Pinkney, David H. *Decisive Years in France, 1840–1847.* Princeton: Princeton University Press, 1986.

Pinkney, David H. *The French Revolution of 1830.* Princeton: Princeton University Press, 1972.

Pissot, Noël-Laurent. *Le mea culpa de Napoléon Bonaparte, l'aveu de ses perfidies et cruautés.* Paris: Aubry, 1814.

P. J. F. D. S. M. *Bonaparte jugé par lui-même dialogue.* Paris: Trouve, 1823.

Planat de La Faye, Nicolas-Louis. *Correspondance intime de Planat de La Faye*. Paris: P. Ollendorff, 1895.

Planat de La Faye, Nicolas-Louis. *Vie de Planat de La Faye*. Paris: P. Ollendorff, 1895.

Planert, Ute. 'Bonapartismus und Nationalismus in der Berliner Klassik. Goethe, Zelter und der deutsche Männergesang', in Axel Fischero and Matthias Kornemann (eds), *Integer vitae: Die Zeltersche Liedertafel als kulturgeschichtliches Phänomen*. Hanover: Wehrhahn Verlag, 2014, pp. 169–92.

Ploux, François. *De bouche à l'oreille: naissance et propagation des rumeurs dans la France du XIXe siècle*. Paris: Aubier, 2003.

Plunkett, John. *Queen Victoria: First Media Monarch*. Oxford: Oxford University Press, 2003.

Poisson, Georges. *L'aventure du retour des cendres*. Paris: Tallandier, 2004.

Poisson, Georges. *Le retour des cendres de l'Aiglon*. Paris: Nouveau monde éd., 2006.

Pollak, Valentin. *Béranger in Deutschland*. Vienna: Verlag des K.K. Staatsgymnasiums, 1908.

Porter, Charles A. *Chateaubriand: Composition, Imagination, and Poetry*. Saratoga, Calif.: Anma libri, 1978.

Porterfield, Todd and Siegfried, Susan L. *Staging Empire: Napoleon, Ingres, and David*. University Park, Pa.: Pennsylvania State University Press, 2006.

Pougetoux, Alain. 'La Colonne Vendôme', in Jérémie Benoît, Agnès Delannoy and Alain Pougetoux, *Napoléon: le retour des cendres (1840–1990)*. Courbevoie: Musée Roybet-Fould, 1990, pp. 74–84.

Pougetoux, Alain. 'La mort de Napoléon', in Jérémie Benoît, Agnès Delannoy and Alain Pougetoux, *Napoléon: le retour des cendres (1840–1990)*. Courbevoie: Musée Roybet-Fould, 1990, pp. 41–55.

Pougetoux, Alain. 'Le masque de Napoléon: de la relique au bibelot', in Emmanuelle Héran (ed.), *Le dernier portrait*. Paris: Réunion des musées nationaux, 2002, pp. 146–57.

Price, Munro. *The Perilous Crown: France between Revolutions, 1814–1848*. London: Macmillan, 2007.

Proger, L. W. 'A Napoleonic Relic', *Annals of the Royal College of Surgeons of England*, 26:1 (1960): 57–62

Pugh, P. D. Gordon. *Staffordshire Portrait Figures and Allied Subjects of the Victorian Era*. Woodbridge: Antique Collectors' Club, 1987.

Pujol, Edouard. *Napoléon, de la vallée du tombeau au dôme des Invalides*. Paris: H.-L. Delloye, 1841.

Pushkin, Aleksandr. *The Queen of Spades and Other Stories*. Trans. Sutherland Edwards. London: Chapman & Hall, 1892.

Puymège, Gérard de. *Chauvin, le soldat-laboreur: contribution à l'étude des nationalisme*. Paris: Gallimard, 1993.

Quigley, Christine. *The Corpse: A History*. Jefferson, NC: McFarland, 1996.

Rachlin, Harvey. *Lucy's Bones, Sacred Stones, & Einstein's Brain: The Remarkable Stories behind the Great Objects and Artifacts of History, from Antiquity to the Modern Era*. New York: H. Holt, 1996.

Ramsey, Neil. *The Military Memoir and Romantic Literary Culture, 1780– 1835*. Farnham: Ashgate, 2011.

Rationalisme napoléonien, ou Napoléonisme. Paris: Ledoyen, 1834.

Regnault-Warin, Jean-Joseph. *Introduction à l'histoire de l'empire français, ou essai sur la monarchie de Napoléon*. 2 vols. Paris: P. Domère, 1821.

Relation de la maladie et de la mort de Napoléon Bonaparte, extraite de plusieurs lettres venues de Sainte-Hélène. Paris: Librairie départementale, 1821.

Relation exacte de la translation des restes mortels de l'empereur Napoléon. Paris: quai des Orfèvres, 1840.

'Reminiscences of Napoleon Bonaparte, on St Helena. By A Lady', *Edinburgh Magazine*, 35 (January–June 1834): 48–55.

Rémusat, Charles de. *Mémoires de ma vie*. 5 vols. Paris: Plon, 1958–67.

Report on the Manuscripts of Earl Bathurst, Preserved at Cirencester Park. London: HMSO, 1923.

Resnick, Daniel Philip. *The White Terror and the Political Reaction after Waterloo*. Cambridge, Mass.: Harvard University Press, 1966.

Retour des cendres de Napoléon: procès-verbal d'exhumation des restes de l'empereur Napoléon. Orthez: Dumesnil et Auboin, n.d..

Riall, Lucy. *Garibaldi: Invention of a Hero*. New Haven: Yale University Press, 2008.

Rials, Stéphane. *Nouvelle histoire de Paris: de Trochu à Thiers, 1870–1873*. Paris: Association pour la publication d'une histoire de Paris, 1985.

Ribe, Georges. *L'opinion publique et la vie politique à Lyon lors des premières années de la seconde Restauration, la réaction ultra et l'expérience constitutionnelle, 17 juillet 1815–9 janvier 1822*. Lyons: Bosc frères, 1957.

Richardson, James L. *Crisis Diplomacy: The Great Powers since the Mid-Nineteenth Century*. Cambridge: Cambridge University Press, 1994.

Robert, Vincent. *Le temps des banquets: politique et symbolique d'une génération, 1818–1848*. Paris: Publications de la Sorbonne, 2010.

Rohan-Chabot, Philippe de. *Les 5 cercueils de l'Empereur: souvenirs inédits.* Paris: France-Empire, 1985.

Rosanvallon, Pierre. *La monarchie impossible: les Chartes de 1814 et de 1830.* Paris: Fayard, 1994.

Rose, J. Holland. 'The Funeral of Napoleon and his Last Supper', *English Historical Review*, 17 (1902): 311–16.

Rose, John Holland (ed.). *Napoleon's Last Voyages, Being the Diaries of Admiral Sir Thomas Ussher (on board the 'Undaunted'), and John R. Glover, Secretary to Rear Admiral Cockburn (on board the 'Northumberland').* London: Fisher Unwin, 1906.

Rosebery, Archibald Philip Primrose, Earl of. *Napoleon: The Last Phase.* London: Arthur L. Humphreys, 1904.

Rosenfeld, Gavriel D. *The World Hitler Never Made: Alternate History and the Memory of Nazism.* Cambridge: Cambridge University Press, 2005.

Ross, Michael. *The Reluctant King: Joseph Bonaparte, King of the Two Sicilies and Spain.* London: Sidgwick & Jackson, 1976.

Rossi, Henri. *Les Corses des services secrets de Napoléon en exil.* Ajaccio: A. Piazzola, 2007.

Rossigneux, André. 'Ali le mameluk', *Bulletin de la Société des sciences historiques et naturelles de l'Yonne*, 65 (1911): 59–75.

Rothney, John. *Bonapartism after Sedan.* Ithaca, NY: Cornell University Press, 1969.

Rouge-Ducos, Isabelle. *L'Arc de Triomphe de l'Etoile: panthéon de la France guerrière: art et histoire.* Dijon: Ed. Faton, 2008.

Roulin, Jean-Marie. 'Le retour des cendres de Napoléon: une cérémonie palimseste', in Corinne and Eric Perrin-Saminadayar (ed.), *Imaginaire et représentations des entrées royales au XIXe siècle: une sémiologie du pouvoir politique.* Saint-Etienne: Publications de l'Université de Saint-Etienne, 2006, pp. 83–105.

Roustam Raza. *Souvenirs de Roustam, mamelouck de Napoléon Ier.* Paris: P. Ollendorff, 1911.

Rowe, Michael. 'Napoleon's France: A Forerunner of Europe's Twentieth-Century Dictators', in Claus-Christian Szejnmann (ed.), *Rethinking History, Dictatorship and War: New Approaches and Interpretations.* London: Continuum, 2009, pp. 87–106.

Rozelaar, Louis A. 'Mémorial de Sainte-Hélène et le Romantisme', *Revue des études napoléoniennes*, 29 (October 1929): 203–26.

Rozelaar, Louis A. 'Le Mémorial de Sainte-Helene et Victor Hugo en 1827', *French Quarterly*, 9 (1927): 53–68.

Ruiz, Alain. 'Bemerkungen zur Entstehung der Napoleon-Legende', in Marion George and Andrea Rudolph (eds), *Napoleons langer Schatten über Europa*. Dettelbach: Röll, 2008, pp. 409–22,

Rye, J. B. 'The Lost and the New Letters of Napoleon', *English Historical Review*, 13:51 (1898): 473–98.

St-Cère, Jacques and Schlitter, H. (eds). *Napoléon à Sainte-Hélène: rapports officiels du baron Stürmer, commissaire du gouvernement autrichien*. Paris: Librairie illustrée, 1888.

Saint-Denis, Louis Etienne (Mameluck Ali). *Journal inédit du retour des cendres, 1840*. Paris: Tallandier, 2003.

Saint-Denis, Louis Etienne (Mameluck Ali). *Souvenirs du Mameluck Ali sur l'empereur Napoléon*. Paris: Ed. SPM, 2000.

Saint-Paulien (M. I. Sicard). *Napoléon, Balzac et l'empire de la Comédie humaine*. Paris: A. Michel, 1979.

Salgues, Jacques-Barthélemy. *Mémoire pour servir à l'histoire de France sous le gouvernement de Napoléon Buonaparte et pendant l'absence de la maison de Bourbon*. 9 vols. Paris: L. Fayolle, 1814–26.

Sammons, Jeffrey L. *Heinrich Heine: A Modern Biography*. Princeton: Princeton University Press, 1979.

Samuels, Maurice. *The Spectacular Past: Popular History and the Novel in Nineteenth-Century France*. Ithaca, NY: Cornell University Press, 2004.

Saugera, Eric. *Reborn in America: French Exiles and Refugees in the United States and the Vine and Olive Adventure, 1815–1865*. Trans. Madeleine Velguth. Tuscaloosa: University of Alabama Press, 2011.

Schlitter, Hanns. *Die Stellung der österreichischen Regierung zum Testamente Napoleon Bonaparte's*. Vienna: F. Tempsky, 1893.

Schmitz, Edgar. 'Das trojanische Pferd und die Restauration. Die Auseinandersetzung um die *Colonne de la Place Vendôme* als Paradigma der gescheiterten Restauration', in Gudrun Gersmann and Hubertus Kohle (eds), *Frankreich 1815–1830. Trauma oder Utopie? Die Gesellschaft der Restauration und das Erbe der Revolution*. Stuttgart: F. Steiner, 1993, pp. 187–96.

Scholz, Natalie. *Die imaginierte Restauration: Repräsentationen der Monarchie im Frankreich Ludwigs XVIII*. Darmstadt: Wissenschaftliche Buchgesellschaft, 2006.

Scholz, Natalie. 'Past and Pathos: Symbolic Practices of Reconciliation during the French Restoration', *History & Memory*, 22:1 (2010): 48–80.

Schroeder, Paul W. *The Transformation of European Politics, 1763–1848*. Oxford: Oxford University Press, 1994.

Seaton, A. V. 'War and Thanatourism: Waterloo 1815–1914', *Annals of Tourism Research*, 26:1 (1999): 130–58.

Seaton, Robert Cooper. *Sir Hudson Lowe and Napoleon*. London: D. Nutt, 1898.

Ségur, Philippe de. *Histoire et mémoires, par le général comte de Ségur*. 7 vols. Paris: Firmin-Didot, 1873.

Seigan, Kôbô. 'L'influence de la mémoire de la Révolution française et de l'empire napoléonien dans l'opinion publique française face à la guerre d'Espagne de 1823', *Annales historiques de la Révolution française*, 335 (2004): 159–81.

Sellin, Volker. 'Der Tod Napoleons', *Francia*, 35 (2008): 273–94.

Semmel, Stuart. *Napoleon and the British*. New Haven: Yale University Press, 2004.

Semmel, Stuart. 'Reading the Tangible Past: British Tourism, Collecting, and Memory after Waterloo', *Representations*, 69 (Winter, 2000): 9–37.

Sessions, Jennifer E. *By Sword and Plow: France and the Conquest of Algeria*. Ithaca, NY: Cornell University Press, 2011.

Sewell, Jr, William H. 'Social Mobility in a Nineteenth-Century European City: Some Findings and Implications', *Journal of Interdisciplinary History*, 7:2 (Autumn, 1976): 217–33.

Shaylor, Joseph. *The Fascination of Books: With Other Papers on Books & Bookselling*. London: Simpkin, Marshall, 1912.

Shorter, Clement (ed.). *Napoleon and his Fellow Travellers*. London: Cassell, 1908.

Shorter, Clement (ed.). *Napoleon in his own Defence*. London: Cassell, 1910.

Shroder, Maurice Z. *Icarus: The Image of the Artist in French Romanticism*. Cambridge, Mass.: Harvard University Press, 1961.

Sibalis, Michael. 'Conspiracy on St. Helena? (Mis)remembering Napoleon's Exile', *French History and Civilization*, 4 (2011): 94–105.

Sibalis, Michael. 'Political Prisoners and State Prisons in Napoleonic France', in Philip Dwyer and Alan Forrest (eds), *Napoleon and his Empire: Europe, 1804–1814*. New York: Palgrave Macmillan, 2007, pp. 96–113.

Simond, Charles (ed.). *La vie parisienne à travers le XIXe siècle: Paris de 1800 à 1900 d'après les estampes et les mémoires du temps*. 3 vols. Paris: E. Plon, Nourrit, 1900–1.

Simonetta, Marcello and Arikha, Noga. *Napoleon and the Rebel: A Story of Brotherhood, Passion, and Power*. New York: Palgrave Macmillan, 2011.

Simonnin, Antoine Jean-Baptiste. *Histoire des trois derniers mois de la vie de Napoléon Bonaparte*. Paris: Chaumerot jeune, 1821.

Sinnema, Peter W. *The Wake of Wellington: Englishness in 1852.* Athens, Ohio: Ohio University Press, 2006.

Skinner, Thomas. *Fifty Years in Ceylon: An Autobiography.* London: W. H. Allen, 1891.

Skuy, David. *Assassination, Politics, and Miracles: France and the Royalist Reaction of 1820.* Montreal: McGill-Queen's University Press, 2003.

Smallman, David L. *Quincentenary: A Story of St Helena, 1502–2002.* Penzance: Patten, 2003.

Smart, John. 'Napoleon on Board the Bellerophon at Torbay', in Clement Shorter (ed.), *Napoleon and his Fellow Travellers.* London: Cassell, 1908, pp. 295–302.

Smith, William. *Napoléon III.* Paris: Marabout, 1983.

La Snapoleonazione. Opera buffa, ovvero il mago don Pilucca Dramma per musica. Cagliari: n.p., 1814.

Sonnenfeld, Albert. 'Napoleon as Sun Myth', *Yale French Studies*, 26 (1960): 32–6.

Soulié, Frédéric. *Le tombeau de Napoléon.* Paris: Marchant, 1840.

Spitzer, Alan B. *Old Hatreds and Young Hopes: The French Carbonari against the Bourbon Restoration.* Cambridge, Mass.: Harvard University Press, 1971.

Staël, Germaine de. *Portrait d'Attila.* Paris: impr. librairie stéréotype, 1814.

Stagg, J. C. A. *The War of 1812: Conflict for a Continent.* Cambridge: Cambridge University Press, 2012.

Stanhope, Philip Henry, Earl. *Notes of Conversations with the Duke of Wellington, 1831–1851.* New York: John Murray, 1888.

Stendhal. *Le rouge et le noir.* Paris: Gallimard, 2000.

Stokoe, John. *With Napoleon at St Helena.* London: Lane, 1902.

Strachey, Lady (ed.). *Memoirs of a Highland Lady: The Autobiography of Elizabeth Grant of Rothiemurchus, 1797–1830.* London: John Murray, 1898.

Stroud, Patricia Tyson. *The Man Who Had Been King: The American Exile of Napoleon's Brother Joseph.* Philadelphia: University of Pennsylvania Press, 2005.

Supplementary Despatches, Correspondence, and Memoranda of Field Marshal Arthur, Duke of Wellington. 15 vols. London: John Murray, 1858–72.

Tardy, Jean-Noël. *L'âge des ombres: complots, conspirations et sociétés secrètes au XIXe siècle.* Paris: Les Belles Lettres, 2015.

Tchernoff, Iouda. *Le parti républicain sous la monarchie de juillet: formation et évolution de la doctrine républicaine.* Paris: A. Pedone, 1901.

Telesko, Werner. *Erlösermythen in Kunst und Politik. Zwischen christlicher Tradition und Moderne.* Vienna: Böhlau, 2004.

Ténot, Eugène. *Paris en décembre 1851: étude historique sur le coup d'état.* Paris: Le Chevalier, 1868.

Thackeray, William Makepeace. *The Second Funeral of Napoleon.* New York: Hugh Cunningham, 1883.

Thibaudeau, Antoine-Clair. *Le Consulat et l'Empire, ou Histoire de la France et de Napoléon Bonaparte, de 1799 à 1815.* 10 vols. Paris: J. Renouard, 1834–5.

Thibaudeau, Antoine-Clair. *Histoire générale de Napoléon Bonaparte, de sa vie privée et publique, de sa carrière politique et militaire, de son administration et de son gouvernement*, 6 vols. Paris: J. Renouard, 1827–8.

Thiers, Adolphe. *La monarchie de 1830.* Paris: A. Mesnier, 1831.

Thomassy, M. *De la sensation qu'a faite en France la mort de Buonaparte, et des écrits publiés à ce sujet.* Paris: chez G.-C. Hubert, 1821.

Thompson, Neville. *Earl Bathurst and the British Empire, 1762–1834.* Barnsley: Leo Cooper, 1999.

Thompson, Victoria E. 'The Creation, Destruction and Recreation of Henri IV: Seeing Popular Sovereignty in the Statue of a King', *History and Memory*, 24:2 (2012): 5–40.

Thornton, Michael John. *Napoleon after Waterloo: England and the St. Helena Decision.* Stanford, Calif.: Stanford University Press, 1968.

Thourel, Albin. *Les accens de la liberté au tombeau de Napoléon.* Paris: les marchands de nouveautés, 1821.

Thureau-Dangin, Paul. *Histoire de la monarchie de juillet.* 7 vols. Paris: E. Plon, Nourrit, 1888–92.

Tomiche, Nada. *Napoléon écrivain.* Paris: Armand Colin, 1952.

Touchard, Jean. *La gloire de Béranger.* 2 vols. Paris: Armand Colin, 1968.

Translation des cendres de Napoléon, de Sainte-Hélène en France. Cherbourg: Lecouflet, n.d..

Trollope, Frances. *Paris and the Parisians in 1835.* 2 vols. London: R. Bentley, 1836.

Truesdell, Matthew. *Spectacular Politics: Louis-Napoleon Bonaparte and the Fête Impériale, 1849–1870.* New York: Oxford University Press, 1997.

Tudesq, André-Jean. *L'élection présidentielle de Louis-Napoléon Bonaparte, 10 decembre 1848.* Paris: Armand Colin, 1965.

Tudesq, André-Jean. *Les grands notables en France. 1840–1849: étude historique d'une psychologie sociale.* Paris: Delmas, 1964.

Tudesq, André-Jean. 'La légende napoléonienne en France en 1848', *Revue historique*, 218 (1957): 64–85.

Tudesq, André-Jean. 'Le reflet donné par la presse', in Jean-Marcel Humbert (ed.), *Napoléon aux Invalides: 1840, le retour des cendres.* Paris: Musée de l'armée, Fondation Napoléon, 1991, pp. 85–91.

Tuite, Clara. *Lord Byron and Scandalous Celebrity.* Cambridge: Cambridge University Press, 2014.

Tulard, Jean. 'Les épurations administratives en France de 1800 à 1830', in *Les épurations administratives: XIXe et XXe siècles.* Geneva: Droz, 1977, pp. 49–62.

Tulard, Jean. *Le mythe de Napoléon.* Paris: Armand Colin, 1971.

Tulard, Jean. *Napoléon II.* Paris: Fayard, 1992.

Tulard, Jean. *Napoléon ou le mythe du sauveur.* Paris: Fayard, 1977.

Tulard, Jean. *La Préfecture de Police sous la monarchie de juillet.* Paris: Impr. municipale, 1964.

Tulard, Jean. 'Le retour des cendres', in Pierre Nora (ed.), *Les lieux de mémoire.* 3 vols. Paris: Gallimard, 1984–6, ii. pp. 81–110

Tulard, Jean. 'Sainte-Hélène et l'opinion française', in Ulane Bonnel (ed.), *Sainte-Hélène, terre d'exile.* Paris: Hachette, 1971, pp. 179–200.

Unwin, Brian. *Terrible Exile: The Last Days of Napoleon on St Helena.* London: I. B. Tauris, 2010.

L'usurpateur remis à sa place dans les cieux, ou arrêt de la Cour céleste, extrait du Journal de l'Empirée. Paris: chez les marchands de nouveautés, 1814.

Vale, Brian. *Cochrane in the Pacific: Fortune and Freedom in Spanish America.* London: I. B. Tauris, 2008.

Vane, Charles William (ed.). *Correspondence, Despatches, and Other Papers of Viscount Castlereagh.* 12 vols. London: H. Colburn, 1848–53.

Vaulabelle, Achille de. *Histoire des deux Restaurations: jusqu'à l'avènement de Louis-Philippe, de janvier 1813 à octobre 1830.* 8 vols. Paris: Perrotin, 1860.

Veauce, Eugène de. *Les masques mortuaires de Napoléon.* Paris: La Pensée universelle, 1971.

Vernon, Bower J. *Early Recollections of Jamaica.* London: Whittaker, 1848.

Vidalenc, Jean. *Les Demi-solde, étude d'une catégorie sociale.* Paris: M. Rivière, 1955.

Vidalenc, Jean. 'L'opinion publique en Normandie et le retour des restes de Napoléon en décembre 1840', in *La France au XIXe siècle: études historiques. Mélanges offerts à Charles Hippolyte Pouthas.* Paris: Publications de la Sorbonne, 1973, pp. 212–24.

Vie civile et militaire de Napoléon Bonaparte, depuis sa naissance jusqu'à sa mort, par L***** R******, officier de l'ancienne armée. 2 vols. Paris: Chassaignon, 1821.

Vielledent, Sylvie. *1830 aux théâtres.* Paris: Champion, 2009.

Vielledent, Sylvie, 'Le retour du "petit chapeau" en 1830', in *Napoléon, de l'histoire à la légende.* Paris: Maisonneuve & Larose, 2000, pp. 351–72.

Viennet, Jean-Pons-Guillaume. *Mémoires et journal: 1777–1867.* Paris: Champion, 2006.

Vigier, Philippe. *Nouvelle histoire de Paris: Paris pendant la Monarchie de Juillet. 1830–1848.* Paris: Association pour la publication d'une histoire de Paris, 1991.

Villenave, Théodore. *Relation des funérailles de Napoléon, exhumation, translation, pièces officielles, etc.* Paris: A. Rigaud, 1840.

Villeroy, Alfred. *Histoire de 1840, annuaire historique et politique.* 2 vols. Paris: Paulin, 1841–2.

Villers, Marius. *Pèlerinage à Sainte-Hélène, ou Souvenirs d'un voyage autour du monde.* Paris: Dureuil, 1829.

Vimont, Jean-Claude. 'Enfermer les politiques: la mise en place progressive des "régimes politiques" d'incarcération', in Philippe Vigier and Alain Faure (eds), *Répression et prison politique en France et en Europe au XIXe siècle.* Paris: Créaphis, 1990, pp. 47–63.

Vincent-Buffault, Anne. *The History of Tears: Sensibility and Sentimentality in France.* Trans. Teresa Bridgeman. New York: Macmillan, 1991.

The Voyages and Travells of the Ambassadors Sent by Frederick Duke of Holstein, to the Great Duke of Muscovy, and the King of Persia: Begun in the Year 1633, and Finish'd in 1634: Containing a Compleat History of Muscovy, Tartary, Persia, and Other Adjacent Countries: with Several Publick Transactions Reaching Near the Present Times. London: n.p., 1669.

Wachtel, Natahn. 'Memory and History: Introduction', *History and Anthropology*, 2 (1986): 207–24.

Wagner, Anne M. 'Outrages: Sculpture and Kingship in France after 1789', in Ann Bermingham and John Brewer (eds), *The Consumption of Culture, 1600–1800: Image, Object, Text.* New York: Routledge, 1995, pp. 294–318.

Walsham, Alexandra. 'Introduction: Relics and Remains', *Past & Present*, Supplement 5 (2010): 9–36.

Waquet, Françoise. *Les fêtes royales sous la Restauration ou l'Ancien Régime retrouvé.* Geneva: Droz, 1981.

Warden, William. *Letters Written on Board His Majesty's Ship the Northumberland and Saint Helena.* Brussels: R. Ackermann, 1817.

Waresquiel, Emmanuel de and Yvert, Benoît. *Histoire de la Restauration, 1814–1830: naissance de la France modern.* Paris: Perrin, 1996.

Watson, George L. de St Macaire. *A Polish Exile with Napoleon*. London: Harper, 1912.

Watson, George L. de St Macaire. *The Story of Napoleon's Death-Mask*. London: John Lane, 1915.

Wehs, D. B. *Some Account of the Political Life of Louis Napoleon*. London: Houlston & Wright, 1859.

Weider, Ben and Hapgood, David. *The Murder of Napoleon*. Toronto: Methuen, 1982.

Welschinger, Henri. *Le roi de Rome. 1811–1832*. Paris: E. Plon, Nourrit, 1897.

Weygand, Maxime. *L'Arc de Triomphe de l'Etoile*. Paris: Flammarion, 1960.

Whidden, Seth. *Authority in Crisis in French Literature, 1850–1880*. Farnham: Ashgate, 2014.

Whitehead, Anne. *Betsy and the Emperor*. Sydney: Allen & Unwin, 2015.

Willms, Johannes. *Napoleon & St Helena: On the Island of Exile*. Trans. John Brownjohn. London: Armchair Traveller, 2008.

Willms, Johannes. *Napoleon. Verbannung und Verklärung*. Munich: Droemer Verlag, 2000.

Winter, Jay. 'Thinking about Silence', in Efrat Ben-Ze'ev, Ruth Ginio and Jay Winter (eds), *Shadows of War: A Social History of Silence in the Twentieth Century*. Cambridge: Cambridge University Press, 2010, pp. 3–31.

Woloch, Isser. *The French Veteran from the Revolution to the Restoration*. Chapel Hill, NC: University of North Carolina Press, 1979.

Wood, Marcus. *Radical Satire and Print Culture, 1790–1822*. Oxford: Oxford University Press, 1994.

Woodward, Christopher. 'Napoleon's Last Journey', *History Today*, 55:7 (2005): 51–9.

Wrede, Martin. 'Le portrait du roi restauré, ou la fabrication de Louis XVIII', *Revue d'histoire moderne et contemporaine*, 53:2 (2006): 112–38.

Wren, Keith. 'Victor Hugo and the Napoleonic Myth', *European History Quarterly*, 10 (October 1980): 429–58.

Wrigley, Richard. *The Politics of Appearance: Representations of Dress in Revolutionary France*. Oxford: Oxford University Press, 2002.

Wu, Duncan. *William Hazlitt: The First Modern Man*. Oxford: Oxford University Press, 2008.

Wurtz, Jean-Wendel. *L'Apollyon de l'Apocalypse, ou la révolution française prédite par saint Jean l'évangéliste*. Lyons: M.-P. Rusand, 1816.

Yonge, Charles Duke (ed.). *The Life and Administration of Robert Banks, Second Earl of Liverpool*. 3 vols. London: Macmillan, 1868.

Young, Norwood. *Napoleon in Exile: St Helena.* 2 vols. London: Stanley Paul, 1915.

Zeldin, Theodore. *The Political System of Napoleon III.* London: Macmillan, 1958.

Ziolkowski, Theodore. 'Napoleon's Impact on Germany: A Rapid Survey', *Yale French Studies*, 26 (1960): 94–105.

Acknowledgements

This is the end of a journey that has taken many years to complete, during which time I developed a relationship of sorts with Napoleon, even if only in my head. On good days it was as though I were having a conversation and getting to know a character who had a lot of interesting but improbable stories to tell. At other times, I felt like one of Napoleon's harried aides-de-camp, woken in the middle of the night to sort out some trivial detail or obliged to dwell on some problem or other before being sent back to bed, which could be any time between three and six in the morning. I hope that the end result of my labour is a work of biography – that is, a work that has attempted to construct Napoleon's life as a work of art.

Biography is a tricky business. If I were to begin this work now, it would be a very different beast from the one I have produced. That is because my own experiences over these years have shaped who I am and because, ultimately, biography is as much a reflection of the author as it is of the subject. I have sifted through the archives and hundreds of works written about the man. In doing so I have tried to portray Napoleon frankly, some might say harshly, when it was called for, sympathetically on other occasions, hoping to break free of the mould in which Napoleon appears to have been set over the years. I am not entirely sure I have understood him as much as I would have liked to. The problem with biography is that it is impossible to 'know' one's subject. Napoleon was, after all, like many individuals, a bundle of contradictions.

In the course of this journey, which has taken me to many places throughout Europe and the Middle East where I would not normally have ventured, I have met a remarkable number of stimulating and fascinating people. This is one of the advantages of being an academic. Writing is largely a solitary pursuit, but the final product is also the end result of a collective effort. Many others, from colleagues and friends to copy-editors, have had a hand in the three books that are the outcome of years of reading, writing and thinking about a man whose impact on Europe and the world was extraordinary. None of this could have been possible in the first place with the support of my agent, Bill Hamilton, and my editor at Bloomsbury, Michael Fishwick. My thanks too to Sarah Ruddick and Jasmine Horsey at Bloomsbury for guiding the manuscript through its final stages. Those who have generously helped in the previous two volumes have already been thanked so let me limit this expression of gratitude to those who have given of their time and knowledge to this book: Gérard Leyris from the Musée Carnavalet in Paris for his help in locating an obscure engraving of Louis-Philippe; Francis O'Gormen for allowing me to cite his unpublished paper; and, for help with the post-Napoleonic era throughout Europe, Sibylle Erle, Charles Esdaile, David Laven, Chad Ludington, Patricia Mainardi and Ute Planert. A number of colleagues were kind enough to read all or part of the manuscript: Michael Sibalis read the chapters on St Helena, while Alan Forrest, Martyn Lyons and Peter McPhee read the manuscript in its entirety. I was again fortunate enough to work with Peter James, an extraordinarily thorough copy-editor. They all not only prevented me from committing innumerable errors but their critiques obliged me to rethink entire chapters and passages, making this a better book in the process. Needless to say, all errors remain my own. Finally, I would like to thank my darling Andrea, who also read, commented on and corrected the manuscript; she constantly challenges me to be a better writer. I hope this book lives up to their expectations.

Index

Beauharnais, Stéphanie de (Grand
  Duchess of Baden), 196–7
Belle-Poule, 199, 204, 211, 214, 216,
  218, 220
Béranger, Pierre-Jean de, 147, 175
Berezina, river, 116
Berry, Charles Ferdinand, Duc de, 124,
  143, 175
Bertrand, Arthur, 204–5
Bertrand, Fanny, 21–2, 26, 30, 33, 44,
  46–7, 61, 72, 81, 85, 89–91, 98, 108–9
  and Napoleon's death, 118–19,
    124, 133
Bertrand, General Comte Henri-
  Gatien, 19–20, 22–4, 26, 42, 45–7,
    59, 61, 63, 65, 71–2, 85, 92, 95, 98
  departure from St Helena, 89,
    109, 128–9
  and Gourgaud's departure from St
    Helena, 87–9
  memoirs (*Cahiers de Sainte-Hélène*),
    88, 153, 156
  and Napoleon's death, 119, 121,
    123–4, 126, 133
  and Napoleon's declining health,
    107–8, 111–14
  and Napoleon's memoirs, 37, 153
  and Napoleon's will, 112
  and return of Napoleon's remains,
    197–8, 204–5
Bicêtre asylum, 211
Bingham, Colonel Sir George, 27, 47, 59
Blakeney, Henry Pierce, 70–1
Blücher, Generalfeldmarschall Gebhard
  Leberecht von, 8, 51
Boigne, Comtesse de, 133, 174
Bonaparte, Caroline, 10
Bonaparte, Catherine, 139
Bonaparte, Elisa, 108
Bonaparte, Jérôme, 139
Bonaparte, Joseph, 76, 104, 139, 157
Bonaparte, Julie, 157
Bonaparte, Letizia, 10, 103, 105–6,
  139, 197

Bonaparte, Louis, 9, 106, 148, 229
Bonaparte, Lucien, 10–11, 83
Bonaparte, Pauline, 10, 92, 106
Bonapartists
  adopt violet as emblem, 137
  and collapse of July
    Monarchy, 230–2
  frequent Chaussée d'Antin, 146
  and July Revolution, 176–8
  and Lamarque's funeral, 227
  and Las Cases' memoirs, 160
  and Napoleon as saviour, 166–7
  and Napoleon's death, 122–3,
    133–4, 136–7, 140, 143
  and Napoleon's will, 113
  and Orleanist regime, 184
  popularity of Bonapartism, 155–6
  reactions to Bourbon restoration,
    169–72
  and return of Napoleon's remains,
    198–9, 203, 208–9, 216, 218, 230–2
  and Second Empire, 233–5
  street clashes with royalists, 179
  threat to Bourbons, 73–6
Botany Bay, 17, 62
Bourbon restoration, 169–71
Boys, Rev. Richard, 96
Brack, Colonel, 138
Brando, Marlon, 235
Braquehais, Bruno, 234
Bro, General, 138
Broglie, Duchess de, 136
Brumaire, coup of, 6, 37, 143, 191
Brune, Marshal, 75
Bullock, William, 8
Bunbury, Major-General Sir Henry,
  16–18, 22, 52
*Buonaparte-phobia ou La malédiction
  rendue facile*, 12
Buonavita, Abbé Antonio, 105
Burton, Francis, 124
buses, horse-drawn, 216
busts, 173–4, 228
Byron, Lord, 131, 144

A Note on the Author

Philip Dwyer studied in Perth (Australia), Berlin and Paris, where he was a student of France's pre-eminent Napoleonic scholar, Jean Tulard. He has published widely on the Revolutionary and Napoleonic eras, and is Director of the Centre for the History of Violence at the University of Newcastle, Australia.

A Note on the Type

The text of this book is set in Linotype Stempel Garamond, a version of Garamond adapted and first used by the Stempel foundry in 1924. It is one of several versions of Garamond based on the designs of Claude Garamond. It is thought that Garamond based his font on Bembo, cut in 1495 by Francesco Griffo in collaboration with the Italian printer Aldus Manutius. Garamond types were first used in books printed in Paris around 1532. Many of the present-day versions of this type are based on the *Typi Academiae* of Jean Jannon cut in Sedan in 1615.

Claude Garamond was born in Paris in 1480. He learned how to cut type from his father and by the age of fifteen he was able to fashion steel punches the size of a pica with great precision. At the age of sixty he was commissioned by King Francis I to design a Greek alphabet, and for this he was given the honourable title of royal type founder. He died in 1561.